Georgetown University Round Table
on Languages and Linguistics 1970

Bilingualism and Language Contact

James E. Alatis
Editor

Georgetown University Press, Washington, D.C. 20007

Bibliographical Notice

Since this series has been variously, and confusingly, cited as *Georgetown University Monograph Series on Languages and Linguistics, Monograph Series on Languages and Linguistics, Reports of the Annual Round Table Meetings on Linguistics and Language Study*, etc., beginning with the 1973 volume the title of the series was changed.

The new title of the series includes the year of a Round Table and omits both the monograph number and the meeting number, thus: *Georgetown University Round Table on Languages and Linguistics 1970*, with the regular abbreviation *GURT 1970*. Full bibliographical references should show the form:

Fishman, Joshua A. 1970. The politics of bilingual education. In: Georgetown University Round Table on Languages and Linguistics 1970. Edited by James E. Alatis. Washington, D.C., Georgetown University Press. 47–58.

CONTENTS

FOREWORD

For twenty-one years now, scholars in linguistics and related disciplines have converged on Georgetown University at the annual Round Table meetings each spring to report on their latest research and to discuss current problems. Twenty papers were delivered at this year's session held on March 12, 13, and 14, 1970. For the first time a Thursday evening session was added to the traditional Friday and Saturday sessions.

The theme of this 21st Annual Round Table was 'Bilingualism and Language Contact: Anthropological, Linguistic, Psychological, and Sociological Aspects.' The meeting was divided into four panels, the first on Thursday evening with three speakers, and the remaining three with five speakers each. To these panels were added two luncheon addresses on Friday and Saturday.

The discussions which followed the delivery of the papers were recorded, and are included as a part of this volume. Subsequent written comments are also given after the first paper, that of Einar Haugen.

Thanks are due to the following graduate and undergraduate students of the School of Languages and Linguistics for their voluntary and invaluable assistance at the 21st Round Table:

Student Committee Chairmen: Frances Reid, Susan Savage, June Hutchinson, George Long, Maria del Rio, and Jane Proctor; Committee Members: Molly Frost, James Holbrook, John Albertini, Dave Strickler, Nadine Dutcher, Hailu Araaya, Paul Stevens, George Lenches, Sister Marie Shiels, Ronald Post, Sister Mary Rimblas, Bettie Mahan, Hai Vuong, Margaret Sheppard, Edith Harper, Barbara Lyons, Linda Feldman, Louis Arena, Dolores Kendrick, Charlise Young, Cathy Sullivan, Nina O'Keefe, Louise Jansen, Sister Sigrid Simlik, Sister Ann Carolyn Kessler, Mary Ann Corley, Barbara Derritt, and Barbara Wyatt.

Special thanks go to Marilyn S. Rosenthal and Marta I. Moia who beautifully coordinated the entire student effort and attended to a thousand and one details which ensured the successful running of the meeting.

I am most grateful to Carol LeClair for her·patience in transcribing the lengthy discussions from the tape recordings, typing and correcting manuscripts, and preparing the final photocopy of the volume.

Finally, I wish to express my warmest thanks to my colleagues, Professors Neil J. Twombly, S J. and Richard J. O'Brien, S. J., for their invaluable attention to detail in the preparation of this manuscript, as well as to Rev. Stephen X. Winters, S. J. for his painstaking and patient proofreading of the final copy.

James E. Alatis
Editor

WELCOMING REMARKS

FRANK FADNER, S. J.

Regent, School of Languages and Linguistics
Georgetown University

Ladies and Gentlemen, Colleagues, Participants and Guests at
Georgetown's twenty-first Round Table Meeting on Linguistics and
Language Studies:

I don't suppose that in these chaotic days of turmoil and bitter debate, of Sturm und Drang, and the threats of Boy Bolsheviki on the
campus, a man could win a popularity contest among the knowing élite
by asserting that humanity owes a debt of gratitude to the advent of
Communist ideology.

And yet the historical record shows that since the rise of Bolshe-
vism and its triumph in a large neighborhood, people in the rest of the
world have become more socially aware: we've been put on our toes
and made to realize the existence of the other man.

In bygone days when static hierarchy ruled the world of thought,
philosophers were content with a stress on the static, individual aspect
of that important creature known as man; and they said of him: Man is
a rational animal.

Now we have come to realize that an equally essential definition of
man stresses his dynamic aspect, his nature, the way he acts; and we
say: Man is a social animal, an intelligent, free animal with an inner
urge or drive to enter the society of his own kind as a necessary means
to his immediate end (life, liberty, and the pursuit of happiness) and
his ultimate end.

This means communication, human language. Hence we also come
up with a third definition of a man, rather waggish if you will: Animal
sapiens nonnunquam loquax, an intelligent animal who has to talk—
now and then!

As I look over the agenda for our Round Table discussions, I am agreeably impressed with its realism. Your Chairman, the Associate Dean, Dr. Alatis, summed up the focus very succinctly for me: Bilingualism and Language Contact: Anthropological, Linguistic, Psychological, and Sociological Aspects. This is certainly a most noble attempt to make our specialty relate, as they say. I wish all God's blessing in your efforts.

Finally, I know I'm speaking the voice of the President and the Board of Directors of the University when I assure you that the mat of welcome has never grown threadbare at the entrance to this place. And that goes for old faces and new ones alike in the congregation.

Thank you.

WELCOMING REMARKS

ROBERT LADO

Dean, School of Languages and Linguistics
Georgetown University

Father Fadner, dear Colleagues: Earlier editions of the now traditional Georgetown University Annual Round Table Meetings have focused on the changing national needs in languages and linguistics: first, on the wartime experience in foreign language teaching and its applicability to peacetime; later, on linguistic theory; then on technology; then on method. Last year's Round Table focused on the linguistic problems of our neighbors next door through sociolinguistic studies and the teaching of Standard English to speakers of other languages or dialects.

The theme of this year's meeting is even more timely and significant, for it reflects what many of us consider a great cultural and linguistic growing up of this great land, a maturation that could hardly have been thought possible ten years ago: the idea that bilingual education is important, that bilingualism is not a disease, that our bilinguals can and should be a great asset to this country. That maturation has been confirmed through the passing by the Congress of the United States of the Bilingual Education Act of 1968. This Round Table could not be more timely, since the seven and a half million dollars spent during the first year of that Act will probably be increased to perhaps twenty-one million dollars during the coming second year.

I take great pleasure in welcoming you to the proceedings of the 21st Annual Round Table Meeting.

INTRODUCTORY REMARKS

JAMES E. ALATIS

Associate Dean, School of Languages and Linguistics
Georgetown University

Let me add my word of welcome to those of Father Fadner and Dean Lado.

Thank you all for coming to share your thoughts with us at this, the 21st Annual Round Table on Linguistics and Language Studies. I especially wish to thank our speakers—and we have a splendid roster indeed—for having responded so magnificently to the call for papers, and for having agreed to come, many from very long distances, to speak to us today. I also wish to thank those whose sponsorship has made this meeting possible: namely, the Administration of Georgetown University in general and of the School of Languages and Linguistics in particular, especially Dr. Robert Lado, whose continuing leadership, understanding, and support are very much appreciated. Without such support, constantly applied, this meeting and others like it would not be possible. Because of his support and the support, implicit or explicit, of such valued colleagues as Father Fadner, our Regent, Father Dinneen, formerly acting Dean and now Head of the Theoretical Linguistics Division, Dr. Charles Kreidler, Head of the Applied Linguistics Division, Father Richard O'Brien, Head of our Publications Department, and all the heads of the various language divisions and the rest of the faculty and staff of the SLL, the planning and preparation of the Round Table have been a pleasure and a joy.

I should like to point out that, as in the case of last year's Round Table, the general theme was selected to assist a new academic program which was established at Georgetown two years ago with the help of the U. S. Office of Education. The program is called the Experienced Teacher Fellowship Program (ExTFP) for Teachers of Standard English

to Speakers of Other Languages or Dialects (SESOLD) and is supported
from funds granted under the provisions of the Education Professions
Development Act (EPDA).

For this program 22 fellows were selected from applicants from all
over the nation and were granted government fellowships; two tuition-
paying participants were also allowed to join the program. The majority of the 24 teachers come from the District of Columbia Public Schools;
there is one from Florida and another from the state of Washington.

The program consists of a highly integrated and coordinated series
of courses leading to a Master of Arts in Teaching (MAT). Among new
courses which were developed to meet the needs of these urban teachers
are: Problems in Urban English, taught by Dr. Roger Shuy of the Center for Applied Linguistics; the Sociology of the Urban Community,
taught by Dr. Veronica Maz; and Practice Teaching, which involves
supervisors and teachers of the District of Columbia Public School
System, and which was coordinated by Mrs. Charles W. Kreidler who
was specially employed for this function. The practice teaching took
place in special facilities of the School of Languages and Linguistics;
classrooms were especially equipped for the program with the installa-
tion of closed circuit television which allowed the practice teachers to
be viewed, video-taped, and evaluated. Elementary school children
from the Sloe School and other children from the Americanization School
came to the University for the month of February and through today. We
had the graduation exercises for these children just this morning. As
part of an integrated colloquium, the participants will be taught some of
the basic elements of Modern Greek in an attempt to demonstrate various methods, approaches, and techniques of language teaching. It is
hoped that teachers will thus become even more sympathetic than
they are already to the problems of students involved in language learning.

Last year Channel 4 in Washington produced a half hour colored film
showing the work done in teacher training in this program. The North-
east Conference financed a film demonstrating how the closed circuit
television was used in teacher training.

It was our hope that this year's Round Table would help round out
the experience of these fellows and assist them in their attempt to integrate all the things they are learning—so intensively—about theoretical linguistics, applied linguistics, and the sociocultural aspects of
learning a foreign language or dialect. We feel that it is perhaps precisely through this specialized program for teachers, and through this
year's Round Table Meeting that Georgetown University could make at
one and the same time a unique, practical, and truly academic contribution to the solution of some of the most pressing social problems of
the day.

Unfortunately, because of severe budget limitations and general fiscal retrenchment, the Federal Government's support of this program is not likely to be continued next year, at least in its present form. This is all the more regrettable since we are certain that the program has had an important impact on the teaching going on in the schools of the District of Columbia and elsewhere. It certainly has had an important impact on Georgetown University.

You will note among the ushers and in the audience a group of participants wearing green and white badges such as the one I am wearing. They are all participants in the ExTFP. I am grateful for their help. And, of course, the incomparable students of the School of Languages and Linguistics in general have once again risen to the occasion to help prepare for what I am sure you will find to be a very productive conference.

To conclude, let me welcome you once again and wish you a fruitful and enjoyable meeting.

LINGUISTICS AND DIALINGUISTICS

EINAR HAUGEN

Harvard University

Abstract. Efforts are being made to establish a new interdisciplinary field under the name of sociolinguistics. In an article entitled 'Sociolinguistic perspective on the study of bilingualism' (1968) Joshua Fishman has charged linguists with 'methodological and theoretical rigidity,' specifically in their conception of language as a 'pure, monolithic' structure, and of language contact as resulting in 'harmful' interference. It will be the purpose of this paper to determine to what extent this charge is justified.

One of the problems that has concerned some of us for a number of years is to ask what contribution linguists could make to the study of bilingualism. In the rapid growth of linguistics that we see taking place before our eyes, there is a danger that the kind of problems which bilinguals face may be neglected. The topic of bilingualism has interested psychologists and educators a good deal more than it has linguists, and much of the literature on the subject is written by non-linguists. This is surprising in view of the fact that linguists are (or ought to be) bilingual by definition, and one would expect them to take an interest in their own problems.

The situation has been acutely pointed up in a free-swinging article by Joshua A. Fishman, who accuses linguists of not being 'truly impartial to the language of bilinguals' (Fishman 1968a: 29). We are told that linguistic research on bilingualism 'has but two basic notions to it, the first being that of two "pure" languages and the second, that of "interference" between them.' The concept of 'languages in contact' is characterized by Fishman as 'the interaction of two entities that normally exist in a pure and unsullied state and that have been brought into unnatural contact with each other.' 'The underlying model of pure, monolithic langue leads the linguist to assume that the inter-action or fusion of two such is "interference", that is, deleterious, harmful, noxious.' The linguist's ferreting out of interference is described as being like that of 'a housewife looking for smears of wet paint ... what structures of language X have rubbed off on lan-guage Y and vice versa?' As a result, we are told, linguists have 'fre-quently failed to familiarize themselves with the communities and speakers from which they have obtained their corpuses of speech' and have overlooked the fact that 'in many ways bilinguals are people like other people' (Fishman 1968a: 29-30).

At first sight one is inclined to take this salvo rather lightly, as a piece of science fiction, since it does not correspond to any con-ceptions harbored by those of us who have carried on research in bilingualism over the past generation. Happily, Fishman does not footnote his charges, so that no one needs to feel hurt. If Joshua's trumpets are going to bring the walls of Jericho down, one would be happy not to be living in that particular city.

Among the linguists who have dealt seriously with bilingualism in America, Uriel Weinreich certainly is preeminent. He introduced the terms that are the particular targets of Fishman's critique, namely 'interference' and 'languages in contact' (Weinreich 1953). As I read Weinreich's book, these terms are entirely neutral and dispassionate designations of important aspects of bilingual behav-ior. He defined languages as being in contact 'if they are used al-ternately by the same persons.' Interference phenomena were 'those instances of deviation from the norms of either language which occur in the speech of bilinguals as a result of their familiarity with more than one language' (Weinreich 1953: 1). I find no reference to these norms as being 'pure' or to interference as being 'noxious'. Instead, Weinreich notes that to the bilingual a 'partial identification' of the two systems is 'a reduction of his linguistic burden'. He discusses the possibility of systemic merger, but for most bilinguals he pre-fers to speak of 'two coexistent systems' (Weinreich 1953: 8). In long-established bilingual communities, however, he recognizes that 'there is hardly any limit to interference' (Weinreich 1953: 81), so that some speakers might be said to have 'only one language with two modes of expression' (Weinreich 1953: 9). As for familiarity with bi-lingual communities, one could hardly overlook the fact that Wein-reich lived in New York and did field work in Switzerland.

As one who from time to time has written on this subject, perhaps I may be so bold as to quote a sentence or two from my own writings. More than thirty years ago, in my first article in Language, I wrote: 'When the speakers of [Norwegian] were transplanted to American soil ... a more or less gradual transformation of their speech became inevitable... [This process is] generally referred to under the inaccurate metaphor of "borrowing", and the result is called a "mixed language"... These terms obscure the fact that what has really taken place is a shift in structure ... correlated to a shift in cultural and social form.' (Haugen 1938: 113) In a 1950 article published in Language I demonstrated that 'the process of learning changes the learner's view of the language' (Haugen 1950: 216). In my Norwegian Language in America I documented the rise of new linguistic norms in bilingual communities; I called them 'bilingual norms' or 'bilingual dialects' (Haugen 1953: 60). (I was therefore somewhat surprised to read in an article by Ma and Herasimchuk [in Fishman 1968b: 644] that linguists had not noticed that 'speakers generate their own bilingual norms of correctness'.) In the same work I inveighed against the views of educated native speakers who rejected the emigrant's language as either 'comical or offensive' (Haugen 1953: 57). The book was based on memories of participation in bilingual communities since childhood and active field work over a period of years. As for admitting that 'bilinguals are people,' I can only say that I am one myself.

The point of these quotations has merely been to demonstrate that Fishman's charges can hardly be based on the work of linguists who have actually concerned themselves with bilingualism. Knowing his writings and his outlook, I suspect that he would exonerate us and other linguists who have worked firsthand with these problems and say that we were not writing as linguists, but as sociolinguists.

The charge is therefore more properly directed at the linguists proper, those who are generally recognized as being in the mainstream of American linguistics. In their writings we find precious little either about bilingualism or any other kind of linguistic variability. If we peek in the standard textbook of American structuralism, H. A. Gleason's Introduction to Descriptive Linguistics (1955, revised 1961), we find that only one of its twenty-eight chapters deals with what he calls 'variation in speech'. Under this heading he throws together borrowing, dialectology, levels of speech, etc. These are all marginal to his definition of descriptive linguistics, which is concerned only with 'minimal contrastive elements and their combinations', i.e. the synchronically defined structure of a single idiolect. If we turn hopefully to the linguists of the New Grammar, who speak freely of 'creativity' in language, there is little change on this point. On the very first page of Chomsky's Aspects we read that linguistic theory is 'concerned primarily with an ideal speaker-listener, in a completely homogeneous speech-community' (Chomsky 1965: 3). Since the bilingual by definition lives in a nonhomogeneous speech community and usually (if not always) falls short of being an ideal speaker, there is little encouragement to bilingual study in this pronouncement.

Any scholar is of course entitled to exclude from his research strategy any set of data he chooses if this enables him to make more powerful generalizations. Sooner or later, however, the excluded data will rise up to haunt him. The appeal to the speaker's native intuition for judgments on grammaticality has shown that each speaker has his own distinct competence, and that this can vary with time and place. Gleason recognized the limitations of his approach and suggested that it might be a valid objective to make 'an empirical description of the range and significance of variation' and to make 'generalizations about linguistic variation as a characteristic feature of language'. He even suggested that such generalizations might become 'the basis for a second type of linguistic science', but found that 'we lack a general term for this discipline as a whole' (Gleason 1961: 392).

In the meanwhile, 'sociolinguistics' has offered itself as a candidate for such a term. William Bright declared linguistic diversity to be the essential criterion of the field in his introduction to the UCLA symposium on sociolinguistics (Bright 1966: 11). From the hardcore linguist's point of view, however, the prefix socio- compromises the term by identifying variation with its social correlates, which he feels are not his primary business. In 1956 I proposed 'dialinguistics' as a possible name for the kind of interlingual confrontation that is now often known as 'contrastive' or 'differential' linguistics (Haugen 1956: 41). I was impressed by the number of linguistic terms in this area that begin with the Greek prefix dia-, all of which suggest variation: 'diachronic' linguistics studies variations in time, 'dialectology' variations in space. Weinreich proposed 'diasystem' for the compound system of bilinguals. In 1954, at a Georgetown lecture, I suggested the use of 'diaphones' and 'diamorphs' to identify interlingually defined phonemic and morphemic units. Recently Dingwall (1964) has used the term 'diaglossic' for a similar operation; the step is short to 'diaglossics' or 'diaglottology'. The disjecta membra are present to constitute a field of dialinguistics, if only a coherent theory and terminology could be developed.

Within such a theory seen from an entirely linguistic point of view, the concept of the 'nonunique' or 'variable' structure would seem to be central. Perhaps the very word 'structure' is unfortunate as suggesting a rigidity which is not characteristic of human behavior. We would certainly have to examine once more whether Meillet's famous dictum of the coherence of language systems is really true. If a language is really un système ou tout se tient, how does it happen that bilinguals find it so easy to accept novel elements into their systems?

There are other well-known linguistic dogmas that require reexamination in the light of the data furnished us by bilingual speakers. One of them is the distinction between langue and parole, now reformulated into English by Chomsky as 'competence' and 'performance'. Mackey began his description of bilingualism (1962: 51) by assigning bilingualism to the domain of parole, as a characteristic of the individual rather than of the group. But every time a bilingual draws upon the resources of his other language, he is by ever so little altering the nature of his competence in both. Every performance alters one's competence by the increment of what one has learned or unlearned during the performance. Our linguistic competences are changing from moment to moment throughout our lives, and there is no set of data which reveals this more clearly than the life cycle of bilinguals.

What I have called a 'bilingual dialect' in the bilingual speech community may prove to be either stable (as in India) or unstable (as in the United States). This is a matter for empirical examination in each given instance. The main thing is that bilinguals exhibit in principle a succession of variable competences, which may be infinite in number, since they represent points on a continuum from one language to another. The concept of the variable competence is one that needs to be developed in order to account not only for the interferences of bilinguals, but for all kinds of idiolectal, dialectal, social, and historical variation. Only in this way can we get away from the stultifying logico-mathematical formalism and devise models that reflect more accurately what speakers actually do.

It is not my intention here to outline a full-scale theory of bilingualism, only to suggest a few lines of inquiry, some of which are well represented in the literature, and others less so. The characteristic features of bilingual behavior include the complementary processes of learning and unlearning one's two codes, and one's success in switching from one to the other. While a first language is learned step by step as the child matures, a second language has to establish its structure under constant reference to the first. If we recognize that every item and every rule that is established in the second language adds to the competence of the speaker, which grows and expands with each successful performance, we will accept the concept of variable competence. On the way from monolingualism to bilingualism the learner passes through stages that may be called (with Nemser 1969) 'learner's systems', some of which can be studied in children and an entirely different set in adolescents or adults. Generative linguists speak glibly of 'adding' or 'deleting' rules, as if one could just write it into the learner's system. But each item and each rule in a second language is somehow related to those of the first, and each one is the response to an opportunity and a need for learning.

The gradual 'build-up' of competence in the second language may be matched by a gradual 'unlearning' of the first language. An extreme example of this occurs in aphasics, which as Roman Jakobson showed many years ago (1941) proceeds in the inverse order to the

learning. A mild form of it is observed in immigrants who lose flu-
ency in their native language after some years in a new linguistic environment. To some extent the first language is dismantled—by the
forgetting of words, complex sentence structures, subtleties of meaning. The same person may be building up one language and partly tear-
ing down another; or better still, he is rebuilding his first language to
suit the occupancy of a new personality. The German language can
here provide us with a handy set of tags: if we call the building-up a
language an Aufbau and the aphasic dismantling an Abbau, the bilingual's restructuring can be called an Umbau. This is the goal of all the
studies of bilingual interference: in what way has a language been
rebuilt or umgebaut because of the coexistence with another language
in the minds of bilingual speakers?

This conception of the symbiosis of languages and the ever varying
competences of individual speakers and speech communities is as far
as possible from the rigid conception of monolithic systems for which
linguists were castigated, and not without reason, by Joshua Fishman.
Linguists have an opportunity to study the infinite variability of language more clearly and easily among bilinguals than among monolinguals. I would be glad to scuttle the word 'interference' if it is felt
to imply a condemnation. It would have been nice if someone had
started calling the same phenomenon 'enrichment', for it can easily
be argued that the bilingual who reaches into his other language for
an expression is in fact enriching his effective range of communication, for he is using a word or a form that feels right to his interlocutors. However, the term 'enrichment' is as loaded as 'interference',
and if we want a really neutral word, we will have to accept some such
term as 'transfer', originally launched by Zellig Harris. Only in normative grammar does it make sense to speak of 'interference', for
then the speaker is violating a rule laid down by fiat and not by custom.
But that is another problem entirely.

It is my conviction that linguistics can profit by becoming dialin-
guistic, and that the problems of bilinguals can receive a linguistic
solution if linguists are willing to settle for a variable rather than a
static competence.

REFERENCES

Bright, William, ed. 1966. Sociolinguistics: Proceedings of the
    UCLA Sociolinguistics Conference, 1964. The Hague: Mouton.
Chomsky, Noam. 1965. Aspects of the theory of syntax. Cambridge,
    Massachusetts: The M. I. T. Press.
Dingwall, William Orr. 1964. Diaglossic grammar. Ph. D. disser-
    tation, Georgetown University. Washington, D. C.

Fishman, Joshua A. 1968a. Sociolinguistic perspective on the study
of bilingualism. Linguistics 39.21-49.
_____ et al. 1968b. Bilingualism in the barrio. Final report,
U. S. Department of Health, Education and Welfare. New York:
Yeshiva University.
_____. 1968c. Readings in the sociology of language. The Hague:
Mouton.
Gleason, Henry A. 1955 (rev. ed. 1961). An introduction to descriptive linguistics. New York: Holt, Rinehart and Winston.
Haugen, Einar. 1938. Phonological shifting in American Norwegian.
Language 14.112-120.
_____. 1950. The analysis of linguistic borrowing. Language 26.
210-231.
_____. 1953. The Norwegian language in America: a study in
bilingual behavior. Philadelphia: University of Pennsylvania Press
(reprinted 1969, Indiana University Press).
_____. 1954. Problems of bilingual description. Georgetown
University Monograph Series on Languages and Linguistics, No. 7,
9-19.
_____. 1956. Bilingualism in the Americas: a bibliography and
research guide. University, Alabama (Publications of the American Dialect Society, No. 26).
Jakobson, Roman. 1941. Kindersprache, Aphasie und allgemeine
Lautgesetze. Uppsala. (Språkvetenskapliga Sällskapets i Uppsala
Förhandlingar 1940-1942).
Mackey, William F. 1962. The description of bilingualism. Canadian Journal of Linguistics 7.51-85. (Reprinted in Fishman 1968c,
554-584).
Nemser, William. 1969. Approximative systems of foreign language
learners. Yugoslav Serbo-Croatian-English Contrastive Project,
3-12. Zagreb, 1969.
Weinreich, Uriel. 1953. Languages in contact. Findings and Prob-
lems. (Publications of the Linguistic Circle of New York, 1).
New York.

DISCUSSION

Esperanza Medina-Spyropoulos, Georgetown University, graduate
student: Professor Haugen has just mentioned that there is little encouragement from Mr. Chomsky's pronouncement by the fact that bilinguals are neither ideal speakers nor live in a homogeneous community; and I was very glad to hear it, since I have long been puzzled by
this dogma of the 'ideal speaker-hearer' in regard to the limited bearing of the generative-transformational model on the problem of sociolinguistic studies. For most sociolinguists are mainly interested in

'performance', that is, the actual interactions of the 'real' speaker-hearer. I would think that performance is not the residual and secondary (and irrelevant) behavior that some linguists imply it is. (I have discussed this matter briefly with Dr. Alatis.) Now, Chomsky has admitted that he works within a Cartesian framework, and such an approach seems to be, in my opinion, diametrically opposed to the sociolinguists' main interest—performance. If Mr. Chomsky has followed in his tradition a view of language that denies the significant role of the sociocultural factor, my question is, how is it feasible for some of the well-known, contemporary sociolinguists to regard the system of generative rules as a point-by-point model for the actual construction of a sentence by a speaker? In order to do sociolinguistic work we must collect representative samples of 'natural' speech, right? Then, should we not first modify and refine the model of the theory which is based on formal logic and which operates on a circumscribed inventory of unnatural strings? With all due respect to Mr. Chomsky's theory, it seems to me that his model of grammar would have to be developed to include the societal aspects of language structure.

Haugen: If you are asking if you should continue to work with Chomskian principles, this is something that each student will have to settle for himself. At least in a purely transformational syntax there is no concern with the relationship of one speaker's speech to that of other speakers. Variations are simply not admitted in the grammar. But, as I said in my paper, this is clearly a strategic decision and the problem is, if you choose to use Chomsky's theory, how it can be modified so as to admit sociological variation. I can see ways in which it could be done, and I have heard papers, for example, one given at this conference last year by David DeCamp, showing one approach. William Labov's approach is rather different. Personally, I feel closer to Labov's than to DeCamp's; but I follow them both with great interest. I did not condemn one or the other approach, but indicated that the structuralists as well as the generativists have by and large been disinterested in the problems of linguistic variation.

Frank Ponce, Jr., District of Columbia Teachers College: Being myself a bilingual and having spoken Spanish from a Spanish mother and a Mexican father and never having experienced a bilingual problem as such, I ask Dr. Haugen if perhaps we should not distinguish between 'learned' and 'unlearned' immigrants or emigres to a country. My parents had a tremendous problem because they were learning English, or have been learning it for years, and they speak English every day better and better; but their Spanish is being infiltrated by English more and more. The question, then, is should we distinguish the learned from the unlearned person arriving in a country and living in a community?

Haugen: Yes, of course there is a difference between educated and uneducated speakers, particularly by virtue of the ambition that has been instilled in the educated speaker to speak a so-called pure language.

Ponce: What I mean is, I think that in the person, the professional, even in the newly arrived emigre or immigrant, there is an attempt to anchor both languages, not just one, and in the case of, say, a Portuguese community in Rhode Island, as such, there isn't this need to anchor the native language; it is kind of spoken with a certain love and sentiment. It isn't just a matter of teaching the language to others.

Haugen: Even educated speakers deviate from the norms of their native language. This has been amply demonstrated. I remember specifically Susan Ervin-Tripp's studies of educated Frenchmen in Washington, D.C., whose speech was full of Anglicisms which they were themselves completely unaware of.

Ponce: I just seem to fear a danger on the part of the linguists to throw into the same 'caldron' the person who is a bilingual, using it in one way, and the person who is a bilingual, using it in another field, or aspect of life. Thank you very much, Dr. Haugen.

Subsequent written comment by Joshua A. Fishman, Yeshiva University: I did not respond to Haugen's paper, although I was in the audience when he read it, because it left me with the puzzled impression that he ended by adopting the position that he had initially criticized me for, and that his final words were words of agreement rather than disagreement with me. I therefore asked Haugen for a copy of his talk, which he was kind enough to provide, and Dr. Alatis for permission to reply in writing, which he was kind enough to grant.

In examining the text of Haugen's talk I find my puzzlement fully corroborated. After initially taking me to task for my purportedly exaggerated critique of traditional linguistic approaches to societal bilingualism—by the way, it was only societal bilingualism with which my paper dealt—Haugen concludes that the 'conception of the symbiosis of languages and the ever varying competences of individual speakers and speech communities is as far as possible from the rigid conception of monolithic systems for which linguists were castigated, and not without reason, by Joshua Fishman.' Further on Haugen also offers 'to scuttle the word interference, if it is felt to imply a condemnation

... (for) only in normative grammar does it make sense to speak of "interference", for then the speaker is violating a rule laid down by fiat and not by custom.' In the space of four pages Haugen turns from differing with me to ostensibly agreeing with me on most scores.

I only conclude that Haugen was upset by the novelty of a social psychologist criticizing linguistics, but that he felt that it was quite proper for himself, a distinguished member of the linguistic fraternity, to make the same criticisms, adding a few neologisms of his own coinage in the process. Unfortunately, however, Haugen failed to understand the true nature of my critique; and, therefore, while belatedly accepting it (when restated in his own terms), he simply demonstrates throughout his paper the truth of my basic contention that linguistics, as essentially a code-centered discipline, cannot without difficulty be used in any examination of societal bilingualism, the latter being not a code-centered phenomenon at all, but rather a societal phenomenon.

Thus, in criticizing Chomsky, Haugen claims that 'the bilingual by definition lives in a nonhomogeneous speech community,' failing to recognize that in a diglossic bilingual community life is all of one interwoven cloth and that no heterogeneity is necessarily present, whether in terms of discordant values, languages, groups, or behaviors. If Chomsky is to be amended it is only to point out that bilingual speech communities (and I have argued for a decade that dislocated and enfeebled immigrant bilingual groups in the USA are very poor examples of what well established, diglossic bilingual speech communities are really like) are as homogeneous as monolingual ones—or, to put it more accurately, that they are each equally integrated via their societal norms of communicative and behavioral appropriateness, even though they both reveal several varieties of speech differentially employed by the various networks within them.

Haugen, even though he is a reconstructed linguist, one who has always shown great interest in societal reality, fully demonstrates how difficult it is to grasp that reality when blinded by the biases of linguistic terms and linguistic concepts. Throughout his paper Haugen refers to the bilingual's 'two codes', thus permitting to enter through the back door the very artificiality that he has purportedly ejected through the front. However, my own article, which he questioned, struggled to reveal that there were possibly many (not just two) varieties in a diglossic bilingual community and that these might well be differently utilized by such a community's various networks, not all of which needed to control the entire repertoire range of the community as a whole. Thus there might well be some for whom varieties A and B were essentially indistinguishable from their parallels in neighboring monolingual speech communities, but other networks might not control A and B at all, and all networks might more intimately use A' and B', or A" and B", or even a variety designatable as A"B".

My major disappointment with Haugen's paper is not, however, that he does not understand me. It is, rather, that he does not understand societal phenomena. While he suspects that the social correlates of language might not be the linguist's primary business, he nevertheless believes that with some new terms (mostly of his own coinage) linguistics as a discipline can cope with societal bilingualism in perfectly adequate fashion. However, this is his basic error. Societal bilingualism is a phenomenon of social reality. It is not a discipline, and, therefore, no discipline (no, not even that queen of all sciences, linguistics) can do it justice. It will take a truly interdisciplinary effort in order to explore societal bilingualism and it was the purpose of my cited paper, and of several papers and books that have since followed it, to suggest some approaches for such exploration. Linguists are invited to join, if they are willing to become more than disciplinary apologists.

Written comment by Haugen on Fishman's reply: It appears from Fishman's remarks that it is difficult to conduct an interdisciplinary discussion without inviting misunderstanding. He is confused by the fact that I attacked his 1968 Formulations while agreeing with many aspects of his criticism. I found his summary of the linguists' position inaccurate and tendentious, with its attribution to us of terms (or concepts) like 'unsullied', 'unnatural', and 'noxious'. I brought forth evidence (which has not been controverted in his reply) that those linguists who have written seriously on bilingualism have never used such terms or implied any negative attitude to bilingualism as such.

My general stance is therefore not a disagreement with Fishman's criticism of linguists, but a contention that he has overstated his case and tossed out the baby with the bath. I would emphasize rather the neglect of bilingualism by linguists than their failure to understand it. The contention that linguists (including myself) have failed to 'understand societal phenomena' may or may not be true (who does 'understand' them?). But it remains to be shown that bilinguals do not operate with 'two codes' (or more)—why call them 'bilinguals' otherwise? Once they have reached the stage Fishman calls A″B″ (which is allowed for in Weinreich's and my writings), they are no longer bilinguals; they have created a new koine (or creole or pidgin). That people of various degrees of bilingualism live together in one community and that they interact in different 'networks' is a truism which I have not only not denied but indeed supported by examples in my writings.

I regret that my (modest) coinage of terms should have called forth Fishman's barbs; his own penchant for innovation is hardly a secret. The notion that linguists should abandon their established terminology (because it 'blinds them to reality') is hardly viable, unless one that offers great advantages is produced. Linguists must continue to study language, in all its varieties, in their own terms, while social psychologists provide insights from their discipline(s) concerning the correlation of these varieties with 'societal phenomena' on all levels. They are 'invited to join, if they are willing to become more than disciplinary apologists'—I cannot phrase the problem better than by echoing Fishman's invitation. Interdisciplinary research is not a one-way street.

THE DISCOVERY OF UNIVERSALS
IN MULTILINGUALISM

ROBERT J. DI PIETRO

Georgetown University

Abstract. At last year's meeting of this same Round Table, David DeCamp spoke of ways to incorporate sociolinguistic inquiry within the theoretical framework of language developed by linguists. The need to reconcile diverse areas of language-related research is especially evident with regard to multilingual situations. In the study of multilingualism, the linguist is joined not only by the sociologist but by the psychologist and the anthropologist as well. With the variety of research in mind, several pronouncements about multilingualism are examined and discussed as being possibly universal. It is felt that finding universally valid processes at work in multilingualism is essential if the future research of linguists, sociologists, anthropologists and psychologists is to proceed on some common ground. Otherwise, we shall be forced to continue our multilingual studies in bits and pieces. The quest for universals is certainly not new to linguistics (see, for example, Universals of Language, edited by J. Greenberg, 1963; Universals in Linguistic Theory, edited by E. Bach and R. Harms, 1968). The present paper, however, takes a different tack, which is to explore the universals of language contact.

'The quest for universals is organically linked with all other manifestations of a unitary attitude toward language and linguistics' (Jakobson 1963: 277). With these words, Roman Jakobson concluded his contribution to the epoch-making conference on language universals held at Dobbs Ferry, New York, some nine years ago. The steady growth of a 'unitary attitude' toward the study of language has been evident throughout the last decade and will become, I predict, one of the significant characteristics of linguistic studies in the decade that is beginning. Joseph Greenberg, who pioneered in the search for language universals, has been joined in his work by an ever-increasing number of linguists.

Several important works were published in the late 60s to mark the next important milestone in the positing of language universals after the Dobbs Ferry Conference. Lenneberg's Biological Foundations of Language was the first, in 1967, to assert that the 'biological properties of the human form of cognition set strict limits to the range of possibilities for variations in natural languages' (Lenneberg 1967: 374-5) and that 'the universal ... features of language will appear to be inextricably intertwined with physiological peculiarities' (Lenneberg 1967: 76). The assertion that human language is species-specific not only points up the need to provide physiological and psychological correlates for linguistic universals, but also shows the ways in which these correlates are to be established.

The distinction between 'accidental' and 'essential' universals which was related to language by Hockett (1963) is further elaborated upon by Chomsky and Halle (1968) in their The Sound Pattern of English. Since the linguist is interested chiefly in defining the range of possibilities in human language, he should be careful to cull out those language features which arise only as the result of historical development, the extinction of particular languages, or other 'outside' forces. To repeat a well-known example, if all languages in which nasalized vowels are distinctive were to become extinct due to some war or epidemic, the fact that all remaining languages have only oral vowels would be accidental. Moreover, there would be no restriction to prevent the remaining languages from developing new sets of nasalized vowels.

In the same year that Chomsky and Halle published The Sound Pattern of English, Bach and Harms (1968) edited a series of papers by Fillmore, Bach, McCawley, and Kiparsky under the title of Universals in Linguistic Theory. These papers had been presented in 1967 at a symposium on the topic of universals held at the University of Texas, Austin. In their introductory remarks, Back and Harms state: 'It is no longer of any interest to describe one after another language without regard to the relevance of the facts to general linguistic theory' (Bach and Harms 1968: vi). While the papers themselves were testimony to the lack of agreement on specific universals, all seemed to concur in the belief that to promote the general understanding of language was the most important task of linguistics.

As we extend our view to the universal aspects of language, we should not, however, be overly critical of the self-contained structural descriptions of the 40s and 50s. We must remember that structural linguistics had rightly reacted against the nonformal, speculative grammar of classical tradition. A great debt is owed to the structuralists for clearly demonstrating that Greco-Latin grammar could not serve as the universal basis for all languages. Faced with the task of analyzing so many unknown languages of the world, the formulation of universals simply had to be set aside. Only after a significantly large body of data about the world's languages had been amassed, could it be considered more rewarding to shift the focus from what is unique in each language to what is shared by all.

Concomitant with the search for universals is the deemphasis on the so-called arbitrariness of language—a notion which has been extended beyond its usefulness. As a matter of fact, the assumption that the structures of all languages are formed arbitrarily has always been bothersome in application, especially as regards the study of multilingualism. It could be reasoned that if languages are arbitrary in their structures, their distinctiveness must depend on the unique ways in which this arbitrariness can be expressed. Therefore, for an individual to speak more than one language, he must 'possess' more than one 'unique' linguistic system. This reasoning led linguists to interpret the kinds of theoretical organization multilingual individuals must have as 'coexistent' systems hooked together by some sort of code-switching mechanism.

Another conclusion was that the language systems of multilinguals could either be maintained separately or merge somehow. Psychologists began experimentation on 'compound' or 'balanced' versus 'coordinate' multilinguals. Semantic differential tests were devised to determine various kinds of multilingual performance. Most significantly, such studies came to include speculations on intelligence. The question was asked in many ways: are multilingual individuals more or less intelligent than monolinguals? Peal and Lambert (1962) have compiled an excellent survey of such studies. As one reads their report, one is impressed with how literally the psychologists have taken the theoretical constructs of linguists as a basis for their tests and how minimal is any consideration of the sociological contexts in which each case of multilingualism functions.

The body of data on multilingualism has grown to be immense and highly diversified in recent years. Not only have linguists and psychologists studied the phenomenon but sociologists and anthropologists, as well, have contributed much through their respective disciplines. This diversification has been not only welcome but essential to the growth of the study of language contact. We have now reached a point, however, where the lack of a unitary attitude will retard further theoretical development. Fishman (1968a, b) has already criticized what he calls 'immaculate' linguistics for not paying greater attention to sociological factors. He has also assaulted psychologists for producing 'ethnocentric' tests of multilinguals dependent on speed of reaction. While the sociologists, themselves, are not totally innocent of their own social biases and parochial attitudes, it is not difficult to see that many aspects of multilingual study are being obscured because of the lack of a unified theory. [1] The positing of a body of universals acceptable to all disciplines concerned with the study of multilingualism is seen as an important contribution to this end.

Finding universals in multilingualism requires some prior understanding both about the nature of universals in general and about man and the kinds of social structures he builds for himself. It is important to realize that the generalizations arising from the study of many specific cases do not automatically become universals. While generalizations are usually true, universals do not admit exceptions. For this reason, the form in which a universal is stated, must include a clarification of the circumstances in which it holds true. Furthermore, it must incorporate an appeal to logic. To give an example of how the procedure goes, let us consider the element of social stratification vis-à-vis language. Labov (1966) has shown that the various layers of social stratification correlate with features of language in New York City. These features are called 'linguistic variables' and they may be syntactic, lexical or phonological. Labov centers upon the pronunciation of [r], the variation of which he associates with socioeconomic stratification.

Even if we should find similar cases in many other speech communities, we could not advance Labov's observation to the status of a universal, as it stands. The assertion that language variables correlate with socioeconomic status would not admit the logical possibility that levels of social stratification may exist with no correlation to language. It is altogether possible that stratification which depends on human patterns of dominance and subordination could be marked in some other form of social interaction, such as in commercial transactions, religious ritual, or in marriage. [2] At least one sociologist, Dennis H. Wrong (1969), believes that social inequalities can exist without even fitting into any ordered pattern of stratification. It is not difficult to show that sociologists can and have studied social stratification without direct reference to language (see, for example, Heller 1969).

Since the language of a community is one of the major tools serving the functions of that community, the marking of societal primes such as dominance and subordination are bound to have linguistic correlates. In fact, a careful study of a community's language has traditionally helped anthropologists to understand much about family relationships, taboos, and so forth. Despite our intuitions about the correlation between linguistic and socioeconomic status, any universal dealing with such correlations would have to be expressed in a careful way, such as the following: <u>If a community is socially stratified and there is</u>

variability in the language of that community, then some of the variability of language must relate to the social stratification. In order to disprove such a universal, one would have to show that a community exists in which there is observable social stratification and observable variability in the language spoken by the community but that none of the language variability correlates with the social stratification. Speculations about the presence of elements of stratification in all societies do not affect the validity of the universal because the socially marked variability of language derives from society and not vice versa.

The power of any universal lies in the implications it brings to subsequent research. The one which I have proposed actually has greater implications for the study of the social structure of communities than for multilingualism in itself. It suggests to the sociologist and the anthropologist that clues to social structure can be found in language. Our main concern in this paper, however, is with the quest for universals that center on language, itself, and specifically on language contact. In regard to the latter, I have only two to propose. The first concerns the stability of language usage in a multilingual community and the second has to do with the nature of language convergence.

Before pursuing the matter in greater detail, it is well to point out that the reference to 'multilingualism' in this paper subsumes all situations involving the use of more than one language. Thus, no special status is given to two-language contact. The literature on language contact situations indicates some disagreement among investigators as to what terms are most appropriate. For some, a distinction is made between bilingualism (i.e. situations involving two languages only) and multilingualism (situations with more than two languages). Many use 'bilingualism' as the cover term for all cases involving two or more languages. Since it is not even clear that cases with two languages in contact are more common than those with more than two, I have chosen 'multilingualism' as the general term. I take this measure with full awareness that some of the specifics might vary. It remains to be proven, nevertheless, that two-language contact should be distinguished qualitatively from three- or four-language contact. Incidentally, I do adhere quite closely to the traditional requirement that 'languages in contact' be those used alternately by an individual in carrying out the usual functions of community life. In this way, different languages spoken by different individuals living in adjoining communities are excluded from the definition. Many so-called multilingual nations are primarily composed of separate monolingual communities contained within the same political boundaries. Any multilingualism that occurs in such situations is usually found along the 'periphery' of the communities, where individuals serve in a role of liaison between the monolingual groups.

Multilingual speech communities are groups of socially interacting individuals who share the same culture and the same languages for communication. In this way, we restrict our definition from including, ipso facto, the presence of English- and Spanish-speaking people in many American cities. While multilingualism might characterize one or the other group, the mere fact that they share some communal functions does not make the situation a multilingual one.

Discussion of Proposed Universal No. 1. In surveying the many parts of the world where languages are in contact, the investigator cannot help but speculate on the relative stability of each situation. Rubin (1968) has described what seems to be a relatively stable multilingualism in Paraguay. In that country, communication relating to specific domains of activity is either in Spanish or in Guaraní. Since there are certain domains associated predominantly with either language, the multilingual character of the nation is rendered stable. Ferguson's diglossia (1964) can be equally understood as a type of stable multilingualism in which only one of the codes is given the status of language. In the Arabic-speaking countries of the world, for example, a classical form of the language exists as the only 'correct' one along side a colloquial variety. The latter has no official status but is associated, nonetheless, with its own domains of social interaction. As a student of mine once said in reporting on the diglossia of Egypt, if a person were to inappropriately use classical Arabic to purchase a loaf of bread, he would run the risk of being considered insane. Other diglossic situations have been reported in Haiti (Stewart 1962) and in German-speaking Switzerland (Moulton 1962). Gumperz (1969) reports on highly stabilized multilingual communities in India where separate languages function in a type of diglossic relationship while the speakers retain an awareness that they are different languages.

Since stability is a relative matter, it would be difficult to draw any conclusion as to how long a given community of speakers will remain multilingual. At the base of the matter is a criterion of simplicity, statable as follows: Given two or more codes (i.e. languages) to convey the same set of messages, all but one will be abandoned. As both Mackey (1968) and Fishman (1968a) have observed, no community of speakers needs more than one language to communicate. For this reason, we cannot assume that when different speech communities merge into one, the result will always be stable multilingualism. What can be observed, however, is the relationship between multilingualism, when it does occur, and the association of each language with specific domains of social interaction. Thus, we might propose the following as a universal:

(1) The presence of multilingualism in a speech community depends on the association of each language involved with specific domains of social interaction.

The implication is that the stability of multilingualism is a function of the time period in which the community gives each language dominance in specific domains of interaction. A perfect balance of multilingualism in which, say, English and Spanish would be used equally as well for all domains of interaction is highly transitory and represents the step just before a new stage of monolingualism in one or the other language.

Discussion of Proposed Universal No. 2. The second universal concerns modifications of each of the languages used in multilingual communities. In his study of India, Gumperz (1969) observed that two or more languages spoken in the same community differ significantly from the same languages spoken in separate, monolingual communities. He concludes that the uniqueness of each language involved in multilingualism varies with the type of social interaction and context. The implication is that the longer two or more languages remain in stable multilingualism the more they will tend to converge. Examples are given from genetically unrelated languages like Marathi and Kanada which have developed impressive similarities with each other in communities where they are in contact.

Before we make it axiomatic that multilingual contact causes languages to converge, we must anticipate the difficulty of verification. Is there a point where two or more languages will converge to total merger? Or is there a cutting-off point where they will simply stop and reverse the polarization, going instead toward greater divergence? A more specific problem is predicting the ways in which they will grow more or less alike. Can we state categorically that it will be in the set of morphophonemic rules? Or in the underlying syntax? Or semantically? It appears that such a decision procedure would be very difficult to establish.

In view of such problems, we might consider multilingual convergence and divergence on a more abstract plane. We could begin with the observation that languages are in a state of constant change whether or not they are involved in multilingual contact. With each new speaker that is born, a new language competence is created, with its own grammatical specifics. As generations pass and the directions of social interaction are realigned, the language in its Saussurian sense of langue changes. To take a concrete example, we claim that the French of Canada would change and drift away from the French spoken in France regardless of whether or not it had contact with English in Canada's multilingual communities. The fact that English does co-exist with French in Canada means that the directions of change in Canadian French would be consequently affected by that contact. To refute this assertion would be tantamount to saying that languages are not affected by their social contexts. Or, alternatively, we would have to deny that English as the other language involved in this case of multilingualism is part of the social context in which both it and Canadian French are spoken. The universal that we extrapolate must be couched in very general terms but is, nevertheless, fundamental in the study of language distance:

(2) Given that a language is in a constant state of change and is susceptible to the social pressures and contexts in which it is spoken, contact with another language in the multilingual situation will be a factor in determining the direction of change in that language.

Although we leave unspecified the directions and the extent of change, the way is opened to experimentation with psychological and linguistic theories of competence, together with the study of socially relevant domains of interaction. If accurate, our second universal should help us go beyond the finite state taxonomic descriptions which characterize contemporary multilingual studies and enter a stage in which we will be equipped with the theoretical tools to predict the outcome of specific instances of multilingualism and even theorize about hypothetical cases.

Whether one will agree or not that the universals proposed in this paper are useful, I hope that I have at least made a case for developing a unified approach to the study of multilingualism through the uncovering of natural laws. Techniques of language planning by emerging nations and the organization of educational programs are only two of the many areas which would profit from an awareness of universals of the kind discussed here.

In distinction to DeCamp's (1969) proposal at last year's Round Table conference to incorporate sociolinguistic markers into an integrated theory of language, the present paper has dealt with the theory of multilingualism itself. Giambattista Vico, the father of the social sciences, saw the need long ago for a unifying force in any type of research. He wrote, in 1725: 'The great fragments of antiquity, hitherto useless to science because they lay begrimed, broken, and scattered, shed great light when cleaned, pieced together, and restored.' (See translation by Bergin and Fisch, 1968, and commentary by Tagliacozzo and White, 1969).

NOTES

[1]Hoffman (1968), for example, discusses the expression of male aggressiveness among Puerto Ricans living in New York City under the title of 'machismo'. Giving a Spanish label to it hides the important point that male agressiveness probably exists in all societies but manifests itself in different ways. At any rate, the overt expression of agressiveness in sexual terms has much to do with the age of the subject. The biological aspects of such behavior are often totally ignored by sociologists.

[2]Labov, himself, concludes that the natives of Martha's Vineyard, as opposed to New Yorkers, are 'essentially single-style speakers' and 'show relatively little change in their linguistic behavior as the formality of the social context changes'. (See Labov, 1966: 4).

REFERENCES

Bach, Emmon and Robert T. Harms, editors. 1968. Universals in linguistic theory. New York: Holt, Rinehart and Winston, Inc.

Bergin, Thomas G. and Max Harold Fisch, translators. 1968. The new science of Giambattista Vico. Ithaca, New York: Cornell University Press.

Chomsky, Noam and Morris Halle. 1968. The sound pattern of English. New York: Harper and Row.

DeCamp, David. 1969. Is a sociolinguistic theory possible? In MSLL No. 22, 157-173.

Ferguson, Charles A. 1964. Diglossia. In: Language in culture and society. Dell Hymes, editor. New York: Harper and Row, 429-439.

Fishman, Joshua A. 1968a. Sociolinguistic perspective on the study of bilingualism. Linguistics 39, 21-49.

_____. 1968b. Bilingualism in the barrio. Vols. I, II. Final report on contract no. OEC-1-7-062817-0297. U.S. Office of Education, Washington, D.C.

Greenberg, Joseph, editor. 1963. Universals of language. Cambridge, Massachusetts: M.I.T. Press. Second printing 1966.

Gumperz, John J. 1969. Communication in multilingual societies. In: Cognitive anthropology. Stephen A. Tyler, editor. New York: Holt, Rinehart and Winston, 435-449.

Heller, Celia S., editor. 1969. Structured social inequality. New York: Macmillan.

Hockett, Charles F. 1963. The problem of universals in language. In: Greenberg 1963.

Hoffman, Gerard. 1968. Puerto Ricans in New York: a language-related ethnographic summary. In: Fishman 1968b, 20-76.

Jakobson, Roman. 1963. Implications of language universals for linguistics. In: Greenberg 1963.

Labov, William. 1966. The social stratification of English in New York City. Washington, D. C., Center for Applied Linguistics.

Lenneberg, Eric H. 1967. Biological foundations of language. New York, J. Wiley.

Mackey, William F. 1968. The description of bilingualism. In: Readings in the sociology of language. J. A. Fishman, editor. The Hague, Mouton, 554-584.

Moulton, William G. 1962. What standard for diglossia? The case of German Switzerland. In MSLL no. 15, 133-144.

Peal, Elizabeth and Wallace Lambert. 1962. The relation of bilingualism to intelligence. Psychological Monographs, General and Applied, 76, no. 546.

Rubin, Joan. 1968. National bilingualism in Paraguay. The Hague, Mouton & Co.

Stewart, William A. 1962. Functional distribution of Creole and French in Haiti. MSLL no. 15, 149-159.

Tagliacozzo, Giorgio and Hayden V. White, editors. 1969. Giambattista Vico: An international symposium. Baltimore, Johns Hopkins.

Wrong, Dennis H. 1969. Social inequality without social stratification. In: Heller 1969, 513-520.

DISCUSSION

John Gumperz, University of California, Berkeley: I would like to comment on a paper of mine that Professor Di Pietro mentioned. That paper is one of a series of two in which I dealt with different aspects of the same problem. In that particular paper I was interested in the linguistic overlap between codes as they are used within the community. I did not go into the question of why two codes are kept separate. This was done for a purpose; it is impossible to make statements about social phenomena without careful ethnographic research. In order to be able to tell exactly why codes are used as they are I would have to do at least another year of field work.

I feel that there is much too much talk on the part of linguists and others about social causes of linguistic change and bilingual behavior. Having lived in the communities in question I do have some hypotheses which might explain the persistence of bilingualism. There is reason to suspect, for example, that speakers in the community assign priority to ethnic identity in friendship formation. But in order to make that as a categorical statement I would have to validate it by investigating the relationship between ethnic identity and friendship formation empirically. In other words, to deal with problems like Professor Di

Pietro suggests, I think we need an ethnography that is specifically concerned with these problems. Too many of our bilingual studies try to extrapolate from the linguistic to the social phenomena without adequate evidence.

Marion Walter, Millersville State College, Millersville, Pennsylvania: I would like to have Dr. Di Pietro distinguish between 'drift' as a direction of change in the home, the cultural center of life, and 'shift', that is the change away from the original patterns of the language, where an immigrant's language or dialect is concerned.

Di Pietro: I purposely avoided such terms as 'drift' and 'shift' because, as I said at one point in the paper, languages would change anyway whether they are in monolingual, bilingual, or multilingual contact. But when they are in contact in the way I have explained here, you must consider the other language as part of that context which will then structure the change one way or the other. Now if, as a result of Professor Gumperz's type of investigation into the ethnography, we can come to an understanding of how some sort of societal prime such as 'friendship' in this particular culture will affect language change more than other primes, then we are on our way to uncovering some of the universals. I have no intention to disclaim the work done by the sociolinguists. As I said at the end of my paper, you have got to piece all bits of research together; they have all got to make sense, they cannot be saying different things about the same thing.

BILINGUALISM AND THOUGHT

JOHN MACNAMARA

McGill University

Abstract. Recent studies conducted by linguists, anthropologists, and psycholinguists in the area of semantics make it possible to have a fresh look at the semantic processes of bilinguals. The new insights result in no small measure from the shedding of strict behavioristic constraints—without, however, abandoning the techniques developed in association with behaviorism. My paper will review with, hopefully, appropriate comments the work which has been done on the relationship between bilingualism and thought. The topics that arise include bilingualism and IQ, the coordinate-compound distinction, the Whorfian hypothesis, the problem-solving capacities of bilinguals and ethno-semantics.

If Whorf's hypothesis were true, if it were the case that differences among languages caused substantial differences in cognitive functioning, the bilingual person would be in a curious predicament. In his cognitive functioning, the bilingual would have to conform to one of three patterns, and each of the three would involve serious inconveniences. He might when using L_1 or L_2 always function cognitively in the manner appropriate to L_1 say; he would then have great difficulty in understanding speakers of L_2 or in being understood by them. Alternatively, he might always function cognitively in a manner appropriate to neither language and run the risk of understanding or being understood by nobody. Or he might have two cognitive systems, one for each language. He could then communicate with speakers of either language but he would have great difficulty in 'communicating' with himself. Whenever he switched languages he would have difficulty in explaining in L_2 what he had heard or said in L_1.

The implications which I am drawing from Whorf's hypothesis may seem preposterous, but I think that they follow logically. The differences in cognitive functioning which Whorf attributed to linguistic variables in syntax and vocabulary are far-reaching and profound. And though Whorf does not, to my knowledge, emphasize the effect which such differences might have on communication across language boundaries, the effects must surely be grave.

Our unwillingness to believe that the bilingual finds himself in the predicament I describe above is the measure of our unwillingness to accept the Whorfian hypothesis. But there are other grounds for caution. Psychologists, as Joshua Fishman (1960) points out, have been hard pressed to find any evidence in favor of the hypothesis. Only in its weakest form, only when it is taken as referring to the relationship between the suitability of vocabulary items to denote certain objects and some dependent cognitive functioning, is there support for Whorf in the psychological literature (see Lenneberg 1967, and Miller and McNeill 1969). Moreover, many of us instinctively join Church (1958) and Black (1959 and 1969) against Quine (1960) and numerous other philosophers in the view that one cannot establish a man's ontology from either his vocabulary or his grammar.

One is a little surprised, then, to hear Lounsbury (1969) say that in their thinking about limited areas of vocabulary and the related cognitive structures 'the leading social anthropologists of today incline ... in the direction of complete relativism' (Lounsbury 1969: 14). Lounsbury is referring specifically to kinship systems, but his remarks can presumably be extended to cover other folk taxonomies. The root reason for the prevailing opinion is the hope, perhaps even belief, that the componential analysis of folk taxonomies reveals psychological entities. Indeed several of the leading exponents of the art, Goodenough (1956), Frake (1962), Mathiot (1969), and Wallace (1962) have made statements which suggest that they are laying bare the bases used by people in classifying their environment. On the other hand, it is only fair to point out that this belief has been seriously questioned several times by social anthropologists themselves; see, for example, Burling (1969), Hymes (1969), Lounsbury (1969) and Wallace (1965). The claim that componential analysis reveals psychologically valid entities runs into Burling's (1969) objection that any set of terms can be analyzed, or systematically divided, in several different ways. Since each division demands a set of components somewhat different from any other division, and since the choice of one division rather than another is arbitrary, it follows that the psychological validity of the resultant components is highly questionable. Moreover, as Vermazen (1967) observes in discussing a similar problem connected with Katz and Fodor's (1963) model of lexical structure, there is no principled way of selecting components or bases of classification. We can effectively distinguish men from women, for example, on the basis of skin texture, body outline, length of finger nails, hair ribbons and the like without ever needing to carry the study further. The seemingly obvious candidate for component status, then, need not be the one which people generally employ. The truth is that we know very little about the bases which people use for classifying the most familiar objects in their environment (see Polanyi 1968), and it is unlikely that language on its own should provide the answer.

The point of all this is to emphasize once again the lesson which psychologists drew from their studies of Whorf's hypothesis. Linguistic evidence on its own can be used to support linguistic conclusions only, never psychological ones. Since anthropologists have seldom gone beyond linguistic evidence in their analyses of folk taxonomies, it would be premature to make claims of psychological validity for their componential systems. It follows, too, that one would be unwise to base claims for Whorfian relativism on such analyses.

Coordinate-compound distinction

The coordinate-compound distinction to which I now want to turn is closely related to Whorfian relativism. Indeed I hope to show that in some of its forms it is a veiled version of such relativism. It was mainly Uriel Weinreich (1953) in his book, Languages in Contact, who drew the attention of psychologists to the distinction. In that book he tentatively suggests that on semantic grounds bilinguals seem to fall into three types, which I shall call by the names which have subsequently become standard. 'Coordinate' bilinguals are those for whom the corresponding pair of terms in two languages signify a single 'semanteme'. 'Compound' bilinguals are those for whom corresponding terms signify a single semanteme. 'Subordinate' bilinguals are those for whom a term in L_2 signifies first a term in L_1 and signifies a semanteme only indirectly. The three types may be illustrated by means of Weinreich's own diagrams in which he uses the Russian word kniga 'book' together with the English word book.

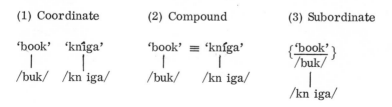

(1) Coordinate   (2) Compound   (3) Subordinate

In Ervin and Osgood (1965) the subordinate type is subsumed into the compound one and criteria are given for judging to which of the two remaining types a bilingual belongs. Compounds are those who either learned one language through the medium of the other, as in old-fashioned language classes, or learned both languages in the same context, the home for instance. The coordinates or 'true' bilinguals are those who learned the two languages in different contexts, such as L_1 at home and L_2 at school (presumably by the direct method) and at work. Ervin and Osgood's illustration of the two types are shown in Figure 1 in which $\underline{S}$ and $\underline{R}$ stand for sign and response respectively,

FIGURE 1.

Coordinate	Compound
S_A $\overset{r}{\underset{m_1}{}}$--------$\overset{s}{\underset{m_1}{}}$ R_A S_B $\overset{r}{\underset{m_1}{}}$--------$\overset{s}{\underset{m_1}{}}$ R_B	S_A $\overset{r}{\underset{m}{}}$--------$\overset{s}{\underset{m}{}}$ R_A S_B R_B

$\underline{r}$ and $\underline{s}$ stand for 'mediating processes or meanings', and the subscripts $\underline{A}$ and $\underline{B}$ stand for different languages as do the sub-subscripts 1 and 2 in the diagram for coordinates. Not wishing to start old battles all over again, I will rest content with two observations about this theory. It falls heir to all the criticism that Chomsky (1959), Fodor (1965) and others have made of $\underline{S}$-$\underline{R}$ attempts to handle the phenomena of language. In addition, and here I am sure its authors would agree today, it is quite inadequate as a representation of the lexical structure which must be employed by anyone who speaks a natural language. Space permits me to do little more than refer to a number of sources: Chomsky (1965), Katz (1966), Katz and Fodor (1963), Katz and Postal (1964), Macnamara (in press), Macnamara and O'Clerigh (1969), Quillian (1967 and 1968) and Weinreich (1966). Among the principal weaknesses of the Ervin and Osgood model is the fact that it makes no provision for denotation as distinct from connotation or for emotive meaning as distinct from either. Moreover the model does not discuss the problem of selecting an appropriate meaning from among the many meanings of a polysemous term, although this is one of the major criteria which a satisfactory semantic theory must meet.

I fear that the man whose lead I have long followed in the study of bilingualism has added somewhat to the confusion which surrounds the coordinate-compound distinction. In some recent papers (Lambert

1966, Lambert and Rawlings 1969, Segalowitz and Lambert 1969) he shifts the distinction between coordinate and compound bilingualism to one between early and late bilingualism. Compound bilinguals are those who acquire both languages in their homes before they go to school; coordinate bilinguals are those who began to acquire their second language after school age. In this new way of classifying bilinguals he is joined by Stafford (1968) and by Stafford and Van Keuren (1968).

But to return to the point of departure! Through all the variations in the interpretation of the terms, 'coordinate' and 'compound', the distinction has always been a semantic one and for Ervin and Osgood, unless I am mistaken, it was a Whorfian one. Ervin and Osgood's compound bilinguals had a single set of 'representational mediation processes' for the two languages, whereas their coordinates had two sets of such processes, one for each language. Since mediation processes in their system are caused by signs or stimuli, it is fair to say that differences between languages cause different cognitive, nonlinguistic, mediating processes. For example, French uses the word couper in connection with the cutting of hair with a scissors and also the cutting up of a joint of meat with a knife; standard English divides the function of couper between cut and carve respectively. It follows that a coordinate French-English bilingual could well have different mediating processes associated with couper and cut. Admittedly, Ervin and Osgood seek to avoid the resultant inconveniences by suggesting that across languages the differences between translation equivalents are mostly slight. But as the above example shows this is not true. Ervin and Osgood also permit of elaborate connections between the coordinate's parallel mediating processes, in order to account for translation. Such connections might seem at first to preclude the plight of the Whorfian bilingual who cannot communicate with himself, who when he switches to L_2 can never make out what he has heard or said in L_1. But Ervin and Osgood's additional associations will not preclude this difficulty; they are not equivalent to an instruction 'compare and contrast', and make good any differences discovered by having recourse to other linguistic materials and other mediation processes. Yet only by means of such an instruction and a device to operate it could a person with something like 'coordinate systems' ever switch languages without becoming hopelessly lost.

Lest you think that I am being unfair to the Ervin and Osgood model, permit me to point out two other related difficulties. The model has no system which would permit of two sets of mediating processes associated with a single term and for permitting context to select between them. Yet the cutting of hair with a scissors and the carving of meat with a knife might well give rise to distinct mediation processes which might well compete for possession of a Frenchman's head when couper was encountered. Furthermore, Osgood's semantic system, like all the other ones which have since been proposed, does not handle grammar. Apart from anything else, this means the model is confined to pairs of lexical items; hence it cannot guard against the inconveniences I have outlined by systematically relating viande with couper in one expression and cheveux with couper in another expression so as to ensure that only the appropriate mediating processes are elicited.

On the subject of research into the coordinate-compound distinction I have little to add to what I wrote in the Journal of Social Issues in 1967. I then considered the evidence for the distinction to be exiguous, and I have seen no reason since to change my mind. I agree with Diller (1967) that the distinction as it stands is most likely a 'conceptual artifact', and I am fearful for the sturdiness of the tall cognitive and personality structures, which Diebold (1968) builds upon it. Perhaps my basic trouble is my belief that nothing like an adequate semantic system has been worked out for any language, let alone related semantic systems for two languages in bilingual harness.

This need not mean that we abandon work on the semantic systems of bilinguals; it is rather an invitation reculer pour mieux sauter. I suspect that the original inspiration for the coordinate-compound distinction owes more to instances of semantic interference than to Whorfian relativism. This sort of interference is well-known; it is beautifully illustrated for example by Professor Mackey (1962 and 1965). For instance, the Irish word lámh is the nearest equivalent to the English word hand in the sense of human member. However, unlike hand, lámh includes 'arm' in its denotation. If we start out not from words but from semantic fields we find numerous situations which I have previously illustrated with the French word couper serving the function of the English words cut and carve in at least some of their senses. It seems to me that such differences between the semantic systems of languages might well give rise to a whole range of bilinguals who vary in the extent to which they keep the semantic systems of their two languages distinct. Furthermore, I agree with Kolers (1963) and Fishman (1964) that the manner in which a person has learned his languages is unlikely to fix his semantic systems for life. Some may start out with fused semantic systems and gradually sort them out; others may start out with separate systems but gradually permit them to merge. Indeed, as John Gumperz (1964) has pointed out, it may be that distinct semantic systems can be maintained only by a person who makes a great conscious effort to do so, and much good language teaching is aimed precisely at achieving this effect.

At this point I want to forestall a possible source of confusion. The sort of distinction between semantic systems of which I have been speaking does not at all suggest a Whorfian relativism. It does not suggest that an Englishman either carves meat differently from a Frenchman, or perceives the carving of meat differently from a Frenchman, or is in the least different from a Frenchman in his approach to meat, simply because as an Englishman he has a special term for the action of slicing meat with a knife. Neither is there any suggestion that an Irishman's knowledge of anatomy is more confused than that of an Englishman. All I want to suggest is that when a well-educated Irish-English bilingual cashes the terms in the two languages, he may get different semantic values for the words lámh and hand; a bilingual who does not know the languages so thoroughly is likely to get the same value for both words, even when he should not. It follows that when the well-educated bilingual needs to denote precisely that which the word hand denotes, he has to go beyond the word lámh and either add a modifying expression or choose a different lexical item.

It may help to be more precise about the advantages of employing a distinction based on degree of semantic interference rather than the coordinate-compound distinction. The first is clarity. Any clarity which the coordinate-compound distinction seemed to have was deceptive. Weinreich said that kniga and book might denote different 'semantemes' for a coordinate bilingual, but he did not clarify what he meant by a 'semanteme' or how the two semantemes related to these words might differ. The differences between Ervin and Osgood's coordinates and compounds are securely locked inside the head where no one can see them. In contrast, I am tying semantic interference to denotation and more specifically what I might call 'denotational extent'. In the limited illustrative materials which I have used, lámh has a wider denotational extension than hand, and cut has a narrower denotational extension than couper. At a less concrete level, conscience (French) has a wider denotational extension that conscience (English).

Admittedly, I am not proposing any formal model of information processing or language processing, but then I do not believe that formalism in these areas is profitable at the present time. Formalism often results in hardening of the intellectual arteries; I for one feel freer when working from a nonformal base to explore the broad strategies of semantic functioning. One such strategy must call for an ability to relate the incoming linguistic message to stored information and to systems which process such information. Quillian (1968) points out that a highly likely sense for an ambiguous symbol can frequently be determined simply on the basis of frequency of association. For instance, frequency suggests the meaning 'down tools' for strike in (1) though other meanings are possible.

(1) The foreman called a strike.

The problem discussed by Bar-Hillel (1964: 174-179) is rather different. He noted that the meaning 'enclosure in which children play' is determined for pen in (2) on the basis of the relative sizes of boxes and pens in the sense of 'writing instruments'.

(2) The box is in the pen.

The successful interpretation of the word pen in (2), then, depends on access to stored information and also on the ability to carry out some computations on such information at the moment of recall. This follows from the fact that few will have readily available as a piece of information the fact that boxes are rarely small enough to fit inside even a large writing pen. Since we could presumably use the relative sizes of writing pens and any other physical objects with which we are familiar, it is more parsimonious to hypothesize a function which permits us to compare sizes, whenever such information is required, than to store the results of innumerable comparisons. On the assumption that this is correct, I would suggest further that such information is for the most part stored and processed nonlinguistically and probably unconsciously.

Ulric Neisser (1967) has recently made an excellent case for the theory of analysis by synthesis in perception. In essence, the theory proposes that on the basis of partial information one can usually form a correct hypothesis about that which one is perceiving. Applied to language this means that on the basis of partial information, linguistic, nonlinguistic, and stochastic, one can usually form a correct hypothesis about that which someone is trying to communicate. One of course tests the hypothesis against further information which comes one's way and if necessary modifies the hypothesis. My reason for mentioning the theory here is to suggest that if it is correct in broad outline—and it seems to be—we must visualize the human language user as a far more dynamic agent in his approach to speech than either Whorf or bilingual theory builders seem to imagine. Moreover, it seems likely that linguistic processes are only a small part of the cognitive functioning which is associated with either the production or the interpretation of speech. Furthermore, this very dynamism is surely the reason that the bilingual does not end up in any of the impasses to which Whorfian theorizing and the Ervin and Osgood model of coordinate and compound bilingualism seem inevitably to lead.

Bilingualism and IQ

The issues of which I have been speaking raise other more far-reaching issues which unfortunately I can do little more than allude to in this paper. The suggestion that linguistic functioning is to a great extent dependent on nonlinguistic functioning of many sorts is bound to disturb many philosophical spirits. However, it ties in nicely with the theory of Vygotsky (1962) and the oft-repeated theory of Piaget (see, for example, 1963 and 1965) that the origin of thought is distinct from that of language, and that insofar as the two are related in the early stages, language is the dependent partner. The investigations of Piaget's student, Sinclair-de-Zwart (1967 and 1969) support this theory and suggest that even in school children the development of basic cognitive schemata owe little to language, but rather that developments in language which occur at this time are dependent on prior nonlinguistic growth.

Essentially in the same tradition are recent papers by Bever (1970), Hebb, Lambert and Tucker (1970), and Macnamara (1970) all arguing for a much closer integration of nonlinguistic cognitive functioning with linguistic functioning than has been common in most of the recent discussions of language acquisition. In my paper, I attempt to establish the thesis that the majority of linguistic universals are due to certain essential features of human intelligence. These are the features which ensure that mathematics, logic and science are essentially the same the world over; these are the reason that every language is translatable into every other language; these are the basic reason for disbelieving Whorf.

Such communality in human intelligence has been obscured by the development of psychometrics and by the accompanying emphasis in psychology on individual differences. From their earliest beginnings intelligence tests have been designed to reveal individual differences in intelligence; they have never been designed for the purpose of revealing the essentials of intelligence. No analysis of IQs, then, however sophisticated or however comprehensive, could ever reveal what intelligence is; so it is little wonder that psychometric discussions on the topic have been barren. I suspect that the results of concentrating on IQs and on individual differences have been even more baneful than fruitless discussion of the nature of intelligence; I suspect that they have drawn attention away from factors which contribute to the development of intelligence. If I may be permitted to point a moral, one notices how interesting studies of child language became when in the early 1960s scholars abandoned the individual differences approach of earlier years and focussed instead upon the essentials of the process in which children differ very little. A similar moral can be drawn from the experimentally feeble and statistically naive investigations of Jean Piaget which have yielded results of such interest which have been replicable the world over.

This is the background against which I would like to pose the question so often posed by students of bilingualism, does bilingualism affect intelligence? Against such a background one wonders what the question might mean. I have never seen the question discussed in this context, but it seems unlikely that bilingualism should have any effect upon the development of the basic, common, cognitive structures. The question, however, has usually been translated into the form, does bilingualism affect IQ? In that form it is almost trivial. An indefinitely large number of factors can affect IQ without having any direct bearing on what we intuitively recognize as intelligence. Among such factors is command of language. Under certain circumstances bilingual children have frequently been found to have a poorer command of their school language than their unilingual counterparts—see Macnamara (1966). Under similar circumstances bilinguals have generally scored a lower mean verbal IQ than unilinguals, but not a lower mean nonverbal IQ—see Darcy (1953 and 1963). It seems then that grasp of the language variety in which an IQ test is couched can affect the outcome of the test—an honest but hardly a surprising discovery.

What does all this amount to? Instinctively I want to say that the results just mentioned do not mean that bilinguals are more stupid than unilinguals, they have only been made to appear so. I well realize, however, that deficiencies in the standard version of a school language can constitute added difficulty in schoolwork. Tom Kellaghan and John Macnamara (1967) have shown that such difficulties can arise from something other than ignorance of certain words, idioms and syntactic structures; they can arise from a fairly generalized unfamiliarity with and poor control of the standard language, at least in written form, so as to affect a student's problem-solving ability adversely. To conclude, then, bilinguals probably have need of some special help with language; poor control of the school language could well prevent a child from developing competence in several important areas of schoolwork. Granted that difficulties with the language are overcome, however, there is no reason to believe that bilingualism of itself should affect school progress in any way, adversely or beneficially. But of course a second language usually means access to a whole new world of people, literature and ideas, and so bilingualism can be an enormous advantage.

Before passing on to the last section, it is worth pausing for a moment to consider where the study of bilingualism and IQ fits in with Whorfian relativism and the coordinate-compound distinction. There is probably no direct connection between them; nevertheless they are all related to some more general view of the connection between language and thought. The fears, or hopes, which caused people to study the relationship between bilingualism and IQ seem to spring from the general view that language either constitutes or creates intelligence. It is not difficult to see how such a view is related to Whorfian relativism and to the Ervin and Osgood models for coordinates and compounds. It follows then, that the basic objections to both Whorfian relativism and the Ervin and Osgood semantic models can also be used against a direct causal connection which would make intelligence dependent upon bilingualism.

Bilingualism and creativity

The whole study of creativity which has waxed and waned over the past ten years seems to be bedevilled to an even greater degree than the study of intelligence. The enterprise to explain creativity in school children has had two main objectives: (1) to prove that something could be measured which was largely independent of IQ; (2) to purify measures of this 'something' and use them to establish a range of individual differences in it (see Dacey and Madaus 1969). Very little attention indeed has been paid to this 'something' or to the notion of creativity or to the relationship between creativity and intelligence. The fact that measures of creativity were designed almost entirely for the purpose of revealing individual differences in creativity meant that they were bound to miss the essentials of creativity, just as IQs miss the essentials of intelligence. The requirement that IQs and measures of creativity should as far as possible be orthogonal meant that the whole enterprise was committed from the outset to the trivial task of establishing that intelligence and creativity can differ in some peripheral ways. It is hardly unfair to say that the enterprise has been barren.

The whole thrust of Jean Piaget's life work has been to show that intelligence is essentially creative. If anything, he has attributed too much creativity to the mind and failed to stress the fact that the neonate must have a great deal of mental structure to explain intellectual creativity. Be that as it may, however, the main point is that the most important body of investigation into the nature of human intelligence results in the conclusion that the mind is essentially creative. Hardly a happy augury for studies of creativity which start from the assumption that the two are different in kind. To Piaget's work may be added the body of theoretical and empirical work on language which clusters around the writings of Noam Chomsky. Chomsky stresses the creativity involved in the use of natural language and others (see, for example, McNeill 1966) have found that the process of learning a language is a creative one. Perhaps the study of creativity would not have been so fruitless if it had been appreciated from the start that what its investigators were hunting for was not creativity at all, but rather unusual creations. That would not have given the investigators any greater guarantee of validity for their measures, but it would have set them free of the constraint that sought to justify the notion of creativity by showing that it could be distinguished from IQ.

Students of bilingualism have also wondered about the possibility that bilingualism should make people more creative. As I imagine Professor Lambert will discuss the evidence later in the conference, I will be brief. Both he and I are cautious about claims that bilingualism 'generates' creativity, though he tends to be more optimistic than I do. Apart altogether from the theoretical considerations which I mentioned, I am not impressed by the evidence that has been produced to indicate that bilinguals tend to be more creative than monolinguals. Taking the theoretical considerations into account, in particular the total absence of any indications of validity for measures of creativity in school children, I am of the opinion that the topic of bilingualism and creativity comes under Wittgenstein's rubric: wovon man nicht reden kann, darüber muss man schweigen.

Conclusion: Wanted: a theory of semantics

The saying that it is part of wisdom not to know (ignorare) certain things is attributed to Erasmus. I am not sure that I know what it means, but I would like it to include a counsel to realize and admit when we do not know something. Most of the topics which I have discussed have led me to make negative statements: I do not believe that there is any evidence to justify claims of Whorfian relativism; I do not believe that there is any evidence that there are two different sorts of bilinguals, coordinate and compound, at least as these have been described in the literature; I do not believe that bilingualism is directly related to intelligence; I do not believe that bilingualism is directly related to creativity. I want to add one other disclaimer to these: I am not even sure that the pair of concepts which are dissociated in each of these four statements are essentially unrelated. In other words, I am not even sure that any negativism is justified.

The reason is that each section of this paper is about the relationship between language and some aspect of thought and we have no semantic theory which even remotely approaches adequacy. Furthermore, I am not at all convinced that the empirical investigations to which I have alluded in this paper have contributed much to the building up of such a theory. Yet without an adequate theory of semantics, psychology and linguistics (and possibly philosophy) rapidly reach an impasse. One has the impression of one vogue succeeding another without any substantial progress. For what it is worth, my feeling is that valuable insights are going to come only through careful studies of infants, the development of their psychological functioning as a whole, of their classification of objects and the bases of such classification, of the assumptions which they make or do not make in their approaches to the world about them and in their approaches to language, of their ability to generalize, and the like. Furthermore, we need more careful studies of how language learning relates to other psychological developments. Among such studies, the analysis of bilingual language learning will have an honorable position. The road will be longer and more arduous, I imagine, than that which led to the major discoveries of modern physics, but the rewards will, I hope, be greater and less pregnant with destructive power.

REFERENCES

Bar-Hillel, Joshua. 1964. Language and information. Reading, Massachusetts, Addison-Wesley.

Bever, T. G. 1970. The cognitive basis for linguistic structures. In J. R. Hayes, ed., Cognition and language learning. New York, Wiley.

Black, Max. 1959. Linguistic relativity: the views of Benjamin Lee Whorf. Philosophical Review 68: 228-238.

_____. 1969. Some troubles with Whorfianism. In Sidney Hook, ed., Language and philosophy: a symposium. New York University Press, 30-35.

Burling, Robbins. 1969. Cognition and componential analysis: God's truth or hocus-pocus? In Stephen A. Tyler, ed., Cognitive anthropology. New York, Holt, Rinehart and Winston, 419-428.

Chomsky, Noam. 1959. Review of verbal behavior by B. F. Skinner. Language, 35: 26-58.

_____. 1965. Aspects of the theory of syntax. Cambridge, Massachusetts, M. I. T. Press.

Church, A. 1958. Ontological commitment. Journal of Philosophy, 55: 1008-1014.

Dacey, John S. and George F. Madaus. 1969. Creativity: definitions, explanations and facilitation. Irish Journal of Education, 3: 55-69.

Darcy, Natalie T. 1953. A review of the literature on the effects of bilingualism upon the measurement of intelligence. Journal of Genetic Psychology, 82: 21-58.

_____. 1963. Bilingualism and the measurement of intelligence: review of a decade of research. Journal of Genetic Psychology, 103: 259-282.

Diebold, Richard A. 1968. The consequences of early bilingualism in cognitive development and personality formation. In E. Norbeck, D. Price-Williams and W. M. McCord, eds., The study of personality: an interdisciplinary appraisal. New York, Holt, Rinehart and Winston, 218-245.

Diller, Karl C. 1967. 'Compound' and 'coordinate' bilingualism—a conceptual artifact. Paper presented to the Linguistic Society of America, Chicago, Illinois (mimeo).

Ervin, Susan and Charles E. Osgood. 1954. Second language learning and bilingualism. Journal of Abnormal and Social Psychology. (Supplement), 49: 139-146.

Fishman, Joshua A. 1960. A systematization of the Whorfian hypothesis. Behavioral Science. 5: 232-239.

_____. 1964. Language maintenance and language shift as a field of inquiry. Linguistics, 9: 32-70.

Fodor, Jerry A. 1965. Could meaning be an r_m? Journal of Verbal Learning and Verbal Behavior, 4: 73-81.

Frake, Charles O. 1962. The ethnographic study of cognitive systems. In Thomas Gladwin and William C. Sturtevant, eds., Anthropology and Human Behavior. Anthropological Society of Washington. Washington, D. C.

Goodenough, Ward H. 1956. Componential analysis and the study of meaning. Language, 32, 195-216.

Gumperz, John J. 1964. Linguistic and social interaction in two communities. In John J. Gumperz and Dell H. Hymes, eds., The Ethnography of Communication. American Anthropologist, Special Publication 3: 137-153.

Hebb, Donald O., Wallace E. Lambert, and G. Richard Tucker. 1970. Language, thought and experience. McGill University, Department of Psychology, (mimeo).

Hymes, Dell H. 1969. Discussion of Burling's paper. In Stephen A. Tyler, ed., Cognitive anthropology. New York, Holt, Rinehart and Winston, 428-431.

Katz, Jerrold J. 1966. The philosophy of language. New York, Harper and Row.

_____, and Jerry A. Fodor. 1963. The structure of semantic theory. Language 39: 170-210.

_____, and Paul M. Postal. 1964. An integrated theory of linguistic description. Cambridge, Massachusetts, M. I. T. Press.

Kellaghan, Thomas, and John Macnamara. 1967. Reading in a second language. In Marion D. Jenkinson, ed., Reading instruction: an international forum. Newark, Delaware, International Reading Association, 231-240.

Kolers, Paul A. 1963. Interlingual word associations. Journal of Verbal Learning and Verbal Behaviour, 2: 291-300.

Lambert, Wallace E. 1969. Psychological studies of the interdependencies of the bilinguals two languages. In Jaan Puhvel, ed., Substance and structure in language. University of California Press, 99-126.

_____, and Chris Rawlings. 1969. Bilingual processing of mixed-language associative networks. Journal of Verbal Learning and Verbal Behaviour, 8: 604-609.

Lenneberg, Eric H. 1967. Biological foundations of language. New York, Wiley.

Lounsbury, Floyd G. 1969. Language and culture. In Sidney Hook, ed., Language and Philosophy: A Symposium. New York University Press, 3-29.

Mackey, William F. 1962. The description of bilingualism. Canadian Journal of Linguistics, 7: 51-85.

_____. 1965. Bilingual interference: Its analysis and measurement. Journal of Communication, 15, 239-249.

Macnamara, John. 1966. Bilingualism and primary education. Edinburgh University Press.

_____. 1967. The bilingual^s linguistic performance—a psychological overview. Journal of Social Issues, 23: 58-77.

_____. 1970. The cognitive basis of language learning in infants. Montreal: Department of Psychology. McGill University, (mimeo).

_____. In press. Parsimony and the lexicon. Language.

_____, and Anne O Cléirigh. 1969. Studies in the psychology of semantics: the projection rules. Dublin: Educational Research Center, St. Patrick's College, (mimeo).

Mathiot, Madelaine, 1969. The semantic and cognitive domain of language. University of California, Los Angeles, (mimeo).

McNeill, David. 1966. The creation of language by children. In John Lyons and Roger J. Wales, eds., Psycholinguistic papers: the proceedings of the 1966 Edinburgh Conference. Edinburgh University Press, 99-115.

Miller, George A., and David McNeill. 1969. Psycholinguistics. In G. Lindzey and E. Aronson, eds., Handbook of social psychology, vol. 3. Reading, Massachusetts, Addison-Westley, 666-794.

Neisser, Ulric. 1967. Cognitive psychology. New York, Appleton-Century-Crofts.

Piaget, Jean. 1963. Langage et operations intellectuelles. In Problèmes de psycholinguistique. Symposium de l'association de psychologie scientifique de langue française. Paris, Presses Universitaires de France.

_____. 1965. La formation du symbole chez l'enfant: Imitation, jeu et rêvs, image et représentation. (3rd edition). Neuchatel, Delachaux et Niestlé.

Polanyi, Michael. 1968. Logic and psychology. American Psychologist, 3, 27-43.

Quillian, M. Ross. 1967. Word concepts: a theory simulation of some basic semantic capabilities. Behavioral Science. 12: 410-430.

_____. 1968. Semantic memory. In Marvin Minsky, ed., Semantic information processing. M.I.T. Press, 216-270.

Quine, Willard Van Orman. 1960. Word and object. New York, Wiley.

Segalowitz, Norman, and Wallace E. Lambert. 1969. Semantic generalization in bilinguals. Journal of Verbal Learning and Verbal Behaviour. 8: 559-566.

Sinclair-de-Zwart, Hermina. 1967. Acquisition de langage et développement de la pensée. Paris, Dunad.

_____. 1969. Developmental psycholinguistics. In David Elkind and John H. Flavell, eds. Studies in cognitive development: Essays in honor of Jean Piaget. New York, Oxford University Press: 315-336.

Stafford, Kenneth R. 1968. Problem solving as a function of language. Language and Speech. 11: 104-112.

_____, and Stanley R. Van Kauren. 1968. Semantic differential profiles as related to monolingual-bilingual types. Language and Speech. 11: 167-170.

Vermazen, Bruce. 1967. Review of an integrated theory of linguistic descriptions by J. J. Katz and P. M. Postal, and the philosophy of language by J. J. Katz. Synthese, 17: 35-365.

Vygotsky, Lev S. 1962. Thought and Language. Cambridge, Massachusetts, M. I. T. Press.

Wallace, Anthony F. C. 1962. Culture and cognition. Science, 135: 351-357.

_____. 1965. The problem of the psychological validity of componential analysis. In E. A. Hammel, ed., Formal semantic analysis, Menasha, Wisconsin, American Anthropological Association. 229-248.

Weinreich, Uriel. 1953. Languages in contact. Publications of the Linguistic Circle. New York, no. 1.

_____. 1966. Explorations in semantic theory. In Thomas A. Sebeok, ed., Current trends in linguistics, vol. 3. The Hague, Mouton: 395-477.

DISCUSSION

Einar Haugen, Harvard University: This paper covers areas that I think all of us are interested in, which in some ways are crucial to the whole problem of bilingualism and the things we have been thinking about.

I've had occasion in the last few months to review the entire literature on bilingualism in the Americas and write a research report on it (for Current Trends in Linguistics). I've uttered many rash opinions there on some of the subjects that Professor Macnamara has spoken so well about. One or two things I would like to add to them.

We start with this matter of bilinguals being thought to be mentally inadequate because of their performance on intelligence tests. This, I think, is deeply and seriously connected with the fact that 'bilingual' is used in many circles as a pejorative term to refer to people who are socially disadvantaged in other ways. In the Southwest, I know, to say of someone, 'Oh, he's just a bilingual' often means he is a Mexican child who has not learned enough English in the home to profit adequately from English teaching in the school. The term 'bilingual' has come to be a euphemism for a linguistically handicapped person, while the kind of bilinguals that we define in academic terms are simply not considered.

As for the compound-coordinate distinction, this builds ultimately on a partial misunderstanding of Uriel Weinreich's book (1953). I have reread very carefully what he wrote on this subject. He was very skeptical about the notion that people could be classified as compound or coordinate. He merely wrote that some signs in the language could be stored as compound signs and some as coordinate, while, in addition, some could be subordinate. In other words, he made it a trichotomy, not a dichotomy. The subordinate signs belong characteristically to language students in our classes, those to whom we teach the language through a dictionary or through translation. In a paper given to the Linguistic Society a couple of years ago by Karl Diller, the whole concept of compound and coordinate as used by the psychologists was shown to be badly defined. Recent experiments by Lambert have shown greater skepticism than his earlier ones with regard to the value of this distinction.

Now let's take a look at the linguistic relativity hypothesis, which was developed in this country by Benjamin Whorf. The problem is not whether Whorfianism is true, but rather why some people believe in it. The Whorfian hypothesis is certainly wrong in its strongest form, as when Whorf suggested that relativity could have been discovered in Hopi more easily than in English. Relativity was not discovered in English at all, but in mathematics. It is a mathematical statement and has no clear relation to natural languages. This is what we have mathematics for: to be able to say things so that they are universal and not tied to a particular language. The so-called 'Whorfian' hypothesis goes far back into history, as recent studies have shown. The Germans have been very strong on it, and one reason may be that they were eager to show that German somehow was different from all other languages and therefore better. This does not mean that the hypothesis is absolutely wrong by any means; I think that in a weak form we all have to accept it. Anyone who is a bilingual knows that it feels different to talk one language than to talk another. You talk about different things, and you talk about things from different points of view. The problem is how to capture this difference. I suspect it is basically semantic, as Professor Macnamara was saying: we need a semantic theory, not the kind of gross measures that have been used so far. My apologies to the Whorfians—I think they've got something, but as yet they haven't told us what it is.

William F. Mackey, Université Laval: I think Professor Macnamara started something by bringing up the Whorfian hypothesis. I would simply like to add something which may clarify the issue. The so-called Whorfian hypothesis is not a single hypothesis; it really is two hypotheses, and you can accept one without accepting the other. The first one has to do with relativity, with linguistic relativity, meaning that languages slice up reality in a different way. I think this is evident; and anyone who has done any translation would admit it. The other hypothesis is what you might call the hypothesis of determinism; meaning that, because languages do slice up things in different ways, people speaking them are forced to think in different ways. Now, this is something that we can easily deny. We can accept the relativity part of the hypothesis without accepting the determinism part of it. I think this is what Professor Haugen had in mind.

Robert Lado, Georgetown University: I'm very much encouraged by Professor Macnamara's paper. We're conducting an experiment at this time to test the hypothesis that language and thought are sufficiently distinct to be measured separately and, furthermore, that in language in use, that is, in linguistic performance, thinking is central and we search for utterances within the rules and patterns of a language to refer to thinking. Thinking is understood as mental activity of any variety. A language is a symbolic system used by the speakers of a linguistic community to refer imperfectly to their thinking and to make noises that trigger another person's brain and stimulate him to do his thinking. This experiment is in an advanced stage at the present time, and I was delighted to see the interest shown in the topic under discussion.

Dell Hymes, University of Pennsylvania: Professor Haugen's account of linguistic and anthropological history can hardly be allowed to pass without a comment. The remarks he made attach to both Boas and Sapir. Both were concerned to interpret grammatical structures as forms of thought, although the degree to which each saw grammar as giving form to thought, or as simply an outer form, may have varied. Boas saw himself as carrying on the approach of Steenthal, the interpreter of von Humboldt. Sapir was probably the originator of the term 'linguistic relativity'. Whorf was conscious of the continuity of his work with that of both. Yet Boas and Sapir were both born German Jews; Boas came to this country partly because there was little academic future for him in Germany. Sapir's last years were clouded by denial of admission to the Faculty Club at Yale. Boas denounced and fought against racism and national superiority to the moment of his death. Neither can hardly be thought to have taken the view they did out of sympathy with German nationalism and superiority. As to Herder and von Humboldt, while others may have made out of some of their efforts on the association between language and cultural identity a kind of nationalism which became vicious and invidious, they were hardly motivated by that same concern. They were concerned to understand individuals and to study the differences among peoples in a sympathetic way. It was, after all, Herder who motivated the break with the Enlightenment's ahistorical and a priori approach to cultural differences; in turn he coined the word einfühlen for a mode of understanding. So I think that this explanation hardly bears any further comment.

With regard to the Whorfian hypothesis itself there is a great deal to be said, too much to be said in a brief space, but I think that many of the comments tonight show a considerable ignorance of the history of philosophy and western thought. It is simply not an all or nothing proposition. It is quite clear, as Lewis Feuer showed many years ago, that systems of philosophy pass from one language community to another, showing the degree to which thought and philosophical insight is independent of language. There are also many well documented cases of the effect of language upon the transmission of philosophical thought, as when the translation of Aristotle's philosophy into Arabic forced the choice, necessary in Arabic, between those copulas which indicated merely a connection and those which indicated a claim on existence, and led to differences in the interpretation of his thought in that language which were then passed on into medieval thought. So it is not an all or nothing thing. I think that what perhaps needs to be explained is why people are so ready to dismiss the possibility that their language conditions their thinking.

Robert J. Di Pietro, Georgetown University: I would like to disagree with Dr. Macnamara, and say that science is nationalistic. I subscribe to a science magazine which often makes reference to 'French' science, 'German' science, and 'American' science. The only difference is that in this country we tend to think science is American, so we don't bother to use the adjective 'American' when we talk about it.

Macnamara: I'm not an American, though.

Di Pietro: Fine.

Macnamara: I don't even live in the U. S.

Di Pietro: If you talked to scientists from various countries you would find that they are not adverse to saying that this is 'French' science, this is 'German' science, or this is 'Japanese' science. For example, the Japanese now have a satellite in orbit, and they have been very careful to point out in the news reports that this effort has been totally Japanese, including both the satellite and the rockets, and has had no connection with America.

And the point about thought through language: it is strange that people would be willing to say that somehow thought is not influenced by language, but would probably accept the notion that language is a tool of man's communication. If we make the analogy of language to a tool, we must also see that tools are shaped by man and they, in turn, shape the tasks that man does. If, for example, you take your Volkswagen to a Volkswagen mechanic, you do it because you know he has the tools to fix Volkswagens. The fact that he has the tools to fix Volkswagens means that if you have a Chrysler you had better not take it to him. The tools that man has at hand shape and limit the kinds of things that he does with them. I'd say that the work of the coming decade had better involve more than semantics. I think part of it should involve some understanding of the kinds of contact and the levels of language which are affected in language contact. One of the things I thought of putting in the universals but which I withdrew, was the notion that phonology is far more resistant to change through contact than is semantics. I know of many immigrants to the United States—professors and blue collar people alike—who very quickly forget the words for particular things in their own language and substitute the English word or an anglicized form of the original word. Lexical substitution happens very readily, while persons living among speakers of other languages may go for 25 years and still retain much of their original pronunciation. So there must be some sort of structure there, but I think it would be rash to propose it as a universal. I think the work of the decade to come should include not only studies in semantic fields and how they are affected in language contact, but also the relationship between semantics, syntax, and phonology.

A. Bruce Gaarder, U.S. Office of Education: I offer a bit of a footnote to the remarks by Professors Macnamara and Haugen regarding the 'stupidity' of bilinguals. This may not have come to your attention. Recently in California through the work largely of certain psychologists, there was a random study made of children, Spanish-speaking children, Spanish surnamed children, who had been classified as mentally retarded but educable and, therefore, placed in special education classes. I recall some of the figures: they made a random selection of 45 of these children and then had them retested with a Spanish language test and by a competent psychologist—competent in Spanish and psychology— and 42 of the 47 were completely above the range of intelligence which would have placed them among the retarded children. This has now resulted in a court order in the United States District Court, Northern District of California, which will require that all such children be retested through the Spanish language and using psychologists who are competent in the Spanish language.

Macnamara: I wonder if I may make some irenic remarks on the subject of Whorfianism? When I was objecting to Whorfian relativism I didn't suggest that one didn't feel different when speaking one language rather than another; I didn't suggest that one didn't speak about different topics; I didn't suggest that some translations could be inadequate. In fact, my remarks about the differences in the semantic systems related to different lexicons surely suggest the contrary. They surely make room for the sort of differences that arise in translating Aristotle from Greek into Arabic.

William A. Stewart, Education Study Center: I was interested by your remarks, Professor Macnamara, on the role of bilingualism and intelligence-testing. You may have hit on an important aspect of a controversy which, though actually quite old, has recently been reactivated in this country, and this time with a decidedly pedagogical focus. The controversy concerns the apparent gap between Negro and white population means on IQ tests. Now I mention this because, whatever the differences may be between Negroes and whites in the United States, they certainly do not involve the use of totally distinct languages. Thus, while you can laugh away the debate on IQ performance differences involving groups which speak very different languages (only one of which is recognized in the testing procedure), the American Negro case is bound to bring you up short. What I think it may indicate is that differences in language which are much more subtle than full bilingualism (in the traditional sense) may produce a similar effect. Although there has been a tendency for middle-class Negroes and white liberals to pooh-pooh the linguistic differences between whites and Negroes in the United States as 'inconsequential'—probably because of a fear that it is racistic to recognize Negro-white behavioral differences—some of us feel that the 'inconsequential' structural and functional differences between standard English and nonstandard Negro dialect may actually contribute to IQ score differences. And it is likely that differences in learning styles and heuristic styles will also play a part. At any rate, the climate of opinion is currently such that few will see the implications which your remarks on the relation of bilingualism to IQ scores have for the one case in terms of which the issue is really going to be fought to the end—that of the American Negro.

THE POLITICS OF BILINGUAL EDUCATION

JOSHUA A. FISHMAN

Yeshiva University

Abstract. Our childhood lessons in civics—particularly the chapters once studied on 'how a bill becomes a law'—have not really prepared us to cope with the realities of influencing legislation. Were this not the case then we would realize that the latter is a never-ending process requiring continual attention and cultivation, rather than self-satisfaction and mustering out of forces at the end of a session in which the votes and the authorizations have seemingly gone our way. However, in this respect we—language scholars and language teachers interested in bilingual education—have fully confirmed our amateur political standing—a standing shared with most citizen groups—by retiring from the field of battle once the authorization for funds has been approved. That is when the real action first begins.

A well organized and constantly active lobbying group is imperative if authorizations are to be increased and are to become actual appropriations, if appropriations are to become actual expenditures, if bilingual education is to become widely available rather than largely restricted to the Spanish-speaking poor, and if the major education, language teaching and ethnic forces of this country are to effectively bring their considerable combined strength to bear on behalf of true bilingual education. Some techniques and approaches peculiarly suited to the initial organizational stage of a bilingual education lobby are suggested.

Unlikely Dreams Can Come True. As the 'Language Resources Project' which I headed from 1960-1963 was drawing to a close, I began to put the finishing touches on a report which was ultimately to appear as the volume Language Loyalty in the United States. I wrote

the report itself during a fellowship year at the Center for Advanced
Study in the Behavioral Sciences, commonly known as the 'Think Tank'
or the 'leisure of the Theory Class'. Those of you who know it—in the
beauty of its location, overlooking the Stanford campus and the lower
Bay—will understand what I mean when I suggest that it provides the
scholar with opportunity for even more detachment from the trials and
tribulations of society than does his ordinary academic existence.
There it was that I first wrote my chapter on the 'preservation' of our
unrecognized non-English language resources. There it was that I first
suggested that one of the necessary steps for the preservation of American bilingualism was an agency of government that would be responsible for safeguarding and augmenting the cultural and linguistic resources
that our country has so often ignored and even snuffed out. I distinctly
remember feeling triply removed from reality while writing that particular chapter, for few things seemed as unlikely then as the possibility
that within five years there might be a Bilingual Education Act and at
least some of the funds and staff needed to make it functional.

If such unlikely dreams can be realized in this age of miracles, then
it may not be too unrealistic to hope that language scholars, language
teachers, and other genuine friends of bilingual education will yet learn
how to influence and strengthen the Bilingual Education Act and how to
put its funds to better use. After all, we have arrived at a day and age
when interest groups—even those on college campuses—engage in concerted action as never before in order to attain their goals. It is my
hope that the friends of bilingual education too can rise to a more active
position than that of going to conferences, writing and reading papers,
and agreeing to spend the funds that come their way as a result of the
efforts of those who refuse to be even once removed from the real world
of affairs and of power.

Having devoted the past decade entirely to academic matters pertaining to bilingualism and to sociolinguistics more generally, it may also
be that I now want to atone, in part, for my own sins by trying to 'tell it
as it is,' rather than delivering yet another academic paper and leaving
the responsibility for influencing the Act itself entirely to professional
politicians.

Some Lessons in Elementary Actmanship. Our childhood lessons in
civics—particularly the chapters once studied in 'how a bill becomes a
law'—have not really prepared us to cope with the realities of influencing legislation. Were this not the case, we would realize that the latter
is a never-ending process requiring continual attention and cultivation
rather than self-satisfaction and mustering out of forces at the end of a
session in which the votes and the authorizations have seemingly gone
our way. However, in this respect we—language scholars and language
teachers interested in bilingual education—have fully confirmed our

amateur political standing—a standing shared with most citizen groups —by retiring from the field of battle once the authorization for funds has been approved. That is when the real action begins. What we have not realized—and probably do not really comprehend to this very day—is that an authorization is just that and nothing more. However, once authorizations are signed and the jubilant citizen groups go home to celebrate their little victories, the legislative process gets down to the real business of appropriations. Authorizations are not appropriations! Hardly any educational appropriations are as much as 50% of what their respective authorizations mentioned. The final authorization for the Bilingual Education Act was 45 million dollars over a three-year period. We were sufficiently inexperienced to be elated by the immensity of that paltry sum. How naive we were! The appropriation was only 7.5 million dollars and it provided nothing beyond a one-year period! (See Table below.)

FUNDS FOR BILINGUAL EDUCATION
UNDER TITLE VII: ESEA

Fiscal year	Authorization	Appropriation	Expenditure
1968	15 million	————	————
1969	30 million	7.5 million	7.5 million
1970	40 million	21,250,000	————
1971	Senate Sub-committee on Educ. recom. 80 million		
1972	100 million		
1973	135 million		

This, too, we must learn. While authorizations may cover several years most appropriations are for one year only and, therefore, without constant attention on the part of those who are interested, appropriations may be conveniently allowed to lapse or may be cut drastically. No amount of talk about grandiose new authorizations will prevent this unless constituents and lobbyists are immediately at hand and vocally so. Thus, this fall the Senate Subcommittee on Education recommended an authorization for bilingual education (in conjunction with considering the extension of the ESEA) of more than three hundred million dollars over a five-year period. After this recommendation had gained the attention and praise it deserved (or, at least, the attention and praise it was intended to elicit), the Senate voted to appropriate a far smaller sum for fiscal year 1970 (some 25 million dollars). This sum the House-Senate Appropriations Conference finally adopted, not without serious attempts to reduce it further (to 15 million dollars). At this point the President's budgeteers, hacking away at the entire HEW appropriation, knocked bilingual education down to 10 million dollars for fiscal 1970 and its final funding is still in doubt.

Appropriations Committees. We were not—and are not today—prepared for the appropriations committees and their ability to emasculate programs or even to gut them entirely. Appropriations committees can and do write limitation riders into acts so that the funds they grant may not be utilized for certain purposes which may well be mentioned in the initial authorizing legislation. Unfortunately, bilingual education is particularly vulnerable to mistreatment at the appropriations stage. These committees—like many other crucial operative committees of Congress—are often controlled by chairmen for whom bilingual education is hardly a live issue. Indeed, one of the reasons that bilingual education has fared so poorly in appropriations committees thus far is that it is viewed as being primarily a regional problem (Southwest, Florida, and the New York Metropolitan area) rather than a matter that all Congressmen and Senators need to worry about. Another and more important reason why appropriations committees have not dealt kindly with bilingual education authorizations is that the entire matter of bilingual education is viewed as just one more anti-poverty measure, one more effort to help the disadvantaged. As such, there are many who take the position that Title I of ESEA and other appropriations are available to combat these two widespread ills and, therefore, why appropriate much more for 'the same purpose again' via Title VII?

It is my considered opinion that the only way to convince appropriations committees to take bilingual education seriously is to convince them (a) that it is not merely a sectional matter, and (b) that it is not merely yet another part of the anti-poverty program. Thus, while it may well be true that whatever has been appropriated for bilingual education in the past few years is primarily due to the Mexican-American vote and the poverty issue, I am convinced that neither of these provide optimal pressure or optimal rationale for the future growth of bilingual education. More about this later.

Lobbying for Bilingual Education. Who can continually try to influence Senators and Congressmen via a flow of information concerning the need for bilingual education? Who can continue to exert pressure —which means personal visits as well as organized calls and telegrams —directed toward members of the appropriations committees? Who can maintain regular contact with thousands upon thousands of language teachers and language scholars so that they will know what pertinent legislation is being considered in Congress and who is for it or against it? Who can bring into action a 'quick contact network' all over the country to elicit the protests and the plaudits that are needed in order to gain Congressional support for bilingual education? Who can watch closely how a new act is being staffed and implemented by the Washington bureaucracy and keep it from being interpreted into an early grave or into a far cry from what its original supporters had had in mind? Obviously, all of these things cannot be done—and done both well and repeatedly—by amorphous citizen groups. What is needed is obviously a lobby for bilingual education. It is equally obvious to me, however, that we cannot at this time hope for an organized lobby that spends all of its time fighting for bilingual education and for that alone. That takes time to establish, and funds, and consensus, and experience—none of which we now have. What then do we have that might pinch-hit for a bilingual education lobby? We have allies who lobby for bilingual education too because bilingual education presents them with another opportunity to obtain funds for the things they are independently interested in.

The organized voices that have been raised on behalf of bilingual education have been of two kinds: educational and ethnic. It is my contention that we who are interested in bilingual education per se (whether as a way to language maintenance, to cultural pluralism, to overcoming the educational retardation of many non-English-speaking learners, or as part of the educational right of every family to self-respect and to cultural integrity) must begin to cultivate friends and influence groups in each of these camps, many of which already maintain lobbies in Washington and throughout the country.

The power of lobbies is that—like mutual funds—they continue to work all of the time, not only when the heat's on. Most Congressmen and Senators are too busy ever to hear about bilingual education in the normal course of events. There is simply too much going on for them to be able to function at any but a highly selective level. At that level only that which is either very well recommended or very powerful gets through the filter imposed for purposes of sheer self-preservation. Lobbyists make it their business to know which of his colleagues any particular Congressman or Senator looks up to or looks upon as bellwethers to be followed in co-sponsoring or supporting bills that are being considered. Lobbyists know to whom in their home territories each Congressmen or Senator is indebted, whom he respects, whom he knows. Lobbyists find individuals favorable to their own positions from among such people and they arrange to take them along when they plan their campaign of visits to Congressman X or Senator Z. These visits go on all of the time, including those times when all concerned

are relaxed, have time, and no vote is pending. Those are the times
when many future votes are gained or lost.

The Education and the Ethnic Lobbies. Among the most effective
friends that bilingual education has had thus far has been NEA in general and its West Coast office in particular. Indeed, when I was invited to testify on behalf of the Bilingual Education Bill in the spring
of 1968, I found that another giving testimony at the same session was
a representative of the Adult Education Section of the NEA. Quite naturally, he not only supported the bill but suggested that its wording be
changed so as to clearly include adult education in its provisions.
Clearly, bilingual education represented another arena in which adult
education and its practitioners could grow and prosper. And why not?
and what about rural education? and special education? and vocational
education? and higher education? and day-care nurseries? and early
childhood education? and reading instruction? and science education?
etc., etc. All of these together (recently conjoined as the Emergency
Committee for the Full Funding of Education Programs) and each of
them separately could be interested in bilingual education—for their
own sake as well as for its sake. One by-product of doing so would be
to counter the currently widespread and erroneous impression that bilingual education is only for the poor; indeed, that it is primarily to
eradicate a disease of the Puerto Rican and Mexican American poor,
namely, greater facility in Spanish than in English!

Which brings us to another lobby that I believe we must cultivate on
behalf of bilingual education, namely the ethnic lobby. When I testified
on behalf of bilingual education, there were several others testifying
who represented various Mexican-American groups and associations.
But where were the Franco-Americans, the Italo-Americans, the
Polish-Americans, the German-Americans, the Ukrainian-Americans,
the Chinese-Americans, the Jewish-Americans, etc., etc.? That
they are potentially very interested in bilingual education may be seen
from the fact that the American Council for Nationalities Services distributed news releases about the 1967 bill in some two dozen languages
to hundreds and hundreds of ethnic publications and radio programs
throughout the country. However, this potential lobby on behalf of bilingual education still remains essentially unorganized and unconvinced.
This is a great pity, I believe, for not only must bilingual education
serve all of them if it is to be a genuine expression of America's
sociocultural and educational maturity (rather than merely a sop to
the 'poor Chicanos', so that they don't become too nasty), but by doing so it can attract a new force in support of education measures
which the education lobby itself might welcome.

The ethnic lobby—and the Congressmen and Senators who respond
to it—often speaks for somewhat insulated and conservative groups

that are disposed to budget-cutting on matters not of explicit interest to them. Since the liberalization of the immigration laws a few years ago—and since the Soviet-American detente—this lobby has been looking around for a 'good disease' to champion. Bilingual education with its implications for ethnic and linguistic maintenance could well entice this lobby and those responsive to it into the general education camp. If we want the education lobby to fight part of this good fight on behalf of bilingual education, we must be on the alert for new allies that we can contribute to the general struggle of the education lobby. The addition of the ethnic lobby to the push for more and for more genuine bilingual education would also help overcome the restricted regional image that bilingual education currently has, and would help give it a more diversified reality and a more varied substance. However, this lobby will remain lost to us, I believe, as long as the Act's poverty criterion excludes them. The poverty criterion must be eliminated from the act, both for sound philosophical as well as for sound tactical reasons!

Coming: Real Bilingual Education. Both the logic and the psychologic of bilingual education are leading in the same direction—in the direction of more genuine concern with bilingual curricula for various models and ideals of societal bilingualism. The day is coming when more and more genuine bilingual education, for all those who want it, regardless of income, mother tongue or language dominance, will be part of the variegated picture of American education. At that time it will not be a mere euphemism for programs in English as a Second Language which, though unquestionably essential, constitute only one part and one kind of dual language education. It will not be just a promissory note to the poor, nor a left-handed contribution to increasingly vocal and organized (though still exploited and dispossessed) Hispanos and Indians. It will be available to my children and grandchildren, and to yours, because it is too good to keep it from all the people. But if that time is to come as quickly as it should, as it could, as it must—without threats and animosities and confrontations—it requires that we become more than merely language scholars and language teachers. It requires that we become political activists, political realists, and political sophisticates, even more so than those who have pressured the Bilingual Education Act into its current stage. Bilingual education needs more than crumbs and deserves more than crumbs. The more rapidly we build it into the concerns of the education lobby and the more we strengthen that lobby with the new friends that bilingual education is in a good position to attract, the more rapidly it will get more than crumbs—which is all it is getting today.

A Practical Suggestion, in Parting. What I have suggested above is merely a 'pitch' and, like any 'pitch', it requires a 'follow through' if it is to amount to anything. The alliance that I have called for (not to mention an even grander alliance incorporating Pan-American business and economic interests, United Nations supporters, and yet others) will not be fashioned spontaneously. It requires a few people, a little money, and a little help to get it rolling. Perhaps this is where we, language teachers and language scholars, could contribute most by taking the lead. Could not TESOL, ACTFL, NEA, and the AATs designate one dedicated and informed person each, to begin with, to form an ad hoc committee in Washington, D. C. ? Could not these leading agencies of our profession pro-rate among themselves the initially modest expenses for the stationery, postage, reference materials, typing, and a bit of travel necessary in order for such an ad hoc group to begin the task? The task is a sizable one, but many others have done it before and some of them would be very willing to show us how and what. We need a clearing house and headquarters for information (e. g. current names and addresses of key Congressmen and their administrative assistants; reports on pertinent legislation pending and amendments needed; material on bilingual education for press, radio, TV, and school boards; reports on successful experiments and projects in bilingual education; analyses of the difficulties encountered, etc., etc.). It is high time for us to do 'our thing'.[1]

NOTES

[1]I am grateful to the following individuals for their comments on the first draft of this paper as a result of which I have made many changes and additions to it: Professor Theodore Andersson (Southwest Educational Development Laboratory), Joe Carter (Administrative Assistant to Senator George Murphy of California), Dr. Bruce Gaarder (Basic Studies Branch, Division of College Programs, Bureau of Educational Personnel Development, USOE), Larry Horwitz (Administrative Assistant to Congressman John Conyers, Jr. of Detroit), and Monroe Sweetland (West Coast Regional Office NEA). Of course, I alone am responsible for the views (or errors) presented and do not mean to imply that the foregoing friends of bilingual education have any responsibility at all for either.

DISCUSSION

Robert J. Di Pietro, Georgetown University: I'd like to say, first of all, that I agree wholeheartedly with Professor Fishman. The problem to me, though, seems that we have to convince not so much the ethnic groups who force the issue of bilingualism, but the general American population, the so-called 'silent majority', that there is a value in knowing and being educated in more than one language. This, I think, is a general problem in the English-speaking world.

Fishman: I'd like to suggest a possible modification of that. Most Americans would agree that it is fine to know other languages. There are just a couple of qualifications that come after that. It is very nice to know other languages (a) provided it is French, (b) provided it is the French of Paris, and (c) provided your parents don't speak French at home.

Robert Lado, Georgetown University: I would like to support the urgent plea of Professor Fishman and I hope that action will follow. I would also like to support the last comments. I fought a battle for ten years to permit the children of speakers of the languages in which we give a major, to major in those languages. I fought hard and I got it through, and then when I spent two years away in Spain on a Fulbright grant, I came back to find it had been pushed aside. There seems to be something that isn't liked in permitting a child of an Italian family to major in Italian or to permit a child of any other language that we teach to major in that language. I would like to support the idea that we should provide a lobby and should move toward really full-fledged bilingual education all the way from prekindergarten to college, and if we succeed in this, the United States will truly be one of the leading nations of the world in this area.

Joan Baratz, Education Study Center: I'd like to broaden the scope of the discussion a little. I think we are not simply talking about language programs and we are not simply trying to educate the country in general and Congressmen in particular about the fact that it would be nice to have multilingual speakers and bilingual programs in this country. We have to recognize that what Mr. Fishman suggests is really attacking a basic fabric of the American dream in terms of what a melting pot is and what America is like. When we are talking about not eradicating the second language through bilingual education, what we are really talking about is kind of revolutionary—we are talking about reconceptualizing what America is and what it should be. It is not a simple language problem.

Fishman: I think that is very true, very well put, but also very desirable; I'm sure it doesn't frighten you and it doesn't frighten me. The major blessing of the current turmoil in our lives is that it is exactly due to the fact that people are reconceptualizing America, are more demanding with respect to new dreams, are more eager to realize dreams that were always there. I'd like to tell you about that best kept secret in the world, a book called <u>Language Loyalty in the United States</u>, which most fully documents the existence of the dream of a bilingual America, a dream that people might be fully accepted in this country not merely by erasing themselves, but by being themselves. That dream has been dreamt ever since the days of the Pilgrims, because they came exactly in order to maintain themselves as they were rather than to change, and so did many groups since then. That has been an American dream for as long and longer than the country has existed, and it is high time that it came to be realized for blacks, for Hispanos, and for immigrants and their children and grandchildren. We are finally coming to realize that this is not the best of all possible countries, that it could be improved in many ways to make it so, and I believe this is one of the most vital avenues of improvement, precisely because it has so long been overlooked by some and denied by others.

P. B. Pandit, Cornell University: I'm really touched by this very eloquent plea to make America a multilingual country. I would like to ask Dr. Fishman, since he has coedited a book on linguistic problems of developing countries where most of the authors have considered the developing countries to be very unfortunate because of the great diversity and variety of languages. Having done so, and having considered countries with many languages as problem countries, I would like to ask Dr. Fishman what would be his interpretation of the American situation when it becomes multilingual. Multilingualism is also looked upon as symptomatic of barriers in communication by these writers; in what way would such multilingualism affect the development of mass media in particular and technology in general?

Fishman: It is quite true that the coincidence between underdevelopment and multilingualism is very high, but it is the same kind of coincidence that John Macnamara and Einar Haugen were speaking about last night: the coincidence between bilingualism and lower IQ scores in this country and elsewhere. There is no necessary connection between these factors. There are several highly stable and economically very advanced multilingual societies in the world today, and there are, as we know, a very large number of very unstable, very miserable, problem-plagued and problem-ridden monolingual countries in the world today. I don't think we have to worry that the Bilingual Education Act or the fostering of genuine bilingualism in the United States for those who want it will be the ruination of the country. The ruination of the country is more likely to come, as it always has in the past, by the insidious implication that by forgetting the problems, by forgetting oneself, by overlooking one's parents, by throwing away treasures that are rightfully one's heritage, one could help the country. I think that is far more of an insidious, unrecognized type of underdevelopment than the kind of multilingual and multicultural development that I have been advocating.

John Gumperz, University of California, Berkeley: I would like to ask Dr. Fishman two questions. Does he feel that too much money is being spent on poverty programs? In other words, he said that the Bilingual Education Act has been associated with poverty programs. We are living in a year that all funds for education are being cut. In my own university we are having something like a 50% cut in EOP programs. This is the first year that we have begun to admit minority group students in large numbers, and it is also the first year that we have no funds to support such students. Now, what would he like to do about this in real terms?

The second question is not related. In a paper which I believe was published in Anthropological Linguistics, Dr. Fishman discusses the language problems of what he calls underdeveloped nations, and specifically choice of national language. In talking about the choice of English—he uses the term 'rationality'—he says rational choices are made when English is chosen. In countries who choose their own native language, the choice is said to be motivated by sentiment. In other words, he implies that people give in to their sentiments when they choose their own native language, but when they choose English this is called a rational decision. Now how does he reconcile this with his position about multilingualism in the United States; is he advocating that we too make 'sentimental' rather than 'rational' choices?

Fishman: We don't happen to have a state legislature backing Yeshiva University, but we have had many cuts too. I'm genuinely alarmed that all these cuts are taking place, and I oppose them as strenuously as I can. Nevertheless, one must take care not to be for bilingual education only if there is money for it, or only if there is enough money for everything else, or only in the end of all things when the state will wither away. Of course, I didn't begin to say that there is too much money for poverty programs in the United States today; I said there was a complete misunderstanding of bilingual education and the Bilingual Education Act; so much so that it was seen as just one more poverty program and therefore, since some Congressmen and Senators have thought that lots of money was being put into poverty programs, they felt there was no need to put any aside for bilingual education if it was just one more minor, funny kind of poverty program. There obviously is not enough money going into poverty programs. However, in pleading for more funds for bilingual education I am not really competing with the poverty programs at all. A country that has been able to waste money the way we have wasted it for the worst causes ought to be able to amply support bilingual education and still have greatly increased funds for the poverty program as well. There is no necessary competition between them and it shouldn't be thought of in that way.

Secondly, it is not at all my conviction that where English or another language of wider communication is chosen, it is actually chosen in terms of more rational appeals, nor that where the national language is chosen for government, education, etc., by a developing country, it is actually chosen in terms of more sentimental appeals. My point is that the actors themselves in the new language drama going on through the Third World commonly approach the problem as if this were the case. That is, the announced appeals on behalf of English or other world languages are that the country will be helped to develop economically; that its ties with the English-speaking countries or other major centers of power will be strengthened; its scientists will be more closely in touch with scientists all over the world; all of these being advanced as very rational, instrumental, and modern reasons. However, when such advice is adopted, the resulting policies always have affective or sentimental consequences as well, since technical and operative integration always leads to sociocultural integration and vice versa. Similarly, those who plead on behalf of the national language often stress the national heritage, the national past, the national beauty, national ideals, national character, and talk about these things as if they were unrelated to or more important than practical, operative, instrumental concerns.

But actually the brunt of my paper was to show that both of these considerations (the instrumental and the sentimental) are always present together, that they always contribute to each other, and that all countries have always, in connection with language problems, given attention to both simultaneously or at different stages in their development. My advocacy of bilingual education in the United States is therefore based on both instrumental and sentimental grounds, precisely because these grounds always cooccur. Our problem is that we have a world which is highly uneven in terms of development and highly variegated in terms of the stages and types of social problems being experienced and, therefore, we do have a world today in which the haves are shouting to the have-nots: 'Be rational, be reasonable, be successful, be like me, ... use English!'

COGNITIVE DEVELOPMENT IN THE BILINGUAL CHILD

VERA JOHN

Yeshiva University

Abstract. In most studies of bilingual children their intellectual development is assessed by means of intelligence tests. The facilitating or inhibiting role of their bilingual experience is evaluated in this fashion. Alternative approaches, based upon recent work on cognitive style, will be proposed in this paper. Views of intellectual development representing contemporary cognitive theory will also be discussed. Of particular interest is the role of visual conceptualization in the bilingual; some examples of instructional approaches with bilingual children will be discussed from the point of view of their possible effects upon broadening or narrowing the child's cognitive development. The recent research of Rohwer in elaborative learning will be considered in this context.

I am delighted, that after an excessively long period of preoccupation with the tested performance of bilingual children, even on the part of scholars, we are now asking questions concerning their thought processes. It is a sign of the times that two panelists have chosen independently the topic of Bilingualism and Thought.

My joy is a response to a concern born during my adolescence spent in a multilingual school. During our heated debates in Switzerland, we were concerned with the relative importance of images and words in the ideational processes of young people raised with several languages. Soon after starting the study of psychology I have learned that such a question had little scientific validity from an operational standpoint. But I was stubborn, and though I learned to ask more scientific questions, my curiosity persisted to this day. During the last decade interest in cognition revived dramatically; neobehaviorists, structuralists, and rationalists are again concerned with the magnificent, centuries-old inquiry into man's mind.

But interests in cognition, thinking, or the mind have had no substantive impact upon the schools in which children with two languages are struggling to learn and survive. The schools are under the influence of the better known approaches of psychologists. Of particular significance is the field of psychometrics, or the measurement of human skills and achievement, which endeavor is still of enormous importance in the planning of curricula, the placement of children, the evaluation of programs for minority children. Labov's powerful attack on educational psychologists, delivered at the Round Table last year, is of significance in this connection. He challenged the theoretical assumptions of the well-known 'deficiency' concepts, as well as the methodological soundness of testing ghetto children in isolation from each other, invoking topics and styles of communicative exchange alien to their world. But in spite of these criticisms the bilingual minority child is continually tested in the traditional way with standardized tools, though specialists will sadly admit that they have no appropriate tests in the childrens' native languages. The child's achievement is therefore assessed in English and is shown to lag behind other groups; witness the Coleman report.

Psychology has had an impact on another facet of the life of the bilingual child in this country. The currently popular TESOL programs show the influence of behaviorist learning theory as well as that of linguistics of the pretransformational era. The oral approach by means of which children are taught to repeat specific syntactical patterns is an illustration of an emphasis upon overt behavior stressed as basic by learning theorists. I have listened to Navajo children repeating in unison as well as individually, phrases such as This is a pencil, These are pencils. TESOL programs appeal to educators who have been seriously criticized for their failure to educate bilingual children successfully. Some of these TESOL programs are carefully thought out, attractively presented, and effectively organized in second-language instruction. But many contemporary linguists criticize these approaches. These linguists speak of language acquisition 'as primarily a cognitive enterprise rather than a behavioral one' (Scott,1970, p. 81).

The emphasis on processes of thought generously laces the writings of Chomsky (1968), Jacobovits (1968), Troike (1970), and others. Their ideas offer stimulating reading to the cognitive psychologist. The field is not limited to speculations. The work of Bever at Rockefeller Institute illustrates one aspect of this emphasis. In studying speech perception he explores the role of attention in the processing of language input. He speaks of fluctuations between outward attention (social attention), and inward attention, the attention to, or thinking about a just heard message. His work, together with the cognitive implications of much contemporary research and theory, presents a challenge to behavioristic approaches to language.

Have we then decisively rejected all facets of behaviorism in approaches to learning, cognition, and language, and does our task consist only in convincing the practitioners among us that they are behind the times?

I do not think so. Great debates tend to strengthen the single factor features of theories, such as reinforcement in the case of learning theorists, or the innate features of the Language Acquisition Device, as in the case of the transformationalists. In distress over the intensity of the debates many research workers tend to a pragmatic position, picking and choosing from several theories. Educators often follow this course.

My own preference is hard to elaborate without a lengthy departure from the topic of this paper. Let me illustrate it, however, with some personal examples of multilingual education.

Peal and Lambert's findings (1962) concerning the cognitive flexibility of coordinate-bilingual children always struck me as highly important. Intuitively, it seems to me that their results may be of particular significance for children raised in instructional settings which afford an 'intellectualization' of their language experience. (Hence, the ensuing debate.) This type of experience characterized my own acquisition of French. My teachers attempted to acquaint me with that specialized use of language for thought which characterizes many French intellectuals, beyond a mastery of the spoken and written language. Their goal was to deepen my understanding, using a multilingual background as a basis for generalizations and contrast. The features of production of French was an end, not a means, of their tuition. I arrived in this country with such an approach to language learning. I was somewhat older than when I learned French; perhaps I lacked that easy mimicry of the young. I plunged into college work with little proficiency in English, and I neglected to pay much attention to the phonology of the English language. (A neglect that did not escape Charles Ferguson.) My primarily cognitive approach to language acquisition was of little assistance when I decided to improve my articulation. The instruction I then received was based on modeling, (for instance, I did not know how to produce the th sound). I was shown with the help of mirrors and drawings. Principles of learning, such as modeling and the use of corrective feedback, were relevant to this aspect of my struggle with the English language; while cognitive approaches, of great benefit to the acquisition of the semantic system, were of little use.

In short, different aspects of language acquisition may well be governed by widely different principles of learning and cognition. In this context, Courtney Cazden's conclusions, based on an experimental study, are of interest. She proposes that young children's acquisition of vocabulary profits from direct tuition, while syntactical growth is strengthened by the child's exposure to well-formed sentences. In the light of such findings, psycholinguists may wish to abandon single-factor theories; and in this way, follow the example of their colleagues, for instance the neurophysiologists, who no longer attempt to embrace with the same set of explanatory principles the knee-jerk and visual memory.

It is my hope, that from the current theoretical debates, multi-layered theories will emerge, taking into account man's propensities to display over-learned habits while also throwing some light on the agility of the human in grasping new knowledge by the well-practiced leaps of the mind. A fruitful arena for such theory is the developmental study of language and thought in various cultural and instructional settings.

One of the considerations, obvious to many of you, I am sure, which impels me to state this plea for a levels-of-analysis approach to theory building in the sciences of language and knowing, is the lack of such an approach to the education of the bilingual child. We observe either a well-intentioned laissez-faire approach in barrio and reservation classrooms, or a proliferation of pattern-drill techniques. As yet, little pedagogical attention has been paid to the applicability of cognitive approaches to second-language instruction. (An important beginning in this direction is Bernard Spolsky's (1970) paper presented at last year's Round Table.) What are some of the approaches to thought of relevance to the bilingual child?

Studies of Cognition. For students of behavior it is hard to deal with entities lodged inside the human mind, but such is the emphasis given to 'structure' in Jean Piaget's theory of intellectual development. Ideas are arranged in a particular body of knowledge or structure, according to the Swiss theorist, and it requires most of the years of growing into adulthood to achieve the necessary formal 'operations' to deal effectively with logically organized knowledge. Operations are a key concept in Piagetian theory; he describes them 'as the essence of knowledge: it is an interiorized action which modifies the object of knowledge. For instance, an operation would consist of joining objects in a class, to construct a classification' (Piaget 1964: 8). Can these operations be taught? Most followers of Jean Piaget would argue against direct tuition.

Professor Kohlberg, a Piagetian psychologist of development, has severely criticized compensatory programs for low-income children because of their highly content-oriented approaches (Kohlberg 1968). He argues in favor of an alternative approach, stressing multiple experiences and activities. Such an approach to education is attempted by the British Infant Schools. The free manner in which children move from activity to activity is in stark contrast with the education of many non-English speaking children in this country. I am referring particularly to those students who spend many hours in structured language activities, stressing production skills. These children receive little, if any, opportunity in conceptually enriching encounters, considered important by the followers of the great Swiss psychologist.

Piaget and Chomsky confront the educationally-minded with the same dilemma. While both emphasize an active organism, stressing operations (Piaget) and hypothesis-testing (Chomsky) as crucial to the development of the human mind and language, neither develops the pedagogical implications of their conceptualizations. There are some cognitive theorists, however, who have attempted to relate theory to educational practice.

Jerome Bruner, whose approach to cognition has been deeply influenced by Piaget, deals with issues of learning and teaching in his book Toward a Theory of Instruction (1966). He is particularly concerned with the study of representations: 'how the child gets free of present stimuli and conserves past experience in a model, and the rules that govern storage and retrieval of information from this model' (p. 10). Bruner postulates three methods of representation, starting with the young child's reliance upon action. This 'enactive' mode bears some resemblance to Piaget's emphasis upon internalized action. Next in the developmental sequence is the 'ikonic' mode in which the child is able to represent the world to himself by an image or a spatial schema which is relatively independent of action.' Thirdly, he speaks of symbolic representation, and the role of language in the development of models of reality. Of significance to the child growing toward this mode of functioning are the dialogues he conducts with adults. To quote Bruner again, he 'suggests that mental growth is in very considerable measure dependent upon the growth from the outside in—a mastering of techniques that are embodied in the culture and that are passed on in a contingent dialogue by agents of the culture.'

Several aspects of Bruner's theory of cognition appear relevant to the development and education of the bilingual child. The importance of the ikonic mode of representation is one of these. Bruner and his co-workers have shown in the research reported in Studies of Cognitive Growth the importance of this mode of thought for children in their earliest years of schooling. Bilingual children often are caught between two languages during those years, thus the instructional use of imagery may be of great assistance to them. In addition, to help foster the development of the symbolic mode of representation as well, bilingual children should have the opportunity to engage in cognitively rich dialogue with adults in their 'dominant' language.

A third area of interest in the recent studies of cognition is the focus on the 'processes' of learning and knowing. I have been particularly intrigued with the work of William Rohwer. The beginnings of his inquiry are rather typical for an experimental psychologist. He was working with paired-associate learning, and his subjects ranged broadly according to age, sex, ethnic membership, and social class. He demonstrated conclusively that when children were taught to 'elaborate' on a word-association pair by constructing a meaningful sentence, their performance increased dramatically.

The logic of this research propelled Professor Rohwer to move into an unusual next step for an experimental psychologist, namely theory-building. In studying self-generated images, sentences, or categories, Rohwer has developed a model of 'imaginative conceptual activity' in contrast with 'formal conceptual activity'. Low-income children profit greatly from instruction when they are encouraged to rely upon the former mode. Similarly, bilingual children could gain from such strategies for learning; these children are often the subject of ridicule for their unconventional use of words and metaphors. Where the child needs to rely upon language-for-the-self in the solution or recollection of tasks, his unique phrasing should not be considered an impediment, but as a creative use of words.

This research is but one example of the new trend in the study of active, individually developed, conceptual learning strategies. 'Learning by discovery' is another approach to open-ended instruction. The greatest benefits this latter method yields is in the development of children's comprehension of subject matter, particularly in mathematics. However, these primarily inductive methods of instruction have been lumped mistakenly with 'progressive education'. In the priorities of the post-Sputnik era, the failure of many school children in spelling and computation has been blamed on educational methods dating from a more permissive and relaxed atmosphere. Hence, the turn toward didactic instruction and programmed learning on the part of many school systems. It is ironic that the beleaguered school administrators have given up on inductive learning at the very time that psychologists are offering promising approaches to the schools.

I do not think that we have to face a similar impasse in the education of bilingual children. My optimism is based upon evidence such as the contribution of linguists to last year's Round Table: Labov, Scott, Troike, Spolsky, all of whom approached their subject matter from a fresh point of view. I am hopeful that these and other attempts at examining levels of language and concomitant processes of acquisition will yield a sophisticated theory of instruction.

Recommendations. As yet, the new insights of linguists and psychologists have had little impact upon the education of non-English speaking children. The classrooms we have observed in the barrios and on reservations reflect a new spirit of optimism; the promise of bilingual education is an exciting one. But in most instances the focus is upon the production skills of these children; their native language is considered a bridge, albeit a necessary one, to the acquisition of the English language.

A theoretical basis for second language instruction is still a hope for the future; lacking an integrated approach, I would like to make a few suggestions for the education of non-English speaking children, based upon ideas drawn from unrelated sources. My primary concern is the young child in pre-school and primary classes.

a. Comprehension: Dr. Troike (1970) made an important distinction in his Round Table presentation of last year between receptive and productive competence. According to his model, an instructional approach stressing receptive competence in individuals acquiring a second language or a second dialect may be a useful goal. This proposal is stressed more fully by Susan Ervin-Tripp (see paper in this symposium). In exploring the lessons of first language acquisition, it is suggested that children and adults should be given training in the development of comprehension skills before they are expected to improve their production skills.

The use of songs, stories, and short skits are effective in exposing young children to a new language. The great success of some television programs (such as Sesame Street) in creating motivation for new learning is of interest. While a primarily passive approach to language development is certainly not a plan I favor, some techniques can be adopted from the mass media to enliven the acquisition of English on the part of barrio and reservation children.

b. Cognitive development: Children convey their growing comprehension of a new language by gestures and pantomine. It is harder to judge whether school is helping them broaden their conceptual mastery of their environment while learning a new language. Teachers often neglect the cognitive aspects of growth. The use of language for purposes of problem-solving unfolds at an accelerated pace between the ages of four and seven, the very time when non-English speaking children are exposed to a second language. Caught between two languages, the young child needs special assistance in organizing his world. The use of ikonic representation, as described by Bruner, is seldom explored in these classrooms, where language and its acquisition dominate the curriculum. Nonverbal materials, as developed by Montessori schools, are also useful in dealing with concepts such as sequencing, size relationships, etc. in the bilingual classroom.

There are a number of programs which have a strong cognitive component, but they are aimed at ghetto children who speak an English dialect, (John and Moskovitz 1970). In addition, most of these efforts are devoid of culturally appropriate content for children whose life differs from that of the middle class child. But teachers can be helped to adapt programs to their own community, and in learning how to use local talents and materials. My experience with the Indian kindergarten programs (jointly sponsored by the National Association for the Education of Young Children and the Bureau of Indian Affairs) was instructive in this regard. The Indian art students together with resource personnel drawn from reservations, people not necessarily skilled in linguistics, helped us to develop a curriculum related to the experiences of the rural Indian child.

    c. Fluency: The non-English speaking child will, at one point in his school life, in a bilingual program, show evidence that he is ready for a more intensive learning experience in his second language. Once his active and enthusiastic participation is insured, the young child is willing to listen to and repeat choral language. The flexibility of the young child, his willingness to imitate, playfully, songs, rhymes, dialogues, speaks in favor of a limited amount of experience that strengthens fluency.

But the emphasis upon comprehension and cognitive development in this set of informal recommendations is offered because I share with many other speakers in this symposium the conviction that ultimately the child becomes a successful learner of languages because he takes an active part in the process of acquisition. He tests his notions about grammar, he experiments with new sounds, he discovers the meaning of words by direct tuition as well as by more indirect routes.

    d. The use of language: Languages are acquired fast, and often forgotten equally fast by young children. Unless instruction in English is related to the life of the bilingual community in which the program is placed, the child will have no reason to practice on his own that which he is learning. Though this seems an obvious thought, its implementation requires more than common sense. Only with a knowledge of the sociolinguistic features of a community can a meaningful language program be developed for the children of barrios and reservations.

REFERENCES

Bever, Thomas. 1967. Presentation to psycholinguistic circle of New York.

Bruner, Jerome. 1966. Toward a theory of instruction. Cambridge, Massachusetts, Harvard University Press.

_____, Rose Olver, Patricia M. Greenfield, et al. 1966. Studies of cognitive growth. New York, Wiley and Sons, Inc.

Chomsky, Noam. 1968. Language and the mind. Psychology Today. I, no. 9.48-51, 66-68.

Jacobovitz, Leon A. 1968. Implications of recent psycholinguistic developments for the teaching of a second language. Paper delivered at San Antonio TESOL Convention.

John, Vera, and Sarah Moskovitz. 1970. Language acquisition and development in early childhood. National Society for the Study of Education. Chicago.

Kohlberg, Laurence. 1968. Early education: A cognitive developmental view. Child Development, XXIX. 1013-62.

Peal, Elizabeth, and William E. Lambert. The relation of bilingualism to intelligence. Psychological Monograph, General and Applied, vol. 76, no. 546.

Piaget, Jean. Cognitive Development in children: The Piaget papers. In R. E. Ripple and V. N. Rockcastle, eds., Piaget rediscovered: A report of the conference on cognitive studies and curriculum development. Ithaca, New York, School of Education, Cornell University. March 1964. 6-48.

Rohwer, William Jr. 1969. Learning, race and school success. Mimeographed paper. Berkeley, California, University of California.

Scott, Charles T. 1970. Transformational theory and English as a second language/dialect. In Alatis, James E., ed., MSLL no. 22. 75-92.

Spolsky, Bernard. 1970. Linguistics and language pedagogy— applications or implications? In Alatis, James E., ed., MSLL no. 22. 143-157.

Troike, Rudolph C. Receptive competence, productive competence, and performance. In Alatis, James E., ed., MSLL no. 22. 63-75.

BILINGUAL EDUCATION: LINGUISTIC VS. SOCIOLINGUISTIC BASES

DELL HYMES

University of Pennsylvania

Abstract. The objectives of the Bilingual Education Program are in part to develop greater competence in English among children of limited English-speaking ability. There are children who need the Program's help, but who may be missed if the Program is permitted to make the same fundamental mistake as does much linguistic theory: to equate competence in a language with competence in ways of speaking.

Children may enter school with English as their first and only language, but with the communicative norms of a different cultural background (and ultimately, language community) governing their use of English in the school situation. In her paper Mrs. Philips presents data from an American Indian case. Here I shall discuss briefly how the linking of 'Cartesian' and 'Herderian' linguistics compounds the confusion cited above, and how a sociolinguistic perspective on the notions of 'language' and 'speech community' may help to resolve it, and to provide a conceptual basis adequate to the empirical problem.

(When Dr. Alatis invited me to participate in this Round Table Meeting, I suggested that he invite Mrs. Philips instead. She is doing empirical research on the problem of the meeting, as I am not. He very kindly asked us both. I see my role as one of sketching the theoretical background to Mrs. Philips' work. I shall try to underscore the significance of the sort of research in which she is engaged.)

Bilingual education is a sociolinguistic subject par excellence. The skills of linguists are both necessary and insufficient. The role of linguistics in research on bilingual education may seem to be a matter only of application of a linguistics already given. The contrary is the case. Research on bilingual education requires a kind of linguistics not yet fully constituted. The use of linguistics in such research challenges linguistics to develop conceptual and methodological tools able to deal adequately with the place of speech in human life—with the place of actual speech competencies in actual lives.

A goal of education, bilingual or other, presumably is to enable children to develop their capacity for creative use of language as part of successful adaptation of themselves and their communities in the continuously changing circumstances characteristic of contemporary life. And linguistics indeed has already addressed itself to this goal, as witnessed by the concern within descriptive theory for the 'creative aspect of language use' (Chomsky 1965, 1966) and the recognition of the role of the child's first language long advocated by many linguists and anthropologists. In both respects, however, linguistics falls short until it is able to deal with ways of speaking in relation to social meanings and situations, until, in short, the starting point of description is not a sentence or text, but a speech event; not a language, but a repertoire of ways of speaking; not a speech community defined in equivalence to a language, but a speech community defined through the concurrence of rules of grammar and rules of use.

The leading view of the nature of linguistic competence and creativity has been dubbed 'Cartesian linguistics' (Chomsky 1966), not as a historically exact label, but in recognition of a direction given to theory of language in the period following Descartes by an emphasis on the nature of mind as prior to experience, and an analytic, universalizing, reconstituting methodology (cf. Cassirer 1955, Ch. I, 'The Philosophy of the Enlightenment'). In similar vein, one may dub a subsequent tradition of thought 'Herderian linguistics' (Hymes 1970a), not as a historically exact label, but in recognition of a direction given to theory of language in the period following Herder (1744-1801) by an emphasis on language as constituting cultural identity (cf. Barnard 1965: 117, 118, 142), and on a methodology of sympathetic interpretation of cultural diversity sui generis—Herder coined the German verb einfühlen—if within a larger universal framework. (The two traditions might be labelled 'Enlightenment' and 'Romantic', but the individual names perhaps are better, in that they less imply two mutually exclusive periods, or simple uniformity within each.)

'Cartesian' and 'Herderian' approaches have contributed much to our knowledge of language. In the past the differences between the two approaches have been salient, but here what matters most is what they have fundamentally in common: isolation of a language as the object of linguistic description; equation of a language with a speech community (or culture); taking of the social functions of language as external, given, and universally equivalent; restriction of study of the structure of language to units and relations based on reference.

The emergence of sociolinguistics is in important part a response to social needs; but as an intellectual stage in the history of linguistics, the recent history of sociolinguistics can be seen as a response to the hegemony of 'Cartesian' and 'Herderian' assumptions, first, by critical analysis of the assumptions themselves, and, secondly, by effort to replace them. Just as Boas, Sapir, Bloomfield, Pike, and others can be seen as concerned to develop concepts and methods adequate to the description of all languages, so the current work of Ervin-Tripp, Fishman, Gumperz, Labov, and others can be seen as concerned to develop concepts and methods adequate to the description of speech communities. And where Boas, Sapir, Bloomfield, Pike, and others had to empty some concepts of normative or ethnocentric content (e. g. 'inflection', 'incorporation' vis-à-vis compounding), extend some (e. g. morphème), and invent others (e. g. phoneme), with regard to grammars, so have contributors to sociolinguistics today the task of emptying, extending, and inventing with regard to the identification and organization of ways of speaking.

Mrs. Philips' work is a contribution to the empirical task. In the rest of my remarks I shall sketch some of the critical analysis associated with it, with regard to 'Cartesian' concepts of competence and creativity, and 'Herderian' concepts of language in the speech community.

The concern with competence and creativity in Chomsky's 'Cartesian' linguistics is an advance toward sociolinguistics, but, on analysis, an advance more nominal than real. To make competence central, rather than la langue, to reconcile the sphere of creativity with that of structure, does focus discussion on actual human beings and their abilities, and regard them as acquirers and shapers of culture, rather than merely as 'culture-bearers'. Just such a transformation was projected for anthropology and linguistics by Sapir in his last writings (see discussion in Hymes 1970b). But whereas Sapir turned attention to 'living speech', understood as requiring that received categories be reconsidered within the matrix of social interaction, Chomsky's 'Cartesian' linguistics seems a cogent, thoroughly thought out perfection of the impulse to the autonomy of language that spurred so much of structural linguistics and in an earlier stage, Sapir himself. From origin as possibly a physico-chemical accident to the assumptions of wholly fluent use free of situation in a homogenous community, any dependence of language on social interaction and adaptation is excluded.

In brief, Chomskyan 'competence' is restricted to knowledge and, within knowledge, to knowledge of grammar. Much of what would nor-

mally be considered part of a speaker's knowledge and ability is excluded. Much of what one would need to study to understand actual individual competence is not 'competence' but 'performance'. In effect,
two senses of 'performance' are confounded: a negative sense, in
which 'mere' performance is that superficial behavior which linguistics must seek to go beneath, and an implicitly positive sense, in
which 'performance' is everything other than grammar that contributes
to acceptable speech. The confusion tends to give the positive contents
of 'performance' the negative association, and in any case, the dichotomy is used to relegate all but grammar to a secondary status. The
constitutive role of social factors is ignored, as is knowledge of them,
yet identification and motivation are found to be key factors in sociolinguistic change (Labov 1966, Le Page 1969). Performances, as
events, have no admitted structure of their own.

The 'creative aspect of language use', like 'competence', promises
more than it contains. It is analyzed (Chomsky 1966) in terms of the
possibility of producing an indefinitely large number of sentences, free
of immediate stimulus control, that are yet appropriate. But a sentence might be new, free of stimulus control, and bizarre. Appropriateness entails a relation to situation. Competent speakers have knowledge of the structure and meaning of sentences and of the structure and
meaning of situations and the relations between the two as well. Just as
'Cartesian' linguistics reduces competence to knowledge of grammar, so
it reduces 'creativity' to novelty.

Those concerned with linguistic aspects of education and with sociolinguistic theory must thank Chomsky for making competence and creativity central to linguistic theory, but must reconstruct the concepts
for themselves. [1]

Cartesian and 'Herderian' linguistics differ most obviously with regard to the place of differences among languages. There is not, to be
sure, a complete opposition. The most celebrated early figure in the
'Herderian' tradition, W. von Humboldt, was concerned with universals
as well as specific difference, as were Boas, Sapir, and Whorf later.
Indeed, what Herder, von Humboldt, and Goethe are linked by is a conception of form that links the individual and universal. The notion of
form is linked to that of creativity, and individuality, both, so that in
contrast to the 'Cartesian' sense of particularity and uniqueness of
personality (language, culture) as negative limitation, such limitation
is seen as positive. It is not the absence of universality, but realization of a universal power. The universal finds realization only in the
actuality of the particular; form is truly acquired only through the
power of self-formation (Cassirer 1961: 20-25). (On this development,
see Cassirer 1950: 224-5, 252; 1955: 32-36; 1961: 20-26. On von
Humboldt as having found his way into the study of language through

his concern with the characterization of individuals and individual peoples, see Lammers 1936 and Leroux 1958: 69, n. 2).

Chomsky treats von Humboldt in terms of his continuity with the general approach of the Enlightenment; he acknowledges but omits much of that aspect of von Humboldt which, according to Cassirer, is his distinctive achievement. He follows von Humboldt in concern with the universal power, but neglects von Humboldt's understanding of form as something not given, but historically emergent and acquired. [2] The treatment of von Humboldt is in keeping with the treatment of competence and creativity.

The 'Herderian' approach, as developed by von Humboldt is indeed the approach needed in sociolinguistics. The focus, however, must be changed from a language, as correlate of a people, to persons and their ways of speaking. The inadequacy of a monolingual approach has long been recognized and, indeed, no one has ever denied the obvious facts of multilingualism, the prevalence of linguistic diversity in the world. The difficulty remains that in informal thought one tends to fall back on the Herderian model of one language, one people, one culture, one community—the Hopi and their language, etc., (on the persistence of 'savage anthropology' of this sort, see Fontana 1968), because we are only beginning to have sociolinguistic models and taxonomies adequate to thinking in terms of multilingual situations. But, as the work of Gumperz, Labov, and others has shown, more than plurality of languages is involved.

First of all, what counts as a language boundary cannot be defined by any purely linguistic measure. Attitudes and social meanings enter in as well. Any enduring social relationship or group may come to define itself by selection and/or creation of linguistic features, and a difference of accent may be as important at one boundary as a difference of grammar at another. Part of the creativity of users of languages lies in the freedom to determine what and how much linguistic difference matters. The alternative view, indeed a view often taken, conceals an unsuspected linguistic determinism. (For a recent issue of this sort, involving the notion of ethnic unit and mutual intelligibility, cf. Hymes 1968.)

Secondly, speech communities cannot be defined in terms of linguistic features alone in another respect. Their definition must comprise shared knowledge both of one or more primary varieties, and of rules for their use. Differential knowledge of a linguistic variety aside (and that is of course of importance), a person who is a member of a speech community knows not only a language but also what to say. A person who can produce all and any of the sentences of a language, and unpredictably does, is institutionalized. For some range of situations, itself to be empirically determined and perhaps varying significantly across communities, a competent member of the speech community knows what to say next. And just as there are Sprachbunde, defined by linguistic features shared across language boundaries, so there are Sprechbunde, defined by shared rules of speaking. (I owe this notion to J. Neustupný). And such sharing of speech rules across languages may extend not only in space but also through time. The Ngoni of Africa, for example, mostly no longer speak Ngoni, but use the language of the people in Malawi whom they conquered. However, they use it in Ngoni ways, ways whose maintenance is considered essential to their identity. Analagous situations obtain in some American Indian communities.

In general, both theory and relevance to education require that one break with the equation between a named language and a functional role. Functional role is primary and problematic (cf. argument of Hymes 1966). The means that serve a given function are to be empirically determined. Beyond cognitive differences possibly attributable to differences of language, there are cognitive differences due to differences in speaking. There is interference not only between phonologies and grammars, but also between norms of interaction and interpretation of speech. One must take the vantage point of the person acquiring competence in speech in a community, and discover the number and organization of ways of speaking that result.

The notions of rules of cooccurrence and rules of alternation, recently developed by Ervin-Tripp are general and neutral concepts for discovering the organization of linguistic features in a community, comparable to concepts developed for discovering phonological and grammatical structure. They rely upon the fundamental notion of contrastive relevance, but generalize it to the contrastive relevance of 'stylistic' features as well as features of reference. (Vowel length for emphasis is as much a contrastive feature of English or Wasco Chinook as /m/ : /n/ to distinguish morphemes.) And the step from the identification of features to organized sets of features is, to repeat, an empirical one, governed by analysis of other components of speech events as well. The step is not, repeat not, taken by automatically referring features to a 'named' language known externally and prior to investigation. Rules of cooccurrence identify styles; rules of alternation identify their social meanings and contrastive relevance in use. (This last is the step that the approach to styles of Pike (1967) fails to take.) The notion 'ways of speaking' calls particular attention to the fact that members of a speech community have a knowledge such that speech is interpretable as pertaining to one or another genre, and as instancing one or another speech act and event.

In sum, there is no quarrel with the 'Cartesian' concern for universals and the human mind. There is much concern with the 'Herderian' concern for individuation and emergent form. Only the focus of theory and description changes, from rules of language to rules of speaking. It is the latter that are fundamental, embracing the former as one constituent. And an understanding of rules of speaking is indispensable to understanding failures and to increasing success in bicultural education.

NOTES

[1]A sociolinguistic critique of 'Cartesian' linguistics is markedly parallel to the critique by Marx of Feuerbach. By substituting 'Chomsky' (or 'Cartesian linguistics') for 'Feuerbach', and 'linguistic' for 'religious', one has a remarkably applicable statement:

'Chomsky resolves the linguistic essence into the <u>human</u> essence. But the essence of man is no abstraction inhering in each single individual. In its actuality it is the ensemble of social relationships.
'Chomsky, who does not go into the criticism of this actual essence, is hence compelled:
(1) to abstract from the historical process and to establish linguistic intuition as something self-contained, and to presuppose an abstract—<u>isolated</u>—human individual;
(2) to view the essence of man merely as "species", as the inner dumb generality which unites the many individuals <u>naturally</u>' (i. e. not socially).
(Quoted from Easton and Guddat 1967: 402.)

I do not think one can abandon some conception of a generic human nature (human essence), as the thesis might be taken as saying; but the man for whom Chomsky's competence and theory is a model is indeed an isolated man in the abstract. There is nothing to be said about men (or women).

[2]One might argue that transformational generative grammar ought by rights to be especially concerned, as was von Humboldt, with individual form. By establishing that marked departures from universal, or natural, features and relations entail costs, it is able to recognize the great extent to which languages, or rather their speakers, pay such costs, and to appreciate the power of the sociohistorical forces that motivate such payment.

REFERENCES

Barnard, F. M. 1965. Herder's social and political thought, from enlightenment to nationalism. Oxford, Clarendon Press.
Cassirer, Ernst. 1950. The problem of knowledge. Philosophy, science, and history since Hegel. New Haven, Yale University Press.

_____. 1955. The philosophy of the enlightenment. Boston, Beacon Press. (Princeton University Press, 1955; German original, Tübingen, 1932).

_____. 1961. The logic of the humanities. New Haven, Yale University Press. (German original, Göteborg, 1942.)

Chomsky, Noam. 1965. Aspects of the theory of syntax. Cambridge, M. I. T. Press.

_____. 1966. Cartesian linguistics. New York, Harper and Row.

Easton, Lloyd D. and Kurt H. Guddat, eds. 1967. Writings of the young Marx on philosophy and society. Garden City, New York, Doubleday.

Ervin-Tripp, Susan M. 1971. On sociolinguistic rules: alternation and co-occurrence. In John J. Gumperz and Dell Hymes, eds., Directions in sociolinguistics. New York, Holt, Rinehart, and Winston.

Fontana, Bernard L. 1968. Savage anthropologists and unvanishing Indians in the American Southwest. Paper read before the 67th Annual Meeting of the American Anthropological Association, Seattle, Washington, November 21.

Hymes, Dell. 1966. Two types of linguistic relativity: some examples from Amerindian ethnography. In William Bright, ed., Sociolinguistics, 114-158. The Hague, Mouton.

_____. 1967. Why linguistics needs the sociologist. Social Research 34 (4): 632-647.

_____. 1968. Linguistic problems in defining the concept of 'tribe'. In June Helm, ed., Essays on the problem of tribe, 23-48. (Proceedings of the 1967 annual spring meeting of the American Ethnological Society). Seattle, University of Washington Press.

_____. 1970a. Linguistic aspects of comparative political research. In Robert T. Holt and John E. Turner, eds., The methodology of comparative research, Ch. VII. New York, The Free Press.

_____. 1970b. Linguistic method of ethnography. In Paul Garvin, ed., The problem of method in linguistics. The Hague, Mouton.

_____. 1971. On communicative competence. Philadelphia, University of Pennsylvania Press.

Labov, William A. 1966. The social stratification of English in New York City. Washington, D. C., Center for Applied Linguistics.

Lammers, Wilhelm. 1936. Wilhelm von Humboldts Weg zur Sprachforschung 1785-1801. Berlin.

Le Page, R. C. 1969. Problems of description in multilingual communities. Transactions of the Philological Society, 1968, 189-212. London.

Leroux, Robert. 1958. L'anthropologie comparée de Guillaume de Humboldt. (Publications de la Faculté des lettres de l'Université de Strasbourg, Fascicule 135.) Paris, Société d'éditions.

Pike, K. L. 1967. Language in relation to a unified theory of the structure of human behavior. The Hague, Mouton.

DISCUSSION [This paper was discussed in conjunction with the following paper. See page 96.]

ACQUISITION OF RULES FOR APPROPRIATE SPEECH USAGE

SUSAN U. PHILIPS

University of Pennsylvania

Abstract. On the Warm Springs Indian Reservation in central Oregon the majority of children now enter school having learned English as a first language from parents who are bilingual speakers of a Sahaptin or Chinookan dialect and English. Comparative observations and tape recordings in Indian and non-Indian classrooms and observations of family interaction in Indian households indicate, however, that the Indians' rules for appropriate social usage of English differ distinctively from those of the surrounding non-Indian populations. And in school the children continue to experience considerable difficulty comprehending and participating in the structured verbal interaction between teacher and students which provides the context and mode for classroom learning.

In this paper discussion will focus on some of the specific ways in which Indian and non-Indian rules for and/or assumptions about appropriate speech usage differ and the consequences these differences have for the Indian children's development of communicative competence. Particular attention will be given to the structure of speech events which are an integral part of classroom interaction, such as question-answer sessions, ordering, and instruction, and to the ways in which the Indian ideas of appropriate roles for the senders and receivers of messages in such speech activities differ from those of non-Indians.

Introduction

Recent studies of North American Indian education problems have indicated that in many ways Indian children are not culturally oriented to the ways in which classroom learning is conducted.

The Wax-Dumont study (Wax, Wax and Dumont 1964) of the Pine Ridge Sioux discusses the lack of interest children show in what goes on in school and Wolcott's (1967) description of a Kwakiutl school describes the Indian children's organized resistance to his ways of organizing classroom learning. Cazden and John (1968) suggest that the 'styles of learning' through which Indian children are enculturated at home differ markedly from those to which they are introduced in the classroom. And Hymes has pointed out that this may lead to sociolinguistic interference when teacher and student do not recognize these differences in their efforts to communicate with one another (Hymes 1967).

On the Warm Springs Indian Reservation, in central Oregon, where I have been carrying out research in patterns of speech usage during this past year, teachers have pointed to similar phenomena, particularly in their repeated statements that Indian children show a great deal of reluctance to talk in class, and that they participate less and less in verbal interaction as they go through school. To help account for the reluctance of the Indian children of Warm Springs (and elsewhere as well) to participate in classroom verbal interactions, I am going to demonstrate how some of the social conditions governing or determining when it is appropriate for a student to speak in the classroom differ from those which govern verbal participation and other types of communicative performances in the Warm Springs Indian community's social interactions.

The data on which discussion of these differences will be based is drawn, first of all, from comparative observations in all-Indian classes in the reservation grammar school and non-Indian or white classes in another grammar school at the first and sixth grade levels. The purpose here is to define the communicative contexts in which Indian and non-Indian behavior and participation differ, and to describe the ways in which they differ.

After defining the situations or social contexts in which Indian students' verbal participation is minimal, discussion will shift to consideration of the social conditions in Indian cultural contexts which define when speaking is appropriate, attending to children's learning experiences both at home and in the community-wide social activities in which they participate.

The end goal of this discussion will be to demonstrate that the social conditions which define when a person uses speech in Indian social situations are present in classroom situations in which Indian students use speech a great deal, and absent in the more prevalent classroom situations in which they fail to participate verbally.

There are several aspects of verbal participation in classroom contexts which should be kept in mind during the discussion of why Indians are reluctant to talk. First of all, a student's use of speech in the classroom during structured lesson sessions is a communicative per-

formance in more than one sense of 'performance'. It involves demonstration of sociolinguistic competency, itself a complex combination
of linguistic competency and social competency involving knowledge of
when and in what style one must present one's utterances, among other
things. This type of competency, however, is involved in every speech
act. But in classrooms there is a second sense in which speaking is a
performance that is more special, although not unique, to classroom
interactions. In class, speaking is the first and primary mode for
communicating competency in all of the areas of skill and knowledge
which schools purport to teach. Children communicate what they have
learned to the teacher and their fellow students through speaking; only
rarely do they demonstrate what they know through physical activity or
creation of material objects. While writing eventually becomes a second important channel or mode for communicating knowledge or demonstrating skills, writing as a skill is to a great extent developed
through verbal interaction between student and teacher, as is reading.

Consequently, if talk fails to occur, then the channel through which
learning sessions are conducted is cut off, and the structure of classroom interaction which depends on dialogue between teacher and student breaks down and no longer functions as it is supposed to. Thus
while the question 'Why don't Indian kids talk more in class?' is in a
sense a very simple one, it is also a very basic one, and the lack of
talk a problem which needs to be dealt with if Indian children are to
learn what is taught in American schools.

Cultural and educational background
of the Warm Springs Indians

Before embarking on the main task of the discussion outlined above,
some background information on the setting of the research, the Warm
Springs Indian Reservation, is necessary to provide some sense of the
extent to which the cultural, linguistic, and educational situation there
may be similar to or different from that of North American Indians in
other parts of the country.

Today the reservation of 564,209 acres is populated by some 1500
descendants of the 'bands' of Warm Springs Sahaptin, Wasco Chinook,
and Paiute Indians who gradually settled there after the reservation
was established in 1855. The Warm Springs Indians have always been
the largest group numerically, followed by the Wasco, with the Paiutes
so small in number that their influence in the culture of the reservation
has been of relatively small significance. Although they spoke different
languages, the Warm Springs and Wasco groups were geographically
quite close to one another before the reservation was established, and
were culturally similar in many respects. Thus after over a hundred

years together on the reservation, they presently share approximately the same cultural background.

The 'tribe', as the Indians of Warm Springs now refer to themselves collectively, today comprises a single closely integrated community with strong tribal leadership which receives the full backing of the people. Until after World War II the Indians here experienced considerable poverty and hardship. Then in the 1950s, they received two large sums of money, first in compensation for reservation land which had originally been purchased from the Indians for considerably less than it was worth, and then in compensation for the loss of fishing rights along the Columbia River when the construction of the Dalles Dam caused their fishing sites to be covered with water. Rather than distribute all these funds to individual members of the tribe, which was the practice on other reservations in the area at that time, tribal leaders invested some of the money in tribal economic enterprises, notably a saw mill where reservation timber is processed, and a small resort.

With the income from these enterprises, and drawing as well on various forms of federal aid available to them, the tribe has developed social programs to help members of the tribe in a number of ways. Chief among their concerns is the improvement of the education of their children, whom they recognize to be less successful in school than their fellow non-Indian students. Tribal leaders have taken numerous important steps to increase the educational opportunities of their young people, including the establishment of a scholarship program for college students, a tribal education office with half a dozen full-time employees supervising the tribally sponsored kindergarten, study halls, and community center courses, and the federally sponsored programs such as VISTA, Head Start, and Neighborhood Youth Corps. Their education office employees also act as liaisons between parents of children with problems in school, and the administrators and teachers of the public schools which the children attend. In sum, the tribe is doing everything within its means to provide the Warm Springs children with the best education possible.

Despite their efforts, and those of the public school officials who are under considerable pressure from tribal leaders to bring about changes in the schools which will result in the improvement of the academic performance of Indian students, the Indians continue to do poorly in school when compared to the non-Indian students in the same school system.

One of the most important things to know about the schools the Indian children attend is the ethnic composition of their classes. For the first six grades, Warm Springs children attend a public school which is located on the reservation. Here their classmates are all Indians and their teachers are all non-Indians or whites. After the first six grades, they are bussed into the town of Madras, a distance of fifteen to thirty miles, depending on where one lives on the reservation. Here, encountering their fellow white students for the first time, the Indian students

are outnumbered by a ratio of five to one. From the point of view of
tribal leaders, it is only when they reach the high school, or ninth
grade, that the Indian students' 'problems' really become serious,
for it is at this point that hostility between Indian and non-Indian is
expressed openly, and the Indian students' failure to participate in
classroom discussions and school activities recognized by everyone.

There is, however, abundant evidence that Indian students' learning
difficulties begin long before they reach the high school. The statistics
which are available on their educational achievements and problems are
very similar to those which have been reported for Indians in other parts
of the country (Berry 1969). On national achievement tests the Warm
Springs Indian children consistently score lower than the national average in skills tested. Their lowest scores are in areas involving verbal
competencies, and the gap between their level of performance on such
tests and the national averages widens as they continue into the higher
grade levels (Zentner 1960).

Although many people on the reservation still speak an Indian language, today all of the Warm Springs children in school are monolingual speakers of English. The dialect of English which they speak,
however, is not the Standard English of their teachers, but one which
is distinctive to the local Indian community, and which in some aspects
of grammar and phonology shows influence from the Indian languages
spoken on the reservation.

In addition, there is some evidence that many children are exposed
to talk in the Indian languages which may affect their acquisition of English. Because older people on the reservation are very concerned
about the Indian languages dying out, many of them make a concerted
effort to teach young children an Indian language, particularly the Warm
Springs Sahaptin. Thus some infants and young children are spoken to
consistently in both Warm Springs and English. Every Indian child still
knows some Indian words, and many informants report that while their
children refuse to speak the Warm Springs Sahaptin—particularly after
they start school—they understand much of what is said to them in it.

The effects of the acquisition of a very local dialect of English and
the exposure to the Warm Springs language on classroom learning are
difficult for local educators to assess because children say so little in
the presence of the teachers. Observations of Indian children's verbal
interactions outside the classroom indicate a control and productive
use of linguistic rules that is manifested infrequently in classroom utterances, indicating that the appropriate social conditions for speech
use, from the Indians' point of view, are lacking. It is this problem
with appropriate social contexts for speaking that will now be considered in greater detail.

Conditions for speech use in the school classrooms

When the children first enter school, the most immediate concern
of the teachers is to teach them the basic rules for classroom behavior
upon which the maintenance of continuous and ordered activity depend.
One of the most important of these is the distinction between the roles
of teacher and student. In this there is the explicit and implicit assumption that the teacher controls all of the activity taking place in the classroom and the students accept and are obedient to her authority. She determines the sociospatial arrangements of all interactions; she decrees
when and where movement takes place within the classroom. And most
important for our present concern with communication, she determines
who will talk and when they will talk.

While some class activities are designed to create the sense of a
class of students as an organized group with class officers, or student
monitors carrying out various responsibilities contributing to the group,
actual spontaneous organization within the student group which has not
been officially designated by the teacher is not encouraged. It interferes
with the scheduling of activities as the teacher has organized them. The
classroom situation is one in which the teacher relates to the students
as an undifferentiated mass, much as a performer in front of an audience.
Or she relates to each student on a one-to-one basis, often with the rest
of the class as the still undifferentiated audience for the performance of
the individual child.

In comparing the Indian and non-Indian learning of these basic classroom distinctions which define the conditions in which communication
will take place, differences are immediately apparent. Indian first
graders are consistently slower to begin acting in accordance with these
basic arrangements. They do not remember to raise their hands and
wait to be called on before speaking, they wander to parts of the room
other than the one in which the teacher is conducting a session, and talk
to other students while the teacher is talking much further into the school
year than do students in non-Indian classes. And the Indian children continue to fail to conform to classroom procedure much more frequently
through the school year.

In contrast to the non-Indian students, the Indian students consistently
show a great deal more interest in what their fellow students are doing
than in what the teacher is doing. While non-Indian students constantly
make bids for the attention of their teachers, through initiating dialogue
with them as well as through other acts, Indian students do very little
of this. Instead they make bids for the attention of their fellow students
through talk. At the first grade level, and more noticeably at the sixth
grade level, with new teachers, Indian students often act in deliberate
organized opposition to the teacher's directions. Thus, at the first
grade level, if one student is told not to put his feet on his chair, an-

other will immediately put his feet on his chair, and he will be imitated by other students who see him do this. In non-Indian classrooms, such behavior was observed only at the sixth grade level in interaction with a substitute teacher.

In other words, there is, on the part of Indian students, relatively less interest, desire, and/or ability to internalize and act in accordance with some of the basic rules underlying classroom maintenance of orderly interaction. Most notably, Indian students are less willing than non-Indian students to accept the teacher as director and controller of all classroom activities. They are less interested in developing the one-to-one communicative relationship between teacher and student, and more interested in maintaining and developing relationships with their peers, regardless of what is going on in the classroom.

Within the basic framework of teacher-controlled interaction, there are several possible variations in structural arrangements of interaction, which will be referred to from here on as 'participant structures'. Teachers use different participant structures, or ways of arranging verbal interaction with students, for communicating different types of educational material, and for providing variation in the presentation of the same material to hold children's interest. Often the notion that different kinds of material are taught better and more efficiently through one sort of participant structuring rather than another is also involved.

In the first type of participant structure the teacher interacts with all of the students. She may address all of them, or a single student in the presence of the rest of the students. The students may respond as a group or chorus in unison, or individually in the presence of their peers. And finally, student verbal participation may be either voluntary, as when the teacher asks who knows the answer to her question, or compulsory, as when the teacher asks a particular student to answer, whether his hand is raised or not. And always it is the teacher who determines whether she talks to one or to all, receives responses individually or in chorus, and voluntarily or without choice.

In a second type of participant structure, the teacher interacts with only some of the students in the class at once, as in reading groups. In such contexts, participation is usually mandatory rather than voluntary, individual rather than chorus, and each student is expected to participate or perform verbally, for the main purpose of such smaller groups is to provide the teacher with the opportunity to assess the knowledge acquired by each individual student. During such sessions, the remaining students who are not interacting with the teacher are usually working alone or independently at their desks on reading or writing assignments.

A third participant structure consists of all students working independently at their desks, but with the teacher explicitly available for student-initiated verbal interaction, in which the child indicates he wants to communicate with the teacher by raising his hand, or by approaching the teacher at her desk. In either case, the interaction between student and teacher is not witnessed by the other students in that they do not hear what is said.

A fourth participant structure, and one which occurs infrequently in the upper primary grades and rarely, if ever, in the lower grades, consists of the students being divided into small groups which they run themselves, though always with the more distant supervision of the teacher, and usually for the purpose of so-called 'group projects'. As a rule such groups have official 'chairmen', who assume what is in other contexts the teacher's authority, in regulating who will talk when.

In observing and comparing Indian and non-Indian participation or communicative performances in these four different structural variations of contexts in which communication takes place, differences between the two groups again emerge very clearly.

In the first two participant structures where students must speak out individually in front of the other students, Indian children show considerable reluctance to participate, particularly when compared to non-Indian students. When the teacher is in front of the whole class, they volunteer to speak relatively rarely, and teachers at the Warm Springs grammar school generally hold that this reluctance to volunteer to speak out in front of other students increases as the children get older.

When the teacher is with a small group, and each individual must give some kind of communicative verbal performance in turn, Indian children much more frequently refuse, or fail to utter a word when called upon, and much less frequently, if ever, urge the teacher to call on them than the non-Indians do. When the Indian children do speak, they speak very softly, often in tones inaudible to a person more than a few feet away, and in utterances which are typically shorter or more brief than those of their non-Indian counterparts.

In situations where the teacher makes herself available for student-initiated communication during sessions in which students are working independently on assignments which do not involve verbal communication, students at the first grade level in the Indian classes at first rarely initiate contact with the teachers. After a few weeks in a classroom, they do so as frequently as the non-Indian students. At the sixth grade level, Indian students initiate such relatively private encounters with teachers much more frequently than non-Indian students do.

When students control and direct the interaction in small group projects, as described for the fourth type of participant structure, there is again a marked contrast between the behavior of Indian and non-Indian students. It is in such contexts that Indian students become most fully involved in what they are doing, concentrating completely on their work until it is completed, talking a great deal to one another within the group, and competing, with explicit remarks to that effect, with the other groups. Non-Indian students take more time in 'getting organized', disagree and argue more regarding how to go about a task, rely more heavily on appointed chairmen for arbitration and decision-making, and show less interest, at least explicitly, in competing with other groups from their class.

Observations of the behavior of both Indian and non-Indian children outside the classroom during recess periods and teacher-organized physical education periods provide further evidence that the difference in readiness to participate in interaction are related to the way in which the interaction is organized and controlled.

When such outside-class activity is organized by the teachers, it is for the purpose of teaching children games through which they develop certain physical and social skills. If the games involve a role distinction between leader and followers in which the leader must tell the others what to do—as in Simon Says, Follow the Leader, Green Light, Red Light, and even Farmer in the Dell, Indian children show a great deal of reluctance to assume the leadership role. This is particularly true when the child is appointed leader by the teacher and must be repeatedly urged to act in telling the others what to do before doing so. Non-Indian children, in contrast, vie eagerly for such positions, calling upon the teacher and/or other students to select them.

If such playground activity is unsupervised, and the children are left to their own devices, Indian children become involved in games of team competition much more frequently than non-Indian children. And they sustain such game activities for longer periods of time and at younger ages than non-Indian children. While non-Indian children tend more to play in groups of two and three, and in the upper primary grades to form 'friendships' with one or two persons from their own class in school, Indian children interact with a greater number of children consistently, and maintain friendships and teams with children from classes in school other than their own.

In reviewing the comparison of Indian and non-Indian students' verbal participation under different social conditions, two features of the Warm Springs children's behavior stand out. First of all, they show relatively less willingness to perform or participate verbally when they must speak alone in front of other students. Second, they are relatively less eager to speak when the point at which speech occurs is dictated by the teacher, as it is during sessions when the teacher is working with the whole class or a small group. They also show considerable reluctance to be placed in the 'leadership' play roles that require them to assume the same type of dictation of the acts of their peers.

Parallel to these negative responses are the positive ones of a relatively greater willingness to participate in group activities which do not create a distinction between individual performer and audience, and a relatively greater use of opportunities in which the point at which the student speaks or acts is determined by himself, rather than by the teacher or a 'leader'.

It is apparent that there are situations arising in the classroom which do allow for the Indian students to verbalize or communicate under or within the participant structures which their behavior indicates they prefer; otherwise it would not have been possible to make the distinctions between their behavior and that of non-Indians in the areas just discussed. However, the frequency of occurrence of such situations in the classroom is very low when compared to the frequency of occurrence of the type of participant structuring in which Indian students fail to participate verbally, particularly in the lower grades.

In other words, most verbal communication which is considered part of students' learning experience does take the structure of individual students speaking in front of other students. About half of this speaking is voluntary insofar as students are invited to volunteer to answer, and half is compulsory in that a specific student is called on and expected to answer. In either case, it is the teacher who establishes when talk will occur and within what kind of participant structure.

There are many reasons why most of the verbal communication takes place under such conditions. Within our particular education system, a teacher needs to know how much her students have learned or absorbed from the material she has presented. Students' verbal responses provide one means—and the primary means, particularly before students learn to write—of measuring their progress, and are thus the teacher's feedback. And, again within our particular educational system, it is not group, but individual progress with which our teachers are expected to be concerned.

In addition, it is assumed that students will learn from each other's performances both what is false or wrong, and what is true or correct. Another aspect of this type of public performance which may increase educators' belief in its efficacy is the students' awareness that these communicative acts are performances, in the sense of being demonstrations of competency. The concomitant awareness that success or failure in such acts is a measure of their worth in the eyes of those present increases their motivation to do well. Thus they will remember when they make a mistake and try harder to do well to avoid public failure, in a way which they would not, were their performances in front of a smaller number of people. As I will try to demonstrate further on, however, the educators' assumption of the validity or success of this type of enculturation process, which can briefly be referred to as 'learning through public mistakes', is not one which the Indians share, and this has important implications for our understanding of Indian behavior in the classroom.

The consequences of the Indians' reluctance to participate in these speech situations are several. First of all, the teacher loses the primary means she has of receiving feedback on the children's acquisition of knowledge, and is thus less able to establish at what point she must begin again to instruct them, particularly in skills requiring a developmental sequencing, as in reading.

A second consequence of this reluctance to participate in speech situations requiring mandatory individual performances is that the teachers in the Warm Springs grammar school modify their teaching approach whenever possible to accommodate, in a somewhat ad hoc fashion, what they refer to as the Indian students' 'shyness'. In the first grade it is not easy to make very many modifications because of what teachers perceive as a close relationship between the material being taught and the methods used to teach it. There is some feeling, also, that the teaching methods which can be effective with children at age six are somewhat limited in range. However, as students go up through the grades, there is an increasing tendency for teachers to work with the notion, not always a correct one, that given the same body of material, there are a number of different ways of 'presenting' it, or in the terms being used here, a range of different participant structures and modes of communication (e. g. talking versus reading and writing) which can be used.

Even so, at the first grade level there are already some changes made to accommodate the Indian children which are notable. When comparing the Indian first grade classes with the non-Indian first grade classes, one finds very few word games involving students giving directions to one another being used. And even more conspicuous in Indian classes is the absence of the ubiquitous Show and Tell or Sharing through which students learn to get up in front of the class, standing where the teacher stands, and presenting, as the teacher might, a monologue relating an experience or describing a treasured object which is supposed to be of interest to the rest of the class. When asked whether this activity was used in the classroom one teacher explained that she had previously used it, but so few children ever volunteered to 'share' that she finally discontinued it.

By the time the students reach the sixth grade, the range of modes and settings for communication have increased a great deal, and the opportunity for elimination of some participant structures in preference to others is used by the teachers. As one sixth grade teacher put it, 'I spend as little time in front of the class as possible.' In comparison with non-Indian classes, Indian classes have a relatively greater number of group 'projects'. Thus, while non-Indian students are learning about South American history through reading texts and answering the teacher's questions, Indian students are doing group-planned and executed murals depicting a particular stage in Latin

American history; while non-Indian students are reading science texts and answering questions about how electricity is generated, Indian students are doing group-run experiments with batteries and motors.

Similarly, in the Indian classes 'reports' given by individual students are almost nonexistent, but are a typical means in non-Indian classes for demonstrating knowledge through verbal performance. And finally, while in non-Indian classes students are given opportunities to ask the teacher questions in front of the class, and do so, Indian students are given fewer opportunities for this because when they do have the opportunity they don't use it. Rather, the teacher of Indians allows more periods in which he is available for individual students to approach him alone and ask their questions quietly where no one else can hear them.

The teachers who make these adjustments, and not all do, are sensitive to the inclinations of their students and want to teach them through means to which they most readily adapt. However, by doing so, they are avoiding teaching the Indian children how to communicate in precisely the contexts in which they are least able, and most need to learn how to communicate if they are to do well in school. The teachers handicap themselves by setting up performance situations for the students in which they are least able to arrive at the evaluations of individual competence upon which they rely for feedback to establish at what level they must begin to teach. And it is not at all clear that students do acquire the same information through one form of communication as they do through another. Thus these manipulations of communication settings and participant structures, which are intended to creatively transmit knowledge to the students through the means to which they are most adjusted, may actually be causing the students to completely miss types of information which their later high school teachers will assume they picked up in grammar school.

The consequences of this partial adaption to Indian modes of communication become apparent when the Indian students join the non-Indian students at the junior and senior high school levels. Here, where the Indian students are outnumbered one to five, there is no manipulation and selection of communication settings to suit the inclinations of the Indians. Here the teachers complain that the Indian students never talk in class, and never ask questions, and everyone wonders why.

Conditions for speech use in the
Warm Springs Indian Community

To understand why the Warm Springs Indian children speak out readily under some social conditions, but fail to do so under others, it is necessary to examine the sociolinguistic assumptions determining the conditions for communicative performances, particularly those involving explicit demonstrations of knowledge or skill, in the Indian community. It will be possible here to deal with only some of the many aspects of communication which are involved. Attention will focus first on the social structuring of learning situations or contexts in which knowledge and skills are communicated to children in Indian homes. Then some consideration will be given to the underlying rules or conditions for participation in the community-wide social events that pre-school children, as well as older children, learn through attending such events with their families.

The Indian child's pre-school and outside-school enculturation at home differs from that of many non-Indian or white middle-class children's in that a good deal of the responsibility for the care and training of children is assumed by persons other than the parents of the children. In many homes the oldest children, particularly if they are girls, assume these responsibilities when the parents are at home, as well as when they are not. Frequently, also, grandparents, uncles and aunts assume the full-time responsibility for care and instruction of children. Children thus become accustomed to interacting with and following the instructions and orders of a greater number of people than is the case with non-Indian children. Equally important is the fact that all of the people with whom Indian children form such reciprocal nurturing and learning relationships are kinsmen. Indian children are rarely, if ever, taken care of by 'baby-sitters' from outside the family. Most of their playmates before beginning school are their siblings and cousins, and these peer relationships typically continue to be the strongest bonds of friendship through school and adult life, later providing a basis for reciprocal aid in times of need, and companionship in many social activities.

Indian children are deliberately taught skills around the home (for girls) and in the outdoors (for boys) at an earlier age than many middle-class non-Indian children. Girls, for example, learn to cook some foods before they are eight, and by this age may be fully competent in cleaning a house without any aid or supervision from adults.

There are other areas of competence in which Indian children are expected to be proficient at earlier ages than non-Indian children, for which the means of enculturation or socialization are less visible and clear-cut. While still in grammar school, at the age of 10 or 11, some children are considered capable of spending afternoons and evenings in the company of only other children, without the necessity of accounting for their whereabouts or asking permission to do whatever specific activity is involved. At this same age, many are also considered capable of deciding where they want to live, and for what reasons one residence is preferable to another. They may spend weeks or months at a time living with one relative or another, until it is no longer possible to say that they live in any particular household.

In general, then, Warm Springs Indian children become accustomed to self-determination of action, accompanied by very little disciplinary control from older relatives, at much younger ages than middle-class white children.

In the context of the household, learning takes place through several sorts of somewhat different processes. First of all, children are present at many adult interactions as silent but attentive observers. While it is not yet clear how adult activities in which children are not full participants are distinguished from those in which children may participate fully, and from those for which they are not allowed to be present at all, there are clearly marked differences. What is most remarkable, however, is that there are many adult conversations to which children pay a great deal of silent, patient attention. This contrasts sharply with the behavior of non-Indian children, who show little patience in similar circumstances, desiring either to become a full participant through verbal interaction, or to become completely involved in some other activity.

There is some evidence that this silent listening and watching was, in the Warm Springs culture, traditionally the first step in learning skills of a fairly complex nature. For example, older women reminisce about being required to watch their elder relatives tan hides when they were very young, rather than being allowed to play. And certainly the winter evening events of myth-telling, which provided Indian children with their first explicitly taught moral lessons, involved them as listening participants rather than as speakers.

A second type of learning involves the segmentation of a task by an older relative, and the partial carrying out of the task or one of its segments by the child. In household tasks, for example, a child is given a very simple portion of a job (e.g. in cleaning a room, the child may begin by helping move the furniture) and works in cooperation with and under the supervision of an older relative. Such activities involve a small amount of verbal instruction or direction from the older relative, and allow for questions on the part of the child. Gradually the child comes to learn all of the skills involved in a particular process, consistently under the supervision of an older relative who works along with him.

This mode of instruction is not unique to the Warm Springs Indians, of course; many non-Indian parents use similar methods. However, there are aspects of this type of instruction which differ from its use among non-Indians. First of all, it is likely to be preceded by the long periods of observation just described when it occurs among the Indians. The absence of such observation among non-Indian children is perhaps replaced by elaborate verbal instructions outlining the full scope of a task before the child attempts any part of it.

A second way in which this type of instruction among the Warm Springs Indians differs from that of non-Indians is the absence of 'testing' of the child's skill by the instructing kinsman before the child exercises the skill unsupervised. Although it is not yet clear how this works in a diversity of situations, it appears that in many areas of skill, the child takes it upon himself to test the skill unsupervised and alone, without other people around. In this way, if he is unsuccessful, his failure is not seen by others. If he is successful, he can show the results of his success to those by whom he has been taught, whether it be in the form of a deer that has been shot, a hide tanned, a piece of beadwork completed, or a dinner on the table when the adults come home from work.

Again there is some evidence that this type of private individual's testing of competency, followed by public demonstration only when competency is fully developed and certain, has been traditional in the Warm Springs Indian culture. The most dramatic examples of this come from the processes of acquisition of religious and ritual knowledge. In the vision quests through which adolescents, or children of even younger ages, acquired spirit power, individuals spent long periods in isolated mountain areas, from which they were expected to emerge with skills they had not previously demonstrated. While some of these abilities were not fully revealed until later in life, the child was expected to be able to relate some experience of a supernatural nature which would prove that he had, in fact, been visited by a spirit. Along the same lines, individuals until very recently received and learned ritual songs through dreams and visions, which they would sing for the first time in full and completed form in the presence of others.

The contexts described here in which learning takes place can be perceived as a sequence, idealized, of three steps: (1) observation, which of course includes listening; (2) supervised participation; and (3) private, self-initiated self-testing. It is not the case that all acquisitions of skills proceed through such phases, however, but rather only some of those skills which Indian adults consciously and deliberately teach their children, and which the children consciously try to learn. Those which are learned through less deliberate means must to some extent invoke similar structuring, but it is difficult to determine to what extent.

The use of speech in the process is notably minimal. Verbal directions or instructions are few, being confined to corrections and question-answering. Nor does the final demonstration of skill particularly involve verbal performance, since the validation of skill so often involves display of some material evidence or nonverbal physical expression.

This process of Indian acquisition of competence may help to explain, in part, Indian children's reluctance to speak in front of their classmates. In the classroom, the process of 'acquisition' of knowledge and 'demonstration' of knowledge are collapsed into the single act of answering questions or reciting when called upon to do so by the teacher, particularly in the lower grades. Here the assumption is that one will learn, and learn more effectively, through making mistakes in front of others. The Indian children have no opportunity to observe others performing successfully before they attempt it, except for their fellow classmates who precede them, and are themselves initiated. They have no opportunity to 'practice', and decide for themselves when they know enough to demonstrate their knowledge; rather, their performances are determined by the teacher. And finally, their only channel for communicating competency is verbal, rather than nonverbal.

Turning now from learning processes in the home to learning experiences outside the home, in social and ritual activities involving community members other than kinsmen, there is again considerable evidence that Indian children's understanding of when and how one participates and performs individually and thus demonstrates or communicates competence, differs considerably from what is expected of them in the classroom.

Children of all ages are brought to every sort of community-wide social event sponsored by Indians (as distinct from those sponsored by non-Indians). There is rarely, if ever, such a thing as an Indian community event which is attended by adults only. At many events, children participate in only certain roles, but this is true of everyone. Sociospatially and behaviorally, children must always participate minimally as do all others in sitting quietly and attentively alongside their elders.

One of the social features which characterizes social events that are not explicitly kin group affairs, including activities like political General Councils, social dinners, and Worship Dances, is that they are open to participation by all members of the Warm Springs Indian community. While different types of activities are more heavily attended by certain Indians rather than others, and fairly consistently sponsored and arranged by certain individuals, it is always clear that everyone is invited, both by community knowledge of this fact, and by explicit announcements on posters placed in areas where most people pass through at one time or another in their day-to-day activities.

A second feature of such activities is that there is usually no one person directing the activity verbally, or signalling changes from one phase to another. Instead, the structure is determined either by a set procedure or ritual, or there is a group of people who in various complementary ways provide such cueing and direction. Nor are there any participant roles which can be filled or are filled by only one person. In dancing, singing, and drumming there are no soloists, and where there are performers who begin a sequence and are then joined by others, more than one performer takes a turn at such initiations.

The speaking roles are handled similarly. In contexts where speeches are appropriate, it is made clear that anyone who wants to may 'say a few words'. The same holds true for political meetings, where the answerer to a question is not necessarily one who is on a panel or council, but rather the person who feels he is qualified, by his knowledge of a subject, to answer. In all situations thus allowing for anyone who wants to to speak, no time limit is set, so that the talking continues until everyone who wants to has had the opportunity to do so.

This does not mean that there are never any 'leaders' in Indian social activities, but rather that leadership takes quite a different form than it does in many non-Indian cultural contexts. Among the people of Warm Springs, a person is not a leader by virtue of holding a particular position, even in the case of members of the tribal council and administration. Rather, he is a leader because he has demonstrated ability in some sphere and activity, and many individuals choose to follow his suggestions because they have independently each decided they are good ones. If, for example, an individual plans and announces an activity, but few people offer to help him carry it out or attend it, then that is an indication that the organizer is not a respected leader in the community at the present time. And the likelihood that he will repeat his efforts in the near future is reduced considerably.

This type of 'leadership', present today among the people of Warm Springs, is reminiscent of that which was described by Hoebel (1954: 132) for the Comanche chiefs:

> In matters of daily routine, such as camp moving, he merely made the decisions himself, announcing them through a camp crier. Anyone who did not like his decision simply ignored it. If in time a good many people ignored his announcements and preferred to stay behind with some other man of influence, or perhaps to move in another direction with that man, the chief had then lost his following. He was no longer chief, and another had quietly superseded him.

A final feature of Indian social activities, which should be recognized from what has already been said, is that all who do attend an activity may participate in at least some of the various forms participation takes for the given activity, rather than there being a distinction made between participants or performers and audience. At many Indian gatherings, particularly those attended by older people, this aspect of the situation is reflected in its sociospatial arrangement: people are seated in such a way that all present are facing one another, usually in an approximation of a square, and the focus of activity is either along one side of the square, or in its center, or a combination of the two.

And each individual chooses the degree of his participation. No one, other than perhaps those who set up the event, is committed to being present beforehand and all participating roles beyond those of sitting and observing are determined by the individual at the point at which he decides to participate, rather than being pre-scheduled.

In summary, the Indian social activities to which children are early exposed outside the home generally have the following properties: (1) they are community-wide, in the sense that they are open to all Warm Springs Indians; (2) there is no single individual directing and controlling all activity, and to the extent that there are 'leaders', their leadership is based on the choice to follow which is made by each person; (3) participation in some form is accessible to everyone who attends. No one need be exclusively an observer or audience, and there is consequently no sharp distinction between audience and performer. And each individual chooses for himself the degree of his participation during the activity.

If one now compares the social conditions for verbal participation in the classroom with the conditions underlying many Indian events in which children participate, a number of differences emerge.

First of all, classroom activities are not community-wide, but, more importantly, the participants in the activity are not drawn just from the Indian community. The teacher, as a non-Indian, is an outsider and a stranger to these events. In addition, by virtue of her role as teacher, she structurally separates herself from the rest of the participants, her students. She places herself outside the interaction and activity of the students. This encourages their cultural perceptions of themselves as the relevant community in opposition to the teacher, perhaps much as they see themselves in opposition to other communities, and on a smaller scale as one team is in opposition to another. In other words, on the basis of the Indians' social experiences, one is either a part of a group or outside it. The notion of a single individual being structurally set apart from all others, in anything other than an observer role, and yet still a part of the group organization, is one which children probably encounter for the first time in school, and continue to experience only in non-Indian derived activities (e.g. in bureaucratic, hierarchically-structured occupations). This helps to explain why Indian students show so little interest in initiating interaction with the teacher in activities involving other students.

Second, in contrast to Indian activities where many people are involved in determining the development and structure of an event, there is only one single authority directing everything in the classroom, namely the teacher. And the teacher is not the controller or leader by virtue of the individual students' choices to follow her, as is the case in Indian social activities, but rather by virtue of her occupation of the role of teacher. This difference helps to account for the Indian children's frequent indifference to the directions, orders, and requests for compliance with classroom social rules which the teacher issues.

Third, it is not the case in the classroom that all students may participate in any given activity, as in Indian community activities. Nor are they given the opportunity to choose the degree of their participation which, on the basis of evidence discussed earlier, would in Indian contexts be based on the individual's having already ascertained in private that he was capable of successful verbal communication of competence. Again these choices belong to the teacher.

Conclusion

In summary, Indian children fail to participate verbally in classroom interaction because the social conditions for participation to which they have become accustomed in the Indian community are lacking. The absence of these appropriate social conditions for communicative performances affect the most common and everyday speech acts which occur in the classroom. If the Indian child fails to follow an order or answer a question, it may not be because he doesn't understand the linguistic structure of the imperative and the interrogative, but rather because he does not share the non-Indian's assumption in such contexts that use of these syntactic forms by definition implies an automatic and immediate response from the person to whom they were addressed. For these assumptions are sociolinguistic assumptions which are not shared by the Indians.

Educators cannot assume that because Indian children (or children from other cultural backgrounds than that which is implicit in American classrooms) speak English, or are taught it in school, that they have also assimilated all of the sociolinguistic rules underlying interaction in classrooms and other non-Indian social situations where English is spoken. If the children are to participate in the classroom verbal interaction upon which the learning process depends, they must first be taught the rules for appropriate speech usage in contexts where talking is necessary.

REFERENCES

Berry, Brewton. 1969. The education of American Indians: A survey of the literature. Prepared for the Special Subcommittee on Indian Education of the Committee on Labor and Public Welfare, United States Senate. Washington, D. C., Government Printing Office.
Cazden, Courtney B., and Vera P. John. 1968. Learning in American Indian children. In: Styles of learning among American Indians: An outline for research, 1-19. Washington, D. C., Center for Applied Linguistics.

Hoebel, E. Adamson. 1954. The law of primitive man. Cambridge, Harvard University Press.

Hymes, Dell. 1967. On communicative competence. MS due to be published in a volume edited by Renira Huxley and Elizabeth Ingram, tentative title: Mechanisms of language development. To be published by Centre for Advanced Study in the Developmental Science and CIBA Foundation, London.

Wax, Murray, Rosalie Wax, and Robert Dumont, Jr. 1964. Formal education in an American Indian community. Social Problems Monograph no. 1. Society for the Study of Social Problems, Kalamazoo, Michigan.

Wolcott, Harry. 1967. A Kwakiutl village and school. New York City: Holt, Rinehart, and Winston.

Zentner, Henry. 1960. Volume II: education. Oregon State College Warm Springs Research Project.

DISCUSSION

Shaligram Shukla, Georgetown University: In your brief paper, Mr. Hymes, you mention Chomsky and his creative aspect of language use, etc. I would like to know what is the noncreative aspect of language use.

Hymes: This, in fact, touches on something which is quite important in language use. Creative, of course, is something for which there is not a single definition, but in Chomsky's use of it and in many people's sense of it, it is very much the sense of novelty, of innovation, of some sort of production of something which is in itself an instance occurring for the first time. That is fundamental and important to language in its role in human life. From an anthropological point of view, of course, one misses in that emphasis an equally, perhaps, important aspect of the role of language in human life which is the saying again of things which are valued, the perpetuation of traditional forms of speech, the satisfactions often of saying something which one's father has said in the same situation, and so forth. This is not necessarily an answer directly to your question, because if one takes the view which I was sketching in the paper, to analyze creativity as such one really has to relate the novelty of the utterance to the situation. One may have the kind of creativity which involves saying something which has been said before. No creativity there, perhaps, from Chomsky's point of view, with regard to the sentences, but if it is new in that situation, the novelty and creativity may be in recognizing the possibility of using this familiar utterance in this new circumstance. If I repeat a list I memorized, that would probably not be very creative.

Shukla: If you remember, in 1958 Charles Hockett said exactly the same thing, that in language you could say something that has never been said before. So why shouldn't people quote Hockett instead of Chomsky?

Hymes: Well, you know, in 20 minutes I don't discuss everybody who may have had something interesting to say. The reason we are discussing Chomsky is because most linguists read Chomsky and, unfortunately, don't read what Hockett said in 1958. I did, in fact, read what Hockett said at a previous Georgetown Round Table on ethnolinguistic implications, and thought it was one of his best articles; but I do think he was a bit hung up on the matter of ritual use. There again one has the same problem of being so hung up on the notion of novelty as to find it a mystery that people will do the same thing again.

Robert J. Di Pietro, Georgetown University: I have a footnote to add to Mrs. Philips' talk. You don't have to go to the Indian schools to find nonvocal children. All you have to do is sit in a foreign language class where students are expected to say something which they haven't really been taught. Also, 'nonvocalism' has been noticed among Welsh children, among black Americans, and among many different groups trying to climb up into another economic class. The anthropological study of such groups often is as revealing of the anthropologist as it is of the people being studied. If it is true that an effort is being made to get the Navajo Indian children to act more like Anglo-Americans, we must also notice among universities and schools in various parts of this country the exact opposite trend in trying to destroy the usual type of teacher-student interaction. There is an attempt to set up new forms of interaction and reduce the authoritarian figure of the teacher and work toward more of a social grouping of student and teacher. Perhaps in succeeding to change the Navajo we will find that we ourselves have been changed.

Hymes: I think that of course it is not alright to decide for peoples what their own goals should be. Generally speaking, the Indians of Warm Springs want to succeed in education. On their own initiative they have used their funds to make it possible for every child who can finish high school to go to college. They themselves are constantly concerned and distressed at the failures as they perceive them in the schools. It was only possible for Mrs. Philips to do this work at Warm Springs because the people at Warm Springs accepted her and in fact considered what she was doing as relevant and of interest to them.

Philips: With regard to what kinds of changes one would want to introduce into a classroom situation, I like to think that it would depend on what the people in the community actually want, and not on any decisions that those of us who are outside of the situation would make for them. And while this kind of thing is possible at Warm Springs because of the small size of the tribe and the strong leadership they have, I don't know that it is possible in some of the other Indian situations. However, I would like for it to be more so; I want to see that kind of thing happening instead of us making the decisions.

Vera John, Yeshiva University: I think the size of the tribe is not necessarily a limiting factor in planning on Indian reservations. I'm sure that Dr. Roessel is going to speak to us during our lunch in greater detail about many important adventures in self-determination and education on the Navajo reservation. Traditional education for Indians has been so bad that throughout Indian communities all over the country there are very, very strong movements, on the part of tribal people, defining the role and purpose of education for Indian children by Indians. The big problem is that educational techniques very often lag behind in helping to implement new objectives, and I think it is in this area that we can be of assistance. That is, I think more and more Indian groups are saying, 'We don't want the secondhand Anglo education that we have been exposed to; we want another form of education.' The question is: Can the consultants, collaborators, and those members of the white community who are accepted in these endeavors, come up with something new? This is our challenge.

Walter A. Wolfram, Center for Applied Linguistics: I'm deeply sympathetic with your concern for functional uses of language, the ethnography of speech. What I would like to have clarified is exactly what you mean by rules. Do you, when you talk about rules, interpret this to be some sort of taxonomic framework for setting up participants, topics, settings, and so forth, into which certain linguistic styles might fit? Or do you conceive eventually of formalizing such types of rules so that they may have some generative type of capacity? At what stage is your development of these so-called rules in terms of their formal representation?

Hymes: Two things to say to that. Usually I mentally use the word 'rules' in quotes, because the conception of 'rule' itself is one which can be debated. Lamb, for example, would argue that it is not proper to speak of rules in this connection. I use the word 'rules' for the same reason that I spoke of Chomsky rather than Hockett: because I'm trying to address linguists and the generally common terminology for dealing with these things, to point out the importance of certain things which are neglected. With regard to what I think the nature of these rules might be, it seems to me that we know rather little about it, that the kinds of notions which I think are most important at this time are those which are developed by Dr. Tripp, for example. In a recent paper of hers she talks about rules of co-occurrence and alternation. That seems to be a very good basis for it because it is a completely general and neutral approach which cuts across many of the difficulties which we have in thinking in terms of whole languages and so forth. One can discover empirically whatever styles or organizations of speech features may be present; and not only co-occurrence which brings together ways of speaking, but also alternation which enables one to deal with their substitution, one for the other, and their contrastive social uses, which is a point which Pike, for example, fails to take in his book. He talks about styles, but it is always complementary in relation to the ordinary linguistic structure, never taking that step to contrast styles in social circumstances. What form these would take is very difficult to say. A lot of people are concerned about this. I don't think anybody has the whole answer. David DeCamp, as you know (he spoke here last year), talks about scaling, and that obviously gets at some things. Dr. Tripp has used flow charts for getting at some kinds of relationships, and that seems to be the most economical and effective way of showing those relationships. It is very much an open matter here, I think.

Esperanza Medina-Spyropoulos, Georgetown University: I would like to comment on one of Professor Hymes' assertions, and I hope that my comments will tie in with Professor Shukla's remarks on the creative aspect of language use. Professor Hymes asserts that there is no quarrel with the Cartesian linguistics. If you will permit me, I would like to change for a moment the title of 'Bilingual Education: Linguistic vs. Sociolinguistic Bases' to read: 'Bilingual Education: Cartesian Linguistic Bases vs. Sociolinguistic Bases' and maintain that there should be, if not a quarrel, a careful evaluation of the Cartesian linguistics if we are to apply its principles to sociolinguistic studies. I would like to echo Professor Andree F. Sjoberg's remarks that the descriptive techniques of transformational linguistics (to which many sociolinguists subscribe) have had the effect of drawing the attention of linguists away from the sociocultural dimension of language. Clearly, the descriptive techniques developed by the generative grammarians represent great improvements in the study of language structure and there is no doubt that their impact will endure the test of time. However, some of the basic assumptions of the followers of Cartesian linguistics must be questioned, mainly their line of reasoning in regard to their view of man in relation to language; it seems to me that we have failed to recognize that there is a fundamental incompatibility between the assumptions underlying Cartesian linguistics and those basic to sociolinguistics as far as the basic view of man, mind, and language. Descartes sought to separate man from society; on the other hand, leading sociolinguists see the study of language as inseparable from the study of society and maintain that linguistic interaction is social interaction. Such a notion appears to be in contrast to that of the Chomskians, who are at present primarily interested in language structure as directly embedded in the fundamental character of the human mind, and apparently seem to exclude interest in societal structures and interactions. In regard to creativity, Cartesian linguists and their followers seem to view creativity in rather mechanistic terms: creativity involves far more than the generation of new sentences; the generation of new strings is essentially an automatic process and it results from the operation of certain grammatical rules which act as calibres or filters, rejecting the structures that are not acceptable. The search is now on for language universals, but once they are discovered, it will also be a rather mechanistic process if all the mind has to do is to select the applicable universals. Professor George Herbert Meade emphasizes the reflective nature of the human mind and says that it is not so much man's ability to create new sentences which sets him apart from the animals, but it is his ability to reflect on what he has said and to reflect on his capacity to conceptualize. In addition, we must remember that the Port Royal method never produced as fine and eloquent linguistic descriptions as did its rival, the empirical method, so I believe that sociolinguists should take issue with Cartesian linguistics to the extent of clarifying with insight their main tenets and adding further refinement to their model; for Chomsky himself speaks of the 'absurdity of regarding the system of generative rules as a point-by-point model for the actual construction of a sentence by a speaker'. (I must give credit to Professor Andree F. Sjoberg, University of Texas at Austin, for his lucid exposition of 'The Socio-Cultural Dimension in Transformational Theory' presented at the Annual Meeting of the Linguistic Society of America, New York City, December 28-30, 1968).

Hymes: I find myself sometimes in a situation having to defend Chomsky first so that after I can criticize him the way I would like to. But in my text, at least, and I hope certainly implicit in the presentation, there is no quarrel with the Cartesian concern for universals in the human mind, which is less than accepting everything that goes under that name. Just to make my position clear, let me read you a footnote which maybe is kind of cute and maybe not. It goes as follows: 'A sociolinguistic critique of Cartesian linguistics is markedly parallel to the critique by Marx of Feuerbach. By substituting "Chomsky" for "Feuerbach" and "linguistic" for "religious" one has a remarkedly apposite statement. (I'm now quoting Karl Marx): "Chomsky resolves the linguistic essence into the human essence, but the essence of man is no abstraction inhering in each single individual. In its actuality it is the example of social relationships." Chomsky, who does not go into the criticism of this actual essence, is hence compelled to abstract from the historical process and to establish linguistic intuition as something self-contained, and to presuppose an abstract, isolated, human individual, and to view the essence of man merely as 'species', (that is in a generic sense), as the inner dumb generality which unites the many individuals naturally (i.e., not socially).

William Stokoe, Jr., Gallaudet College: I'd like to ask Mrs. Philips if she has noted a distinction between the ways that the Indians of Warm Springs Reservation and non-Indians communicate nonverbally; whether the nonverbal communicative interchange suggested by the square formation of social groupings plays a different role in the Indian participant interaction than that in non-Indian participant situations.

Philips: I'm not quite clear on whether you mean that the organization of activity is in itself communicating something, or that by virtue of that organization, other things get done. I would say that this face-to-face kind of organization in itself allows for people to be able to see constantly how everybody is reacting to everything. It implies in itself a type of silent participation that you can't possibly have when all the people are in a room like this facing toward the front. You have little idea how each other among you have responded to the same things that you have responded to, whereas the Indians would. They would know. I think that is one kind of thing that makes a difference.

Stokoe: You mentioned the difference between the imperative and interrogative structures of English which call for specific responses in some cultures. Isn't it so that some kind of signal or a certain kind of response comes from nonverbal cues rather than from the structure of the verbal utterance?

Philips: Yes, in some respects, but that wasn't what I was thinking about in this particular case. I was actually referring to some sociolinguistic discussions of things like questioning and answering (I don't know if anything like this has been published, but papers circulate). There has been some notion that a question implies an automatic response. Thus somebody might point out that a child knows that if he asks a parent a question the parent will have to respond to him. It is a way of engaging somebody in interaction. On the Indian reservation one of the first things that I heard was that it was possible to have an encounter with somebody where you ask them a question and they simply don't answer you, but they might come back and visit you a couple of days later and answer the question that you had asked them! This indicates a difference in the cultural assumptions about what the temporal obligations of the answerer are. That was what I was talking about in this particular case.

THE LINGUISTIC DIVISION OF LABOR
IN INDUSTRIAL AND URBAN SOCIETIES

EVERETT C. HUGHES

Boston College

Abstract.   Nearly all industrial societies have brought two or more ethnic groups together, each occupying certain positions in the economy in a proportion different from the other ethnic groups.   Frequently the ethnic differences include language.   The industrially dominant group, whether more or less numerous than other groups, will probably use a world language.   The other groups, not dominant in industry, often speak a more local language.

In Montreal, Province of Quebec, Canada, both official and widely used languages are world languages completely adapted to the demands of science, technology, commerce and modern government.   French is the language of the great majority of the population; English, of a numerical, but economically dominant, minority.   It makes a good case for study of the functions of two languages in a modern industrial community, for the difference of function cannot be attributed to the characteristics of the languages themselves.

The place of the two languages can best be described in terms of the organization of communication in the particular society.   One great category of transactions consists of those of delivering goods and services to customers or clients.   Some such transactions are impersonal, even made automatic; others are intimate, personal and require subtle exchange of words.   Another category consists of those of managing industrial and commercial organizations.   The top level managers and technologists communicate among themselves and with their peers in other organizations in large, often international, orbits.   In Montreal the language of that communication is more often English than not (as it is to some extent in many parts of the world).   Those top level people also communicate information and instructions downward through the organization. At the middle level and toward the bottom ranks of industrial and commercial organization, personnel are nearly all, or completely French-speaking. At some point translation into French must occur, either in writing or by word of mouth of bilingual individuals.

Thus, there are essentially two kinds of communication. One is horizontal, among people of the same level, either inside the same organization or reaching out into the large world. The other is vertical, predominantly downward, but also sometimes upward. The choice of language for each kind of communication will depend upon what will be effective as between the parties to the language transactions. Given the large French population, horizontal communication in French characterizes many transactions. In the delivery of professional services such as medicine, religion, social services, and education, all parties to the transaction are often of one language. There are two sets of institutions in all these fields: one French-speaking, the other, English. English dominates in industrial vertical communication downward from the top, and out into the larger world of international transactions. But there is a strong movement to change the situation. It is by no means certain what the future division of linguistic labor will be. Multilingual, industrial civilizations are, however, becoming more and more common around the world and deserve detailed study.

In urban and industrial societies in which two or more languages are widely current, who speaks what language to whom, about what, and in what situations? I refer not merely to verbal speech in personal encounters, but to all sorts of uses of language, and not only between individuals but between institutions and publics as well. By linguistic division of labor I mean that in a society where two languages are used, they are not used for precisely the same purposes, one being used more in certain contexts and for certain purposes than the other. The two make a more or less complete system of communication in that community. Of course, where there are two languages of wide use, there are probably also other languages used by fewer people in perhaps fewer contexts. We are ignoring the languages of lesser use in this discussion.

My illustrations will be taken from the one very large city of two main languages which I know fairly well, Montreal, Canada.[1] It is a city in which Mackey's statement about the world is apt: "More and more people are tending to be bilingual through the necessity of becoming poly-social; that is, belonging to one group for one thing and to another for another.'[2]

Two official languages are widely used in Montreal. One is the language of that empire on which, for a number of decades, the sun never set, of most of the continent of North America, thus of the world's greatest industrial complex, and which is at present the dominant language of world business, science, and diplomacy. It is the language of about one-quarter of the population of Montreal, but of a much larger proportion of its financial and industrial transactions. The other language, that of about three-quarters of the population, is also a world language; it had its day as the dominant language of the world, and can now hold its own as a medium for communicating all sorts of human concerns and thought. M. de Gaulle hoped to restore it to world dominance. It is that language which, more than any other, people pretend they can understand, or could understand if only the French were to speak their own language with a true Parisian accent. While it is the language of a social élite, theatre, theology, local and provincial politics, of universities and learned professions in Montreal, it is better designated as the language of the masses of the people and of small rather than of larger transactions.

W. F. Mackey calls such languages as English and French 'great languages' and 'languages of wide distribution'. ' They are often the same languages in which most of the world's knowledge is available—languages which can easily express and communicate not only what is known but also the new findings of modern science and technology. They are also the native languages of countries with the economic wealth and population to be able to diffuse this learning in the form of books, periodicals, films, broadcasts, and to spread this knowledge throughout extensive areas over which the country has some influence. Because of this, these languages develop into very flexible communications media, carrying a varied culture which becomes more and more universal. '

Contact between the dominant languages and those which are tribal, regional, or limited to one continent or subcontinent occurs nowadays wherever these languages of limited currency are found; likewise contacts of people who use languages of limited repertoire with those of wider functions are to be found wherever such limited languages are in use. Where a more limited language is in contact with a dominant language, the dominant language will likely take over some functions which could perfectly well be carried out in the limited language. In the case of the meeting of world languages, as English and French in Montreal, the dominance of one in certain areas of activity may be such that one can say, as does Jacques Brazeau, that 'in several respects French is an unused language'. [3]   The starting point of sociological study of languages is the fact that human societies are systems of interaction; interaction occurs only where there is communication [4] even though it be only the communication of motion from one billiard ball to another. Spoken and written languages are among the chief media of communication, hence of interaction. In the rhetoric of science, presumably each symbol used has but one clearly defined and strictly limited reference to each of the givers and receivers of a message; one hears that even in that case gestures of aggression creep in. It is probably possible to say 'you idiot' or 'I told you so' in algebraic symbols. But, in any case, such limited communication of knowledge is, if not rare, a rarefied form of communication. Situations are generally not so pure, and the symbols and gestures are richer in meaning. One of the purest of situations is that of trade; and trade has been one of the recurrent occasions of meeting of peoples of different languages, hence of inventiveness in communication.

Among the most fascinating phenomena of the contacts of peoples are the 'pidgin' languages and their offspring, the creoles, which arise when there results from migrations new settled classes of people in such contact with each other and in such isolation from others that they develop a code of their own.

The sociolinguists and anthropologists are working hard on the pidgins and the creoles. Others are working on the loss or maintenance of languages in countries that receive immigrants. Still others are working on the bilingualism which results when peoples are in contact. But we sociologists, pioneers as we have often been in study of the contacts of peoples as well as in study of social interaction[5]—which requires communication—have done little with language except to count the numbers of people who claim to speak some one language or combinations of more than one.

R. E. Park and R. D. McKenzie[6] were pioneers in study of ethnic division of labor. McKenzie noted the functions of various Indian, Chinese, and other ethnic groups in the rubber plantation economy of the Malay Peninsula. Park and his students described the symbiotic relations of the various ethnic and racial groups in the plantation and other large-scale commercial agricultural economies of the U.S.A., Brazil, Hawaii, and other regions. The races worked with and for each other with a minimum of social contact. Their communication was limited to that necessary to getting the simple labor of the plantation done. It was the work of these two men that led me to look at French Canada as an economy and society in which French and English each performed certain functions, and to show in tabular form what these functions were in various industries and professions. My students William Roy and Stuart Jamieson had a hand in our early analysis of these relations. But we did not pay much attention to the use of language in the industries and occupations we studied, although of course we used both French and English in gathering our data on the occupational distribution of the ethnic groups in industry.[7]

As students of Park carried out parts of his program of studying ethnic relations throughout the world, it became more evident that contacts between peoples often brought about an industrial revolution for one of them, sometimes for both. [8] Seen from the other end, seldom has any country become urban and industrial without becoming ethnically diverse. 'Industry is always and everywhere a grand mixer of peoples.' (Hughes and Hughes 1952: 63) But it does not beat them at once into a homogeneous batter. Rather it comes about that in the industries management and labor are not of the same ethnic background; and the various staff services are manned often by still other ethnic groups. This has long been known and has been much studied; ethnic succession in industries was one of the topics of interest to the early Chicago human ecologists.

Ethnic differences ordinarily include difference of language. In newer industrial regions, or in older ones which receive immigrant labor, the language of management is more likely a world language while the new labor more likely uses a language of less dominance, one less widely diffused and less versatile in its uses. One could devote much work to observation and analysis of communication in the early phases of linguistic adjustment between management and labor. This may be conceived in many ways. It may be a sort of Robinson Crusoe-Good Man Friday case where there is no previous history of communication. More often there is some supply of people who are bilingual enough to pass on commands and to teach the greenhorns. In a recent novel about life on a Paris automobile assembly line, the French foreman gets the word to a bilingual Algerian worker who initiates newcomers who speak only Arabic. But not much language is required. Given a wrench and a supply of nuts and bolts, one can point to the hole, insert the bolt, tighten the nut, and hand the wrench to the greenhorn without any talk. He can make signs to show the nut must be drawn tight. In fact, the Algerians even initiate a Hungarian worker who has neither French nor Arabic. They even get it over to him to take it a bit easy when the time-study man is approaching. Our purpose, however, is not to go into the natural history of communications where ethnic groups meet in industry and cities, [9] but to talk of the particular case of cities and industrial systems already in a very advanced stage of development but in which there are two main languages in use both at work and in the city and region. These background conditions will and do vary greatly throughout the world, and even as between cities within a given country. The assembly line is but one of many functioning parts of modern industrial and other organizations. It has its own problems of communication on the small scale among fellow workers, and of communication with the rest of the factory, with unions, families and public.

One way of looking at a community, especially a large one, is as a constellation of institutions, that is, a constellation of going concerns all the way from families to huge corporations, public agencies, and government. Communication goes on inside these institutions. Each of them has its own situations of confrontation of people of various categories (offices, roles). For many of these situations there is an appropriate social rhetoric. It may be instruction, command, persuasion, threat. The people in the various roles learn the equations relating words to action, the amount of salt to be taken or to recognize understatement and to be prepared for the worst. I will come back to internal communication and language.

The institutions also communicate with each other at various levels; research institutes with client industries; business with government; unions with management. Some of these inter-institutional communications are highly technical, some are privileged and supposedly locked in top drawers; some are public relations pronouncements meant to be consumed, if not swallowed whole, to be overheard as well as heard.

The institutions also communicate with the publics to whom they furnish goods or services, from which they seek a mandate to carry on and to control certain features of society, goods, and services.

Each institution, each going concern, may be considered a system of communications, with its confrontations between communicators and audiences, and with its own degrees, kinds and speeds of feedback; with its degrees of intimacy and exclusiveness. Some communications are meant only for a few, and it is assumed that those few instinctively keep the secret. Some communications are made in terms which can be understood by only those few who have a particular kind of technical training.

My small contribution to the study of bilingualism is merely the proposition that bilingualism, as a social phenomenon, must be described in the terms of the organization of communication in the particular society. It is the same proposition I insist upon in study of race and ethnic relations in general: that the significant statements concerning them can be made only in terms that have social significance in their own right.

Until now most of what we have on bilingualism is statistics on the statements of people concerning the language they speak, when they learned them and perhaps how well they know them. Some of the applied linguists have already gone a good deal beyond that; many studies are being made of the kind I suggest, but usually in small settings.

We are all customers or clients of the great institutions. Few are the makers and distributors of goods and services who do not appeal to us to believe in their good will towards us and to accept their notions of what is best for us. In a multilingual society, they have to decide in what language to address us, and in what rhetoric.[10] This requires a judgment about the relative number, spending power, social influence, and political power of the publics of the different languages.

But these same service and commercial institutions tend to take on the quality of utilities, which deliver universally desired or required goods and services in highly standardized forms to everyone. The customer-client must be taught how to shop for the goods and how to use the services. A combination of simple instruction in the commoner languages with signs and symbols makes it possible to dispense goods and services with a minimum of talk and writing. As services are mechanized and made more automatic, language encounters of persons are eliminated. The arrangement of goods in a supermart, the packages and the pictures make it possible for the initiated to shop efficiently without talk. A bilingual taped message tells us what to do next about a phone call. The picture on the slot machine, the male or female shoe on the toilet door, the international traffic signs in European countries make it possible for people initiated into modern life to travel, buy groceries, make telephone calls. A Montreal acquaintance tells of seeing a new immigrant woman from North Africa taking something from a shelf in a supermarket to one of the people who put things on the shelves and trying to haggle with him over the price. Elihu Katz reports that Yemenites newly arrived in Jerusalem try to haggle with the bus driver over the fare. Haggling requires a richer language. This is why I emphasize that this standardized communication without talk depends upon the initiation of the public into this scheme of things. The specializing and standardizing of organization and of positions in organizations—known as bureaucracy—depends upon a complementary standardizing of goods, services, and of the wants and behavior of the public. The apparatus for delivering many kinds of goods and services and 'savvy' about that apparatus is so widely diffused that the people of the post-industrial world can get themselves to and from work, can buy food, drink, cigarettes, can post letters, see the movies, and heaven knows what else (sailors never learn the languages of all those ports) with scarcely any verbal exchange. It is as if the day of the silent trade had returned.

But if in certain transactions language has been automated out, in other transactions it returns with all of its power of nuance, nicety, elaboration, and sophisticated imagination and precision. The choice of language becomes itself a gesture of power, of acquiescence, of intimacy, of self-defense, within the limits of the bilingualism of the parties to the transactions. Further, the number and proportion of bilinguals in a population is itself a function of power and of other social relations.

It is characteristic of large business and industrial organizations in Montreal that the top management and technical personnel are unilingual Anglophones. They exchange messages with their counterparts in similar organizations—often with parent companies—in the United States. They belong to clubs of their peers. If they are technical and scientific staff, they read the technical journals and attend scientific meetings and consort with other such staff people and with research people. Their language is English. (At a meeting of medical educators in New Delhi, I overheard the Swede, the Norwegian, and the Dane talking English to each other. When I inquired why, they said if they were talking medicine at home, they would probably talk English among colleagues, but not to patients.) There is thus horizontal communication which, in the upper strata of large organizations, is apt to be done in an international language; and in the dominant language of the economic system of which the local going concerns are part.

Even at this upper level there is horizontal communication with Francophones in Montreal. In our study of white collar careers in Montreal we found the bilingual private secretary. Her function is liaison communication. Usually of upper middle-class French family, she has taken the bilingual secretarial course offered by a certain convent. She has developed to a fine point the art of answering a phone call in the right language, French or English, and of performing all those confidential and diplomatic functions required of a private secretary. These include translation of messages from either language to the other, but also the translation of social gestures. This art of liaison communication is a standard requirement of most large organizations; bilingualism is an extra skill required in performing it in Montreal. One also finds in certain management offices a bilingual executive assistant, a personnel man and other staff people usually playing second fiddle to the number one man of the department. This bilingual man has some of the liaison functions of the bilingual secretary, but he also deals with people lower in the ranks inside the organization.

As one goes down the ranks, it is likely that horizontal communication will circulate in a smaller orbit, and be confined to the one concern or enterprise, except insofar as the members (workers) belong to a union which transcends that enterprise. With the decline of trade or craft unions, and with the emphasis on seniority, guaranteed wages, and on pensions—i.e. on security—workers are more and more bound by interest to a given organization and may thus have less occasion for communication with people of their own level in other organizations. We may state this as the proposition that, in the measure that itinerancy occurs less frequently, there is less close communication among the people of a given level but in different organizations. As one goes downward in large organizations, one might expect that there would be less interorganizational communication.

On the other hand, the need for internal horizontal communication probably does not decrease as one goes downward through the strata. Insofar as it concerns a small group of people who are very much in the same boat, they can use a language peculiar to themselves, or at least not shared with people at other levels or in other sections of the organization in which they work. In Montreal the men in a shop can talk to each other in that special variety of Canadian French called joual, from the way of pronouncing what is in standard French cheval, a horse. I am told that the boys gathering around the water fountain talk joual to each other, saying things the girls must delicately pretend they do not understand. In many Montreal establishments, however, use of standard Canadian French is sufficient guarantee against eavesdropping by management of the higher ranks.

The question then is at what point in the system there is need of bilingualism for internal communication. There is translation at some level in the line of command of many organizations; that is, a point of bilingualism. Sometimes it is a clear point, with an individual foreman passing the English word downwards in French; in some cases he uses his bilingualism to keep a monopoly on both downward and upward communication. Of course, many supervisors manage such a monopoly of upward and downward communication in organizations where but one language is used. Bilingualism is an extra device for the common practice of keeping control of communications. The minor boss who uses bilingualism for controlling downward and upward communication can, by refusing to speak English with aspiring workers under his supervision, make it difficult for them to become functionally bilingual enough to rise in the organization. This possibility exists wherever bilingualism is required for upward mobility.

In the retail establishment, unless it be a small one in a linguistically homogenous neighborhood, bilingualism occurs at the bottom and at the periphery where customers confront salespeople. While many goods are dispensed with little or no verbal exchange, the large department store must still talk to its customers. In earlier times in Montreal the large department stores catered largely to English customers. That day is long past, and with it, the unilingual salesperson. The customer is always right; one must try to answer him in his own language. But some customers are righter than others. There are few retail establishments in Montreal which can ignore or turn away French customers, although some may have some departments which cater to a clientele that might be largely English or at least bilingual enough to be served in English. A department store which did not advertise at all in the French newspapers when I first knew Montreal, this year even carried a full-page goodwill advertisement in the French papers congratulating the French-Canadian people on the occasion of their national holiday, St. Jean Baptiste. The store is thus not merely seeking French as individual customers, but seeks their collective goodwill.

This is accompanied by an almost complete elimination of unilingual English from retail selling, from the point of contact with the public. Previously the book section of a department store was usually completely or almost completely English, and the sales people usually did not speak French. The more general question here is what kinds of goods are retailed in a modern city to one ethnic group only, to two or more ethnic-linguistic groups separately, and finally, what kinds are distributed to all ethnic groups by the same distributing agencies. The trend in the modern consumer society is toward common distributing agencies, since the various groups want essentially the same goods and are so distributed spatially and by social class that there is less and less place in the system for enterprises that cater to only one group. The enterprises which cater to one language group tend to be small and residual; although some can survive on being exotic. A French restaurant may thrive in Montreal by catering to tourists, both local and foreign, but it must be ready to translate its menu verbally into English for customers who can't quite read French.

Schools of all levels, hospitals and clinics, institutions which dispense professional services, social agencies—public and private— form an increasing part of the constellation of institutions. They communicate constantly with individual members of the public. Although there is a demand for protection against the evil eye among Italian businessmen in Boston, and although many Wall Street operators retain the services of fortune tellers and astrologers, and although the chiropractors of Montreal—nearly all French—have recently declared their willingness to give their services free to indigents, the medical services demanded by various ethnic-linguistic groups tend to be more and more alike. The Province of Quebec has three French universities with medical schools which, of course, teach and treat patients in French. Hospitals still are related to religions. Ethnic and religious groups differ somewhat in their demands for medical services; the religious establishments also differ in their conception of disease and treatment, and even as to what services they are willing to perform. Tying off the tubes was formerly not permitted in Catholic hospitals, although there appears to be a change. (In Boston, I was told by a gynecologist that it is no longer Catholic women, but black women who refuse this operation. They want to make sure of the future of the black race.)

There is a dialectic in medicine between the peculiar symptoms and endemic troubles of various cultures, expressed in some of the most particular phrases and concepts of the appropriate language, and the more universal aspects of human physiology, disease, the medical sciences and modes of treatment. A medical team is in a sense multilingual even if its several members and the patient all speak one standard historic language. The translation from patients' complaints to medical diagnosis and effective management may involve a practical nurse, a registered nurse, a clergyman, a social worker, other patients on the ward, and physicians and surgeons of widely differing viewpoints as to what ails people. Add difference of basic culture and language to the differences of professional and lay culture and language, and one has a difficult situation. Sick people are often afraid of death; they wish to die in proper religious and cultural surroundings, in cultural and linguistic comfort. In bilingual Montreal there have been two systems of hospitals, English-Protestant and French-Catholic, each staffed from top to bottom by people of the appropriate language and religion. Hospitals are also training places for nurses and doctors. There is accordingly a full complement of higher educational institutions and training schools in each language and attached to the religious establishment to some extent.[11]

Some French patients get into the English system of hospitals and clinics, through referral or for other reasons; the reverse occurs, but probably less frequently. Doctors work rather exclusively in one system or another. Nurses, as their occupation becomes more and more professionalized and secular, become more interchangeable. French laboratory technicians and physiotherapists, practicing new trades, are more likely to have had training in the same schools as their English colleagues. There is, however, a strong movement to fill out the French system of higher education to include all the specialty training programs of the North American system. That movement requires bilingual teachers, trained in English-speaking schools but now working with French students. The hoped for result is that a French Canadian may have all of his medical needs provided for in institutions of his own language.

Each ethnic medical system might get along with one language internally, if each accepts patients of only one language. Even so, there remains the problem of horizontal communication across the ethnic and language line. There is, in Quebec, a single official College of Physicians which licenses all members of the profession. The staff of that organization is, need one say, bilingual in a very complete way—in technical language and in diplomatic language. Medical sciences are largely international. The recent rash of heart transplants is certainly multilingual; the surgeons of South Africa and Montreal who have performed these operations are all bilingual members of groups which have been known as ethnic minorities, although they are not numerically in the minority in their immediate cities or regions.

This brings up the question of communication among colleagues of two language groups working in the same city or region. One's closest colleagues are generally those with whom he is in daily contact, and with whom he must talk about particular cases and problems. But there is a larger colleagueship of a profession within a country or language community. English-speaking physicians and nurses in Montreal are members of the English-speaking national fellowships, and even of the inclusive North American fellowship. French-speaking physicians are in some measure members of the same fellowship, but they have a more intense provincial fellowship; and they have the alternative of fellowship in the worldwide French community centering in France. To which of these fellowships do they refer their wish for recognition, mutual confidence, for all that is implied in closer colleagueship? If they were to refer only to the French medical community, they would be practically free of verbal encounters which would require use of English. They could lapse into verbal unilingualism, but would have to be bilingual in the reading of medical literature since so much of scientific and medical work is published in English only. The nurses, now that even the Catholic nursing orders have joined actively in modern nursing education and professional organization, seem to find their closer colleagues not among the nursing sisters of Europe, but among the more aggressively professional nurses of North America.

All of the professions, while they may carry on much of their practice with clients of their own language, and may have some closer colleagueship which can be nourished in that language, may have some point or points of contact with a larger community in which other languages are used. Thus bilingualism of various degrees of power of colloquial understanding and expression, of varying degrees of oral and written communications is to be found in modern professional systems. The pressure for bilingualism is the greater on these whose primary language is less dominant in the systems in question.

One could carry this on to the law, where there are confrontations with clients with opposing counsel in the courts, with colleagues, with juries and with judges of lower and higher courts. As a rule where two historic literary languages are current, there are in some respects two systems of law. One who is tried before a court and judged by a jury of another language than his own is likely not to be content with the verdict.

One might also go on to analysis of language and religion. Liturgical bilingualism is very widespread. The priest performs his mysteries in obsolescent language; the laymen live, sin, and are guilty in a vernacular. This institutionalized diglossia becomes holy; people are really torn over whether they want the Mass said in the vernacular. Yet religion is tied with ethnic and linguistic identity. The clergy of various denominations and of various religions are almost by definition not colleagues; at least, not if they and their flocks take their doctrinal differences as heaven or hell choices. But we have seen a growing colleagueship of the clergy of many denominations and nations. How far they can speak to each other in the same linguistic and theological codes is to be seen. In our city of Montreal, there is a huge colleagueship of French-speaking Catholic clergy; let no one believe that they agree with each other on all things! Yet I suppose a Catholic priest, or a brother or nun, can pass more days than almost anyone without use of the English language.

There are in Montreal complete, separate systems of public communication—newspapers, periodicals, radio, television. The public for each language system is so large that there is no resort to the device of programmes or publications which use both language. The bilingual connection is that of getting the news which comes over the wire in one language turned into the other. English dominance is clear; it is the French who must translate news dispatches. How much bilingual readership there is I do not know; most of it is, I suspect, done by French readers. Another connection is that of advertising, an especially interesting case because the words of advertising are meant as stimuli to arouse feeling and move people. Simple translation won't do, as Frederick Elkin has shown.

In this paper I have meant to demonstrate the obvious: that language encounters, hence bilingualism, are a function of social organization. It is social organization which makes the occasions for communication between people. In many parts of the world drastic changes in social organization are bringing people of different languages into contact. In some cases, through various media, one language encounters people of another without personal confrontation. The case from which I have taken examples is of long standing, but the pattern of confrontation is being drastically changed as society itself changes. These changes have in turn aroused old sentiments of nationalism to new liveliness; new demands are made by the French—that Quebec have but one language, that English people and all immigrants learn French, and that the transactions of higher management be carried out in French.

I have presented no organized empirical findings. My own knowledge consists of my experience of linguistic encounters with French speakers in many situations, in various roles, and with opposites of various roles and statuses in relation to my own. I have had students report their encounters. But I have no systematically organized findings. Since I first began considering this problem, there has been a tremendous surge of studies similar to what I have proposed and would like to see done. My proposal, once made but not carried out, was to train an army of observers to pick up language cues quickly and send them to observe a large sample of places where people meet in various roles to carry out transactions, and to record choice and use of language. They were also to have initiated transactions in various situations and to have noted the reactions. Such a study would have included detailed observation of the characteristic linguistic encounters inside various institutions.

It is certain that I am far behind the times with respect to the linguistic changes and politics of the État de Québec as well as concerning the research being carried on there. It is gratifying to learn that research is being carried on in experimentally created situations and that many natural situations are being studied with what amounts to experimental control of pertinent variables. The intent of my paper is, in part, to develop a frame of reference for study of the linguistic division of labor in complicated settings; in part to alert my fellow sociologists to the importance and the fascination of a field they have neglected.

NOTES

[1] The reader is warned that Montreal is in a period of conflict over the appropriate use of the two main languages and over the place of the ethnic groups in business, industry, government, and education. A great deal of research on use of language is being done by sociologists at the Université de Montréal, especially by Prof. Jacques Brazeau, who has also done similar study in Belgium with respect to the Flemings and the French-speaking Walloons. A commission of the Government of Quebec is also considering the matter. A Royal Commission on Bilingualism and Biculturalism, appointed by the Government of Canada some years ago, has issued a number of volumes dealing with the place of French and English in various regions and institutions. Of the several volumes it has thus far issued, the one most pertinent to our discussion is Report of the Royal Commission on Bilingualism and Biculturalism, Book III, The Work World, Part 1, Socio-economic Status; Part 3, The Private Sector, Ottawa: The Queen's Printer, 1969. I regret that I received these volumes so recently that I have not been able to make use of them in this discussion. I should also mention a pertinent thesis: Lussier, Yvon, La Division du Travail selon l'origine au Québec, 1931-1961, M.A. thesis. Université de Montréal, 1967. This is an exhaustive analysis of the numbers and proportions of people of the various ethnic origins in the occupations and industries of the Province of Québec.

[2] Mackey, W. F., Bilingualism as a World Problem. Montreal, Harvest House, 1967: 19-20.

[3] Brazeau, J. 'Language Difference and Occupational Experience,' Canadian Journal of Economics and Political Science, XXIV. 1958: 536.

[4] Park, R. E., and E. W. Burgess, Introduction to the Science of Sociology. Chicago, 1921. Chapter on 'Social Interaction', p. 341 et passim. 'Society stated in mechanistic terms reduces to interaction ... the limits of society are coterminus with the limits of interaction. Communication (is) the medium of social interaction.'

[5] The readers of this doubtless know that a team has been working on choice of language in market transactions in Ethiopia. It is an ideal experimental setting for sociological study of linguistic division of labor. The material is not yet, I believe, in print.

[6]McKenzie, R. D., 'Migration in the Pacific Area' in American Foreign Relations. C. P. Howland, ed. New Haven, Yale University Press, 1930.

_____, 'Cultural and Racial Differences as Bases of Human Symbiosis' in Social Attitudes. Kimball Young, ed. New York, Henry Holt, 1931.

_____, 'Industrial Expansion and the Inter-relations of Peoples' in Race and Culture Contacts. E. B. Reuter, ed. New York, McGraw-Hill, 1934.

McKenzie's work has recently been reissued in Hawley, A., ed., R. D. McKenzie on Human Ecology. Chicago, University of Chicago Press, 1969.

[7]Hughes, Everett C., French Canada in Transition. Chicago, University of Chicago Press, 1943. Phoenix Edition, 1963.

Jamieson, Stuart M., 'French and English in the Institutional Structure of Montreal.' M. A. thesis, McGill University, 1938.

Roy, William H., 'The French-English Division of Labor in Quebec.' M. A. thesis, McGill University, 1935.

[8]See Hughes and Hughes, Where Peoples Meet. 1952. Chapter 5, 'Industrial Revolutions and Ethnic Frontiers.'

[9]Etcherelli, Claire, Élise ou la vraie vie, Paris, Denoël, 1967.

[10]Frederick Elkin of York University, Toronto, has done work not merely on the language of advertising in Montreal, but also on the symbolic rhetoric of advertising directed to the two ethnic groups. See Elkin, 'Advertising Themes and Quiet Revolutions: Dilemmas in French Canada,' American Journal of Sociology, Vol. 75, July 1969: 112-122.

At the meeting of the Canadian Sociological-Anthropological Association of June 1969, a paper was presented on the image of the woman shown in various kinds of advertisements in Montreal. If clothing is being advertised, the woman is young and slim. In advertisements for bread, she is allowed to be more motherly in appearance. This suggests that the language of advertising goes far beyond the use of words.

[11]There is a Jewish hospital in Montreal. Such a hospital serves several purposes. Hospitals are hotels for sick people; Jewish sick people require special food and kitchens. There is often a problem for Jewish doctors to find hospitals they can practice in. Jewish medical graduates do not always find it easy to get internships and residencies of the calibre they are prepared to accept. The language of the Jewish hospital in Montreal is, in general, English; Yiddish is probably used for the comfort of some of the older patients.

DISCUSSION

Gillian Sankoff, Universite de Montreal: I enjoyed Professor Hughes' talk very much. You have talked about the current situation in Montreal which, if I understand you correctly, parallels tendencies in the rest of the world towards increasing bilingualism. In drawing your diagram, however—

Hughes: No, I didn't say that. I said there is a point of confrontation. It has always been there, it was there a hundred years ago, and that is where there is bilingualism.

Sankoff: Right. But you did say, though, that the east-west boundary may be shifting, so that people are more bilingual east of the boundary. I'm wondering to what extent you think that current popular movements advocating French unilingualism are going to have any effect on the situation.

Hughes: If you are in the Catholic Church hierarchy, you don't need to speak English often, unless you go to St. Patrick's Church. There are hierarchies in which there is no need of bilingualism at all, practically none, and they have Latin in which they can write to the Pope, and I believe there are still a few priests who can speak it, at least write it. But there are certain aspects of life in which there is almost a complete unilingual hierarchy, but at some point some of these people have to have outside communication, and that would likely be in English.

William A. Stewart, Education Study Center: Professor Hughes, you spoke of what you called the liaison level, by means of which the managerial level interacts with other levels below it. You mentioned that this liaison level was characterized by a certain amount of divided loyalty. Now, if you'll think for a moment about current trends toward democratization, involving such phenomena as community control of schools, you will see that, just as the traditional managerial elite developed its liaison level for dealing with those below, so popular pressure groups may develop their own liaison level for dealing with those above. And might not this 'popular' liaison level have its own divided loyalties as well?

Hughes: That's right.

Stewart: Now, I was thinking particularly of the possible effect of divided loyalties on education, using the French case in Canada as a sort of comparison for somewhat similar issues elsewhere. We have the case of the Belgians in the Congo, who came to the conclusion that African children should be started in school in their native language, only to have the idea opposed by liaison groups for the Africans who insisted that education for Congolese children be in French throughout.

Obviously, these liaison groups were beset by feelings of divided loyalty; they were in favor of African children, but they were also in favor of the French language. A similar situation seems to be developing in the United States with respect to the pedagogical recognition of Negro dialect. We are witnessing the rise of a cadre of black community spokesmen who like what they call 'black history', and want it taught in the schools, but who don't like the language which was spoken by many of the heroes of that history. They claim to like black children, but they obviously dislike the language spoken by many of those children. They call it 'bad language', and they want it weeded out of the classroom, and stamped out of the child. Now, my question is: Is this divided loyalty a universal phenomenon, or is it a peculiarity of the two situations I have cited? That is, is there a situation developing in which spokesmen for the French Canadians really themselves prefer English, or is there a complete loyalty to the French language all the way?

Hughes: Yes, there is. You never never increased your social prestige in the eyes of your parents or anybody else by becoming anglicized. It is a different situation. It might be in the place where one of the two languages is a local language, is a language of limited use. The only sense in which French is a limited language is that it is not as frequent in the upper levels of industry as is English, but there's a certain amount of prestige in French. French is the language, I think, that more people in the world pretend to speak without being able to speak it than any other.

THEY CAME HERE FIRST

ROBERT ROESSEL

Navajo Community College

The Indian people are the first Americans and are the most rapidly increasing ethnic group in the United States. Over the years, there has been a continuing effort to eliminate Indian culture and language in the process of obtaining the kind of education designed to make the Indian acceptable in the dominant society and 'melt in the melting pot'. Conspicuous by its absence has been any effort to give the Indian one of the most important rights, long enjoyed by many other Americans, and that is the right to be wrong. Indian education was controlled and directed by non-Indians with minimal involvement of the Indian people. Under this system, Indian culture and language was frowned upon and every effort was made in and through the school to destroy both.

Recently there have been two major successful attempts by Indian people to control their education and to demonstrate clearly their ability to provide such direction. The Rough Rock Demonstration School is an elementary school located in the heart of the Navajo Reservation and controlled by a group of seven Navajos who have a total number of four school years between all seven members. This group has made it possible for the education of children attending this school to reflect what Navajo parents want. This includes a bilingual program at the lower primary grade which has, as the language of instruction, Navajo. This includes Navajo history and culture being an important part of the total school curriculum. Under the direction of the Navajo culture center at Rough Rock, a series of books written and illustrated by Navajos has been developed. These books have been used in the classroom with excellent result.

The second major example of successful Indian control can be found at Navajo Community College. This college temporarily located at

Many Farms, Arizona, is the first college located on an Indian reservation and controlled by Indian people. Once again a similar pattern emerges in that, when Indian people are given the chance to control their education, they include in it those elements that are important to them, namely the language and culture. This college has a Navajo Studies Department which offers a broad array of courses dealing with Navajo language, history, and culture. The Board of Regents, the ten-member all-Navajo body, has made certain courses in Navajo language and culture required for all Navajo students. Navajo Community College Press has been established to publish books written primarily by Indians and about Indians. The first publication of the press will be a book written and illustrated by Navajo elders dealing with the 'Origin of the Navajo'.

These two experiences in Indian education show: first, that Indian people have the ability and the desire to direct and control the education of their children and of their communities and second, that when given the opportunity to develop the curriculum, Indian people include as priority subjects courses dealing with their language and culture.

DISCUSSION

(Unfortunately, the questioners cannot be identified in the following discussion, since it took place at a luncheon and their questions were not directed into the microphone.)

Roessel: The question was: Do we use the children and do we use the contacts with their parents and grandparents in collecting and accumulating materials to be used? The answer is: That is exactly the way we collect our materials, by bringing the parents to the school, or going to the homes of the parents, and through the children developing the materials. Those of you who are Navajo authorities—and we have one in the room—will know that we've got literally hundreds of books about Navajos. She has written some of the best, but we have no books, really—unless you consider a biography or an autobiography —that have been generated by the Navajos themselves. But now we are developing a story; one of the books that we will be coming out with soon is a Navajo story of themselves, not the anthropologist's story of the Navajos, and there is a difference.

Question: Do you speak Navajo?

Roessel: I can get by. My wife is Navajo, and her folks don't speak English. We speak Navajo one day a week, and I'm rather quiet that day, but I can get by. I should say 'baby talk Navajo'; I can understand it better than I can speak it, but I don't need an interpreter when I'm with Navajos.

Question: What about publishing companies? Have they published books about Indians?

Roessel: Well, they don't respond. In other words, if you are talking about the publishing companies that would publish books in this area, we no longer attempt to go that route. We are publishing our own books. However, this is changing somewhat now. At the Rough Rock Demonstration School they have established what they call the Navajo Curriculum Center, and have put out books like Coyote Tales, Grandfather Stories, and Black Mountain Boy, a whole series of books written and illustrated by Navajos. They happen to be in English, but now they are printing some in Navajo. These, as I say, are published by the school. Now, different publishers are wanting to take those publications because there is a great deal of demand for them outside of Indian education as well as in Indian education.

Question: Can you justify publishing books about Indians when there are so many different tribes?

Roessel: Just as there are certain major countries in the world to-day where large numbers speak certain languages and they can justify publications in those languages, I think the same thing is true, of course in a more limited way, with the Indians. We have certain tribes of Indians that are large enough to justify it, and other tribes that are not large enough. We have other tribes that don't even have a written language yet. Perhaps only anthropologists or linguists would be able to transcribe the language. But I don't think this would preclude some publications that might be of a general nature, even in English, that could be used for the tribes where the use of the native language is marginal or even nonexistent.

Question: How are the Navajo involved in Navajo Community College?

Roessel: The Navajos have a written language, and the important thing I failed to mention and I'm glad you brought it up, is that both of these schools are controlled by Indians. The president of the college is a Navajo—I work for him—and the director of the Rough Rock Demonstration School is a Navajo. I think this is extremely important, because the Navajo tribe is putting their mouth where their money is. They have provided, not only control through the administrative and policy-making levels, but they have been able to find Navajos to hold down the key jobs, and that is important.

Question: How many different Indian languages are there?

Roessel: There are about 200 different Indian languages. There are at least three different ways to write Navajo that are used rather widely. You could safely say that there is one system, that adopted by the Bureau of Indian Affairs and Robert Young and Willie Morgan, that I think has rather risen to the top in terms of preference.

Question: Do the Navajo have an oral tradition?

Roessel: Yes, they have, and this is the book that I was referring to in terms of the Navajo story of themselves. When I was teaching at Arizona State University, I used to take an extract from some of the Navajo myths—I don't like to use the word 'myths', but the 'Navajo oral traditions'—and ask them to identify it as either being Indian or from the Bible. In many cases they could not make the distinction, it is that beautiful. They have some very beautiful stories.

Question: What is the role in Indian education of the Bureau of Indian Affairs?

Roessel: The Bureau of Indian Affairs is the federal agency that has the responsibility for Indians, and they are responsible for educating about 25 or 30 percent of the Indians in this country today. But still more Indians are in public schools than are in BIA schools. I worked for the Bureau for a number of years and was considered to be a real critic of it, but I think the Bureau of Indian Affairs today is attempting to help implement the kinds of programs we are talking about, where they can be controlled by the Indian people, and where the kinds of Navajo language programs can be cultivated and encouraged, and English as a Second Language being taught in schools where that is also appropriate. So I think that they are not ogres as some people like to make them out to be.

Question: Can the Indians be important politically like the blacks?

Roessel: What kind of Indians are you talking about? In answer to your question, I think that in certain states Indians are or will soon become a rather important force, even politically, but I also think it is naive to think that the Indian can command the kind of attention that certain of our other larger ethnic groups can. The Indians suffer from a very difficult kind of discrimination to fight, and that is indifference. Everybody loves the Indians, but nobody is willing to do anything about it, and Congress doesn't have the reason to really concern itself with the needs of 600,000 people.

Question: Have OEO type programs had an impact on Indian reservations?

Roessel: I think it has had a very profound effect. I think it has made people, and not only those living on and near the Navajo reservation, but the non-Navajos, aware of the contributions and some of the types of positive program that the Indians are developing. These are important for them to understand, because usually proximity breeds problems. I think this has been very evident that these materials and efforts of the Indians to help themselves have gone a long way in terms of improving the attitudes of non-Indians. As you get further away, if you get into the different schools on the reservation, the BIA schools and the public schools are beginning now to copy and use materials that have been prepared in these ventures. We think we are just at the beginning of a really new day in Indian education.

Question: Can bilingual education be meaningful and practical in Indian education?

Roessel: I think the idea is that perhaps at the lower grades they will attempt to do this. Right now only one percent of the teachers at the elementary school level are Indian, so you've got a long way to go before you can find the people that are bilingual in those Indian systems where this would be desirable.

Evelyn Bauer, Bureau of Indian Affairs: I am enormously impressed with the work that has been done at Rough Rock and that is being done at Navajo Community College, but I do feel that now and then the Bureau deserves a bit of defending.

First of all—perhaps a small point, but not really so small—your statement, Dr. Roessel, about children being punished for use of their native tongue. Historically this may have been true. I can say without question this is no longer true, since I have visited dozens and dozens of schools. Oh, I'm sure you could tell me lots of schools where it happens, but as a policy and, I think, probably as a general approach this is no longer true; it has not been my experience. Drs. Alatis, Bosco, Campbell, and Harris have recently been touring around these schools, and they could possibly say more about this, but it is not policy. It has been in the past, but it is no longer true.

Somebody asked what the Bureau is doing and how they are keeping up the start made in bilingual education. I would just like to mention a few of these projects if I may. There is at the present time a bilingual pilot kindergarten project on the Navajo involving six classes. There is an application in now to continue it (this is a program where the language of instruction is Navajo, with English as a Second Language being taught for a portion of each day), if funding is available, through the first and second grades.

There is an application in from Alaska to implement the same kind of program, a pilot project along the Kuskokwim River. These will be six beginning classes (we have in the Bureau of Indian Affairs the beginner level, then first and second grade; not all of our areas have kindergarten), where the language of instruction would be Northern Eskimo.

Also there is the development of materials that is going on—one example is the Hopi-English readers. There is, by the way, a backlog of materials in Navajo as I think probably Dr. Roessel knows. In the late 30s and early 40s there was quite a movement within the Bureau to develop literacy in Navajo among both adults and students, and a number of materials were put out, most of which are still in print, some pre-primers, primers, and some adult materials are available in Navajo.

One other project I would like to mention is one very much like the one that Dr. Nancy Modiano did in Mexico. Dr. Bernard Spolsky at the University of New Mexico is undertaking a three-year research project to determine whether speakers of Navajo become more proficient in reading in English if they are taught to read in Navajo or English first.

I could name many other things. I think, although some of Bureau policy and Indian education has been bad, there are many bright spots.

Question: (could not be determined)

Roessel: I'm not sure that I understand exactly what you are asking, but I would say this. The Navajos are determining the goals toward which these institutions are striving, and in that determination they are not saying in any wise that they do not want the ability and facility with English. They want this. I think they are saying they want this and something more. The Navajo Nation, as they call themselves, perhaps are unique among Indians because of their size. The reservation itself is 25,000 square miles. It is not impossible that some day they may be the 51st state. So they have the context in terms of numbers of people and number of acres, if you will, to do certain things that other tribes may not have the opportunity to do. So they can be a viable system within the broader Arizona, New Mexico, and Utah system, and I think that they will search out for themselves how much of each they want and which roads they are going to walk down. I don't think that in any wise our regents, at least at this point, have said 'This is what we are going to do and that's it.' It is a flexible growing thing as they learn more, as they see more, and as they make more choices, and this is what we are trying to provide them with: the opportunity to make choices. We are trying to point out what the alternatives of some of these choices are and the consequences; but they are able, if that is the question, to identify the kinds of values and the kinds of objectives that they want and these are not always, in fact in many cases are not, incompatible.

Ilo Remer, U. S. Office of Education: The Navajo tribe is a large one and has strong leadership, whereas other tribal groups are smaller and less united. In view of these facts, do you believe that the Navajo experience is transferable to other tribes?

Roessel: I think in some cases it certainly is. Right now there has been a new president elected of the Pine Ridge Sioux in South Dakota. They're now talking of starting a college between Rosebud and Pine Ridge. It may take a combination of some of them. There are other Indian groups outside of the Navajo who are attempting to work with the Bureau in contracting their own education, developing their own curriculum materials, etc., so I think that in many cases it is very transferable. I think even in places in California where you find very small tribal groups in a very large population of Indians, there has been a very real effort to try to get materials prepared that deal with the Indians of California and the curriculum. I do think the basic principles in many cases are transferable.

VERBAL STRATEGIES IN MULTILINGUAL COMMUNICATION

JOHN J. GUMPERZ

University of California, Berkeley

Abstract. Most scholars have dealt with bilingual communication in
terms of the 'code-switching paradigm, ' attempting to specify when,
and under what conditions, speakers use the varieties in question. The
assumption is that one set of forms is specific to certain settings while
others are used elsewhere. There are many instances where this is
indeed the case. In other cases, however, the correlation between
language usage and setting breaks down. This paper is an attempt to
give a detailed analysis of several such cases. Bilingual and bidialectal conversations were recorded in Chicano and Afro-American communities and were analyzed as conversational wholes, using anthropological linguistic techniques. Conclusions show that selection among
alternate codes is meaningful in much the same way that choice among
alternate vocabulary items in meaningful is monolingual societies.

Recent systematic research in the inner city has successfully dis-
proved the notions of those who characterize the language of low income
populations as degenerate and structurally underdeveloped. There is
overwhelming evidence to show that both middle class and non-middle
class children, no matter what their native language, dialect, or ethnic
background, when they come to school at the age of five or six, have
control of a fully formed grammatical system. The mere fact that their
system is distinct from that of their teacher does not mean that their
speech is not rule governed. Speech features which strike the teacher
as different do not indicate failure to adjust to some universally accepted
English norm; rather, they are the output of dialect or language-specific

syntactic rules which are every bit as complex as those of standard English (Labov 1969).

It is clear furthermore that the above linguistic differences also reflect far-reaching and systematic cultural differences. Like the plural societies of Asia and Africa, American urban society is characterized by the coexistence of a variety of distinct cultures. Each major ethnic group has its own heritage, its own body of traditions, values, and views about what is right and proper. These traditions are passed on from generation to generation as part of the informal family or peer group socialization process and are encoded in folk art and literature, oral or written.

To understand this complex system, it is first of all necessary to identify and describe its constituent elements. Grammatical analysis must be, and has to some extent been, supplemented by ethnographic description, ethnohistory, and the study of folk art (Stewart 1968; Hanners 1969; Abrahams 1964; Kochman 1969). But mere description of component subsystems is not enough if we are to learn how the plurality of cultures operates in everyday interaction and how it affects the quality of individual lives. Minority groups in urbanized societies are never completely isolated from the dominant majority. To study their life ways without reference to surrounding populations is to distort the realities of their everyday lives. All residents of modern industrial cities are subject to the same laws and are exposed to the same system of public education and mass communication. Minority group members, in fact, spend much of their day in settings where dominant norms prevail. Although there are significant individual differences in the degree of assimilation, almost all minority group members, even those whose behavior on the surface may seem quite deviant, have at least a passive knowledge of the dominant culture. What sets them off from others is not simply the fact that they are distinct, but the juxtaposition of their own private language and life styles with that of the public at large.

This juxtaposition, which is symbolized by constant alternation between in-group and out-group modes of acting and expression has a pervasive effect on everyday behavior. Successful political leaders such as the late Martin Luther King and Bobby Seale rely on it for much of their rhetorical effect. Kernan in her recent ethnographic study of verbal communication in an Afro-American community reports that her informants' everyday conversation reveals an overriding concern—be it positive or negative—with majority culture.

Majority group members who have not experienced a similar disjuncture between private and public behavior frequently fail to appreciate its effect. They tend merely to perceive minority group members as different, without realizing the effect that this difference may have on everyday communication. This ignorance of minority styles of behavior seems to have contributed to the often discussed notion of 'linguistic deprivation'. No one familiar with the writings of Afro-American novelists of the last decade and with the recent writings on black folklore can maintain that low-income blacks are nonverbal. An exceptionally rich and varied terminological system, including such folk concepts as 'sounding', 'signifying', 'rapping', 'running it down', 'chucking', 'jiving', 'marking', etc., all referring to verbal strategies, (i.e. different modes of achieving particular communicative ends) testifies to the importance which Afro-American culture assigns to verbal art (Kochman 1969; Kernan 1969). Yet, inner city black children are often described as nonverbal, simply because they fail to respond to the school situation. It is true that lower-class children frequently show difficulty in performing adequately in formal interviews and psychological tests. But these tests are frequently administered under conditions which seem unfamiliar and, at times, threatening to minority group children. When elicitation conditions are changed, there is often a radical improvement in response (Labov 1969; Mehan 1970).

The fact that bilingualism and biculturalism have come to be accepted as major goals in inner city schools is an important advance. But if we are to achieve this goal, we require at least some understanding of the nature of code alternation and its meaning in everyday interaction. Bilingualism is, after all, primarily a linguistic term, referring to the fact that linguists have discovered significant alternations in phonology, morphology, and syntax, in studying the verbal behavior of a particular population. While bilingual phenomena have certain linguistic features in common, these features may have quite different social significance.

Furthermore, to the extent that social conditions affect verbal behavior, findings based on research in one type of bilingual situation may not necessarily be applicable to another socially different one. Much of what we know about second language learning or on bilingual interference derives from work with monolingual college students learning a foreign language in a classroom. Other research on bilingualism has dealt with isolated middle-class bilinguals residing in monolingual neighborhoods or with immigrant farmers or their descendants. We know least about the kind of situation where—as in the case of big city Afro-Americans or Chicanos—bilingualism has persisted over several generations and where strict barriers of caste limit or channel the nature of communication between the groups in question. Most importantly, we only have a minimal amount of information about the ways in which bilingual usage symbolizes the values of speakers and the social conditions in which they live.

The accepted paradigm for the linguistic study of bilingualism is the code-switching paradigm. Having observed that linguistic alternates exist at the level of phonology and syntax, we proceed to ask which alternates are used when and under what social circumstances. The assumption is that the stream of behavior can be divided into distinct social occasions, interaction sequences, or speech events. These events are assumed to be associated with culturally specific behavioral norms which, in turn, determine the speech forms to be used. To some extent this is indeed the case.

In every society there are certain performative occasions, such as ceremonial events, court proceedings, greetings or formal introductions and the like, where the form of the language used is strictly prescribed and where deviations also change the definition of the event (Blom and Gumperz 1970). When asked to report about their language usage, speakers tend to respond in such all-or-none terms. Hence, language censuses of urban neighborhoods in the U.S. usually indicate that the minority languages are used for informal, in-group, family interaction, while the majority language serves for communication with outsiders.

Tape recordings of conversation in natural settings, however, frequently reveal quite a different picture. A recent study of bilingual behavior in Texas, for example, reports many instances of what seems almost random language mixture (Lance 1969: 75-76).

(1) Te digo que este dedo (I TELL YOU THAT THIS FINGER) has been bothering me so much.
Se me hace que (IT SEEMS THAT) I have to respect her porque 'ta (BECAUSE SHE IS)
But this arthritis deal, boy you get to hurting so bad you can't hardly even ... 'cer masa pa tortillas (MAKE DOUGH FOR TORTILLAS)

In Texas, such language mixture tends to be disparaged and referred to by pejorative terms such as Tex Mex. It is rarely reported in the literature and frequently dismissed as abnormal. Nevertheless, such apparent language mixture is a common feature of informal conversation in urban bilingual societies.

When asked why they use English in situations where, according to their own reports, the minority language is normal, speakers tend to respond by stating that the English items in question are loan words, words for which there are no equivalents in the home language. But this is not always the case. On a number of occasions, Puerto Rican mothers in Jersey City could be heard calling to their children as follows:

(2) Ven aquí, ven aquí.

If the child would not come immediately, this would be followed with

Come here, you.

Clearly, it would be difficult to justify such alternation on the grounds of ease of expression. There is more to this message than can be conveyed by usage surveys. The English is used for stylistic effect to convey meaning. An English-speaking mother under similar conditions might respond to her child's failure to obey with something like:

(3) John Henry Smith, you come here right away.

Both the English and the Puerto Rican mothers indicate annoyance, but they use different verbal strategies for doing so.

Let me illustrate this point with some additional examples from conversations recorded in Chicano and Afro-American groups in California, and analyzed in more detail in Gumperz and Hernandez (1969). Recordings in question were made by participants in group discussion, who also assisted in the analysis. The tapes were transcribed by a linguist, using detailed phonetic transcription wherever necessary, in order to isolate instances of code-switching. The contextual meaning of code-switches was then determined by a procedure which derives from the apparatus for conversational analysis developed by ethnomethodologists (Sacks 1970; Schegloff 1970). When in doubt, our hypothesis as to what was meant was checked with other participants in the conversation.

In the first two examples, the speakers are a faculty member at the University of California (E), and (M), a social worker in a day care center where E is working as a volunteer. Both speakers are native Americans of Mexican ancestry. The conversation ranges over a number of topics from the speakers' personal experience.

(4) E. What do you dream in?
M. I don't think I ever have any conversations in my dreams. I just dream. Ha. I don' hear people talking; I jus' see pictures.
E. Oh, they're old-fashioned, then. They're not talkies yet, huh?
M. They're old-fashioned. No. they're not talkies yet. No, I'm tryin' to think. Yeah, there too have been talkies. Different. In Spanish and English both. An' I wouldn't be too surprised if I even had some in Chinese. (Laughter) Yeah, Ed. Deveras (REALLY).

(M. offers E a cigarette which is refused.) Tu no
fumas, verdad? Yo tampoco. Deje de fumar. (YOU
DON'T SMOKE, DO YOU? I DON'T EITHER; I
STOPPED SMOKING) and I'm back to it again.

M breaks into Spanish, just as she is about to offer E a cigarette. The
shift is accompanied by lowering of the voice of the type that accompa-
nies confidentiality in monolinguals. She continues to talk about her
smoking problem, explaining that she had given up the habit for awhile,
but that she had begun again during a period when she was visiting a
friend in a local institution. On each visit she would buy a pack of
cigarettes; the friend would smoke some and she would take the rest
home and smoke them herself. Now notice the passage:

(5) E. That's all you smoked?
    M. That's all I smoked.
    E. An' how about ... how about now?
    M. Estos ... melos halle ... estos Pall Malls me los ... me
        los hallaron. (THESE ... I FOUND ... THESE PALL
        MALLS I ... THEY WERE FOUND FOR ME.) No, I
        mean ... that's all the cigarettes ... that's all.
        They're the ones I buy.

Later on M goes on to analyze her struggle with the smoking habit as
follows:

(6) M. MM-huh. Yeah. An' ... an' ... an' they tell me,
        'How did you quit, Mary?' I di'n' quit. I ... I just
        stopped. I mean it wasn't an effort that I made. Que
        voy a dejar de fumar porque me hace daño (THAT
        I'M GOING TO STOP SMOKING BECAUSE IT'S HARM-
        FUL TO ME, OR) this or tha', uh-uh. It just ... that
        ... eh ... I used to pull butts out of the ... the ...
        the wastepaper basket. Yeah. (Laughter) I used to
        go look in the (unclear) ... Se me acababan los cig-
        arros en la noche. (MY CIGARETTES WOULD RUN
        OUT ON ME AT NIGHT.) I'd get desperate, y ahi voy
        al basurero a buscar, a sacar, you know? (Laughter)
        (AND THERE I GO TO THE WASTEBASKET TO LOOK
        FOR SOME, TO GET SOME, YOU KNOW?) Ayer los
        (unclear) ... no había que no traia cigarros Camille,
        no traia Helen, no traia yo, el Sr. de Leon, (YES-
        TERDAY THE ... THERE WEREN'T ANY. CAMILLE
        DIDN'T HAVE ANY, I, MR. DE LEON DIDN'T HAVE
        ANY) and I saw Dixie's bag crumpled up, so I figures

> she didn't have any, y ahi ando en los ceniceros
> buscando a ver onde estaba la . . . (AND THERE I
> AM IN THE ASHTRAYS LOOKING TO SEE WHERE
> THERE WAS THE . . .) I din' care whose they were.

Here again, what someone studying the passage sentence by sentence might regard as almost random alternation between the two languages, is highly meaningful in terms of the conversational context. M is quite ambivalent about her smoking and she conveys this through her language use. Her choice of speech forms symbolizes her alternation between embarrassment and clinical detachment about her own condition. Spanish sentences reflect personal involvement (at least in this particular conversation), while English marks more general or detached statements.

Our next example derives from a discussion session recorded in Richmond, California, by a black community worker. Participants include his wife and several teenage boys. Here we find alternation between speech features which are quite close to standard English and such typically Black English features as lack of post-vocalic r, double negation, and copula deletion.

(7) You can tell me how your mother worked twenty hours a day and I can sit here and cry. I mean I can cry and I can feel for you. But as long as I don't get up and make certain that I and my children don't go through the same, I ain't did nothin' for you, brother. That's what I'm talking about.

(8) Now Michael is making a point, where that everything that happens in that house affects all the kids. It does. And Michael and you makin' a point, too. Kids suppose to learn how to avoid these things. But let me tell you. We're all in here. We talkin' but you see . . .

Note the underlined phrase in passage seven, with the typically black English phrase ain't did nothin' embedded in what is otherwise a normal standard English sequence. On our tape the shift is not preceded by a pause or marked off by special stress or intonation contours. The speaker is therefore not quoting from another code; his choice of form here lends emphasis to what he is saying. Passage eight begins with a general statement addressed to the group as a whole. The speaker then turns to one person, Michael, and signals this change in focus by dropping the copula is and shifting to black phonology.

It seems clear that in all these cases, what the linguist sees merely as alternation between two systems, serves definite and clearly understandable communicative ends. The speakers do not radically switch from one style to another, but they build on the coexistence of alternate forms to create meanings. To be sure, not all instances of code alternation are meaningful. Our tapes contain several instances where the shift into black English or the use of a Spanish word in an English sentence can only be interpreted as a slip of the tongue, frequently corrected in the next sentence, or where it must be regarded merely as a sign of the speaker's lack of familiarity with the style he is employing. But, even though such errors do occur, it is nevertheless true that code switching is also a communicative skill, which speakers use as a verbal strategy in much the same way that skillful writers switch styles in a short story.

How and by what devices does the speaker's selection of alternate forms communicate meaning? The process is a metaphoric process somewhat similar to what linguists interested in literary style have called foregrounding (Garvin 1964). Foregrounding in the most general sense of the term relies on the fact that words are more than just names for things. Words also carry a host of culturally specific associations, attitudes, and values. These cultural values derive from the context in which words are usually used and from the activities with which they are associated. When a word is used in other than its normal context, these associations become highlighted or foregrounded. Thus to take an example made famous by Leonard Bloomfield (1936), the word fox when it refers to a man, as in he is a fox, communicates the notions of slyness and craftiness which our culture associates with the activities of foxes.

We assume that what holds true for individual lexical items also holds true for phonological or syntactic alternates. Whenever a speech variety is associated with a particular social category of speakers or with certain activities, this variety comes to symbolize the cultural values associated with these features of the nonlinguistic environment. In other words, speech varieties, like words, are potentially meaningful and, in both cases, this is brought out by reinterpreting meanings in relation to context. As long as the variety in question is used in its normal environment, only its basic referential sense is communicated. But when it is used in a new context, it becomes socially marked, by virtue of the fact that the values associated with the original context are mapped onto the new message.

In any particular instance of code-switching, speakers deduce what is meant by an information processing procedure which takes account of the speaker, the addressee, the social categories to which they can be assigned in the context, the topic, etc. (Blom and Gumperz 1970). Depending on the nature of the above factors, a wide variety of contextual meanings can be communicated. In the examples cited in this paper, all contextual meanings derive from the basic meaning inclusion (we) versus exclusion (they). This underlying meaning is then reinterpreted in the light of the co-occurring contextual factors to indicate such things as degree of involvement (items 4 and 5), anger (items 2 and 3), emphasis (item 7), change in focus (8). In the following additional example, taken from a graduate student's recording of a Korean-English family conversation, Korean seems to be used simply as a device to direct one's question to one out of several potential addressees.

(9) A. No, the lady used to know us. Ka mirri saram ya, ku wife-uga, mariji, odi University ... yoginga, odinga ... (YOU KNOW THAT MAN, HIS WIFE, I MEAN, WHICH UNIVERSITY ... HERE, OR WHERE ...)

    U. Tokaebbi katchi saenging saram? (YEAH, THE ONE THAT LOOKS LIKE A GHOST?)

    A. Unn. Dr. Kaeng katchiin saram. (YEAH, THE ONE THAT IS LIKE DR. KAENG.)

    L. Do teachers that teach in Japan have to have teaching credentials?

    C. Well, it depends. If you're going to teach in a military installation.

Speakers A and U here are of the older generation of immigrants who are somewhat more imbued with Korean culture. L and C are college students who are probably most at home in English. Thus, A's shift to Korean is interpreted by U as an invitation to respond similarly. L's use of English, along with her topic, mark her message as addressed to C.

On other occasions, switching may simply serve as a sign to indicate that the speaker is quoting someone else:

(10) Because I was speakin' to my baby ... my ex-baby sitter, and we were talkin' about the kids you know, an' I was tellin' her ... uh, 'Pero, como, you know, ... uh ... la Estela y la Sandi ... relistas en el telefon. (BUT, HOW, YOU KNOW ... UH ... ESTELA AND SANDI ARE VERY PRECOCIOUS ON THE TELEPHONE.)

We have chosen examples of code-switching from a number of languages to highlight the fact that the meanings conveyed by code-switching are independent of the phonological shape or historical origin of the alternates in question. The association between forms and meaning is quite arbitrary. Any two alternates having the same referential meaning can become carriers of social meaning.

The ability to interpret a message is a direct function of the listener's home background, his peer group experiences, and his education. Differences in background can lead to misinterpretation of messages. The sentence he is a Sikh has little or no meaning for an American audience. To anyone familiar with speech behavior in Northern India, however, it conveys a whole host of meanings, since Sikhs are stereotypically known as bumblers. Similarly the above-cited statement he is a fox, which conveys slyness to middle class whites, is interpreted as a synonym for he is handsome in black culture. The process of communication thus requires both shared grammar and shared rules of language usage. Two speakers may speak closely related and, on the surface, mutually intelligible varieties of the same language, but they may nevertheless misunderstand each other because of differences in usage rules resulting from differences in background. We must know the speakers' normal usage pattern, i.e. which styles are associated as unmarked forms with which activities and relationships, as well as what alternates are possible in what context, and what cultural associations these carry.

Note that the notion of culture that emerges from this type of analysis is quite different from the conventional one. Linguists attempting to incorporate cultural information into their descriptions tend to regard culture as a set of beliefs and attitudes which can be measured apart from communication. Even the recent work which utilizes actual speech samples by eliciting 'subjective reactions' to these forms or evaluations, going considerably beyond earlier work, does not completely depart from this tradition, since it continues to rely on overt or conscious judgment. Our own material suggests that culture plays a role in communication which is somewhat similar to the role of syntactic knowledge in the decoding of referential meanings. Cultural differences, in other words, affect judgment both above and below the level of consciousness. A person who may have every intention of avoiding cultural bias may, by subconsciously superimposing his own interpretation on the verbal performances of others, nevertheless bias his judgment of their general ability, efficiency, etc.

We know very little about the distribution of usage rules in particular populations. For example, there seems to be no simple correlation with ethnic identity, nor is it always possible to predict usage rules on the basis of socioeconomic indexes. To go back for a moment to the Puerto Rican neighborhood referred to above: While the majority of the Puerto Ricans in our Jersey City block followed usage patterns like those described above, there are others residing among them whose patterns differ significantly. A Puerto Rican college student took a tape recorder home and recorded informal family conversation over a period of several days. It is evident from his recording, and he himself confirms this in interviews, that in his family English serves as the normal medium of informal conversation, while Spanish is socially marked and serves to convey special connotations of intimacy and anger.

It follows that while the usual sociological measures of ethnic background, social class, educational achievements, etc., have some correlation with usage rules, they cannot be regarded as accurate predictors of performance in particular instances. On the contrary, social findings based on incomplete data or on populations different from those for which they were intended, may themselves contribute to cultural bias. The use of responses to formal tests and interviews to judge the verbal ability of lower class bilinguals is a case in point. Rosenthal has eloquently shown that teachers' expectations have a significant effect on learning (1969). When these expectations are effected by misapplied or inaccurate social science findings, education suffers. An incident from a tape-recorded session in Black Language Arts will illustrate the point.

(11)   Student: (Reading from an autobiographical essay) This
                  lady didn't have no sense.
       Teacher: What would be a standard English alternate for
                  this sentence ?
       Student: She didn't have any sense. But not this lady:
                  she <u>didn't have no sense</u>.

It happens that in the above case both student and teacher were black, and the classroom atmosphere was relaxed. Thus, the student felt free to give the response she gave. Had the situation been more constrained, she would not have been able to convey what she really wanted to say.

Our final example derives from classroom observation of first grade reading sessions in a racially integrated California school district. Classes in the district include about 60% white and 40% black, chicano, and oriental children. College student observers find that most reading classes have a tracking system such that children are assigned to fast or slow reading groups and these groups are taught by different methods and otherwise receive different treatment.

Even in first grade reading periods, where presumably all children are beginners, the slow reading groups tend to consist of 90% blacks and chicanos. Does this situation reflect real learning difficulties, or is it simply a function of our inability to diagnose reading aptitude in culturally different children? Furthermore, given the need for some kind of ability grouping, how effective and how well adapted to cultural needs are the classroom devices that are actually used to bridge the reading gap ?

Recently we observed a reading session with a slow reading group
of three children, and seven fast readers. The teacher worked with
one group at a time, keeping the others busy with individual assignments. With the slow readers she concentrated on the alphabet, on
spelling of individual words, and supposedly basic grammatical concepts such as the distinctions between questions and statements. She
addressed the children in what white listeners would identify as pedagogical style. Her enunciation was deliberate and slow. Each word
was clearly articulated with even stress and pitch, as if to avoid any
verbal sign of emotion, approval, or disapproval. Children were expected to speak only when called upon, and the teacher would insist
that each question be answered before responding to further ideas.
Unsolicited remarks were ignored even if they referred to the problem
at hand. Pronunciation errors were corrected whenever they occurred,
even if the reading task had to be interrupted. The children seemed
distracted and inattentive. They were guessing at answers, 'psyching
out' the teacher in the manner described by Holt (1965) rather than following her reasoning process. The following sequence symbolizes the
artificiality of the situation.

(12) Teacher: Do you know what a question is? James, ask
William a question.
James: William, do you have a coat on?
William: No, I do not have a coat on.

James asks his question and William answers in a style which approaches in artificiality that of the teacher, characterized by citation
form pronunciation of ([ey] rather than [ə]) of the indefinite article,
lack of contraction of <u>do not</u>, stress on the <u>have</u>, staccato enunciation as if to symbolize what they perceive to be the artificiality and in-
comprehensibility of the teacher's behavior.

With the advanced group, on the other hand, reading became much
more of a group activity and the atmosphere was more relaxed. Words
were treated in context, as part of a story. Children were allowed to
volunteer answers. There was no correction of pronunciation, although
some deviant forms were also heard. The children actually enjoyed
competing with each other in reading, and the teacher responded by
dropping her pedagogical monotone in favor of more animated natural
speech. The activities around the reading table were not lost on the
slow readers who were sitting at their desks with instructions to practice reading on their own. They kept looking at the group, neglecting
their own books, obviously wishing they could participate. After a
while one boy picked up a spelling game from a nearby table and began
to work at it with the other boy, and they began to argue in a style nor-

mal for black children. When their voices were raised the teacher turned and asked them to go back to reading.

In private conversation, the teacher who is very conscientious and seemingly concerned with all her children's progress, justified her ability grouping on the grounds that children in the slow group lacked books in their homes and 'did not speak proper English'. She stated they needed practice in grammar and abstract thinking and pronunciation, and suggested that given this type of training they would eventually be able to catch up with the advanced group. We wonder how well she will succeed. Although clearly she has the best motives and would probably be appalled if one were to suggest that her ability grouping and her emphasis on the technical aspects of reading and spelling with culturally different children is culturally biased, her efforts are not so understood by the children themselves. Our data indicates that the pedagogical style used with slow readers carries different associations for low middle class and low income groups. While whites identify it as normal teaching behavior, ghetto residents associate it with the questioning style of welfare investigators and automatically react by not cooperating. In any case, attuned as they are to see meaning in stylistic choice, the black children in the slow reading group cannot fail to notice that they are being treated quite differently and with less understanding than the advanced readers.

What are the implications of this type of situation for our understanding of the role of dialect differences on classroom learning? There is no question that the grammatical features of black dialects discovered by urban dialectologists in recent years are of considerable importance for the historical study of origin of these dialects and for linguistic theory in general, but this does not necessarily mean that they constitute an impediment to learning. Information on black dialect is often made known to educators in the form of simple lists of deviant features with the suggestion that these features might interfere with reading. There is little, if any, experimental evidence that the pronunciations characteristic of urban black English actually interfere with the reading process. Yet the teacher in our classroom, for example, spent considerable time attempting to teach her slow readers the distinction between pin and pen. Lack of a vowel distinction in these two words is widespread among blacks, but also quite common among whites in northern California. In any case, there is no reason why homophony in this case should present more difficulty than homophony in such words as sea and see, and know and no.

It is not enough simply to present the educator with the descriptive linguistic evidence. What we need is properly controlled work on reading as such, work which does not deal with grammar alone. Our data suggests that urban language differences, while they may or may not interfere with reading, do have a significant influence on a teacher's expectation and hence on the learning environment. Since bilinguals and bidialectals rely heavily on code-switching as a verbal strategy, they are especially sensitive to the relationship between language and context. It would seem that they learn best under conditions of maximal contextual reinforcement. Sole concentration on the technical aspects of reading, grammar, and spelling may so adversely affect the learning environment as to outweigh any advantages to be gained.

The problem of contextual relevance is not confined to contact with speakers of black English. It also applies, for example, to the teaching of both English and Spanish in bilingual schools. When interviewed about their school experiences, Puerto Rican high school students in New York as well as Texas and California Chicano students uniformly complain about their lack of success in Spanish instruction. They resent the fact that their Spanish teachers single out their own native usages as substandard and inadmissable both in classroom speech and in writing.

It seems clear, furthermore, that progress in urban language instruction is not simply a matter of better teaching aids and improved textbooks. Middle class adults have to learn to appreciate differences in communicative strategies of the type discussed here. Teachers themselves must be given instruction in both the linguistic and ethnographic aspects of speech behavior. They must become acquainted with code selection rules in formal and informal settings, as well as those themes of folk literature and folk art that form the input to these rules, so that they can diagnose their own communication problems and adapt methods to their children's background.

NOTES

Research reported on in this paper has been supported by grants from the Urban Crisis Program and the Institute of International Studies, University of California, Berkeley. I am grateful to Edward Hernandez and Louisa Lewis for assistance in field work and analysis.

REFERENCES

Abrahams, Roger D. 1964. Deep down in the jungle. Hatboro, Pennsylvania, Folklore Associates.
Blom, Jan Petter, and John J. Gumperz. 1970. Social meaning in linguistic structures. In: John J. Gumperz and Dell Hymes, eds., Directions in sociolinguistics. New York, Holt, Rinehart, and Winston (in press).
Bloomfield, Leonard. 1936. Language. New York.
Garvin, Paul, ed. 1969. A Prague school reader. Washington, D. C., Georgetown University Press.

Gumperz, John J., and Edward Hernandez. 1969. Cognitive aspects of bilingual communication. Working Paper No. 28, Language Behavior Research Laboratory, University of California, Berkeley, December.

Hannery, Ulf. 1969. Soulside. Stockholm.

Holt, John Caldwell. 1964. How children fail. New York, Pitman.

Kochman, T. H. 1969. Rapping in the Black Ghetto. In Transaction, February.

Labov, William. 1969. The logic of nonstandard Negro English. In: Linguistics and the teaching of standard English. Monograph Series on Languages and Linguistics No. 22. Washington, D. C., Georgetown University Press.

Lance, Donald M. 1969. A brief study of Spanish-English bilingualism. Research report. Texas A and M University.

Mehan, B. 1970. Unpublished lecture delivered to the Kroeber Anthropological Society meetings, April 25.

Mitchell, Claudia. 1969. Language behavior in a black urban community. Unpublished doctoral dissertation, University of California, Berkeley.

Rosenthal, Robert. 1968. Pygmalion in the classroom. New York, Holt, Rinehart, and Winston.

Sacks, Harvey. 1970. On the analyzability of stories by children. In: John J. Gumperz and Dell Hymes, eds., Directions in sociolinguistics. New York, Holt, Rinehart, and Winston. (in press)

Schegloff, Emanuel. 1970. Sequencing in conversational openings. In: John J. Gumperz and Dell Hymes, eds., Directions in sociolinguistics. New York, Holt, Rinehart, and Winston. (in press)

Shuy, Roger W. 1964. Social dialects and language learning. Proceedings of the Bloomington, Indiana Conference. N. C. Y. E. Cooperative Research Project No. OE5-10-148.

Song, Linda M. 1970. Language switching in Korean English bilinguals. Unpublished manuscript. University of California, Berkeley.

Stewart, W. 1968. Continuity and change in American Negro dialects. The Florida FL Reporter, spring.

Troike, Rudolph C. 1969. Receptive competence, productive competence and performance. In: James E. Alatis, ed., Linguistics and the teaching of standard English. Monograph Series on Languages and Linguistics No. 22. Washington, D. C.: Georgetown University Press. pp. 63-75.

DISCUSSION

William A. Stewart, Education Study Center: As you are aware, I pointed out in my 1962 article on diglossia in Haiti that those Haitians who know both Creole and French often use the two languages as if they were different style levels of a single language. (Stewart, 'The Functional Distribution of Creole and French in Haiti,.' MSLL 15 (1962) pp. 156-59. Repr. in Richard J. O'Brien, ed., <u>Round Table Selected Papers on Linguistics 1961-1965</u> (1968), pp. 467-70.) I suggested that this kind of semantic use of the alternation between two linguistic systems might be characteristic of diglossia situations—at least for those who are really able to use both speech forms. And this brings me to my point. For, when I described Haitian diglossia, I made it clear that any observations about switching between Creole and French applied only to that five percent or less of the population which knew French in addition to Creole. Considering that the remaining 95 percent of the population speaks only Creole, you can see how foolish it would be to assume that popular education in Haiti could start with the assumption of diglossic competence on the part of the average Haitian pupil. The only way in which Haitian education could recognize diglossic competence of this type would be to devise a way of teaching it to the many monolingual Creole speakers. And, of course, the pupils would also have to be taught how to avoid switching into Creole when speaking to monolingual French speakers. Now, applying the foregoing qualifications to the American example you mentioned, it may be almost as counter-productive to assume, as you appear to, that all (or even most) Negro children come to school with a diglossia-like competence in nonstandard dialect and standard English. I know, of course, that it is a tenet of the current Black Revitalization movement that all Negroes are bicultural—and, presumably, bidialectal as well. But I just don't believe that all Negro children in our schools are bidialectal, and I suspect that the majority may not be. I think I know why image-conscious Negroes are now making the claim that they are all bicultural and bidialectal. For the would-be spokesman of the race, who is likely to have come from the super-middle-class, and therefore likes to have little or no direct knowledge of lower-class Negro language and culture, such a claim confers the necessary competence upon him. Also, for Negro apologists, the claim of biculturalism and bidialectalism is a way of rhetorically freeing the Negro from the stigma (in their view, at any rate) of unwanted cultural determinism. Negroes used to insist that the standard-English-speaking, middle-class Negro child was the ideal image which educators should keep in mind. Now, it is apparently the bidialectal and bicultural Negro child. But the lower-class Negro child, who knows but little of standard English and mainstream culture, stands to lose just as much now as before from such image-manipulation. Finally, you suggest that Negro teachers, who are presumably already bicultural and bidialectal, would be most ideal for Negro children. Again, I know that this is another fashionable tenet of the Black Revitalization movement, but again, I simply don't believe that it is necessarily so. I know some excellent Negro teachers, who are as much at home with one language and culture as with the other. But I also know of many more who, whether they are bicultural and bidialectal or not, are nevertheless the last persons in the world to accept the use of Negro dialect in the classroom. Now, all of this is by way of introduction to what I suppose is my question: If the society at large uses only standard English, and many black children use only nonstandard dialect (even though some others may know both), then how is your proposed educational program of bidialectal tolerance (which, frankly, looks to me like an institutionalized way of allowing teachers to ignore the linguistic problem altogether) going to prepare these children for their sociolinguistic needs in the mainstream society?

Gumperz: Bill has raised a number of questions; it would take another paper to answer them all. Let me concentrate on a few points. As you know, the recent literature on black folklore emphasizes the importance of verbal acts such as 'signifying' and 'marking', 'rapping', etc. This richness of folk terminology points out the importance of verbal skills in black culture. Take 'marking' as it is described in Claudia Kernan's recent dissertation (Kernan 1969) for example. Kernan's examples of marking show how choice of speech code serves as a rhetorical device to show someone up. There is considerable ethnographic evidence for urban black communities at least, that although not everyone in those communities is ambilingual—i.e. has perfect control of both styles, code-switching is nevertheless an essential part of everyday communication. What I meant to say is that teachers must be aware of code-switching as a verbal skill which can be used to convey a wide variety of meanings in everyday interaction. We have now been tape recording in Bay area schools for about six months, sometimes turning on the recorder at random and we have yet to find children in Berkeley, Richmond, Oakland—anywhere in that area—who don't show some kind of switching behavior. Ethnographic work is needed to show the communicative significance of this type of phenomenon.

One other point. You ask about the problem of preparing children to live in a monodialectal society. We all agree that literacy in standard English is a major educational goal of primary education. But as anthropologists we are concerned with teacher-student interaction rather than with learning goals. We are studying communication in integrated classrooms in order to determine how differences in interactional norms affect the learning environment.

Robert J. Di Pietro, Georgetown University: As one who has grown up in a community where code-switching went on all the time, I was especially interested in Dr. Gumperz' remarks about associating code-switching with what people mean to say or imply. I was thinking about your example of the lady who was trying to give up smoking and switched from English to Spanish in the middle of what she was saying and how this somehow reflected her ambivalence about the notion of smoking. Couldn't her code-switching have also come from the fact that she lives in a community where English is spoken by the majority of people and that people talk about cigarette smoking being harmful to your health in English? Couldn't she be just simply switching back and forth because the two languages are present? There may be some association between code-switching and the domains of interaction of various types, but its going to be very, very difficult to work out. I know that American-born mothers from non-English language backgrounds will often use the language of their parents in talking to their children about intimate body functions or body parts. They do this apparently as a way of hiding or avoiding taboo words.

The thought has been growing in my mind that so far at this meeting, with everything that we have heard about being better teachers and being able to understand the student better and, as Dr. Gumperz says, about the good teacher as being the one who can talk about each one of the students individually, no one to my knowledge here has yet demonstrated that any of these devices are specific to bilingual, bidialectal, or for that matter, to monolingual education.

Gumperz: If I may just comment on one or two points. To explain our procedure: it is not to count code-switching; we are not interested in code-switching as such. We are interested in an empirical problem: How does a linguist or anyone else for that matter decode a person's intent? Our cultural assumptions provide the background knowledge for interpreting a person's intent. Culture is part of the information we need in the decoding process. When I say, for instance, that the child switches in order to relax the atmosphere, I say this because we have analyzed a number of conversations. We play them back to native judges. We don't ask: When do you use English? When do you use Spanish? or, Why did you switch? We take an actual conversational sequence like: Why did the speaker say this in this particular way? And we get answers like: Because she wanted to be friendly. Because she wanted to show off, etc. We can do this cross-culturally, asking the same questions in different groups. When we take a black group and ask a question, or when we take a white group and ask a question, we sometimes find that we get radically different interpretations of the same message.

There is another point in what Dr. Di Pietro said. The problem is why English came to be associated with the out-group. In another part of this paper I discuss my experience with other groups of Puerto Ricans who have completely different language habits from the ones that I discuss in this paper. They use English for everyday conversation

and Spanish as the marked style. One of the most important problems
in the sociolinguist's study of speech behavior is the fact that there
seems to be no direct relationship between ethnic identity and language
usage patterns. Language usage patterns seem to depend on family
backgrounds, and we don't know how language usage patterns are distributed in larger groups yet. It certainly seems at this point that we
know enough to know that our traditional random sampling procedures
may even obscure significant differences within a community. Sampling is not going to do us any good until we understand some of the
ways in which this sort of behavior is distributed. But what I am
reporting on here is an empirical study of one conversation. I
don't assume that I understand the speaker's intent; I use conversations as a way of learning about the speaker's social norms, culture,
and speech behavior.

THE ANALYSIS OF LINGUISTIC AND CULTURAL DIFFERENCES: A PROPOSED MODEL

CHESTER C. CHRISTIAN, JR.

The University of Texas at El Paso

Abstract. A model of intersecting continua in an n-dimensional space is suggested as a basis for the analysis of languages and cultures, and of their relationships to each other. Such a model would facilitate, for example, the analysis of the language and culture of Mexican-Americans and other bilingual and bicultural groups, as well as relations among and overlapping of languages and cultures in general. Although verbal language is inherently inappropriate for designating continua or multidimensional space, a crude model may be devised by utilizing verbal labels for a three-dimensional space, similar in principle to the psychologist's model for structuring perceptions of color. The concepts of force, resistance, and change may be incorporated into this model. Basic definitions and hypotheses are given with an illustration of the use of a semantic differential questionnaire as one possible technique for partial verification of hypotheses based on the model.

It is futile to attempt to create a science either of culture or of language through the use of the language characteristic of any given culture.[1] Except where words are used entirely and exclusively as substitutes for logical or mathematical symbols, nothing said in ordinary language is capable of verification, either in terms of tautological or of empirical processes.[2] This is the principal reason that social scientists and linguists who are concerned with the behavioral aspects of language usage have a closer kinship to politicians or priests than to physical scientists; most of what they say is valid only so long as their followers believe them.

This is an admission of the fact that what I have to say is invalid, since the only way I can say it is in ordinary language, and the only followers I have are my wife and a couple of friends. My excuse for presenting this paper is that this is the only audience I have ever had where it seems to me possible that someone may have the type of background and mentality to be able to offer criticism which is meaningful to me, and perhaps suggest techniques for development of the symbolic structures required for an exact statement of the hypotheses presented. [3]

It will perhaps clarify this presentation to inform you that the early development of these concepts was based entirely on the contrasts in reference systems observed in the United States among different groups of English-speaking people. At that time I knew no other language than English, and assumed that the distribution of ways of perceiving reality in other countries would show a similar distribution to that found in the United States. [4] It now seems evident that the distribution among those who speak Spanish is significantly distinct from the former, to the extent that communication between most native speakers of Spanish and native speakers of English seems as imprecise and as unsatisfactory as any one-hundred dollar misunderstanding. To state it in another manner, it appears that the theoretical range of alternative patterns of meaning and behavior in each culture is similar, but that economic, social and cultural pressures make the practical range of alternatives distinct. For example, in the United States one can choose any one of thirty-two flavors of ice cream; this is not the same as being offered the choice between ice cream and frijoles refritos. The former is, I believe, characteristic of the false alternatives our society offers; most of the authentic alternatives are offered only in other societies.

In an attempt to discover the genuine alternatives among patterns of life offered by contemporary cultures, I tried to identify each possible system of meanings which would imply a logically consistent set of behavior patterns. At first it seemed that each system of meanings would utilize a characteristic vocabulary, and that it would be possible to identify groups of words which would refer to a given system of meanings. It became evident, however, that most key words which represent important meanings are used in different ways by people who have different frames of reference; using the same words provides the illusion of communication, and in normal social relations the illusion is more important than the fact. In order to study the facts of meaning, it seemed necessary to create a private vocabulary. [5]

To define and interrelate the group of systems from which all possible meanings and all possible sets of behavior patterns might be derived, I created five logical categories representing five frames of reference: the material, the historic, the structural, the dynamic, and the universal. All meanings, I felt, could be assigned to one or more of these categories, and a systematic relation to these meanings could be established for any given act. Later, the study of the philosophy of science made it seem advisable to divide these categories into two groups, with the material, structural, and universal in one group representing cognitive meanings, and the historic, dynamic, and (for the sake of theoretical equilibrium) cosmic in the other group, representing emotive meanings.[6] The popular terms most closely associated with the cognitive frames of reference were identified as technology, science, and metaphysics; those associated with the emotive as ritual, art, and mysticism, both groups in their presumed order of abstraction from concrete or universal experience.

Before becoming acquainted with the Spanish language and the culture of those who speak Spanish, it seemed that meanings in the emotive categories were becoming increasingly subsumed under the corresponding cognitive categories, and that this was an inevitable, and probably not regrettable, result of the progress of modern civilization.[7] In the process of learning Spanish, however, I became aware of a heretofore unknown degree of vitality in the emotive categories; it seemed that the language and culture of those who speak English could be identified as belonging in general to the set of frames of reference designated material, structural, and universal, while those of Spanish-speaking people emphasized the historic, dynamic, and cosmic frames of reference.[8] While hundreds of quotations, especially in Spanish, may be taken from descriptions of both cultures to illustrate, if not confirm, this assumption, my own conclusions were first derived not from literary works, but from interviews with prostitutes in El Paso, Texas and Ciudad Juárez, Chihuahua. They were confirmed later in teaching Mexican-American high school students who made me realize that the language of Cervantes acts to form the system of meanings to which they respond most naturally just as it did to form those which he represented in his works.

Although the United States-Mexican border has the reputation of diluting and deforming both the language and the culture of each of the groups in contact, it is an area where representatives of each group can be observed simultaneously, and where differences are therefore more readily apparent. The great Mexican poet and former diplomat Octavio Paz confesses in his book El laberinto de la soledad that he had not noted the unity of Mexican culture until he could observe in Los Angeles, California its contrast with the dominant culture of the United States.[9] Those living in the border area who speak both English and Spanish have had an opportunity during an entire lifetime to observe differences between the two cultures. The observations of people who speak only one language have been limited in that they have been able to perceive only the superficial manifestations of each culture, but there exists a large population of persons who speak both languages and participate in both cultures. Of this group, approximately 3,000 attend the University of Texas at El Paso, and on several occasions I have asked groups of them to characterize the 'North American' and the 'Latin American' by calculating the degree to which each group can be characterized by one or more adjectives listed in contrasting pairs. Although unsystematized, the meaning of one of each pair generally would refer to an emotive frame of reference, and the other to a cognitive one. Indications are that students conceive the North American as cognitively oriented and the Latin American as emotively oriented. [10]

The words considered most important in the description of 'Latin Americans' are, in the order of importance assigned to them by one group of bilingual university students: happy, romantic, religious, passionate, courteous, brave, sensitive, simpático, faithful (the woman to her husband), idealistic, poor, impetuous, natural, unfaithful (the husband to his wife), and anarchic. The corresponding adjectives used to describe 'North Americans' are: organized, practical, wealthy, materialistic, optimistic, strong, industrious, insensitive, worthy of admiration, egotistical, religious, brave, artificial, responsible, and happy. These fifteen adjectives were selected from a group of fifty. It is noteworthy that only three, happy, religious, and brave are used to describe both groups; however, they are considered very important in their application to Latin Americans, and of relatively minor importance in relation to North Americans.

In each survey, the results have been quite similar, not only those obtained by students living on the border but also when they have come from a variety of nonborder states. Similar results were also obtained in a series of several thousand interviews in Lima, Peru, in which respondents were asked to characterize the 'North American' and the 'Peruvian'. Furthermore, the adjectives considered most important in the characterization of each group are very similar to those which have been used by philosophers, essayists, reporters, and other writers who have had the opportunity to observe both cultures. Additional confirmation may be found in the contemporary Latin American novel, where members of Latin American cultures are described as acting in ways people described by the adjectives used might be expected to act.

All this does not necessarily mean that the students of Mexican descent, the Anglo students, the Spanish and Latin American writers, and the contemporary novelists are correct in their views. Any good social scientist would expect that where there is such close agreement either nothing is being said or everyone is wrong. It is certainly true that if, for example, we define 'happy' in terms of an income of ten thousand dollars per year or more for a family of five, there are many more happy North Americans than there are Latin Americans. And if we define 'romantic' in terms of a disposition to divorce one's spouse upon falling in love with another person, North Americans are undoubtedly more romantic than Latin Americans. On the other hand, Latin Americans may be better organized than North Americans in terms of family relations. In terms of provisions for responding to male sexual demands, they may be more practical.

The problem is not in the adjectives we have chosen, but in the language itself, the natural ambiguity of ordinary forms of expression and description. However, by creating the proper type of model, it is possible to lend precision to ordinary language and even to use it, although to a very limited degree, as an element in scientific theory.

Let us take the example of color. In the United States and in Africa people are generally divided into blacks and whites. In English, this is not only a color division; black suggests superstition, cruelty, depression, death, and other negative concepts. White suggests purity, cleanliness, honesty, holiness, and other celestial qualities. If we offered a semantic differential questionnaire to English-speaking people, asking them to describe the degree to which North Americans are white and Africans are black, it would be impossible to get them to react without reference to connotations unrelated to the physical perception of color so that, although the results of the questionnaire might be shown to be highly uniform, they would be invalid.

On the other hand, we could create a simple scientific model by defining black and white in terms of reflectance. We could then measure the amount of light reflected from the tips of the nose of a representative sample of North Americans and of Africans, locate each on a reflectance continuum, and make a curve of the resulting distribution. We could then formulate such hypotheses as 'Africans are blacker than North Americans,' and 'The less light reflected from the tip of the nose, the less living space each person will occupy,' and make exact measurements to determine the degree of reliability of our statements.

We could even place red, brown, and yellow people on this same continuum, but here our model would be much less reliable; red, brown, and yellow would be defined in terms of shades of gray, and a millionaire in Miami Beach might be blacker than a San Francisco Chinaman. Here again science could come to the rescue, though, with a three-dimensional model representing hues as well as shades. We could create a model, in fact, with one hundred, two hundred, or three hundred thousand distinct elements, and identify every human being by the shade and hue of the tip of his nose. And in order not to call anybody yellow, we could identify each combination by a number.

In a model such as this, each element is defined in terms of its relationship to each other element in the system. Any word utilized in referring to one or more elements of the system is therefore defined in a completely arbitrary manner. If we want to divide the continuum from black to white into three segments, for example, we can call one segment black, one gray, and one white. We can divide it into five segments if we wish, adding 'light gray' and 'dark gray'. We could even add 'light black' and 'dark white' since we need not be constrained by the limitations of ordinary language. The important thing is not the word, but the position with reference to the model. In this sense, every color could be identified precisely by three numbers. Any word representing a color could be identified as a range of three-number sets.

In the model for the analysis of language and culture herewith suggested, terms would be defined in a similar manner. Two intersecting continua, for example, would define the six frames of reference mentioned: material, structural, universal, historic, dynamic, and cosmic. The two continua might be designated 'concrete' to 'transcendent' and 'cognitive' to 'emotive'. These continua might be defined as series of 'points of reference', with a 'frame of reference' resulting from the delineation of any area of contiguous points.

The popular terms previously mentioned—technology, science, metaphysics, ritual, art, and mysticism—could be located within the model just as pink, purple, maroon, or pardo can be located within the model of color, without ambiguity in the theoretical sense, or with ambiguities made explicit by empirical processes. There is no theoretical reason that this could not be done for every word in any language.

All meanings might be defined in terms of only one dimension—concrete to transcendent, for example—just as all colors may be defined in terms of black and white. But most phenomena would involve a combination of meanings, just as most objects reflect a combination of colors. And the frame of reference in terms of which a given meaning is defined is as important as the color of the light by means of which a given object is viewed.

These two dimensions are not adequate for defining all meanings, of course. A third continuum which may be one of the most important in defining the contrast between the culture of English-speakding and that of Spanish-speaking people might be termed the personalist-collectivist continuum. [11] This might be conceived as intersecting with the two aforementioned continua and, if we continue to divide the concrete-transcendent continuum into three sections (concrete-abstract-transcendent), we will have twelve possible frames of reference.

There is no theoretical reason why we could not continue to the point where we are able to define thousands or even hundreds of thousands of possible frames of reference, but ordinary language begins to fail when we go beyond twelve; that is, the degree of failure becomes more evident and therefore more nearly intolerable. Ordinary language is, at best, a three-dimensional phenomenon, just as is the ordinary mind.

Metaphysicians (pure mathematicians) liberated themselves from the three-dimensional world only yesterday and we still do not have the tools they used to make their escape.[12]

A mathematical elaboration and systematization of this theoretical model could, I believe, reveal many unjustified assumptions implicit in discussions of societies and cultures now defined as traditional and modern, rural and urban, progressive and static, democratic and autocratic, empirical and magical, developed and underdeveloped, Mexican-American and Anglo-American, etc. The greatest error of most social scientists is in trying to understand cultural differences in terms of the system of meanings found in their native language. The greatest deficiency of linguistics is in the failure of most linguists to attempt to understand the nature of the society in which a given language is produced.

I would like to suggest literature as a possible bridge between linguistics and social science, but that must be reserved for another occasion. In any case, I would suggest the necessity of mathematical or logical models to firm up the swampy grounds of both social science and sociolinguistics before we can have much confidence in a bridge.

Meanwhile, although we know too little about the nature of language and cultural differences to understand what is happening—much less the significance of what is happening—in our bilingual programs, what I have said implies to me the critical importance to education of bilingual teaching. There is no way to understand systems of reference other than one's own except by entering into them, and every door leading into another is labeled 'x'. That 'x' stands for a language.

NOTES

[1]Edgerton defines a 'natural language' as 'a set of systematically manipulated verbal symbols for an essentially arbitrary view of the world (Weltanschauung) or reality, which is largely a heritage from previous generations and which is fundamentally a function of the circumstances in which those linguistic ancestors have lived.' M. Edgerton, Jr., 'The Study of Languages: A Point of View,' Liberal Education Vol. LI, No. 4 (December 1965) p. 517. This definition implies not only the limitations of language as an instrument of science, but also the persistence of culture and the relation of language to culture. These characteristics make it almost impossible to avoid reification when attempting to use such a language to represent abstract ideas. It is for this reason that terms such as 'mass' and 'force' in physics have been the object of so much controversy. It is really unimportant that such terms 'have no meaning'; it is important that they can be assigned specific functions in a given symbolic system.

[2]In its ideal form scientific research combines the abstractness of purely symbolic reasoning such as is found in mathematics and symbolic logic with the concreteness of iconic records such as is provided by the direct transformation of phenomena into representations which can be symbolized within the framework of the theory to which they are relevant. This is why many philosophers of science insist that the only meaningful statements are those which have perception terms as predicates (or can be transformed into such statements), those which are convertible into pointer-readings or ostensive definitions, those which are in principle verifiable, etc. See A. J. Ayer, Language, Truth, and Logic (London 1936) pp. 99f. Also Alexander Johnson, A Treatise on Language (University of California 1947) p. 350.

Some philosophers of science prefer not to attribute meaning to tautological or analytical statements. Thus when we affirm that 2 x 2413 = 4826 we are asserting nothing which is empirically meaningful; we can 'verify' this statement by placing 2413 objects next to 2413 others and counting the two sets as one, but all we are doing is verifying the fact that we are using the terminology according to the rules we have set up for its use. However, without the complex tautological systems we have there would be no science, because the logical applications of our propositions would not be clear enough to offer the possibility of empirical verification. This is now the case with social science and sociolinguistics. We have excellent tools for observation, but the logical systems we use are of the most primitive kind.

[3]Of the many and varied mathematical models which have been devised in the past century, there have been few which have come to the attention of social scientists and linguists. But many of the latest systems and techniques have been used in an ingenious application to competitive strategies in human society, the 'Theory of Games'. This theory assumes what I call in this paper a 'material frame of reference'. It is notable for the manner in which distinct mathematical models are combined in their application to socioeconomic phenomena. Work on this theory has been heavily subsidized by the Department of Defense of the United States due to the many military applications derived from it. While the work itself is too difficult for the nonmathematician, there is an amusing and instructive popularization of it. See Oskar Morgenstern and John von Neumann, Theory of Games and Economic Behavior (Princeton University 1947), and John MacDonald, Strategy in Poker, Business and War (New York 1950). Some of the basic principles of the use of mathematical applications to social data are discussed in Walter Firey, 'Mathematics and Social Theory, ' Social Forces, Vol. 29, No. 1 (October 1950).

[4]This is an assumption which I believe to be the inevitable result of the use of a single language. Here scientists are often more culture-bound than ordinary citizens, failing to distinguish between meanings

which are a part of their scientific system and more general cultural meanings of which the scientific system is a part. Thus a culture which regards scientific meanings as less important than other and contradictory meanings is by definition inferior to a culture which offers the scientist greater prestige and a larger income than it offers, for example, to priests and poets. Emphasis on noncognitive values seems particularly disagreeable to the scientist, and even more so to the technologist. But we are constantly learning how better to 'use' people who hold to emotive (or 'sacred') values; we have come a long way since Dale Carnegie. Margaret Mead seems to have suggested that where people cannot be used, they can be hospitalized; she has said that the contemporary urban community does not tolerate unduly visible expressions of emotion, adding: 'Quite small shifts in mood can be identified or treated ... The first time someone doesn't do what he usually does—the first time a prompt bill-payer neglects his debts, the ardent churchgoer doesn't go to church—something is wrong that should be stopped.' Quoted in the Austin American-Statesman, April 2, 1967.

[5] This language was intended to be literally private, nothing more than a means of clarifying my own thinking. At that time I did not know that this could be done far more effectively through the use of symbolic systems which had already been developed. By the time I learned of the existence of such systems, it was too late to devote the necessary time to master the basic techniques of using them. The problem has been stated by John Kemeny in referring to the need of psychologists for mathematical techniques: 'So, the psychologist has to use mathematics. And it would be rare luck if the mathematics he needs should all fall within one branch of mathematics. How can we hope to give him the mastery he requires, when it is a full-time occupation for the mathematician? Of course, he may master a few standard techniques. But every indication is that theoretical psychology is growing too rapidly to allow this kind of narrow acquaintance with mathematics ... The usual answer seems to be that the psychologist should consult a mathematician when he needs to have a mathematical problem answered. But which mathematician should he ask? And will the mathematician who knows no psychology be able to understand his problem? John G. Kemeny, 'A Mathematician's Point of View,' in Francis Sweeny, S. J. The Knowledge Explosion: Liberation and Limitation (New York: Farrar, Straus & Giroux, 1966) p. 92.

[6] The least satisfactory word in this group is 'historic'. I am attempting to suggest all meanings and acts which are time-related, or which derive their significance from time processes. For example, the use of a fork as an instrument for eating, although it has a technical or material component, is essentially determined by the historic frame of reference, the use of a necktie to an even greater extent, and

the repetition of a given prayer to a still greater degree. Also, 'historic' is intended to include personal experience; it refers to individual as well as collective rites. Thus, associating 'historic' with 'emotive' is not intended to suggest 'emotional', neither with respect to ritual, art, or mysticism. Detached contemplation can be as important in the emotive as in the cognitive frames of reference, and each system has its own rules of validity.

[7] This seems to be to a great extent a result of the suppression <u>as an emotive process</u> of the emotive by Protestant culture. The details of the process are perhaps best expounded in Max Weber, <u>The Protestant Ethic and the Spirit of Capitalism</u> (New York: Charles Scribner's Sons 1958). The result of the process is that ritual becomes a part of the material frame of reference, and technology becomes a ritual. This is the type of interrelation of meanings which the suggested model might be capable of elucidating.

[8] Positivists in Latin America have been on many occasions frustrated and baffled by the intransigence of their fellow citizens who insist on maintaining 'archaic' values. Francisco Bulnes, for example, wrote in 1899: 'The great Latin delusion is the belief that art is the highest, almost the only object of national life. Latins bend every effort to being artists in religion, and turn out idolators; they strive to be artists in industry, and impoverish themselves; even in science they want to be artists, and they fail to understand the scientific method ... Latins set themselves to be the great artists of politics, and the result is that a republic becomes for them a perfectly impossible system of government.' Francisco Bulnes, <u>El porvenir de las naciones hispanoamericanas ante las conquistas recientes de Europa y Norteamérica</u> (México, 1899) p. 85. In the same year, José Enrique Rodó called on the youth of Latin America <u>not</u> to accept the value system of Europe and the United States; he admitted that 'their culture ... has an admirable efficiency insofar as it is directed practically toward the accomplishment of immediate goals,' but insisted that it could produce neither saintliness nor heroism. José Enrique Rodó, <u>Ariel</u> (México 1963) p. 114. But cognitively-oriented societies find little use for heroes, artists, or saints—products of the emotive frames of reference.

[9] Octavio Paz, <u>El laberinto de la soledad,</u> 3d ed. (México 1963). 'I lived for some time in Los Angeles, a city in which more than a million persons of Mexican origin live. At first sight the traveler is surprised by the vaguely Mexican atmosphere of the city, impossible to express in words or concepts. This Mexicanness—pleasure in adornment, carelessness and ostentation, passion and reserve—float in the air. And I say that they float because they do not mix or fuse with the other world, the North American world, made of precision and efficiency.'

[10]A list of adjectives in contrasting pairs was given to each person, who indicated the degree to which the North American and the Latin American could be characterized by either one of each pair. For example:

poor   __ __ __ _____ __ __ __   wealthy
        3   2   1   0   1   2   3

3 = very poor or very wealthy, 2 = fairly poor or fairly wealthy, 1 = somewhat poor or somewhat wealthy, and 0 = lack of information or too much variation for a valid characterization.

[11]In terms of the model, I believe that the balance of evidence would show that the frame of reference of people who speak Spanish is preponderantly concrete, emotive, and personalist; that of people who speak English preponderantly abstract, cognitive, and collectivist. Of course the situation is extremely complex, and that is why a complex model is needed—not only to represent emphases, but also interrelations, forces, conflicts, etc.

[12]Brathwaite states that 'it has been a fortunate fact in the modern history of physical science that the scientist constructing a new theoretical system has nearly always found that the mathematics he required for his system had already been worked out by pure mathematicians for their own amusement.' R. B. Brathwaite, Scientific Explanation (Cambridge University 1953) p. 1. There may be many systems worked out by pure mathematicians 'for their own amusement' which would be applicable in social science and linguistics, but most social scientists and linguists, like myself, would be hard put to recognize one.

REFERENCES

Ayer, Alfred Jules. 1936. Language, truth and logic. London, Christ College, Oxford.

Brathwaite, Richard Bevan. 1953. Scientific explanation. Cambridge, Cambridge University Press.

Bulnes, Francisco. 1899. El porvenir de las naciones hispanoamericanas ante las conquistas recientes de Europa y Norteamérica. Mexico, D. F., El Pensamiento vivo de América.

Edgerton, M., Jr. 1965. The study of languages: A point of view. In Liberal education, Vol. LI, No. 4, December.

Firey, Walter. 1950. Mathematics and social theory. In Social forces, Vol. 29, No. 1, October.

Frank, P. 1941. Between physics and philosophy. Cambridge, Harvard University Press.

Johnson, Alexander Bryan. 1947. A treatise on language. Los Angeles and Berkeley, University of California Press.

Kohler, Wolfgang. 1938. The place of value in a world of facts. New York, Liveright Publishing Corporation.

McDonald, John Dennis. 1950. Strategy in poker, business and war. New York, Norton.

Morgenstern, Oskar and John von Neumann. 1947. Theory of games and economic behavior. 2d revised ed. Princeton, Princeton University Press.

Morris, Charles William. 1946. Signs, language and behavior. New York, Prentice-Hall.

Paz, Octavio. 1963. El laberinto de la soledad. 3d ed. México.

Rodó, José Enrique. 1963. Ariel. 3d ed. México, Espasa-Calpe Mexicana, Colección Austral.

Kemeny, John G. 1966. A mathematician's point of view. In The knowledge explosion: liberation and limitation. Francis W. Sweeney, ed. New York, Farrar, Straus and Giroux.

Weber, Max. 1958. The protestant ethic and the spirit of capitalism. Talcott Parsons, trans. New York, Charles Scribner's Sons.

Whitehead, Alfred North. 1926. Science and the modern world. New York, Macmillan.

DISCUSSION

Ruth Landman, American University: I would like to accept Miss Moore's invitation and return to the last sentence of the paper just read about bilingual education, to raise a point which seems to me very important, particularly in reference to Spanish-speaking bilingual education. If we are talking in terms of bilingual education of immigrants in the United States, in the case of most Mexican Americans we are talking about a language which is by now approximately one to three generations removed from Mexican Spanish as it was brought here, and I'm curious to know what do we do with the kinds of problems that come up with educating speakers of nonstandard English if we now introduce bilingual education to speakers of nonstandard Spanish through a training program of teachers who are learning standard Spanish in order to teach school subjects. In other words, are we distorting the culture of the Mexican Americans, possibly the Puerto Rican Americans too, in a further way by introducing a bilingual education through the format of teachers trained in the normal educational channels?

Christian: I don't give the importance to two or three generations removed from Mexican Spanish that you apparently give. I have found with my students, who are 90 percent native speakers of Spanish (since I teach in Spanish, Anglos generally don't take my courses), that no matter what form of Hispanic background they have had, they live within the frame of reference of Spanish culture, even going back as far as several centuries. I've used a number of times the example of the 16th century Spanish novel <u>Lazarillo de Tormes</u>. I think that his attitudes, his values, are illustrative of those of many of the migrant children and of poorer Spanish-speaking children in general.

Landman: I found in a California community that the school teachers in a bilingual program are commenting that they have an easy time with the newly arrived Mexican immigrant children, of whom they have a few, and they have a very difficult time with the local California Spanish-speaking children because these children don't know 'proper' Spanish.

Christian: I would take it as the purpose of the bilingual programs to give these other children 'proper' Spanish. I do realize that in many cases we have children coming from Mexico who can advance in language usage within one year to a point where students we have had in the United States have not advanced in eight or nine years. I don't attribute that to lack of language ability on the part of the latter; I attribute it to defects in the school system.

Wolfgang Wölck, Indiana University: I believe that what you said about the distribution of evaluative factors along the cognitive and emotive scale as applied to, in this case, English and Spanish, would be found true for any difference between majority and minority languages, particularly if you have the majority speakers rate the minority speakers and vice versa. Given the time, I could add here some of the experiences that we had in running a language attitude test in Peru with Quechua-Spanish bilinguals.

Christian: You can also find this contrast, for example, between the philosophy of Unamuno and any European philosopher of this century or the last if you want. You can find it as a contrast between Mexican and U.S. philosophies: between Vasconcelos, for example, who was not exactly a deprived person, and William James or John Dewey and North American philosophers in general. You can find in the literature of Latin America and Spain the same basic contrast with the literature of North America. I think that there are a thousand ways that you can find it. I agree that the emotive is generally more important in rural cultures; also, it is generally more important in traditional cultures. There are many other dimensions to that problem, but I think that we can't analyze the problem except in terms of a model where values are recognized as intrinsic to certain social groups. It may not be desirable to remove or destroy these values and replace them with other values which happen to seem to us more palatable at the time. I was very much interested in what Vera John had to say

about New Mexico, and would like to point out that in Aldous Huxley's
Brave New World New Mexico was, I believe, a refuge for those who
couldn't adjust in spite of all to the brave new world.   I would like to
consider that a reason why I live near New Mexico.   It would be com-
forting to have an escape route open in case the blessings of modern
life become intolerable.

THE FIRST SEVENTY-SIX
BILINGUAL EDUCATION PROJECTS

A. BRUCE GAARDER

U. S. Office of Education

Abstract. The essay provides an analytical scheme and criteria
for judging the probable effectiveness of bilingual schooling projects,
applies the scheme and criteria to the first seventy-six such projects
funded by the Office of Education under the Bilingual Education Act,
and offers some comments and criticism of the entire program.

This essay examines certain salient features of the plans of operation
of the first seventy-six bilingual schooling projects supported by grants
under the Bilingual Education Act. It reveals what appears to be, in a
large majority of them, such inadequate attention—time, resources, and
understanding—to the other tongue, as compared to the attention paid to
English that, on the whole, the concept of bilingual education represented
by these plans of operation seems to be something less than the legislation and its advocates intended. I say 'appears' and 'seems' because the
analysis was made from close reading of the official plans of operation,
plus addenda and other correspondence in the files of the U. S. Office of
Education, plus returns from a questionnaire sent to the project directors, rather than from direct observation of the projects in action. The
qualifiers are required too because the development of language competency in children takes several years, and at this writing only the first
half-year of the five years of the supporting grants has elapsed. [1]

The Congress couched its extraordinarily generous and innovative
legislation in support of dual-language public schooling in terms that
permit both the ethnocentrists and the cultural pluralists to see what
they want to see in the Act. It could mean the merest token obeisance
to the non-English mother tongue (N-EMT) and the culture it repre-

sents, or it could—as a fictitious example—support production for one
of the American Indian tribal groups of a full panoply of teaching materials in their language for all the school subjects, the complete training of a corps of native speakers of that language and full implementation of the resulting curriculum from kindergarten through the twelfth
grade, plus schooling for the parents in their native tongue. English,
of course, could never be excluded.

The Office of Education has interpreted bilingual education officially
to mean the use of two languages, one of which is English, as mediums
of instruction ... for the same student population, in a well-organized
program which encompasses part or all of the curriculum, plus study
of the history and culture associated with a student's mother tongue.

As one might expect, of the 76 projects some—quite within their
rights—proposed the use of the child's mother tongue for purposes of
instruction as a 'bridge' to English, to be crossed as soon as possible
and then eliminated entirely or virtually so in favor of English as the
sole medium. With these our special quarrel is that the bridge seems
usually to be a one-way affair with no encouragement to pass back and
forth freely, and is sometimes so short as perhaps not to reach the
other side of the abyss. Most of the projects have planned to give a
much more substantial role to the mother tongue as a medium of instruction in the regular school subjects. Many profess to aim for
equal emphasis on the two languages and seek to develop in their pupils
equal competence in the two. Here it is evident in most cases that,
whether consciously or unconsciously, the emphasis is very far from
equal.

In the plans of operation of all of the projects, there is a profession
of emphasis on the 'history and culture' of the child who has a mother
tongue other than English. They want to strengthen his 'sense of identity', his 'self-concept'. Here—as will be seen later in this essay—the
disparity between aims and means is enormous. Every project attempts
to provide improved and intensified instruction in English. This component, in most cases the principal focus of the project plan, cannot be described in this limited essay. Finally, each plan provides in-service
training for its project teachers and aides, and occasionally, for other
personnel. Suffice it to say, for the purpose of this brief overview, that
the in-service training included in most cases a short orientation session
before the fall term began, and periodic sessions are held during the academic year focused on the other culture, the teaching of English as a second language, and the teaching of and through the N-EMT. The important
point to note is that this work is conducted in the great majority of the
cases by the local project director or the bilingual coordinator.

A brief overview of the entire program:
76 separate projects in 70 different cities, each project to be funded for
5 years if work is performed satisfactorily.

Language (in addition to English)		Projects
Spanish		68
Spanish and Sioux	1	
Spanish and Pomo	1	
Spanish and Keresan and Navajo	1	
Spanish and Chinese	1	
Mexican-Americans	58	
Puerto Ricans	7	
Puerto Ricans and one other		
language group	2	
mixed Spanish-speaking	2	
Cherokee		2
Chinese (Cantonese)		1
(plus the one noted above)		
French		1
Japanese		1
Navajo		1
(plus the one noted above)		
Portuguese		2
		76
In elementary schools only		54
In secondary schools only		8
In both		14

Most projects have begun the first year very modestly, with only one or a few classes of pupils at one or two grade levels only. Some are more ambitious. All expect to expand year by year for five years.

Total first year cost of 76 projects	$7,500,000
Average cost	98,684

Are the 'other-medium' teachers (those expected to teach some or all of the regular school subject areas through the children's mother tongue) adequately prepared for bilingual schooling? There is evidence that most of them are not. In most of the plans of operation the qualifications of the staff are carefully set forth. Forty-nine call for mere 'bilingualism', or 'conversational ability' in the other tongue. Six want 'fluent' bilinguals; at least one specifies the ability to read, write, and speak the two languages; some say the teachers will be 'hopefully' or 'preferably' bilinguals. On the other hand, eleven either identified or demanded well qualified people; and in fifteen there is at least one person educated abroad and some were seeking one or more such teachers. The ethnic groups differ markedly in respect to teacher qualification, with the highest requirements found among those with easiest access to literacy, notably the Portuguese, Chinese, French, and Puerto Ricans.

In about 20 cases the plans contain no requirement that the director and other key project leaders be more than 'bilingual', and in at least 28 cases not even that limited knowledge of the non-English tongue is demanded. Again, in a score of cases the specific requirements for the director and other key persons in respect to competence in the other language and the culture it represents are high.

The above and following comments on teacher adequacy should be read with the knowledge that to a large extent the projects expect to depend on the teaching services of aides, sometimes called para-professionals, 'bilingual' individuals usually drawn from the community, rarely required to be literate in the non-English tongue, and paid disproportionately low wages. Sometimes the aides work with bilingual teachers. In other projects only the aides are expected to be bilingual, and the regular teachers, the 'master' teachers are Anglos. Much can be said in favor of bringing into the schools persons who represent fully the usually under-represented ethnic minorities. But if those representatives obviously have less professional status, less training, less authority and receive less money than the teachers, the other-medium side of the project is getting less than a full, fair trial.

One plan calls for 40 bilingual aides at two dollars per hour to 'encourage and energize the parents'. In another plan of operation for grade one (and eventually grades 1-3) the aides alone are to be bilingual, their English must be 'demonstrably competent', but they need only 'conversational competency' in the other tongue. Yet the hope is that they somehow are to be given 'the factual basis to permit a useful comparison and analysis of the differences between Spanish and English as spoken languages in the classroom' and are expected to prepare teaching materials. In still another case the merely bilingual kindergarten and preschool aides will be given in-service training in language development in both tongues in 'contrasting usage, translation, relationships, vocabulary development, concept development, and pronunciation', and they are expected to 'improve the oral language facility' of both pupils and parents.

What is mere, hopeful, even fluent bilingualism or 'conversational ability' in two languages? Since most of the projects plan to use their own local teachers, and since the American school system has provided virtually no opportunity for child speakers of non-English languages to maintain and develop those languages—indeed, it has commonly discouraged and denigrated such speaking—the merely bilingual person is a product of the very kind of schooling which bilingual education aims to correct. Members in most cases of social groups with strong oral traditions rather than literary ones, given a first chance at literacy at age 15 in the ninth grade under Anglo foreign language teachers who seldom speak the child's tongue and invariably use books designed for Anglo beginners, how many such bilinguals will have read as many as five books or written 50 pages in their mother tongue? There is indeed the possibility of college study of the tongue, and in some few cases the vita notes such college work. The most favored case recorded notes that each teacher has at least 21 college semester hours of Spanish. An elementary school teacher with a college major in a foreign language is a rarity indeed, and none turned up in the data. Nor is the weakness lessened by the assurance of two directors (who had set no special requirements for their bilingual aides) that the secretary is expected 'to read and write' and 'translate the materials'. A third plan of operations sets no requirements beyond 'bilingualism' for the teachers, but specifies that the project secretary must be proficient in writing both languages: 'Accurate spelling and punctuation is a priority need for the secretary.'

A quick look at what the other-medium teachers and aides are usually expected to do affirms the weakness of their training. 'They are expected to teach through the non-English tongue such subject fields as mathematics, science, the social studies, and language arts.' There is a common belief that the person who speaks two languages can say anything in one that he can say in the other. That is simply not true. The most common situation finds such a speaker facile in one or more 'domains' of usage in one language, and in other domains in the other. Perhaps small talk and intimacy in one, business and formality in the other. Facility in the terminology of a game or a sport or a technology in one language, expression of religious feeling in the other. Arithmetic in only one. Professional matters in only one. Everyday affairs can probably be conducted in either, but no one can stand up and invent authentic translations of mathematics teaching terminology or the terminology of any other school subject.

'They are expected in most of the projects to create or assist in the creation of teaching materials in the non-English tongue.' Little need be said here to make the point. It is currently lauded pedagogy to encourage teachers to choose freely among teaching materials and adapt them as needed in order to adjust to the pupils' individual differences, but how many teachers can be expected to write their own books? A few project plans of operation gave examples of locally produced writing in the other tongue. Some were well done. Most are exemplified by the following:

A formal letter:
Hemos estado trabajando bajo considerable obstáculos con respeto a la escritura de la proposición ... La fecha ... adelantada dos días para darles el beneficio de discusiones...

A printed announcement:
Si Ud. desea conversar con el professor, por favor márquelo
en el espacio destinado a ello.... Su firma justificará que
Ud. revisó la libreta de notas ... Poner una nota es algo muy
importante en la Escuela, además de ser el deseo de las
Escuelas Públicas de _____, a fin de interpretar mejor
a los alumnos y ayudar así a los padres.... Para un avance
satisfactorio, es indispensable una asistencia regular y a
tiempo.... Hábitos De trabajo Significa que siempre debe
estar preparado con sus materiales y tareas, siga y escuche
las direcciones que se le dan.

A formal letter to the parents:
... Uds. puede ayudar a su niño tener éxito en el colegio.

A formal printed announcement:
Hablando diariamente, escuchando, leyendo y escribiendo,
son las pericias del idioma inglés.... Substantivos vívidos
y verbos como canyon y amontonar se acentúan.

Educational theory about success in school:
El suceso de un niño ...

Teaching materials:
Si alguien en un carro quiere que vaya con el, tenga cortes,
pero marchase y no entre su carro.
Maria, agarra tres pelotas. Ensename dos modos para
decirme que tienes tres pelotas.

Formal publication:
Advancemos: Mano en Mano

Must one be a pedant to be disturbed by these examples of inordinate
influence from English and violation of the structure of Spanish? I
think not, for the implication in all but possibly one of the Title VII project plans is that the other-language medium, whether Spanish, Cantonese, French, or whatever, will be its 'standard' form. No one has
yet claimed that San Francisco Cantonese, the Portuguese of Providence, and the Spanish of San Antonio are separate linguistic systems
whose exquisite aberrations should be polished and respected and set
apart from the vulgar standard by their own contrastive analyses.
One plan states that its bilingual teacher aides will be trained in 'standard South American Spanish'. The exception noted calls for someone
to prepare 'material in barrio Spanish', but not to the exclusion of
standard writings.

In one plan the measurement of behavioral objectives includes listening to tapes of three sentences each in Castilian Spanish and British English and repeating them in 'Mexican Spanish' and 'United States English'. This particular plan of operation emphasizes speech and drama at the junior high school level.

Since almost all of the project plans require the same bilingual teachers to be responsible for both the non-English and the English side of the program, these teachers are expected to represent and present authentically, fully, fairly, two cultures: that of the United States and that of the non-English mother tongue child's forbears. In most cases they must somehow interpret a third culture, the amalgam, because the Puerto Ricans in continental United States, and Mexican-Americans and Franco-Americans find that their cultural patterns are in essential ways different from either of the two parent cultures.

It is at the bastion of biculturalism rather than at the bastion of language alone that bilingual education will succeed or fail, and it is here that the doubts gnaw most painfully.

First of all, is it fair to expect a product of the amalgam, a product of the educational system and policy which bilingual education seeks to correct, to represent fairly and powerfully both of the parent cultures? Does not biculturalism—a word which appears repeatedly in the projects' aims—imply double perspective, not the perspective of two eyes, but of two pairs of eyes? The use of the same persons to explicate both cultures—rather than two sets of persons, one for the English medium and United States culture, one for the non-English medium and the culture it carries—is matched in a number of project plans by the decision to have the teachers and aides themselves produce the classroom materials dealing with the other history and culture. In some projects the history books and others in this area will be translations of United States, English language texts.

The following examples illustrate some of the ambivalence and uncertainty regarding the other-tongue history and culture:

> One project means to establish in the children 'a detachment towards the Spanish and English languages to enable the student to function in either his native or Anglo-Culture (sic) whenever he so chooses.' Can language be thus successfully detached from culture?

> One program 'encompasses bilingualism with diglossia', by which is meant '... the socio-cultural context in which language learning takes place.' But 'many children's books have been translated into Spanish' (not, it should be understood, by the project's personnel) and 'children's songs, singing games, and rhythmic activities will be translated into Spanish ... '

In one plan the Mexican-American child is expected, on completion of the 'Texas Government and History' course through Spanish, to demonstrate 'respect for himself as an individual by over (sic) acceptance of various levels of ability and differing physical characteristics in others.' Could this be the same as acceptance of one's lot?

'Cultural readings for literature, interdisciplinary materials from the social sciences and science materials will be translated (to Spanish) and modified for language instruction.' Yet the purpose of these culturally oriented materials is supposedly to develop pride in the child's own heritage, to give him a new point of view, not merely the same one presented through another language.

In still another project, the teacher responsible for bicultural activities must have a high degree of competency in both tongues 'because of requirements of both accurate and idiomatic translations.'

As noted, the applicant for a Title VII bilingual education project has the right to propose the degree of emphasis on the non-English language and culture that his wisdom dictates. This is not the same, however, as declaring intention to do one thing and then, unwittingly, describing conditions which can be expected to frustrate that intention.

One project expects to develop the ability of all children, both N-EMT and EMT (English mother tongue), to pursue ordinary school subjects in either language, but it will teach the language arts and mathematics to N-EMT children in that tongue only enough to avoid retardation.

One project seeks 'to develop his (the child's) ability to function in and through two languages' and develop his 'competence needed to employ two linguistic systems separately and consciously as mediums for speaking (reading and writing) and thinking in the total curriculum ... ' But in the third year of the project, reading in Spanish will be included only if sufficient funding is available and community approval can be determined, and such subjects as mathematics will be taught in English only. Two other projects are virtually identical in this respect.

A hint of some notion of the concept of diglossia comes in one plan of operation which seeks to develop 'coordinate bilingualism'. The plan states that ' ... those areas in which the student must succeed in high school and college—for example, mathematics—will be taught in English ... ' and 'those areas which the student associates with his own background, for example, native literature ... ' will be taught in Spanish.

One project means to 'develop curriculum authentic in respect to Mexican-American culture, ' but for the program development specialists there is a formal requirement of expertise in setting 'behavioral objectives' and no such requirement as a knowledge of Spanish.

One project aims at a 'true, balanced bilingual program', but 'English will become the major medium of instruction during the second grade. '

In one of the plans, which provides work through the N-EMT in language, mathematics, and the social studies, only the aides are bilingual. The children show that they are learning 'by responding in classes where the real teacher is Anglo to or through translators (sic) if necessary. '

The plans of operation of the 76 projects are not entirely clear about the amount of time that will be devoted each day to instruction using the N-EMT as the medium. There is uncertainty on this point because the expression 'bilingual program' sometimes means both tongues, sometimes only the N-EMT. Thus, in one, the 'bilingual' part is four hours daily, but the breakdown, during the first quarter year, is three hours of ESL, and one of history taught through English and the N-EMT; and during the second quarter there are two hours of ESL, and two hours of history divided between the two languages. At least four programs favor the N-EMT. Thirty-four are either bridges or favor English markedly. Only six aim eventually to provide bilingual schooling at all grade levels, 1-12.

One project seems to have scheduled only 10-15 minutes' work daily in the other language. Another aims 'to provide an opportunity for any student to become truly bilingual', yet it schedules only 25 minutes daily for the mother tongue as a medium.

The adverse criticism explicit and implied in much of the foregoing is not the whole story. Many strong, promising features are to be found among the 76 projects.

Both Albuquerque and Grants, New Mexico, see clearly that mere bilingualism does not prepare a teacher for this work.

Brentwood, California makes a point of the need for full literacy in both languages for teachers and aides.

Chicago makes two important points: (1) that the 'bilingual' is not necessarily 'bicultural' and may not be able to interpret fairly the other culture; for this purpose they want foreign exchange teachers, and (2) they clearly separate the languages, one in the morning, the other in the afternoon. New Haven also stresses the importance of not mixing the languages during a single class period.

One of the Del Rio, Texas projects has called on experienced teachers from Mexico for help with Spanish-medium tests, and has planned one three-day in-service training session in Acuña, Mexico. Edinburg, Texas arranged for its teacher trainers and the teacher in charge of Spanish language literacy to come from Mexico.

Gonzalez, California sees the importance of employing teachers who are 'conversant with Spanish language approaches to the subjects taught', and declares that its staff 'will make an effort to avoid producing materials in areas where specialized professional competence is of prime importance.' The Naples, Florida project also stresses the employment of teachers able to give training through Spanish in all subject areas.

The Lansing project expects its other-medium teachers to have the baccalaureate and both bilingual and bicultural skills: ' ... ability to discuss in Spanish some of the major language learning problems of the bilingual child and the history and culture of the Spanish-speaking American. '

Laredo, Texas (Laredo Independent School District) seemingly alone among the projects, recognizes the extra burdens of dual-medium teachers and has budgeted an annual bonus of 300 dollars for each one. Its plan also calls for bringing from Mexico a special teacher to be in charge of staff and materials development. The Laredo project's bilingual teachers are required to take the Modern Language Association Proficiency Test (in Spanish) for teachers and advanced students.

The Laredo, Texas (United Consolidated Independent School District) bilingual teachers all have earned at least 21 college semester hours in Spanish.

The New York Bronx project includes a six-weeks summer extension, three hours daily, alternating the languages, in language, reading, and mathematics. The New York Two Bridges project plan offers half of each day for native tongue subject matter classes, and views itself as building a bridge not to English, but on which the children can move easily back and forth.

The Providence, Rhode Island plan seeking to assure that the N-EMT children develop full capacity for conceptualization through the mother tongue, gives less than equal time to English until the participants are in their fourth year of school. English as a second language study begins, nevertheless, in grade one, and they expect to achieve beginning literacy in English in grade two. They employ different teachers for each medium and secure educated, experienced trainers from abroad for the N-EMT work.

Milwaukee sees the importance of uniting its bilingual schooling project with the efforts of its regular foreign language teachers at the high school level, and will offer a history and culture course for both groups of students together.

The Rochester project provides different teachers for each of the mediums, insists on high literacy of all teachers and aides, plus demonstrated ability to teach school subjects through Spanish, and keeps the languages separated in time and place.

Whatever the strengths, whatever the weaknesses of the 76 bilingual schooling projects (and this essay gleaned from written accounts rather than direct observation cannot describe them with complete certainty), they need help. If bilingual schooling, the noblest innovation in American education, is to succeed, it must have close, objective, encouraging attention from all sides. The projects need, above all else, formative evaluation by knowledgeable outside observers who—with the gentle pressure of the Office of Education's authority and responsibility to continue each grant only so long as the work is performed satisfactorily—can help each project to become a model of its kind. Without radical strengthening some could probably never become models. They should either be strengthened or abandoned.

Bilingual schooling needs assistance from research-oriented scholars and other investigators who will answer some of the questions which project directors and teachers are asking:

(1) How can project directors ascertain quickly and fairly the degree of scholarly competence of persons who might be employed as teachers or aides in the non-English medium?

(2) How can the difference between requiring teachers to work through two languages and having separate teachers for each of the languages be made plain? (The cost is not a serious factor, for the length of the school day is fixed and each teacher usually works alone with a class at any given time.)

(3) Bearing in mind the plague of constant borrowing and interference between the tongues in bilinguals who do not maintain separate domains in their lives for each tongue, how can the relative merit of keeping them separate (or mixing them) in respect to time, place, and teacher in the school be determined?

(4) What are the administrative and legal impediments to bringing able, experienced teachers and other personnel from abroad, and how can they be overcome?

(5) How can school materials of all kinds be produced for teaching American Indian children their own languages and through those languages as mediums of instruction?

(6) There is need for a means of measuring the extent to which N-EMT children—even very young children—possess and control that tongue.

(7) There is a great need for a search abroad for teaching materials written originally in the other language, both corresponding to the regular school curriculum in the project schools, and dealing with the 'history and culture' of the N-EMT child's people and their forbears as viewed by themselves through their own language.

There are questions of methodology. Millions of young children three to eight or thereabouts have learned a second language in a complete, effortless, largely mysterious way, but the literature contains no record of anyone's having 'taught' one to a child.

(8) The main problem is to maintain at maximum effectiveness the circumstances which are known to facilitate natural learning by children when the new language is the necessary, unavoidable means to their involvement in pleasant, significant situations far beyond language itself, and still permit experimentation with highly structured lessons (drill, etc.) designed to increase the speed of learning.

(9) Should parents whose English (or any other language) is heavily flawed be asked to speak English to their small children as a means of helping them learn that language?

Their efforts will tend to offset those of the child's English teacher, and their failure to stress the mother tongue will offset the efforts of the mother tongue teacher.

(10) What is the minimum amount of language contact time short of which children's ability to learn naturally a second language becomes ineffective? (One of the 76 bilingual schooling projects schedules only a 10-15 minute period daily for the second language.)

Beyond the concern for developing and refining the 76 projects and others like them and realizing, in school, the full potential of bilingual education, there are broader concerns yet unvoiced for the role of the non-English tongues—certainly this is applicable to Spanish—in the streets, the shops, the offices, the homes. Put otherwise, is it really possible to make a child vigorously literate in his mother tongue if that vigor and literacy are not somehow matched in public places and in the homes? Do children really read eagerly and widely if their parents read reluctantly and seldom? If there are very few books, few newspapers and almost no magazines? Can two languages co-exist stably in the same speakers and be expected to serve exactly the same purposes? Will not bilingual schooling, if it succeeds in raising the educational level of the bilinguals, thereby increase their control of English, their social and geographical mobility and so hasten the disappearance of the other tongue?

These are concerns for the adults, the parents, the intellectuals and, yes, for teachers of these tongues as 'foreign' languages. 'Bilingual education', we saw earlier, can serve the ends of either ethnocentrism or cultural pluralism.

NOTES

[1] The author gratefully acknowledges much help and cooperation from the Office of Education staff which administers the Bilingual Education Act. Since their inception the projects have undergone constant modification to improve their effectiveness.

DISCUSSION

Gerard Hoffman, Yeshiva University: I was particularly gratified to hear Dr. Gaarder's remarks, especially in light of his initial comment that the programs are supposed to focus on those whose mother tongue is not English. In observing our own project and in planning for the future—we are located in first grade at the moment and we expect to expand down and upward from kindergarten through grade 5 eventually—and in talking to people involved in other Title VII programs besides ours, I find that there is some sort of contradiction in the use of the term 'bilingual education', especially in the minds of the people on the Board of Education with whom we have to deal, and the people in the local schools, namely the warning that Dr. Fishman made this morning that through Title VII Bilingual Education we are creating a monolingual people in English. I see that by use of the term 'bilingual education' instead of 'mother tongue instruction' there has been some confusion on the part of some people, and I wonder if Dr. Gaarder or somebody else in the Office of Education would comment on that.

Gaarder: I would like to have Miss Moore, who really knows more about this than I do, comment. Let me say this before she does begin, that I feel ashamed because it seems that I have, and I have indeed, emphasized some negative aspects. I simply ran out of time; the full paper will be published.

Margaret Moore, U. S. Office of Education: Would you repeat, please?

Hoffman: It seems to me that there is some confusion in the case of people we should be trying to reach—the nonlanguage teachers, the educators who are not versed in the field of bilingualism. There is some confusion in their minds as to the purpose of the bilingual act. I believe many of them feel that it is to create, not a bilingual community among the various groups that we are dealing with, but to give them a basic education in their native language with the eventuality of making them English speakers, or finishing their education in English rather than fostering bilingualism throughout the grades. There seems to be a tendency on the part of local educators to see bilingual education phasing out as you go up the grades.

Moore: There are various patterns of bilingual education throughout the Title VII projects. Some projects are following the approach that he has described. There are others that are not, but which are following a full bilingual program. Some projects have chosen not to develop an ideal, all-grades bilingual program. Perhaps for some the reason for choosing another pattern is related to the matter of educating school people in terms of attitudes and awareness of what bilingual education is. Perhaps for some the reason is related to their own analysis of local needs. I admit there are a variety of patterns depending on local needs, etc. Yet there are still those who are following the full bilingual concept.

The law stresses the use of at least two languages, and one of those languages must be English since that is one tool that the students will need in order to function in our society. But the law doesn't spell out specifically which patterns should be followed. Projects discovered early in the first year of operation that there is a problem choosing the pattern best suited to their needs. However, a pattern that is only an English as a Second Language program is not recognized by us as being the same as a bilingual education program.

Robert Lado, Georgetown University: This is Lado from Georgetown, a bilingual. I visited four or five or six—I don't know how many —of these 76 projects with Dr. Andersson and a number of others about a year ago, and I think that I share with Dr. Gaarder the high ideals that he has. I would like to see this America of ours really get there quickly, but I think that if he expects these first projects to achieve these ideals from the start, he is going to impose some impossible demands on this bilingual program, and I would like to give a little testimony, a couple of minutes.

I will mention two things I discovered when we visited these projects in San Antonio that may give us the magnitude of these problems, and then some very optimistic impressions. First, the taxi driver who took me to the hotel was a bilingual Mexican speaker, and I made him talk. I wanted to know how he felt about bilingualism, and he had very strong ideas. He said he did not want his daughter to study Spanish (he told me this in Spanish) because he wanted his daughter to marry a big shot from Washington. And I told him that I was from Washington, but that I was married and had many children, and besides that I liked studying Spanish and English. The problem, then, is that this negativism toward bilingual education is all over, and I do not think we can expect these 76 projects to change the United States from top to bottom overnight. This is asking too much, and if Dr. Gaarder is asking that much, then we are all going to fail and we might as well forget it. But we can expect other things.

I saw some schools where the bilingual programs were going on, and in one school I saw children watching four tubes with a transparent, colorless liquid in them, and they were being asked to reason, to see if they could discover if these four tubes had the same kind of liquid in them—they all looked like water. A child would make a statement, and he or she would be asked to come up to the front of the class and do something to the tubes—smell them, shake them, or pour them into something else—and the material inside the tubes would do different things. Then they would proceed to another step of reasoning in Spanish concerning some introduction to science. Then English-speaking children would do this in Spanish also, and Spanish-speaking children would do this in English in another class. To me this was so exciting that I said (and this is what Dr. Fishman says), 'I wish that my children could have the advantage of this kind of bilingual growth in intellectual as well as linguistic material.' Of course the answer was, 'Your children cannot have this because they are not in the poverty category.' And this is Dr. Fishman's recommendation, that we should strive to expand the bilingual education to those who are not in this $3,000 a year family income bracket. This is the optimistic impression which I got.

Then, on the negative side: In that same school I went to the library; I wanted to see how many books they had in Spanish, and the librarian didn't know. So I located Ferdinand the Bull in Spanish, and a couple of others like that. In my report to the office staff, I asked if something could be done about getting more Spanish books, or French books, or whatever, and I was encouraged by the tremendous effort that is being made to do this. This year, for example, a major program is going on to get Spanish books from all over the world into these schools.

Another impression on the negative side: In one school into which I walked, all the heroes on the walls were those heroes who became famous by fighting and beating the grandparents of the bilinguals in school. I assure you that my heart beat more slowly. The atmosphere according to the pictures was not bilingual or bicultural. On the other hand, in another school in the same district the pictures were bicultural, so much so that one of the members of the visiting team begged to see if he could get some of these pictures, and I think they are now hanging in Hawaii.

I think the situation is very promising. We cannot expect these 76 projects to turn America around overnight, but there is enough of a dawn here that we should support it at this time.

Eleanor Sandstrom, Title VII Project Director in Philadelphia: May I just try to get a statement across, because I am concerned about what Dr. Lado has just said, and I am very concerned that this fear of turning America around too soon is going to help the baby die instead of helping the baby grow. And one of my tremendous concerns is for some more directional effort from U.S.O.E. to support those areas where we are committed to bilingual education and 'real bilingual education for both Anglo and Latino children in our particular city', and where we are trying to teach children in both languages, and we continually have to answer to the climate of school administrators who are concerned about whether these things are good or bad for their children. I would hope that groups such as TESOL and the Linguistic Society will support the things that both Dr. Fishman and Dr. Gaarder had to say here today.

BILINGUAL EDUCATION PROGRAM IN IRELAND: RECENT EXPERIENCES IN HOME AND ADULT SUPPORT, TEACHER TRAINING, PROVISION OF INSTRUCTIONAL MATERIALS

COLMÁN L. Ó HUALLACHÁIN

Linguistic Institute of Ireland

Abstract. The 13th Round Table Meeting heard Father Ó Huallacháin's views on Bilingual Education in Ireland, when he spoke of applied linguistics as a key to possible improvements in the system.

In the light of experiences since 1962 he now speaks of further use to be made of advances in the language sciences.

The Irish bilingual education program has characteristics profoundly different from some of those listed under Section III of The Bilingual Education Program Title VII, Elementary and Secondary Education Act of 1965, as amended. Section IV, however, lists certain activities which have recently received special attention in Ireland:

Establishment of closer cooperation between the school and the homes of children in the bilingual program;

Preservice and inservice training to prepare persons participating in bilingual education programs as teachers;

Development and dissemination of special instructional materials.

1.1 Speaking at the 13th Annual Round Table Meeting (1962) on 'Bilingualism in Education in Ireland'[1] I described the decline of the ancestral Irish language and the adoption of a variety of English by the vast majority of the population, and I told of the 40-year-old policy of the Irish Government to restore Irish as a means of ordinary communication all over the country. I remarked that anybody acquainted with the factors involved would expect that the attainment of such an aim

would have required at least as much expense, research, and adjustment of administration as was provided for national defense, electri-
fication, housing, exploitation of fuel and mineral resources, but that
nobody could seriously allege that such efforts had been made.

1.2 There is no need for me now to modify either that account of
the general situation or the following observation which I made on the
particular subject we are dealing with: 'Bilingualism is more a feature
of the schools than of life outside them, and this is having its inevitable
repercussions on the work of the schools.'[2]

1.3 During the past eight years, however, statements of policy and
advances in the language-related sciences have been made about certain
activities which are listed under Section IV of the United States <u>Bilin-
gual Education Program Title VII, Elementary and Secondary Education
Act of 1965, as amended,</u> and though the Irish bilingual program has
characteristics profoundly different from those listed under Section III
of that document, it may be of interest to give an outline of our recent
experiences in connection with: (1) establishment of closer cooperation
between the school and the homes of children in the bilingual program;
(2) preservice and inservice training to prepare persons participating
in bilingual education programs as teachers; and (3) development and
dissemination of special instructional materials.

2.1 For the vast majority of pupils, Irish is learned at school as a
second language. It is the first official language of the Republic of
Ireland; English is also an official language. Government policy was
reaffirmed in a White Paper published in 1965:

> The national aim is to restore the Irish language as a gen-
> eral medium of communication[3] ... Nevertheless, for a con-
> siderable time ahead, English will remain the language chief-
> ly used outside the Gaeltacht (Irish-speaking areas) for var-
> ious purposes. ... Because of our geographic position and the
> pattern of our economic and social relationships, a competent
> knowledge of English will be needed even in a predominantly
> Irish-speaking Ireland. With effective use of modern teach-
> ing methods and facilities ... the standards of literacy and
> fluency required in English for all our needs can be main-
> tained and general educational standards raised, while our
> knowledge of Irish is advanced and its use extended to realize
> the national aim ... No Irish child can be regarded as fully
> educated if he grows up without a knowledge of the Irish lan-
> guage. The educational system will be seriously defective if
> it does not provide for the teaching of Irish to all children...[4]

2.2 Official policy on the use of Irish as a medium of instruction is
as follows:

The Minister for Education considers that it is not advisable that a general plan to secure teaching through Irish in all schools should be drawn up until further investigation of the general effects of teaching through a language other than the home language have been made. [5]

The use of Irish as a medium of instruction for other subjects in primary schools will be allowed by the Department of Education only when the teacher is competent to give such instruction and where the pupils have sufficient Irish to profit by it. [6]

3.1 Mackey's typology of bilingual education[7] is a considerable help towards describing our present system so that it can be related meaningfully to others (though adequate means are not yet available to us for quantifying variables). It also helps to show clearly the extent of the problems to be faced in Ireland in matters such as teaching a second language which may be used as a medium of instruction, and enlisting or maintaining home and adult support at this stage of a bilingual programme which has been in operation for decades.

3.2 In the half dozen areas where Irish can still be said to be the dominant medium of communication between a total of between 50,000 and 100,000 people (out of a population of 4 million in Ireland, 3 million of them being in the Republic), the system is as follows: Children from bilingual homes (Irish dominant) attend 210 primary and 30 postprimary schools in which Irish is the sole medium of instruction (though there is still a serious lack of textbooks in Irish at postprimary level, so that English language textbooks are used in certain subjects). English is taught as a subject in all these schools. The surrounding area is bilingual, but Irish still dominates. The nation as a whole is, practically speaking, monolingual (English); but there is fairly widespread knowledge of Irish and some is used (see 7.3 to 7.5).

3.3 Three patterns can be discerned in the rest of the country.

3.4 A. In the six counties of Northern Ireland, there are no bilingual schools. In the hour and a half per week allowed for optional studies from 4th to 7th standards, 156 primary schools (out of a total of 1,369) taught Irish as a subject in 1967-68. At postprimary level Irish was taught as a subject in 34 grammar schools (out of 80) and in 33 intermediate schools (out of 66). [8] The area is monolingual (English).

3.5 In the Republic of Ireland also the majority of schools are single medium English; but Irish is taught as a subject in the vast majority of them (in all 4,450 primary schools and 861 postprimary schools —596 secondary, 262 vocational, 3 comprehensive—which receive Government support). [9] Home-school-area-nation pattern is as follows: Home—monolingual English (small minority bilingual or monolingual Irish); school—single medium English (with some official encouragement to use Irish as the medium of school organization, communication between staff and between staff and pupils); area—usually monolingual English; nation (see section 1.2).

3.6 B. In 427 of the primary and 108 of the secondary schools the pattern is: Home—monolingual English (small minority bilingual or monolingual Irish); school—dual medium, but unfortunately so far no precise analysis has been made of the courses and number of courses taught through each medium; area—usually monolingual English; nation (see section 1.2).

3.7 C. Finally, there are 69 of the primary schools and 51 of the secondary schools in which the pattern is: Home—monolingual English, or bilingual, or monolingual Irish; school—single medium Irish (with English taught as a subject and the anomaly of English textbooks being used for certain courses, though the classroom instruction is through the medium of Irish); area—monolingual English; nation (see section 1.2).

3.8 It is not possible to ascertain now the number of people in Ireland who have been educated according to the above patterns of schooling. However, an indication of the position is to be found in the results of a postal questionnaire sent to 924 people (who had already been interviewed as a random sample of the population of the Republic).[10] The response rate to the questionnaire was 75%, 686 persons. 93% of those who answered said they could not speak Irish before they went to school. At primary school 99% were taught Irish as a subject. In 46% of cases Irish was also used as a medium of instruction. Only 8% did all their subjects (except English) through Irish, but 38% did some subjects through Irish. 40% of the respondents attended postprimary schools. 36% learned Irish as a subject. 17% used it as a medium in other subjects also—6% in all other subjects (except English), 11% in some other subjects.

4.1 For more than half a century the training of teachers of Irish as a second language in primary and postprimary vocational schools has been deeply influenced by advocates of the Direct Method. Such teachers are now being provided with planned and pre-tested materials to make it easier for them to put their principles of teaching into action more efficiently and consistently as soon as they have been introduced to certain modifications of technique. In the case of some secondary teachers, a somewhat more radical adjustment is necessary as their formation often did not give such prominence to teaching language for communication. Preservice and inservice courses for all teachers provide training in the use of the new materials. Our experience is that the success of such training depends on the prior provision of teaching materials in which the teachers have confidence. If training in the teaching of English and in the use of a second language as a medium of instruction still require attention, it is partly because a certain amount of linguistic work and further development of materials seem to be a necessary prerequisite.

5.1 Urgency and lack of personnel caused the major part of recent activity to be directed towards improving the teaching of Irish, but there is a keen awareness of the need for improvement in the teaching of English. Indeed a start has been made experimentally on the provision of planned aids for helping native speakers of Irish and speakers of rural varieties of Hiberno-English to gain a confident command of a variety of the language more acceptable in domains in which they felt themselves socially disadvantaged, because of the influence of the ancestral language on their spoken English. [11]

5.2 One result of this may be a help in maintaining the pattern of bilingual schooling characteristic of Irish-speaking areas (single-medium Irish with English as a subject) and reduction of possible opposition to favoring the extension of dual-medium or single-medium Irish schooling elsewhere. A common cause for lack of support for the privileged position of Irish has been the fear of undue lowering of standards in English. Studies[12] in this area have highlighted a problem which has to be faced, assessed, and solved in the light of behavior and attitudes in Ireland. Opportunities for making the relevant assessments and proposing solutions based on objective evidence are developing, but only gradually.

6.1 Seven years ago the government appointed an applied linguist to make a study of contemporary spoken Irish in Irish-speaking areas, so as to provide a basis for scientific planning of the teaching of the language to nonnative speakers. As a result of collaboration with the staff of the Department of Education, Inspectors and Teachers, and scholars from other academic institutions, teachers and learners now have been provided with:

(1) A phonemic analysis of the target language, with a textbook[13] and taped course to prepare teachers to give instruction correctly on the sounds of Irish; also directives for pronunciation based on structural dialectology[14] (certain experimental work on this matter is still incomplete).

(2) A computerised analysis of the vocabulary, morphology, syntax of hundreds of thousands of words of conversational Irish. The result, Buntús Gaeilge I[15] (Foundations and beginnings of Irish), is the basis of a complete audio-lingual-visual course for primary schools, each stage of which was tried out under the supervision of inspectors in at least 100 schools and modified as a result of suggestions by teachers and inspectors before being made available generally. This course is now in use in every primary school (outside Irish-speaking areas) in the Republic (about 4,500 schools). An

additional remedial course was prepared and is being used in postprimary schools where pupils had not reached the standard now being aimed at as a result of the 'new methods'.

6.2 One of the practical advantages sought from the above projects was the attainment of uniformity of target in the organized teaching of Irish as a second language: all were directed to pay attention first to mastery of definite structures which objective research had indicated as being most useful for communication with native speakers conversing on ordinary topics. This degree of uniformity has allowed various agencies—commercial firms included—to produce ancillary materials such as workbooks, language games, and fiction books which are acceptable to learners from end to end of the country.

6.3 A second advantage was a greater ease in linking extra-school teaching to what goes on in the school system—thus providing for parental help and encouragement to children as well as adult retention or reactivation of Irish learned at school. The first application of this idea took the form of a popular language-learning course on radio and television (with accompanying booklets)[16] in 1967-68.

7.1 Buntús (Foundations and beginnings of Irish) on a nationwide television program for a year and a half provided a definite widely-known talking point which served as the point of departure for an exploration of the possibilities of another aspect of research which is urgently needed in our situation—seeking information about popular reactions and results. Through association with research designed to elicit information about the television program and its future development, it was possible for educators to employ (to a limited degree) survey techniques so as to get indications of: (1) self-assessment of Irish-language attainment and use of Irish among the people in general, and (2) domains in which Irish is considered most likely to be acceptable as a medium.

7.2 The survey, based on a probability sample of 1,200 adult individuals (aged 15 years and over) living in the Republic of Ireland, was carried out by Irish Marketing Surveys Limited on behalf of and in collaboration with the Linguistic Institute of Ireland. It was preceded by nondirective interviews in the form of group discussions (eight of which were conducted during April and May 1968 with mixed groups of men and women who were selected to be representative of those who had the opportunity to get acquainted with the teaching program—on TV, radio, or in the booklets). Findings and hypotheses which resulted from these groups formed the basis of a structured questionnaire which was first used in a pilot survey among 40 individuals, then modified in accordance with indications thus obtained and finally used in 924 interviews between 26th July and 16th August, 1968.[17]

7.3 Of the total sample (924 respondents), 18% said they did not study Irish at school. (However, 3% of those who did not study Irish at school said that they were either fluent or fairly fluent in the language, and 12% said they had some knowledge of it. 85% of them said they had no Irish.)

Irish was studied at school by 82% of the total sample (924). 50% took it at primary school only, 29% at postprimary as well, while 3% learned Irish outside school or pursued it to university level. [18]

32% of the total sample said they knew no Irish; 53% claimed to know some; 11% said they were fairly fluent, and 4% that they were fluent. [19] Self-assessment of present competence was as follows in relation to the level to which the language was studied at school:

Of the 50% who learned it at primary:
　9% fluent/fairly fluent
　63% some knowledge
　27% no knowledge
Of the 29% who learned it at postprimary also:
　33% fluent/fairly fluent
　61% some knowledge
　6% no knowledge
Of the 3% who studied Irish outside school or at the university:
　40% fluent/fairly fluent
　60% some knowledge

7.4 25% of the total sample claimed that Irish was spoken 'some of the time' in their homes. 1% said it was spoken 'much of the time', while another 1% said it was spoken 'all the time'. [20]

7.5 25% also said that they either spoke or read Irish at least occasionally nowadays. [21]

Of those, 82% said that they speak Irish on occasions such as the following: with friends (24%), public speaking/praying (22%), with children (22%), reckoning/praying/cursing (14%), with the family (10%), with teachers (5%), business (4%), in class, with school friends (4%), singing Irish songs (2%), with neighbors (2%), with people from Irish-speaking areas (1%), at work (1%). (Other occasions mentioned made up 6% of the answers.)

Of the same 25%, 72% said they listen to Irish: on radio/television (56%), in conversation (30%), at school (1%). (Other answers 4%).

Of that 25% of the sample, 57% said they read some Irish: books (35%), periodicals (15%), application forms (2%). (Other answers 5%).

Of that 25%, 23% write Irish occasionally: correspondence (11%), schoolwork (7%). (Other answers 3%).

7.6 The 25% who speak or read Irish were asked if they found their knowledge of the language to be of any practical use to them, and more

than half (53%) answered affirmatively: helping children with homework (27%), talking to people in Irish when necessary (24%), help
towards getting a job (17%), reading official forms or documents (12%).

8.1 Linguistic work is now going on (Buntús II) to help provide the
bases for further courses in Irish for students who have assimilated
the basic structures (Buntús I) and so attained a degree of competent
and correct communication. An analysis is being made of Irish written by native speakers of the language and published over the last fifteen years. At the same time textbooks for teaching other subjects
through the medium of Irish are also being analysed to find out what
structures and vocabulary are required for each course and at each
level. This should facilitate testing to see if pupils have achieved a
sufficient command of the second language to pursue studies through
it profitably. At the same time those who teach Irish or who teach
through Irish can have their attention directed to points which need
careful watching if the advantages of doing studies through a second
language are not to be outweighed by pupils and teachers allowing
themselves to drift into substandard speech and writing when using
the new medium outside formal Irish classes.

8.2 Work has yet to commence on objective tests of language
achievement.

8.3 The possibilities of using social surveys to help in the preparation of instructional materials are also being explored. Each one
of a random sample of 924 persons[22] was confronted with sixteen hypothetical situations and asked to assess the likelihood of Irish being
used in them. Here is how the questions were asked: 'I am going to
read out a number of situations where people might or might not speak
Irish among themselves. I do not mean people who are necessarily
very fluent in Irish. As I read out each situation, please tell me how
likely it would be that a few short Irish phrases might be used.' Respondents were asked to express the extent of likelihood in each case,
using a five-point scale ranging from 'extremely likely' to 'most unlikely'. The situations are given in TABLE I in order of likelihood
(not in the order of presentation to respondents).

TABLE 1.

Situation	Likely	Fairly likely	Unlikely
People visiting Irish-speaking areas	86%	11%	3%
Talking to people who like to speak Irish	68%	22%	8%
Helping children with homework	58%	28%	12%

Situation	Likely	Fairly likely	Unlikely
At a Céilí (traditional social evening)	53%	23%	22%
Meeting of two old friends who had learned Irish together at school	48%	25%	27%
Thanking people for helping at a social function	40%	23%	47%
Talking with teacher when bringing children to and from school	37%	26%	36%
Irish people meeting abroad	35%	25%	40%
Talking to children going to or returning from school	34%	34%	31%
Crowd at a Gaelic (football, etc.) game	29%	27%	44%
Talking to an official—such as a post office official	17%	24%	58%
Saying grace before meals	15%	22%	61%
Talking on the telephone to a friend	7%	11%	82%
Asking for a ticket on bus	5%	10%	86%
In a restaurant (asking for a table, menu, bill)	3%	6%	90%
Visit to doctor	2%	5%	92%

Designers of materials for teaching Irish get some evidence from these figures to help them direct teaching towards the results which are seen as most likely to be useful (thus heightening the motivation of both learners and teachers). This is particularly necessary when the extra-school situation is having adverse repercussions on learning the second language. Similar attention to popular reactions to domains of use should prove fruitful also in choosing subjects to be taught through the medium of the second language.

NOTES

[1] Report of the Thirteenth Annual Round Table Meeting on Linguistics and Language Studies, Georgetown University, 1962, 75-84.

[2] Ibid., 77.

[3] The Restoration of the Irish Language, Government Stationery Office, Dublin, 1965, 4.

[4] Ibid., 4-5.

[5] Ibid., 106.

[6] Ibid., 12.

[7]William F. Mackey, 'A Typology of Bilingual Education', Report on National Conference on Bilingual Education, Washington, D. C., 1969, 25-52.

[8]Liam Mac an tSagairt, 'An Ghaeilge agus Cúrsaí Oideachais sa Tuaisceart', An Sagart, Winter 1968.

[9]These figures are for 1967-68; they include the schools in Irish-speaking areas mentioned above, 3.2.

[10]See below, 7.2.

[11]Planned for the Linguistic Institute of Ireland by Máirtín Ó Murchú, University College, Cork, and carried out in collaboration with him by Gearóid Ó Crualaoich of the same University College.

[12]John Macnamara, Bilingualism and Primary Education. A Study of Irish Experience, Edinburgh University Press, 1966. Seán Kelly, P. McGee, 'Survey of reading comprehension', New Research in Education, I (1967), 131-134.

[13]An tSr. Annuntiata le Muire and Colmán L. Ó Huallacháin, Bunchúrsa Foghraíochta, Government Stationery Office, Dublin, 1966.

[14]Máirtín Ó Murchú, 'Common Core and Underlying Forms, a suggested criterion for the construction of a phonological norm for Modern Irish', Ériu, XXI, 1969, 42-75.

[15]Buntús Gaeilge, Réamhthuarascáil, Government Stationery Office, Dublin, 1966.

[16]Tomás Ó Domhnalláin, Buntús Cainte, Government Stationery Office, Dublin, 1967.

[17]See Appendix 1.

[18]See Appendix 2, Table 2, also Appendix 3.

[19]See Appendix 2, Table 3.

[20]See Appendix 2, Table 4.

[21]See Appendix 2, Table 5.

[22]See above, 7.2.

APPENDIX 1

SURVEY: THE SAMPLE

(1) Method of selection. The survey was based on contacts with, and individual respondents sought from, a probability sample of 1,200 households or private dwellings in the Republic of Ireland.

Prior to sampling, the Republic was divided into its traditional geographical regions: County Dublin, Rest of Leinster, Munster, Connaught/Ulster. We selected 70 district electoral divisions, except in the case of 'urban districts' where the complete urban district formed single primary areas. In constituting a stratified list of primary samling areas from which the sample was drawn, several DED's in rural districts were grouped together to constitute a single primary area.

The purpose of this merging of DED's being to reduce the heterogeneity of population content of primary areas.

Copies of current electoral registers were obtained for all selected primary areas. These constituted a sampling frame for the selection of the required number of sample dwellings. Electors listed in institutions or in respect of business premises were excluded.

A sample of the remaining electors was drawn with equal probability —the number of electors selected being equal to the number of sample dwellings allocated to the relevant primary area.

On contacting the household or private dwelling selected, interviewers were instructed to list all the eligible respondents, aged 15 and over, in that household and select one individual for interview. The method adopted for the selection of the interviewee involved use of a Kish selection grid. Interviewers were not permitted to take any substitutes for such individuals selected but not interviewed.

Interviewers were instructed to make up to three calls at each address in order to establish contact with the household, and up to a further three calls, if necessary, to obtain an interview with the selected individual.

This report is therefore based on the 924 successful interviews carried out. This sample is broken down as follows:

UNWEIGHTED BASE:	924
Age	
15–24	138
25–34	145
35–44	174
45–54	167
55–64	126
65 and over	174
Social class (based on occupation of head of household)	
ABC1: upper, upper and lower middle class, white-collar occupations	174
C2DE: skilled, semi and unskilled working class and other low income households	406
F1: farmers or farm managers of 30 acres or more	218
F2: farmers having less than 30 acres, farm laborers	126
Sex	
Male	437
Female	487
Area	
County, borough	235
Other urban	148
Rural	541

Region	
Dublin	229
Rest of Leinster	204
Munster	275
Connaught/Ulster	216

(2) Weighting. The method of sampling meant that the sample of private dwellings was selected with probability proportional to the number of electors listed in the electoral registers for each dwelling. It was therefore necessary to correct this at the analysis stage by applying arithmetic weighting to each successful interview.

In applying these weight factors, it was assumed that each dwelling's probability of selection was also proportional to the number of persons, aged 21 and over, enumerated in the household during the contact interview.

It was also necessary to apply a further stage of weighting to correct for the differing chances of selection of the eligible respondents (all adults aged 15 and over) once the household had been contacted, to ensure that each individual should have an equal contribution to the final tabulation. The individual's chances of selection were of course determined by the total number of eligible individuals in that household.

In order to calculate the weight factors required, the interviewer enumerated both the number of adults aged 15 or over in each household, and also the number aged 21 and over. At the analysis stage each interview was therefore adjusted by one of the following weight factors: (1) the number of eligible adults in the household aged 16 and over, (2) the number of electors registered at that address.

Example: Weight factors given to interview.

	Number of persons in household aged 21 or more on last birthday:					
Number of persons aged 15 or over:	1	2	3	4	5	etc.
1	1.0					
2	2.0	1.0				
3	3.0	1.5	1.0			
4	4.0	2.0	1.3	1.0		
5	5.0	2.5	1.7	1.3	1.0	
etc.						

APPENDIX 2: TABLES

TABLE 2.

Base	Total	Sex		Age						Class			
		Male	Female	15-24	25-34	35-44	45-54	55-64	65+	ABC1	C2DE	F1	F2
All learning Irish at school	739	346	391	136	140	168	149	82	64	149	317	177	96
	%	%	%	%	%	%	%	%	%	%	%	%	%
Primary school	63	67	61	39	60	71	72	83	80	19	75	68	87
Secondary school	33	30	35	59	37	25	24	13	13	72	22	31	12
Classes outside school or university	4	4	4	2	6	2	4	3	6	11	3	1	1

TABLE 3.

Base: Total sample	Total	Sex		Age						Class			
		Male	Female	15-24	25-34	35-44	45-54	55-64	65+	ABC1	C2DE	F1	F2
	924	434	487	138	145	174	167	126	174	174	406	218	126
	%	%	%	%	%	%	%	%	%	%	%	%	%
Fluent	4	5	3	4	7	4	2	2	4	8	2	3	5
Fairly fluent	11	11	10	26	8	13	7	5	3	23	8	9	6
Some knowledge	53	51	55	59	66	66	60	42	23	49	54	56	50
No knowledge	31	32	30	11	20	17	31	50	66	19	35	30	37
Don't know/no reply	1	1	1	-	-	1	-	2	3	1	1	1	2

TABLE 4.

(Irish at home)	Total	Sex		Age						Class			
		Male	Female	15-24	25-34	35-44	45-54	55-64	65+	ABC1	C2DE	F1	F2
Base: Total sample	924	434	487	138	145	174	167	126	174	174	406	218	126
	%	%	%	%	%	%	%	%	%	%	%	%	%
All the time	1	2	1	1	1	3	∅	1	2	∅	2	-	4
Much of the time	1	1	∅	-	2	1	-	-	1	1	∅	-	1
Some of the time	25	22	27	29	28	30	31	16	10	34	28	13	21
Never	73	74	72	71	69	65	63	81	84	64	70	85	73
Don't know	∅	∅	∅	-	-	1	∅	2	3	∅	∅	2	2

TABLE 5.

(Do you read or speak Irish at all nowadays?)	Total	Sex		Age						Class			
		Male	Female	15-24	25-34	35-44	45-54	55-64	65+	ABC1	C2DE	F1	F2
Base: Total sample	924	434	487	138	145	174	167	126	174	174	406	218	126
	%	%	%	%	%	%	%	%	%	%	%	%	%
Yes	25	27	24	44	31	29	22	11	11	39	25	18	21
No	73	71	74	55	69	70	78	85	84	60	74	80	75
Don't know/no reply	2	2	2	1	-	1	∅	4	6	1	2	2	4

APPENDIX 3

Categories of secondary schools in which instruction is given through Irish (Source: Government Department of Education, Dublin):

A.1 Schools in which Irish is the medium of instruction in the subjects of the curriculum taught in the school (excepting English and modern languages insofar as these languages are taught through their own medium) and, in addition, is the ordinary language used by teachers and pupils.

A.2 Schools in which there are one or more class groups for whom Irish is the medium of instruction in all the subjects taken by them (excepting English and modern languages insofar as such languages are taught through their own medium) and, in addition, for whom Irish is the ordinary language used by both teachers and pupils.

B. Schools in which Irish is efficiently taught and in which at least one other subject is taught through Irish to one or more classes.

INTERFERENCE, INTEGRATION AND THE SYNCHRONIC FALLACY

WILLIAM F. MACKEY

International Center for Research on Bilingualism
Université Laval

Abstract. One of the most difficult operations in analyzing the language behavior of bilinguals is that of separating the integration of foreign elements into their code from the interference of such elements in the messages. The operation is made more difficult if it has to be performed within the framework fashioned by the fictitious synchronic/diachronic dichotomy. In place of this, the concept of language as an evolving code is more applicable to the analysis of the speech of bilinguals. A method is suggested to help distinguish interference from integration. Results of preliminary experimentation with the method are discussed.

The purposes of this paper are (1) to examine the effects of synchronic description in distinguishing between interference and integration in cases of language contact, and (2) to suggest alternative methods of description suitable for the analysis of systems in motion.

0. Introduction

Let me begin by adopting the now old-fashioned practice of introducing and defining my key terms. By interference, I mean the use of elements of one language or dialect while speaking or writing another; it is characteristic of the message. By integration I mean the incorporation into one language or dialect of elements from another; it is characteristic of the code. What I shall call the 'synchronic fallacy' is the belief that one can describe a language as if at any one point in time its code were stable.

We shall first consider the implications of (1) this 'synchronic fallacy', see how it relates to the distinction between (2) integration and interference, study the possible ways of (3) measuring integration, and analyse the quantitative relationship between (4) integration and availability with sample measurements.

1. The synchronic fallacy

A code is a convention. In language it is a social convention adopted by a speech community. But at any one point, certain elements of the code are preferred to others. At any one point in time, some language signs entering the code will be adopted quickly while others will be integrated gradually; any of these may disappear quickly or gradually, independently of their rate of adoption. Since the language code and its systems are in constant motion, the most appropriate description is not a synchronic analysis but a quantum description. Because a detailed treatment of this question would lead us into a discussion of general linguistic theory, which is evidently beyond the concern of this conference, I shall be content to refer to a recent paper which I have called 'Toward a Quantum Linguistics' (Mackey 1970b), and (1) to reproduce a remark which I made at the International Seminar on the Description and Measurement of Bilingualism in 1962 (Kelly 1969) on the limitations of synchronic description before explaining why it is not suited for describing (2) the entropy of evolving codes.

1.1 Limitations of synchronic descriptions

Almost all modern linguistic theories of language, including those of Saussure, Bloomfield, and Hjelmslev, have postulated a dichotomy between diachronic and synchronic linguistics. This postulate has been workable with the type of analysis made up to now—descriptive and historical grammars. But it is a fiction, ignorable only under two conditions: (a) where language change is so slow and minute as to be imperceptible within the same generation, and (b) where the refinement of analysis does not go beyond distinctive features.

Since language must evolve, there must be variation and vacillation; otherwise we would always be dealing with dead languages. The speed of language evolution through vacillation varies according to the social elements of control—likely to be different in illiterate and bilingual communities.

In bilingual communities, the incidence of interference contributes to the degree of vacillation, and consequently to the speed at which one or more of the languages or dialects evolve. So that degrees of change which in an unilingual situation will take many generations may, under the impact of bilingualism, be realized in one.

If this is the generation whose language use is being described, the investigator is faced with what appears to him either as interference or as a code with a high degree of free-variation. Both are illusions conditioned by the postulate that we are dealing with one or two synchronic codes. And the treatment of bilingual material as synchronic becomes more and more complex as one multiplies cases, because in any evolving code the degree of individual variation is a function of the rate of change.

And it is precisely the speed of this evolving code in situations of language contact that makes its description and measurement so difficult. What has to be described and measured is a two-dimensional continuum, one of which is continually alternating at the moment the other is inconsistently vacillating.

The point I want to make here is that this fiction of the synchronic, which has served so well in generating the abstractions of descriptive and transformational grammars, becomes quite unreal when used to describe the unstable and rapidly evolving systems of nonliterate communities and of languages in contact. This fallacy which assumes a fixed code or norm has led the students of language contact up a blind alley at the end of which was the impossibility of distinguishing between the two fundamental notions in the linguistic study of bilingualism, namely between integration and interference or, if you will, between interference in the code and interference in the message—since the same term has been used for both. This fiction of synchronic description has also made it difficult to determine when interference in the code is no longer interference, that is when it becomes part of the language. At what point, for example, did French words like <u>ignorance,</u> <u>nation,</u> <u>page,</u> <u>lingerie,</u> and <u>liqueur</u> become part of the English language?

Let us now go back to Saussure's original analogy where he compares a language to a game of chess, in which the state of the board is constantly changing according to certain fixed rules which the players must follow (Saussure 1915: 125-27). This is an often quoted analogy used to explain the classical dichotomy between diachronic and synchronic linguistics. The game can be described diachronically in terms of the moves of the players according to the rules, or synchronically in terms of the resulting distribution of the pawns on the board at any given point in time. The analogy and the dichotomy have indeed been useful as a basis for the elaboration of descriptive grammars and dictionaries of standardized languages, the very standardization of which is a factor in attenuating the natural variation and evolutionary tendencies of language.

Since few speakers will deviate greatly from the norm, and these may be limited to groups that are peripheral in space and time—dialects speakers, the very young and the very old—the number of people so deviating will not be in the majority, especially in those few languages which have a long tradition of standardization. Even for these highly standardized languages, the analogy is far from perfect, since if one were to freeze this linguistic game of chess at any point in time, in addition to finding some pawns in some squares and others in others, one would find a number of pawns between squares, some emerging ones on one edge and entering ones on the other edge of a number of squares, squares of different sizes and dimensions, pawns of different sizes, shapes and colors—bishops with the features of horses and horses becoming bishops—and procedures which were laxer or stricter than others in a game where the rules are forever changing.

1.2 The entropy of evolving codes

In other words, we would find a state of entropy, of continual transformation within the system. For all living languages are in a perpetual state of entropy—some more than others, and at some times more than at other times.

Repeated interference from another code tends to increase this entropy, whereas literacy and standardization tend to decrease it. Two related unwritten languages will tend to blend into one more quickly than will two equally related languages with standardized written forms used by most of their speakers. And in formally standardized codes, interference will reach the point of resistance earlier than in nonstandardized languages, for the gap between what speakers of standard languages say and what they know they should be saying becomes quickly more apparent and tends to promote in the literate community such formalized defenses as purism, irredentism, and language repression.

In the permissible range of variation in usage, the entropy of a language is affected by the degree of tolerance of the people who speak it. Some communities tolerate interference more than do others. This tolerance may have historical determinants; but it is also related to literacy, standardization and language contact. In nonliterate communities it may be wider than in literate societies. In unilingual communities, it may be less than in multilingual groups where the incidence of use of linguistic features from several languages by any individual may actually form a single continuum (Le Page 1968). And in nonliterate, multilingual groups, the range of tolerance may even become identical to mutual intelligibility achieved by a speech economy whose norm is the sum of all operant codes. In such situations, the new elements entering the speech of individuals from another language or dialect may do so entirely by chance and never be heard again; or they may be repeated with such consistency as to give the impression that they have been transferred to the other language and integrated into its code. Yet there is no indication in the occurrence of these elements in the stream of speech whether they represent such cases of integration or cases of interference. How then can one distinguish between integration and interference?

2. Integration and interference

One of the most difficult puzzles in the study of bilingualism has been the separation of cases of integration (borrowing) into the code from cases of interference in the message. It involves two problems: (1) the problem of identification, and (2) the problem of relativity.

2.1 The problem of identification

When we listen to an item from another language used in a stretch of speech, we have at first no direct way of knowing whether the item has been integrated into the code of the speaker or whether he is bringing it in from another code. We do not know whether the presence of the foreign item is the result of integration into the code or interference in the message.

It is indeed possible to study one independently of the other. The sorts of integration into the code, generally called language borrowing, have been masterfully classified and analysed by Haugen in a much quoted article (Haugen 1950). It has also been the subject of some extensive treatises (Deroy 1956).

Some indication of the integration of a word into the code may be had by observing the way it is used in the message. If it is combined with the native morphology and phonology it is likely to be more integrated than if it is not so used. For example, the English verb check when used in the French sentence, Il l'a checké hier, would indicate some degree of integration. So could a word whose pronunciation is made to conform to the phonological structure of the native language (e. g. Spanish estek from steak). But integration into the morphological and phonological systems is very often impossible to observe in any stretch of speech containing items from another language. For example, the English word cute in the French sentence, Elle est bien cute, could be a case of borrowing or a case of interference, if we had to rely only on textual evidence. Witness also the pronunciation of integrated trade names in the radio advertising of bilingual communities.

If a French-speaking bilingual uses the word sweater in a stretch of speech, we have no way of knowing whether the word sweater has replaced chandail in his French, or whether he is simply introducing this word from his English code for anyone of many possible social or psychological reasons. If we discover that he does not know the French

word for <u>sweater</u> and that the word <u>sweater</u> is his French way of saying <u>chandail,</u> we know that we are not up against a case of interference.
On the other hand, if he does know how to say <u>chandail</u> in French, this
may or may not be an indication that his use of the word <u>sweater</u> is a
case of interference. Here we are up against the question of bilingual
doublets such as were common in 13th and 14th century England, where
English words, like <u>help,</u> and their French equivalents, like <u>aid,</u> were
used indifferently and sometimes together. For the desire of the bilingual speaker to make himself understood by his fellow bilinguals
can induce him to use both his codes as an extra guarantee. We find
this even in the writings produced during the bilingual periods of a
country's history; in the literature of Medieval England, for example,
we can read such French-English stretches of bilingual redundancy as
<u>ignoraunce, thet is unwisdom (The Ancren Riwle, c. 1225), lord and</u>
<u>sire, faire and fetisly</u> (Chaucer), <u>olde and auncyent doctours, glasse</u>
<u>or mirrour</u> (Caxton). Were these cases of integration or of interfer-
ence?

2.2 The problem of relativity

Even in highly literate communities there is a permissible range of
variation in usage, and on close examination we find that instead of a
fixed code and a positive norm, we have an unstable code and a relative norm. The word 'norm' of course, can be ambiguous, meaning
either what people expect or what people do. Here we will take the
norm to mean what people do and say, not what they say they do. And
since all people do not always do the same things in the same ways,
the norm is relative. If it were not, languages would be eternal; they
would never change.

New elements are continually entering a language and old elements
are dropping out. But this intake and fallout is not sudden; it does not
happen the day a new grammar or dictionary comes off the press to
consecrate its contents as the norm. It is a gradual process which is
observable but not observed. It takes place in time at a rate which is
highly variable. And the variability of the rate is a function of numerous factors—some stable and others unstable.

The stable factors are all internal; that is, they have to do with the
nature of language and the nature of numbers. Their stability depends
on the characteristics of the system in which they operate and on its
dependence upon the other systems of the language. The fewer elements there are in the system, the more stable the system. A phonological system with less than a hundred units and a limited number
of structures is inherently more stable than a grammatical system
with a thousand units and more structures. For the number of phonemes in a language constitutes a very small class—usually much less

than a hundred items. The loss or addition of a single phoneme, therefore, is likely to disturb the system more than the loss or addition of a
grammatical form. For example, if the English language were suddenly to be deprived of the /t-d/ phoneme distinction, the whole system of
systems which makes up the language would be affected more than it
would by the loss of the -ive/-ove grammatical distinction between
present (drive, dive, strive ...) and past (drove, dove, strove ...).

This is perhaps why most items entering the code into its larger
classes have both low redundancy and high information content. In the
smaller classes of linguistic items, the probability of integration of a
foreign element into the code is necessarily lower; but its probability
of interference in the message is correspondingly higher. Because of
this, its redundancy is high and its information content low. For example, when getting the hang of a foreign accent, the strange sound which
consistently replaces a certain allophone in the stream of speech does
not on each recurrence add much new information to the message. We
come to expect it and to take it for granted, for it can be predicted. In
other words, the more predictable the interference, the less it interferes. Grammatical items, in turn, are more stable than items of the
vocabulary, which may contain more than ten thousand active elements.
These are much more loosely systematized than are elements of the
grammar and are consequently less stable.

The inherent degree of stability of a language element, which depends on its function in the system or subsystem to which it belongs,
is modified by external factors such as social change and dialect or
language contact.

In bilingual communities there will be those who always use certain
forms from their other language and who know no other, and yet are always understood because most of their interlocutors are bilingual.
There will be for a given concept, those who know both terms and use
only one. Those who know both forms and use them indifferently. In
other words, the question of whether or not a given element belongs to
both codes or only to one does not take a yes/no answer. It is also a
matter of degree. If everyone uses one and only one form, that form—
even though it comes from and still exists in the other language—is part
of the bilingual's languages. It can be said to have been 100% integrated
into the other languages (e.g. the word wrench in the French of some
Acadians is almost as integrated as is the word sugar in English).

On the other hand, if only half of the population have integrated the
form into their code, it can be said to be 50% integrated. The percentage may range anywhere from near zero to 100%. Integration into a
code is a matter of degree. But if integration is a matter of degree,
what we need are techniques for determining the extent to which the use
of a foreign item may be considered normal. In other words, we need
methods for measuring the degree of integration.

3. Measuring integration

By what criteria can we measure the extent to which a foreign item has become part of a language code? We can take our measures either (1) from the message or, (2) from the code.

3.1 Measuring from the message

By collecting samples of the speech of bilinguals, it is possible to identify and quantify the foreign elements that are introduced. This can be done from the point of view of their frequency or from the point of view of the range of occurrence.

From the point of view of frequency, it seems reasonable to suppose that, if the norm is what people use, the more frequently people include a foreign element in their speech, the more normal it is. How can we then determine the number of times people use a given word or form? One way of finding out is by counting the number of times that word or form comes up in suitable samples of speech or writing. With this in mind, we obtained samples of the free speech of some fifty Acadian bilinguals. After making extensive tape recordings of the unrehearsed conversation of these bilinguals, we computed the frequency of occurrence of English items in their French speech (Mackey 1966).

It soon became evident, however, that the occurrence of an item from the other language depended largely on what the bilingual happened to be talking about at the time his conversation was being recorded. When he was talking about airplanes, the word <u>wing</u> was likely to occur more often than it did when he was talking about horses, in which case, the word <u>hoof</u> was more likely to occur. On the other hand, a very small but important part of the vocabulary always recurred, no matter what he was talking about; it included words like <u>est</u>, <u>à</u>, <u>de</u>, and <u>je</u>— most of them grammatical words. If one of these words were to be replaced by its equivalent in the other language, the number of times it was so replaced could presumably be used as a measure of its degree of integration into the receiving language. But such words—partly because they are the most highly related to the most systematic and structured areas of the language—were seldom replaced. The few that did occur belonged to classes, like conjunctions, representing the least structured of the structure words. If they ever did enter the language, structure words did so only after many of the content words of the general vocabulary had already been affected. Moreover, the criterion of frequency of occurrence is valid for only a small portion of the total number of elements in the language, and these include the grammatical units. For the bulk of the vocabulary, the frequencies depending as they do on the field or the situation, are unstable and therefore unreliable (Mackey 1965a).

An approach making use of frequency of occurrence is the measurement of the degree of consistency of usage. If a foreign form is consistently used to the exclusion of any other, it may be assumed that the form has been completely integrated into the code. But how can one prove that the usage of such a form is one hundred percent consistent? Another difficulty arises when the degree of consistency varies continually from one situation to the next. This makes the degree of consistency difficult to measure, especially when one considers the multiplicity of situations in which individuals in a multilingual community may be involved. Yet the possibility of measurement has been demonstrated in a study distinguishing consistency of usage in various socioeconomic classes of society using as many as five different styles per person (Labov 1966).

Another way of determining the degree of integration would be by counting the number of texts in which a word occurs (range). Although the most frequent words are also those which occur everywhere (have the greatest range), some words are likely to occur in certain texts more than in others. If a man is talking about the production of eggs, the words hen and chicken are more likely to occur than they would if he were talking about the production of light bulbs, paper cups, or iron ingots. But the fact that these words did not occur when talking about eggs would not indicate that they were unimportant to the speaker.

Many important words are seldom used, even in situations to which they are relevant. We do not often write or talk about our tongues or our noses, but this does not mean that we have little knowledge of or use for these words. When we need them, they are available. Secondly, the number of texts is no indication of the complete range of coverage; it would be difficult to cover all the multitude of possible things about which each individual in a population may want to talk. Finally, with range as with frequency, we are dealing with the usage—with the message as it were, rather than directly with the code which produces the message out of an infinite number of possible messages.

What we need is a criterion of integration that deals directly with the code and is likely to expose the bulk of the vocabulary covering the maximum number fields in which it is likely to be used.

3.2 Measuring from the code

Attempts have been made to suggest ways of finding evidence of integration into the code. These include tests of availability, acceptability, and translatability. Let us first examine the uses of availability.

Availability is a measure of the potential of the items in a code. Whereas frequency of textual occurrence is a suitable measure of language forms which must be used, availability is the appropriate measure for words which may be used. These include the thousands of nouns, verbs, adjectives and adverbs which are more or less at the disposal of the bilingual speaker. How can we get at this storehouse of vocabulary? One way is by asking the subject to supply an inventory. This can be accomplished through a formal test. This availability test has the speaker list items on each code according to any number of semantic fields. To return to the above example of sweater/chandail, we have seen that the occurrence of one in the context of the other language was no indication of integration into the other language. What then would an availability test indicate? If a bilingual includes sweater on top of the list of French words for clothing, and chandail at the bottom of the list, we know that both items are part of his French code; if he lists only sweater in his French code, it is likely that it may have replaced the word chandail, unless that term is used with a different meaning, which is often the case for integrated items in bilingual communities. If in a recorded text therefore, we were then to find the word sweater, we could discount it as a probable case of interference. In other words, we first ask the bilinguals to identify their codes before analyzing samples of their speech to decide the extent to which there is interference or switching between codes.

Availability is not integration, but it can be used as a measure of the degree to which an item comes to mind as belonging to one code or the other of the bilingual. It has been used only for the nongrammatical elements of a language—those which serve as labels for concept categories, especially concrete nouns. Although this does not mean that we exclude abstractions, it does seem fitting that a new measure should start as close as possible to the concrete in order to permit easier evaluation. But how can such a measure be applied to a whole population and its language codes?

One way of measuring the availability of an item in a population is to take a representative sample of that population and have each person supply an inventory of the items in each conceptual, or semantic field (for example, food, clothing, housing, etc.). The type and number of conceptual fields depend on the detail and amount of information desired (Mackey 1969). For example, in the field of clothing we ask each person to supply a list of words he uses for clothing in a given language. Some words will appear on most lists, others on only a few. The number of lists on which a word appears indicates the number of people to which the word has most readily occurred within the time limit (in this case, a quarter of an hour per field). This can be stated as a percentage of the population including the word in their vocabulary of that particular field. In the case of a bilingual population, if one asks for the vocabulary of one language, one may get certain items which really belong to the vocabulary of the bilingual's other language. This may indicate a number of possibilities. The bilingual may know only the item in his other language, or not know to which language the item belongs.

Or he may know both items, but remember one of them more readily than the other.

If he indicates items of the other language in the list, they may well be the only items he knows for the concept that comes to his mind. But we do not have enough evidence to assume that this is always the case. We can only say that these items come more readily to his mind than do the others.

We can assume that you can get at the code which a person has in his head by asking him to write it down. If he does not include an item, however, it does not necessarily mean that it is excluded from his code. Its exclusion or inclusion may be a function of the number of responses, which, in turn, is a function of the time taken to produce the inventory, up to the limit of the total vocabulary of the individual in a given field (Mackey 1969a).

From the inventories, we know the number of persons who have indicated a foreign word as part of their code. We do not yet know the number of persons who understand the native word and yet list the foreign word. This, however, can be checked through a test of translatability (see below). Such a test would tell us whether or not a person knows a word, but not how well he knows it. Persons with an effort of memory and enough time may be able to retrieve the native word. This is borne out in interviews with bilinguals. In such interviews, we find the subjects saying such things as: 'My grandmother used to say something like this'. But because the native word is not uppermost in their minds, they will use the foreign word instead. Forgetting is relative, gradual, and a matter of degree.

It seems safe to assume, therefore, that in the bilingual, French-English Acadian materials that we have analyzed and will use as examples, any given French word is understood and remembered to a certain degree. In a given field, the possibilities are the following: (i) the French word can be excluded (E. = zero), (ii) the English word can be excluded (F. = zero), (iii) both can be excluded (E. + F. = zero), and (iv) either can be dominant.

How can we measure this dominance? We assume that in any given field the inclusion of one word rather than another is an indication that that word has been better remembered. There is a whole literature on word association which seems to bear out this assumption (cf. Marbe's law, Thumb and Marbe 1901). For example, if a person includes the words <u>sweater</u> and <u>scarf</u> and excludes <u>leggings</u>, as types of clothing, we can assume that when thinking or talking about clothing, the corresponding words and the objects to which they refer come more readily to mind.

If for the thing 'sweater' however, the bilingual can remember only the name used in the second language, we can assume that although the object comes to mind, it is associated more readily with its name in the other language. In a group of bilinguals, some will include the concept 'sweater', others will not. Of those who include it some will give the French word (chandail) in the French list; others will include the English word (sweater) in the French list, indicating that it is uppermost in their mind. If all do this, it is that word and not its counterpart in the native language that is uppermost in the minds of most people.

If a hundred people were to include the concept 'sweater' in an inventory of their clothing, it may be assumed that that concept is available to 100% of that population. Out of this hundred who have included the concept if fifty were to put the word sweater in the French list, it may be assumed that the English word is uppermost in the minds of half the people. It has been integrated to that extent into the vocabulary likely to be available. Its degree of integration is 50%, meaning that a person taken at random from those who are likely to use either sweater or chandail is just as likely to use the one as he is to use the other. The probability of sweater being the word is .5 and the probability of chandail is also .5 in situations in which the concept is going to be expressed.

What is true for a hundred people is also true for a thousand, or for any number. And if this number is a valid sample of the population, it can be said that in the given bilingual population the word sweater, no matter what its degree of availability, or its importance in a given semantic field, would have just as much chance of coming to the mind of any person chosen at random as would the word chandail. The words are equally probable and their degree of integration (as expressed by this probability), is equal. This probability (.5) is neither a measure of its likelihood of occurrence (frequency), nor of the number of spoken or written texts in which it is likely to occur (range), nor its importance for a given field (availability). It simply says for a given population in a given field that a specific concept ('sweater') is just as likely to be expressed in English as it is in French. It does not say how many people use both words and to what extent, although this is information that could be obtained with a slight refinement of the technique (see below), which could also indicate for those using such doublets whether they are given different or the same roles as far as meaning or domain is concerned (for example, distinctions between les gars, les garçons, les gosses, and les boys).

The availability test is not the only possible technique enabling us better to distinguish integration from interference. There are also the tests of acceptability and translatability.

The acceptability test was suggested a few years ago by Nils Hasselmo at the Unesco International Seminar on the Description and Measurement of Bilingualism (Kelly 1969: 121-41), and later developed by him in a study of American-Swedish bilinguals (Hasselmo 1970).

The purpose of the test is to obtain a range of possible variation of selected items likely to occur in the normal, everyday speech of the bilinguals. The degree of acceptability of an item is indicated by the average score of a given group of subjects judging recorded sentences on a four-point scale. It is obtained by having each subject in a representative group of bilinguals rate constructed and actually observed test sentences containing elements from the other language. Each sentence is rated as to whether, speaking to a friend in the community, the subject would 'say it that way' almost always, sometimes, never (but others would), or never (and others neither). The results reported showed a complete range of degrees of acceptability.

Another access to the code of the bilingual may be had through a test of translatability, also suggested by Hasselmo. It tests the bilingual's ability to furnish equivalents in his other language. Testing procedures are similar to those used for obtaining indices of acceptability. Here the bilingual hears words from one of his languages in the context of the other and is asked to supply the equivalent form in the language of the text. The equivalent must cover essentially the same content as the test item. If the bilingual is unable to supply a suitable equivalent, it may perhaps be assumed that the item actually belongs to his other code, or to both. For example, in the French sentence, <u>Je voulais enlever la roue, mais j'ai perdu mon wrench</u>, one bilingual whom I tested was unable to find the French equivalent of <u>wrench</u>, insisting that it was after all a French word. Preceding translatability, Hasselmo has a test of identification to find out in which language the bilingual classified a selected group of items, identifying those which he thinks had been taken over from the other language. The results also showed a continuum, ranging from complete identification with one language to complete identification with another.

To sum up, we can try to separate a bilingual's codes in three different ways: (i) by asking him what items each code contains (availability), (ii) by asking him to separate items according to the code to which they belong (acceptability), and (iii) by asking him to transfer items from one code to the other (translatability). These different tests may really be measuring different things. An item which is not very acceptable may yet be the most readily available. We find such conflicts in situations of language contact and dialect contact, like the one exemplified in Stephen Leacock's remark before an audience in England whom he suspected of despising his Canadian accent—'I don't like it any better than you; but it's the best I can do.' A word may also be easily translated and identified as belonging to one language, and yet be more highly available than its equivalent in the other language.

Before any of these measures are used extensively, it would be important to find out the extent to which they are related and in what respect one might be used as a check on the others. It would seem, for example, that translatability could be inversely proportional to acceptability.

By correlating the results of such tests it seems possible to determine the borrowed items in the bilingual's codes. This would add precision to the quantitative immediate-constituent analysis of recorded samples of typical speech behavior of individual bilinguals to determine the pattern and degree of interference and alternation (Mackey 1965b). It would mean giving the same three tests to representative samples of the bilingual population and calculating the percentage of integration of each item into the other language. Since I have not yet replicated acceptability or translatability tests on a group, I can supply here only an example of the use of the availability test on a sample bilingual population to obtain indications of the degree of integration of items from one code to the other.

4. Integration and availability: Sample measurements

Let us now see how these proposed measurements from the code would work on a sample population. We shall limit our demonstration to the use of availability indices as a measure of integration. The indices will be taken from a survey of the French of almost 2,000 young Acadian (French-English) bilinguals out of a bilingual population of some 200,000 representing about a third of the inhabitants living in an area of 28,000 square miles (New Brunswick). We shall describe (1) the scope and method of investigation before treating, and (2) the types of analysis and the results obtained in establishing integration probabilities.

4.1 Scope and method

The investigation covered a sample population of some 2,000 (1,745) bilinguals under 19 years of age. This sample population produced 33,510 pages of French vocabulary inventory which yielded a total of 887,550 word tokens in 27 semantic fields.

Because of the great volume of material gathered, we decided to limit the first analysis to the responses of the youngest age-group (under 13) in twelve areas and to 16 semantic fields (see Table 1).

This involved the analysis of 11,456 questionnaires which represented the responses of 702 informants in 16 semantic fields, yielding 286,400 tokens.

An analysis of these word tokens, with the aid of a computer, yielded 64,031 different written forms, each of which had to be brought together by hand under the appropriate word type. For example, the forms quetelle, quettil, quitel, and ketel, along with their frequencies, had to be rewritten under their word type, kettle.

The net result of this work was a list of 10,521 word types representing the total available French vocabulary of the 700 young bilinguals in the 16 semantic fields, as supplied by them in the five to seven hours of cumulative testing time. Most of this vocabulary (about 90%) was indeed French; but there were significant numbers of English words, and also loan-blends, Canadianisms, and even neologisms of the bilingual's own creation (see Table 2).

Each of these 10,521 word types was then put on a punch-card along with the number of bilinguals in each age-group supplying the word. A computer program was then elaborated which would: (i) arrange the words in semantic fields, (ii) total the frequencies for each word type, (iii) within each semantic field arrange the words in decreasing order of frequency, (iv) calculate for each word its percentage of the total response, (v) list the rank of each word, and (vi) print out the results with all words grouped according to the semantic fields and ranked according to percentage of total response.

The results, as printed out by the computer, appeared in some 250 pages of tables. Each table had 12 columns which successively indicated the word, its rank, its percentage of the total population listing it, and the totals and percentages for each age-group(see Table 3).

4.2 Analysis and probabilities

The 702 informants aged 8 to 12 (reduced for some fields to 661), completed a total of 11,456 questionnaires in 16 semantic fields, produced a total of 286,400 word tokens representing 64,031 word forms, which were later reduced to 10,521 word types.

Of these 10,521 different word types, 4,731 (44.1%) appeared only once. The number varied according to the semantic field, the fewest being in the field of clothing (128) and the greatest number being in the field of pastimes (536).

On top of each list, word types with the highest response, which accounted for 75% of the total, were all in French. Most of the code integration from English into French was found in the lower 25% of the list, indications that the commonest words in the French language of these bilinguals were still French.

The proportion of words replaced to words retained was about 3/17, that is, the lists supplied an average of 3 English words to 17 French words. But the proportion varied according to the semantic field. For the parts of the body, it is one English word for 26 French words (English 11, French 285); whereas for the field of cooking, the proportion of English to French is 1/5 (111/540) (see Table 2).

Some words, however, were counted as neither English nor French. These included 20 so-called loan-blends, 165 Canadianisms, and 418 neologisms. Under loan-blends were listed such French expressions as station à feu, constructed on an English model (fire station). Under Canadianisms, we included those items constructed from French materials but peculiar to the area from which they came, for example, moulin à coudre. Under neologisms, we listed all unidentified forms, many of which seemed to be of the informant's own invention; for example, words like licerpitant. For the distribution of these three categories by semantic field, see Table 2.

But this distribution of the everyday vocabulary of the young Acadian bilinguals between English and French is not sufficient to reveal the relative importance of the French or English terms in the community. We are interested in knowing what this large percentage of English replacements actually represents, of determining the extent to which English, the transmitting language, has entered the French, the receiving language, of the community. It is evident that not everyone has replaced the French term by the English word, because for most English words we have also the French equivalents. For each word we are able to tell the percentage of our bilingual population preserving the French word when speaking in French. For most words, these form a majority of the population. For example, whereas 95% of the bilinguals speaking French would use the word manteau, only 3% would use the word coat. There were some terms, however, like flashlight, mixer, map, pickles, office, and manager, where the English term seems to be ousting the French in the speech of the community.

We were now in a position to determine the extent to which ($\underline{Lt}$) the transmitting language (English) had been integrated into the ($\underline{Lr}$) receiving language (French) of the bilinguals.

4.2.1 Probabilities

The first step was to extract all available English items ($\underline{At}$) from the French inventory, and then to search the inventory for French equivalents ($\underline{Ar}$). In each case we listed the percentage of the population which included the words and compared both figures. For example, in the semantic field of clothing 94.7% included manteau, and only 3.1% listed coat. Whereas in the field of cooking, three times more people listed mixer or mix-master (6.9%) as included the French equivalent (mélangeur 1.8%). For other items, like flashlight, there was no French word listed by a single person.

Knowing the percentage of the bilingual population which include in their inventory of one language ($\underline{Lr}$) a given item from the other ($\underline{Lt}$) or another language (if more than two languages are involved), it is possible to calculate the probable degree of integration ($\underline{pI}$) of a vocabulary item ($\underline{V}$) of the transmitting language ($\underline{Lt}$), in this case English, as a replacement for a vocabulary item in the receiving language ($\underline{Lr}$), in this case French, since it would be equal to the availability of the transmitted item ($\underline{At}$) over the sum ( ) of the availability of both items ($\underline{At} + \underline{Ar}$). Or,

$$pI \; (VLt \; > \; VLr) = \frac{At}{A}$$

In other words, we divide the combined percentages ($A = At + Ar$) by
the percentage listed for the transmitting, or lending, language and
state the results as a proportion of 100. For example, in the inventories of French words for clothing, 11.4% of the bilinguals listed <u>foulard</u>,
and 6.6% included <u>scarf</u>. The latter has therefore an integration probability of

$$pI = \frac{At}{A} = \frac{6.6}{6.6 + 11.4} = \frac{6.6}{18} = .367$$

This would mean that if the word <u>scarf</u> were to appear in a stretch of
French speech recorded in the area, the probability that it is part of the
code would be .367. If, on the other hand, the word <u>flashlight</u> were to
appear there would be a probability of almost 1.00—that is, it is almost certain that it had been completely integrated into the local code.
If the word <u>head</u> appeared, however, the converse would be true; it is
almost certainly not part of the local code and the probability would be
almost 1.00 for a case of interference—not of integration. In other
words, interference would be inversely proportional to integration. The
more an item is integrated into a code, the less likely that its appearance in the message—in the speech of a bilingual—would be a case of
interference.

4.2.2 Relationships

Finally, what is the relationship between integration and availability?
Are they completely independent, or are they related? If so, to what
extent?
A first approximation to an answer may be studied by plotting the one
against the other. If we therefore take all the words in the sample selected from the 16 semantic fields and plot their degrees of availability
(At + Ar) (first two columns in Table 4) against their probability of integration (last column of Table 4), we can see that the distribution of
the points of relationship is not haphazard (see Figure 1 on Integration
as related to Availability). There is an observable tendency for these
points to cluster low in the availability scale. In the sample examined,
most items entering the code are the least readily remembered.
If we take a closer look at the appended Figure, we notice the following: (a) None of the words from the transmitting language (English) represents concepts that are highly available (upper right corner of Figure).
Is this necessarily so, or does it reflect the fact that the basic French
vocabulary of these young bilinguals is still exclusively French? (b)

Few highly available words have entered the code from the other language (upper half of Figure). Is this because a highly available item is more strongly associated with its most usual form, or is it simply an indication of the fact that few of the important French words have been replaced? (c) The great majority of the replacements occurred in words supplied by less than a third of the sample population (lower third of Figure). (d) More than 90% of the correlations are below the diagonal line leading from the highest degree of availability to the lowest probability. Most of those above the line represent pairs which pose special semantic problems, like those of imbalance in semantic diversity (e.g. E. map = F. carte géographique; carte = map, postcard, card) (Mackey 1969). These should be checked against the results of translatability tests.

An overall glance at the figure might give the general impression that the probability of a foreign item being integrated into the other code of the bilingual is inversely proportional to its degree of availability. These figures are quite insufficient to enable one to come to such a conclusion. In the first place, they are based on only 10% of the integrated data to be found in the analysed part of the sample, since the intention is simply to illustrate a method of expressing the relativity of integration. Secondly, the data are taken from only 16 general semantic fields in a single geographical area, and within a limited age-group.

What the figure does illustrate, however, is that, for this particular age-group within the particular geographical area and language community, the probability of integration of their most important (available) concrete words is in general not high enough to oust the native equivalents. If, however, we were to present a breakdown by semantic field, some fields might show a line of a different angle, a different delineation of the pattern of relationships, in which many important words might show a high probability of integration. If we were to use subjects speaking highly mixed languages we would presumably get other patterns. In other words, the analytic procedure illustrated here might be useful to indicate the degree of mixture of languages and dialects in contact.

It may be that most items entering the code of a language start at a low level of availability, but only after the probability of remembering the native word has declined sufficiently to make the probability of the foreign equivalent dominant. Whether or not this is always the case can be decided only after extensive surveys and widespread experimentation with different semantic fields, different populations and different languages.

The results presented here are valid only for the Acadian areas of the Canadian Maritimes, particularly those in New Brunswick, for a limited age-group, and for a few of the most concrete and universal

semantic fields. It would now be necessary to extend the analysis to
other semantic fields and other age-groups in order to find out whether
or not the relationship between integration and availability changes
with age and area.

Conclusion

Until then, we may hazard the following general conclusions on the
analysis of integration as distinct from interference:

(1) Conventional synchronic analysis is unsuited to the de-
    scription of mixed and rapidly changing codes.
(2) Code integration is relative.
(3) Its relativity can be measured.
(4) Interference can be stated in terms of this relative inte-
    gration.

This may not be the only way out of the dilemma; but I should be satisfied if this paper gives some indication that a way can be found.

TABLE 1.

Sample Population: Age and Area Distribution

Age-group	Town	County	No. of bilinguals
8-9	St-Jacques	Madawaska	35
8-9	Bathurst	Gloucester	26
9-10	St-Jacques	Madawaska	35
9-10	Bathurst	Gloucester	25
9-10	Shippegan	Gloucester	100
9-10	Petit Rocher	Restigouche	90
9-10	Drummond	Victoria	36
10-11	Bathurst	Gloucester	31
10-11	Shédiac	Westmorland	26
10-11	Rivière-du-Portage	Gloucester	40
10-11	Rogersville	Kent	33
10-11	Tracadie	Gloucester	37
10-11	Ste-Anne	Madawaska	35
10-11	St-François	Madawaska	28
11-12	Bathurst	Gloucester	27
11-12	Campbellton	Restigouche	29
11-12	Tracadie	Gloucester	83
Total			702

TABLE 2.

Semantic Fields: Distribution of Vocabularies

Semantic Field (in French)	French	English	Canadian	Blends	Neol.	Totals
1. The body	285	11	3	0	24	323
2. Clothing	248	94	5	0	13	360
3. Housing	569	84	10	0	13	676
4. Furniture	474	80	16	0	9	579
5. Food	346	104	3	2	33	488
6. Meals	332	61	2	4	9	408
7. Cooking	549	111	11	0	14	685
8. Schooling	597	83	11	0	13	704
9. Heating and light	477	56	4	0	41	578
10. City life	760	109	2	0	33	904
11. Town and village	605	112	8	1	18	744
12. Transport	501	103	5	0	37	646
13. Farming	688	64	16	4	36	808
14. Animals	249	44	3	0	41	337
15. Games	874	189	30	5	45	1, 143
16. Occupations	951	106	36	4	39	1, 138
Totals	8505	1401	165	20	418	10, 521

TABLE 3. Sample Page of Computer Print-out

Cuisine

Age Population	rank	9 – 12 700		9 61		10 267		11 203		12 123	
		%	pop.	%	pop.	%	pop.	%	pop.	%	pop.
Poêle	1	92.5	605	68.8	42	95.8	256	94.5	192	93.4	115
Table	2	82.2	538	86.8	53	85.3	228	74.8	152	85.3	105
Chaise	3	78.1	511	70.4	43	80.8	216	72.4	147	85.3	105
Armoire	4	74.3	486	63.9	39	79.7	213	59.6	121	91.8	113
Cuillère	5	68.3	447	26.2	16	48.6	130	110.3	224	62.6	77
Couteau	6	64.5	422	32.7	20	50.1	134	92.1	187	65.8	81
Fourchette	7	62.8	411	29.5	18	48.3	129	93.1	189	60.9	75
Assiette	8	52.9	346	22.9	14	41.1	110	75.3	153	56.0	69
Chaudron	9	39.6	259	26.2	16	47.1	126	36.4	74	34.9	43
Tasse	10	37.6	246	18.0	11	32.5	87	48.2	98	40.6	50
Plat	11	35.0	229	18.0	11	42.3	113	34.4	70	28.4	35
Verre	12	35.0	229	21.3	13	27.7	74	43.8	89	43.0	53
Frigidaire	13	30.1	197	9.8	6	36.7	98	25.1	51	34.1	42
Réfrigérateur	14	29.9	196	32.7	20	22.4	60	31.0	63	43.0	53
Radio	15	24.1	158	8.1	5	29.2	78	20.6	42	26.8	33
Laveuse	16	22.4	147	8.1	5	23.9	64	19.7	40	30.8	38
Sink	17	22.0	144	9.8	6	29.9	80	20.1	41	13.8	17
Boite	18	21.8	143	1.6	1	19.4	52	21.1	43	38.2	47
Evier	19	21.4	140	24.5	15	13.8	37	25.1	51	30.0	37

Table 3 is continued on pp. 216–217.

TABLE 3 (Cont.)

Cuisine

Age Population	rank	9 - 12 700 %	pop.	9 61 %	pop.	10 267 %	pop.	11 203 %	pop.	12 123 %	pop.
Porte	20	17.7	116	34.4	21	19.4	52	5.4	11	26.0	32
Horloge	21	16.6	109	4.9	3	13.8	37	13.7	28	33.3	41
Bol	22	15.2	100	13.1	8	11.6	31	24.6	50	8.9	11
Soucoupe	23	14.5	95	3.2	2	13.8	37	15.2	31	20.3	25
Fenêtre	24	14.3	94	32.7	20	12.7	34	5.4	11	23.5	29
Tiroir	25	14.3	94	1.6	1	20.9	56	9.8	20	13.8	17
Pan	26	13.9	91	8.1	5	20.2	54	8.3	17	12.1	15
Lumière	27	13.7	90	19.6	12	17.6	47	6.8	14	13.8	17
Salière	28	12.8	84	.0	0	8.2	22	22.6	46	13.0	16
Can	29	11.4	75	6.5	4	13.1	35	14.7	30	4.8	6
Grille-pain	30	11.3	74	8.1	5	4.4	12	21.1	43	11.3	14
Poivrière	31	11.1	73	.0	0	6.7	18	20.6	42	10.5	13
Sécheuse	32	11.1	73	3.2	2	9.3	25	13.7	28	14.6	18
Pompe	33	10.8	71	3.2	2	8.2	22	9.3	19	22.7	28
Balai	34	10.5	69	6.5	4	10.8	29	5.9	12	19.5	24
Bombe	35	10.3	68	6.5	4	11.6	31	10.3	21	9.7	12
Rideau	35	10.3	68	9.8	6	11.2	30	5.9	12	16.2	20
Vaisselle	37	9.7	64	6.5	4	10.1	27	6.8	14	15.4	19
Télévision	38	9.4	62	9.8	6	13.4	36	6.4	13	5.6	7
Planche à repasser	39	9.3	61	8.1	5	8.2	22	7.8	16	14.6	18

Toaster	39	9.3	61	1.6	1	10.4	28	9.3	19	10.5	13
Cafetière	41	9.0	59	4.9	3	8.9	24	9.3	19	10.5	13
Portrait	42	8.7	57	4.9	3	7.4	20	5.4	11	18.6	23
Batteur d'oeufs	43	8.5	56	8.1	5	10.8	29	7.8	16	4.8	6
Sucrier	43	8.5	56	1.6	1	4.8	13	16.2	33	7.3	9
Téléphone	43	8.5	56	3.2	2	9.3	25	8.3	17	9.7	12
Pot	46	8.4	55	1.6	1	2.9	8	16.7	34	9.7	12
Miroir	47	8.2	54	6.5	4	8.6	23	5.4	11	13.0	16
Thépot	48	7.9	52	.0	0	6.3	17	14.7	30	4.0	5
Lavabo	49	7.7	51	1.6	1	9.7	26	4.9	10	11.3	14
Beurrier	50	7.1	47	1.6	1	4.1	11	12.3	25	8.1	10
Fauteuil	51	7.0	46	4.9	3	2.2	6	3.9	8	23.5	29
Chaise berceuse	52	6.8	45	4.9	3	10.4	28	4.4	9	4.0	5
Bouilloire	53	6.4	42	.0	0	7.4	20	3.4	7	12.1	15
Couteau à pain	53	6.4	42	1.6	1	1.4	4	15.2	31	4.8	6
Nappe	53	6.4	42	3.2	2	3.3	9	9.8	20	8.9	11
Banc	56	5.9	39	1.6	1	9.2	25	3.4	7	4.8	6
Casserole	56	5.9	39	9.8	6	6.3	17	6.4	13	2.4	3
Garde-robe	56	5.9	39	3.2	2	7.1	19	3.4	7	8.9	11
Fourneau	59	5.8	38	19.6	12	5.2	14	1.9	4	6.5	8
Calendrier	60	5.6	37	3.2	2	4.8	13	2.4	5	13.8	17
Fer à repasser	60	5.6	37	1.6	1	5.2	14	6.4	13	7.3	9
Crucifix	62	5.5	36	.0	0	6.3	17	3.9	8	8.9	11
Chantepleure	63	5.0	33	1.6	1	6.7	18	5.4	11	2.4	3
Machine à laver	63	5.0	33	.0	0	2.9	8	6.4	13	9.7	12
Couteau à viande	65	4.8	32	.0	0	2.2	6	10.3	21	4.0	5
Cup	65	4.8	32	.0	0	2.9	8	11.8	24	.0	0
Eau	65	4.8	32	6.5	4	4.8	13	5.9	12	2.4	3

TABLE 4.

Integration Probabilities: English into French

English (At) >	French (Ar)	pI
1. The body		
brain .3%	cerveau 15.2%	0.019
jaw .1%	mâchoire 1.6%	0.058
2. Clothing		
sweater 8.7%	chandail 86.9%	0.091
jumper 1.1%	_____ 86.9%	0.012
suit 8.1%	habit 13.6%	0.373
scarf 6.6%	foulard 11.4%	0.366
belt 5.2%	ceinture 17.5%	0.229
slacks 5.2%	pantalons 78.1%	0.062
coat 3.1%	manteau 94.7%	0.031
skirt 2.3%	jupe 61.1%	0.036
overalls 1.6%	salopettes 5.9%	0.213
tie 1.1%	cravate 46.2%	0.232
boots .2%	bottes 29.7%	0.006
_____ .2%	bottines 18.3%	0.108
slippers .1%	pantoufles 13.6%	0.007
3. Housing		
sink 4.8%	évier 6.0%	0.444
attic 2.3%	grenier 26.3%	0.080
plug .7%	prise de courant .4%	0.636
4. Furniture		
sink 12.2%	évier 18.0%	0.403
_____ 12.2%	lavabo 13.5%	0.474
fridge 3.7%	réfrigérateur 28.8%	0.113
_____ 3.7%	frigidaire 31.0%	0.106
desk 3.2%	pupître 17.9%	0.151
bathtub 2.8%	bain 11.7%	0.193
lights 2.5%	lumières 18.2%	0.120
chesterfield 2.3%	sofa 41.6%	0.052
_____ 2.3%	divan 8.6%	0.211
washer .7%	laveuse 44.3%	0.001
_____ .7%	machine à laver 5.9%	0.010
5. Food		
bean 4.7%	fève 30.0%	0.013
pickle 2.6%	cornichon 1.0%	0.722
corn .5%	blé d'Inde 25.7%	0.019
radish .1%	radis 4.7%	0.020
6. Meals		
cup 10.2%	tasse 84.9%	0.107

TABLE 4 (Cont.).

English (At) >	French (Ar)	pI
napkin 6.6%	serviette 18.3%	0.265
glass 1.0%	verre 87.9%	0.001
salt .4%	sel 9.3%	0.041
fork .3%	fourchette 99.7%	0.030
7. Cooking		
sink 22.0%	évier 21.4%	0.506
_____ 22.0%	lavabo 7.7%	0.740
can 11.4%	boîte 21.8%	0.343
toaster 9.3%	grille-pain 11.3%	0.451
mixer 2.7%	mélangeur 1.8%	0.600
mix-master 4.2%	_____ 1.8%	0.700
8. Schooling		
map 40.3%	carte géographique 21.1%	0.656
_____ 40.3%	carte 13.5%	0.749
pen .1%	plume 63.9%	0.001
_____ .1%	stylo 6.0%	0.016
pencil .1%	crayon 90.3%	0.001
9. Heating and light		
flashlight 19.1%	lampe de poche 0%	1.000
bulb 7.8%	ampoule 15.3%	0.337
heater 2.5%	chaufferette 10.1%	0.198
fireplace 2.1%	foyer 4.5%	0.318
oil 1.3%	huile 73.5%	0.173
furnace 1.2%	fournaise 68.7%	0.171
stove .4%	poêle 94.3%	0.004
10. City life		
office 11.5%	bureau 3.1%	0.787
post office 6.5%	bureau de poste 21.3%	0.233
fire station 1.5%	poste de pompier 4.4%	0.254
barber 1.3%	barbier 10.2%	0.113
_____ 1.3%	coiffeur 6.2%	0.173
11. Town and village		
bowling alley .4%	salle de quilles 5.2%	0.070
bank 1.8%	banque 14.3%	0.111
drugstore .6%	pharmacie 2.7%	0.181
fire station .4%	poste de pompiers 1.5%	0.210
_____ .4%	station de pompier .6%	0.400
_____ .4%	bâtisse à incendie .2%	0.666
liquor store .4%	commission des liqueurs 2.5%	0.137
city hall .2%	hôtel de ville .9%	0.188
12. Transport		
truck 19.8%	camion 74.8%	0.209

TABLE 4 (Cont.).

English (At) >	French (Ar)	pI
trolley 3.2%	tramway 4.0%	0.444
streetcar .2%	_____ 4.0%	0.047
boat .6%	bateau 89.7%	0.006
steamer .4%	bateau à vapeur 1.2%	0.250
13. Farming		
digger 1.5%	bêcher 1.8%	0.454
bin .3%	bacul .3%	0.500
row .1%	sillon 9.8%	0.010
flower .1%	fleur 12.6%	0.007
weeding .1%	esherbage 5.0%	0.019
spray .1%	arroseur 5.2%	0.018
14. Animals		
buffalo 2.8%	bison 10.7%	0.207
raccoon 1.2%	raton laveur 5.3%	0.187
cat .9%	chat 98.1%	0.090
lamb .6%	agneau 7.8%	0.071
beaver .4%	castor 27.8%	0.141
pig .4%	cochon 72.1%	0.005
deer .3%	chevreuil 56.0%	0.005
monkey .3%	singe 33.3%	0.008
15. Games		
basketball 11.3%	ballon-panier 21.0%	0.349
race 3.8%	course 25.1%	0.131
bowling 2.6%	quilles 24.1%	0.097
checkers 2.3%	dames 32.8%	0.065
volleyball 2.3%	ballon-volant 5.1%	0.310
cards .3%	cartes 48.0%	0.006
16. Occupations		
manager 4.6%	gérant 3.4%	0.575
boss .3%	_____ 3.4%	0.081
nurse 2.6%	garde-malade 37.5%	0.064
_____ 2.6%	garde 2.1%	0.553
engineer 2.5%	ingénieur 8.5%	0.227
cook 2.1%	cuisinier 14.8%	0.124
plumber 1.0%	plombier 26.5%	0.037
farmer .9%	fermier 36.7%	0.023
_____ .9%	cultivateur 8.5%	0.095
driver .6%	chauffeur 23.2%	0.252
garageman .6%	garagiste 15.3%	0.037
milkman .4%	laitier 9.5%	0.040
lumberjack .3%	bûcheron 24.5%	0.012
reporter .1%	journaliste 6.4%	0.015
secretary .1%	secrétaire 9.6%	0.010

INTEGRATION AS RELATED TO AVAILABILITY

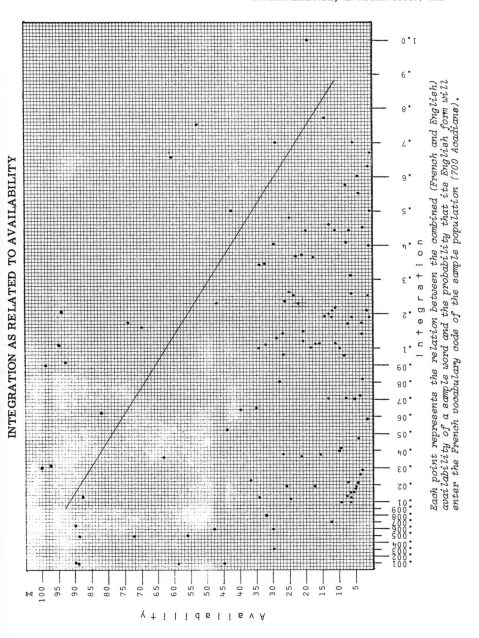

Each point represents the relation between the combined (French and English) availability of a sample word and the probability that its English form will enter the French vocabulary code of the sample population (700 Acadians).

REFERENCES

Bousfield, W. A., and W. D. Barclay. 1950. The relationship between order and frequency of occurrence of restricted associative responses. Journal of experimental psychology 40: 643–647.

Brotsky, S. J., D. C. Butler and M. L. Linton. 1967. Association time, commonality, and the test-retest reliability of free association responses. Psychonomic science 9: 319–320.

Chomsky, N. 1964. Degrees of grammaticalness. The structure of language: Readings in the philosophy of language. Jerry Fodor and Ferrold Katz, eds. Englewood Cliffs, New Jersey: Prentice-Hall.

Coleman, E. B. 1965. Responses to a scale of grammaticalness. Journal of verbal learning and verbal behavior 4: 521–527.

Deroy, L. 1956. L'emprunt linguistique. Paris: Les Belles Lettres.

Diebold, A. R. 1961. Code-switching in Greek-English bilingual speech. Georgetown University Monograph Series on Languages and Linguistics 15: 53–59.

Fishman, J. A. 1964. Language Maintenance and language shift as a field of inquiry; a definition of the field and suggestions for its further development. Linguistics 9: 32–70.

Green, E. 1963. On grading phonic interference. Language Learning 13: 85–96.

Gumperz, J. J. 1964. Linguistic and social interaction in two communities. American anthropologist 66 (6, Part 2): 137–153.

Hasselmo, Nils. 1970. On diversity in American-Swedish. (Unpublished paper). Mimeographed, University of Minnesota.

Haugen, E. I. 1950. The analysis of linguistic borrowing. Language 26: 210–231.

Herdan, G. 1966. How can quantitative methods contribute to our understanding of language mixture and language borrowing? Statistique et analyse linguistique. Paris: Presses universitaires de France, 17–39.

Hill, A. A. 1961. Grammaticality. Word 17: 1–10.

Jakobovits, L. A. and Lambert, W. E. 1961. Semantic satiation among bilinguals. Journal of experimental psychology 62: 576–582.

Kelly, L. G., ed. 1969. Description et mesure du bilinguisme/ Description and measurement of bilingualism. Toronto: University of Toronto Press (for the Canadian Unesco Commission).

Labov, W. 1969. Contraction deletion and inherent variability of the English copula. Language 45: 715–762.

Lambert, W. E. 1955. Measurement of the linguistic dominance of bilinguals. The journal of abnormal and social psychology 50: 197–200.

Le Page, R. B. 1968. Problems of description in multilingual communities. Transactions of the Philological Society of Great Britain 1968: 189–212.

Mackey, W. F. 1965a. Language teaching analysis (chapter 6). London and Bloomington: Longmans and Indiana University Press.

_____. 1965b. Bilingual Interference; its analysis and measurement. The journal of communication 15: 239-249.

_____. 1966. The measurement of bilingual behavior. Canadian psychologist 7: 75-92.

_____. 1967. Bilingualism as a world problem. Montreal: Harvest House.

_____. 1969. Concept categories as measures of culture distance. Quebec: I. C. R. B. (prepared for Man, language and society. The Hague: Mouton (in the press).

_____. 1970a. Optimization of the population-response ratio in lexicometric sampling. Quebec: I. C. R. B. (To appear in Tijdeschrift voor Toegepaste Linguistiek).

_____. 1970b. Toward a quantum linguistics. Quebec: I. C. R. B. (prepared for the Linguistic Department Seminar of McGill University).

_____. Theory and method in the study of bilingualism. London: Oxford University Press (in the press).

Maclay, H., and M. D. Sleator. 1960. Responses to language: Judgment of grammaticalness. International journal of American linguistics 26: 275-282.

Quirk, R , and J. Svartvik. 1966. Investigating linguistic acceptability. The Hague: Mouton.

Saussure, de F. 1915. Cours de linguistique générale (5 ed., 1960). Paris: Payot.

Thumb, A. and Karl Marbe. 1901. Experimentelle Untersuchungen über die psychologischen Grundlagen der sprachlichen Analogiebildung.

Weinreich, U. 1953. Languages in contact; findings and problems. New York: Linguistic Circle of New York (Series: Linguistic Circle of New York, Publications, No. 1).

_____. 1957. On the description of phonic interference. Word 13: 1-11.

DISCUSSION

Einar Haugen, Harvard University: This is not really a question, but an exclamation of delight! This last paper of Professor Mackey's comes as an example of convergence on our part in thinking about bilingual problems over these many years. I have recently had occasion to review his writings as well as my own on the subject, and have come to the conclusion that we are headed inevitably toward a new kind of linguistics, which is clearly suggested in the paper we have just heard. I hope that Professor Mackey will go on and develop it as he has indicated; I don't intend to do so.

Let me just say that I have been more and more unhappy with the kind of simple dichotomies that have been handed out to us in linguistics since the work of Saussure, one of which was mentioned in the paper. The other one that was implied in the discussion was the dichotomy between <u>langue</u> and <u>parole</u>. I have the impression that Professor Mackey accepted this one, whereas he was rejecting the diachronic-synchronic one. I think one could take the other side on this issue. My feeling is that Saussure's <u>langue</u> was an ambiguous term, which referred either to the individual's code or to the code of the community. In the case of bilingual studies, we have to arrive at the concept of an individual code, the competence of the individual. In referring to the whole social group we would then speak of variable competence, as I did in my paper. I'm glad that Professor Mackey wasn't here to hear it, so that there can have been no collusion between us. The concept that bilinguals show interference in the structure of their languages is also wrong because the intermediate norms do not need to be described in terms of interference at all. On this point I am in full agreement with Joshua Fishman's criticism. Although I seemed to be attacking him in my paper, I agree with him that 'interference' is not a good term. We should introduce the concept of intermediate norms and recognize that even the standard norms are intermediate ones that happen to have been accepted in a given social group.

Mackey: I would like to say something about the <u>langue</u>-<u>parole</u> distinction. As a product, I might say, of the Geneva School, I have found it very difficult to destroy the very foundations of my linguistic thinking. I would say that instead of this distinction, we could consider only the entire speech economy as a variable and quantifiable code.

Wolfgang Wölck, Indiana University: I would just like to add a small point which is really in total agreement with what Professor Haugen already said, namely that it seems useless to maintain the idea of separate <u>langues</u> both in the sense of grammar and in the sense of language. Because in talking about bilinguals, we are still too tempted to refer to different codes, and I still find a little of that implication even in Professor Mackey's presentation. In view of recent research begun quite eminently by Professor Gumperz, I think we have to realize that the bilingual's competence—and I think the word 'competence' here is better—is quite different from the monolingual's, and cannot be measured or even compared to the monolingual's individual codes. I think we would make much better headway if we started describing the grammatical concept of the bilingual in terms of what he actually uses, and then to see, perhaps, in what it differs from the monolingual's concept.

Ranko Bugarski, University of Belgrade and University of Chicago: While I have appreciated Dr. Mackey's paper very much, I would like to address a rather general question to him. I'm not sure that everybody would necessarily agree with the rather broad statement that phonological systems are inherently more stable than grammatical systems. I wonder what kind of evidence one might adduce in support of this statement.

Mackey: I think there is plenty of evidence. If you study the history of languages, the rate of vocabulary change is much more rapid than the rate of sound change. Grammar, I think, comes in between. My reasoning is simply this: If you have a lot of items in a system, one of these items is more likely to change than it is in a system with only a few components. This is the point. For example, if you have only 36 phonemes it is very difficult to do without one of them and still have the same system. Whereas if you have something like half a million words, if one, two, three, or more change, it doesn't very much affect the system. This is purely numerical reasong.

Bugarski: May I clarify my question? I did not ask about phonology and vocabulary—we all know that the word stock changes at a relatively fast rate—but about phonology and grammar. While I can see the numerical basis of your reasoning, I am not convinced that this is what in fact happens, and so I asked you to provide some actual evidence.

Mackey: Yes, this would be something worth studying quantitatively. It just seems to me reasonable that the grammatical items are likely to change more quickly. For example, this is very much the case in the history of Latin. Several grammatical forms, including case endings, fall out as a result of much fewer phonetic changes. I think this hypothesis deserves to be tested.

Thomas F. Magner, Pennsylvania State University: I have a question for Father Ó Huallacháin. How can you convince the school children of Ireland that it is worthwhile to speak Irish Gaelic? Are the sessions of your Parliament conducted in Irish? Are there any television programs in Irish? Is the language used extensively in the cities?

Ó Huallacháin: To my mind the plain truth is that the children at the moment are not convinced that it is worth learning. That is why I don't think the thing will continue as a stable situation. There was a time until about ten years ago when learning Irish was accepted as 'something that was done', but I think that what we have to reckon with is just simply the advance of time and the fact that parents now

who have gone through the school system see their own children going
through the same thing and know that they themselves don't use Irish,
so that their encouragement is missing. It is my job here simply to
state the facts. I wouldn't like to conceal my regret that this is so.
But the fact is that Irish is losing out, and I can see no possibility of
the thing changing unless people like those in Parliament use the language more. There is an extraordinary national double-think involved.
At present the amount of Irish on television and in the cities is not
enough to motivate alert and sincere young people by showing them
that it is a language worth learning for use.

Haugen: I would like to ask Father Ó Huallacháin—I can't pronounce
it either. (I'm told that Hooligan is the same name, only anglicized.)
I would hate to see Irish disappear in Ireland, although I realize that
all efficiency and all rules concerning bilingualism point in that direction. If a community can get along with one language, it will never use
two, and the problem is what tone here maintains a second language.
What about Latin in the school system of the United States? How many
people in the United States speak Latin? And yet we teach it in more
high schools than any other language now being taught. What is the
reason? Because English is half Latin. So in somewhat the same
sense—that of giving continuity to the nation—you feel this is more
significant than the effort that pupils have to put forth to learn some
of it. I don't know if this agrees with your point of view.

Ó Huallacháin: Indeed it does; that _is_ my point of view! By the way,
thank you for the allusion to our contribution to the English language—
my family was renowned for its lawlessness! In the same tradition, I
sympathize with your views about the value—and difficulty—of maintaining Irish, but my experience convinces me that it is necessary to
put the problem clearly before the people now. It is very difficult to
analyze the attitudes involved. There is a certain kind of language
loyalty which is a part of the culture, but it seems that it is not a language loyalty which causes people to use the language at present. So
it is a thing to be investigated. I'm sure that there are other communities—perhaps minority communities in the United States—who may have
similar problems. But I don't think these things can be general. When
you think of it, the Irish in the United States are really a most extraordinary group; that is, when you think of how they deliberately abandoned their language as compared with other ethnic groups, it is quite
extraordinary.

William L. Higgins, U. S. Office of Education: With reference to
Dr. Haugen's allusion to Latin's preeminence in American high schools,
the latest statistics which I have heard regarding the study of Latin—

and this was some five years ago—put Latin in third place, after Spanish and French. Latin is chiefly maintained by institutional factors which are fast losing importance. One of the factors which will now help lay Latin to rest is the recent abandonment by the Catholic Church of Latin as an ineffective means of communication, even in a ceremonial context. As long as French and Spanish are being taught chiefly for institutional purposes—to fulfill college entrance or exit requirements—rather than for integrational purposes—to communicate with or to become a member of a non-English speaking community—then they too will follow Latin and Greek into a dead area in our educational system.

As the institutions of higher learning—the graduate schools and colleges—abandon the foreign language requirement for entrance and for graduation, and the high schools need no longer insist on foreign languages as an obligatory group of studies, French and Spanish instruction may become more effective as it adjusts to an optional basis for integrational purposes. Hopefully the trend will then be to start such instruction in the elementary schools where it has its only real chance of success. Perhaps the bilingual efforts which we are discussing at this conference may show the way.

SOME COGNITIVE CONSEQUENCES
OF FOLLOWING THE CURRICULA
OF THE EARLY SCHOOL GRADES
IN A FOREIGN LANGUAGE[1]

W. E. LAMBERT, M. JUST[2] AND N. SEGALOWITZ[3]

McGill University

The paper was presented by the first author at the Twenty-first Annual Round Table Meeting on Linguistics and Language Studies, Georgetown University, 1970.

Abstract. This is a report of a longitudinal study of elementary school children learning a foreign language (French) by using the language as the medium of instruction. It describes the program and its origins and the procedures used to evaluate the (end of year) progress of two classes of English-speaking children who have followed the first three years of schooling entirely or principally in French. Because this program was developed to satisfy a community-wide desire to promote effective bilingualism, the results of the experiment are viewed with much more than an academic interest by parents, teachers, and school administrators, not only those involved in the program but also those contemplating similar programs in other communities.

The results of the experiment to date indicate that the type of bilingual training offered these children is extremely effective, even more so than was originally expected. The similarity of the findings for two different sets of classes, involving changes in teachers, methods of instruction, and modes of testing and analysis, speaks well for the stability and generality of the effects produced by the experimental program. These effects demonstrate a very high level of skill in both the receptive and productive aspects of French, the major language of instruction; a generally excellent command of all aspects of English, the home language of the children; and a high level of skill in a nonlanguage subject matter, mathematics, taught through the foreign language only. Attention is also given to the effects of the program on children's thinking and conceptual development. The potential usefulness of this approach to bilingualism for other ethnolinguistic groups in other settings is also discussed.

This is the second report of an experimental program to teach elementary school children a foreign language by using that language as the medium of instruction. The first report (Lambert and Macnamara 1969) described the program and its origins and the procedures used to evaluate the end-of-year progress of a class of English-speaking first graders who had followed the first year curriculum entirely in French. Because this program was developed to satisfy a widely-accepted community desire to promote effective bilingualism, the results of the experiment are viewed with much more than an academic interest by parents, teachers, and school administrators, not only those involved in the program, but also those contemplating similar programs in other communities. The first year results were extremely encouraging in that the pilot class of experimental children demonstrated high level skills, relative to native speaking control classes, in all aspects of both French and English as well as in mathematics, a nonlanguage subject matter, also taught through French. However, certain aspects of their word associations in both languages indicated that they relied more on the stereotyped common verbal sequences of French and English than did the control children, suggesting that the program may have presented them with a difficult challenge, at least for the first year. This report compares the end-of-year performances of a new set of first grade classes—the followup classes—comprising different groups of experimental and English and French control children; its purpose is to assess the stability and generalizability of last year's results. These comparisons are presented in Part I. In Part II, the pilot class is followed through the second year of the program which remained all French except for fifty minutes of instruction each day given by a teacher of English.

Part I. A replication with the follow-up classes of first graders

General procedure. The overall plan is essentially the same as that of last year's study, described fully by Lambert and Macnamara (1969). Briefly, the purpose of this year's study was to reexamine the effects, on the linguistic and mental development of first grade children, of two years' schooling (Kindergarten and Grade I) conducted exclusively in a foreign language. Equal attention was given to possible retardation in native language skills, to progress made in the foreign language skills, and to relative achievement made with the content of the actual program of study. Accordingly, new classes of control children were selected for purposes of comparison: English Control I, a group of 26 first graders in the same school as the majority of the experimental class, but following the standard English language program; English Control II, a first grade class of 28 children in a progressive school in Montreal's Westmount area; and a French control class of 25 first graders from a French-Canadian school, also in the same district as the experimental class. The follow-up experimental class comprised one class of 25 children in one English elementary school and another class of 13 in a second elementary school, each class with its own French-speaking teacher. As was the case with the pilot groups, all of the experimental children had attended a French kindergarten for approximately two hours a day in the year preceding Grade I, while all of the control children had attended kindergarten classes conducted in their native languages.

Every attempt was made to discourage administrators and teachers from screening out any children, especially in the experimental class, who might be considered as potentially slow learners or otherwise un-likely to cope with the French program. Although the parents of one or two children were discouraged, two children with 'perceptual problems' nevertheless stayed in the class and they subsequently adjusted well and are now indistinguishable in their performance from the other children. Table 1 presents a breakdown of the range of intelligence scores for pilot and follow-up classes on the Progressive Matrices Test (Raven 1956). Note that for all classes, there is a broad range of scores and there was obviously no selection of only the brightest students for either of the experimental classes. As is evident in Table 2, there are no reliable differences in mean intelligence scores among follow-up classes; a comparable table for the pilot classes is given in Lambert and Mac-namara (1969: 88).

Even though all the schools involved in the study are in essentially middle social class districts, each child's mother was nevertheless interviewed in detail about aspirations, values, and child training practices that have been found to influence academic intelligence and academic achievement (see Bloom 1964, Dave 1963, and Wolf 1963). The interview schedules developed by Dave and Wolf to assess these home characteristics were adapted for our purposes; this year's revised version was shorter than that used for the pilot classes, and they are not directly comparable. Class comparisons are presented in Table 2; note that a reliable difference among groups occurred on only one of the five major themes, that of 'home guidance and facilities for school learning', where the English Control II class rated reliably lower than all others. It is clear, then, that in general the groups are comparable on most of the characteristics that are known to affect school achievement,

TABLE 1: Class Comparisons of Raven's Intelligence Scores at Start of First Grade

Percentiles	Scores of the standardization group*	Percentages of students falling in percentile groups			
		Experimental classes	English Control I classes	English Control II classes	French Control classes
		Pilot F-U	Pilot F-U	Pilot F-U	Pilot F-U**
95	23 or over	14 25	11 48	24 33	8 29
90	21-22	27 11	32 5	8 11	13 9
75	17-20	32 36	11 33	40 26	63 43
50	14-16	18 25	11 9	20 22	8 5
25	11-13	9 0	32 5	8 7	8 5
10	10 or less	0 3	5 0	0 0	0 0

*A sample of 300 Dumphries (Scotland) children, 6 years of age, at start of Grade I.

**F-U = Follow-up.

TABLE 2: Group Comparisons of Mean Scores on Measures of Intelligence and Components of Socioeconomic Status, Grade I Follow-up Classes

	Experimental N = 38	Eng. Cont. I N = 26	Eng. Cont. II N = 28	French Cont. N = 25	F-ratio
Intelligence, September testing Raven scores	19.74	21.35	20.39	20.40	n.s.
Home and family characteristics Emphasis on education	3.79	3.50	3.59	3.70	n.s.
Quality of linguistic environment	3.56	3.58	3.69	3.38	n.s.
Home guidance and facilities for school learning	3.83	3.62	3.18	3.80	6.40[a] df 3,105 p<.01
Enrichment of home environment	3.52	3.55	3.43	3.14	n.s.
Educational facilities	4.25	4.14	4.07	4.13	n.s.
School attendance Percentage of school days missed	4.14	6.85	5.74	1.47	10.46[b] df 3,118 p<.01

TABLE 2 NOTES: [a]The multiple-group comparison tested with the Newman-Keuls technique (Winer 1962), reveals that the English Control II group is reliably lower (at either the .01 or .05 levels) than all other groups.

[b]The Newman-Keuls test shows that the French Control class has significantly fewer absences than all other groups (.01 level) and that the English Control I class has significantly more absences than the Experimental class (.05 level).

i.e. intelligence and socioeconomic type factors. Still, to further insure comparability on these salient factors, a covariance procedure was employed again, following the scheme of Snedecor (1956); see also Lambert and Macnamara (1969). This technique statistically adjusts each of the dependent variables for initial differences in I.Q. and home environment characteristics. The adjusted mean scores were then tested by analysis of variance.

There was no evidence, in terms of attendance, to suggest that the experimental program was more demanding (see Table 2). The only reliable difference was that between the French Control class (least absences) and the English Control I class (most absences). Visits to the classes during the year turned up no apparent differences in discipline or attention problems.

As in the 1969 study, no attempt was made to equate classes on the basis of quality, efficiency, or personalities of teachers. However, the school principals were confident that all the first grade teachers were fully trained and experienced and all had selected elementary teaching as their specialty. Both teachers of the Follow-up Experimental classes were from France, with teaching experience both in France and in Canada; they know little or no English.

The curriculum worked out for the experimental classes drew on programs used both in French Canadian and European French first grades; all text materials were in French and were published in Canada. The plan was to cover the same content and course requirements as expected by the English Protestant School System of Greater Montreal.

Thus, although teachers from France are involved in the program, it is essentially Canadian in content and in purpose. The kindergarten program, conducted almost exclusively in French by two very skilled and experienced teachers from Europe, stressed vocabulary development and listening comprehension through art, music and play, and encouraged spontaneous verbal expression in French. Because of this preliminary experience, the first grade teachers were able to relate to the children as though they were French-speaking, albeit somewhat slow and bewildered during the first few weeks. Special emphasis should be given to the kindergarten experience. It may turn out to be a crucial feature of the success of this and similar programs.

French was the only language used by the first grade teachers from the first day on. Since the classes were both part of a typical English elementary school, once outside class the children encountered English only at recess and going and coming to school. Also, weekly courses in physical education, music, and plastic arts were conducted in English.

In an attempt to reduce the 'Hawthorne' effect of having only the one group treated as an 'experimental' class, special care was taken to choose control classes that also were somewhat special. The French control class, for example, is part of a well-publicized school-wide experiment in modern methods of teaching mathematics, and the school from which the English Control II class was drawn is reputed to be progressive and experimental, especially with methods of teaching English and French as school subjects.

Measures used with Follow-up Grade I classes

Essentially the same battery of tests was administered to the Follow-up classes as was used with the Pilot classes: these are described by Lambert and Macnamara (1969: 89ff.). The following modifications or additions were introduced, however, with numbers referring to placement in Table 3: (5) The Peabody Picture Vocabulary Test; the first 85 items were scored; (6) Listening Comprehension in English, a new test. An entire class listened to two stories narrated in English, first in its entirety and then in two parts. After each part, six questions were asked and the children responded by encircling a 'yes' or 'no' on their answer sheets. There were 24 questions asked, giving a maximum score of 24.

(7) Word Association Analysis. The following changes were made in classifications. In view of the theoretical significance of 'syntagmatic' and 'paradigmatic' type responses, special attention was directed to them. When an associational response satisfied the criteria for more than one category, it was classified with the following priorities: category a was given priority over b - f, category b was given priority over c - f, etc.

(a) Syntagmatic. Stimulus and response words occur in immediate sequence (forward or backward) or are separated by a single determiner (a, to, the) in ordinary continuous speech. The sequence must be one likely to occur in children's speech, e. g. dead-drunk is not considered syntagmatic for children of this age, although it is for adults. The word not following a verb stimulus was classified as syntagmatic, e. g. allow— not.

(b) Paradigmatic. Responses occur in the same word class (e. g. noun, verb, adjective) as the stimulus word (even if each can also occur in other classes). The opposite or negation of a word was considered paradigmatic, e. g. clear — unclear. Softly — hard was called

paradigmatic because it was presumed that the children were responding hard to the soft stem of softly. Furthermore, hard may be an ad-
verb, as is softly, e.g. He hit the ball hard. Similarly, color – red
and five – six were classified as paradigmatic.

(c) Semantic clusters. Responses that are semantically related to
the stimulus word but do not fit categories a or b, e.g. eat – plate.

(d) Rhyming responses, e.g. say – day.

(e) Transformations (excluding negation) of stimulus words, e.g.
kill – killing.

(f) Idiosyncratic: no obvious relation between the stimulus and response, e.g. run – spinach.

(8) Speaking Skills: Story Retelling (English and French). Each
child was individually presented with a tape-recorded story consisting
of six or seven sentences. The child retold the story in his own words,
and his output was tape-recorded. For the Experimental class, half
of the children received a French story on one day and several days
later an English story, while the other half had the English first, then
French. Counts were made of the following features of each child's
story: the number of adjectives; the number of different adjectives;
the number of nouns; the number of different nouns; the number of
verbs; the number of different verbs; the number of grammatical errors; and his overall comprehension of the story, rated on a 5-point
scale, ranging from poor to excellent (in French, from nul or mal to
excellent, with native speakers of French as the point of reference).

Ratings. The stories were then randomized on a master tape so that
the judges could not tell from which class any child came. Two balanced bilinguals, acting independently as judges, then rated the stories
on the same 5-point scale for the following linguistic skills: 'overall
expression', consisting of ease of talking, word choice, thought patterns, and errors of substance; 'grammatical correctness'; 'enunciation' (in French, 'enunciation' and 'liaison'); and 'rhythm and intonation'.
Each child's score is the average of the two judges' ratings.

(9) Speaking Skills: Story Creation (English and French). Each child
was presented with a series of comic strip type pictures. For this test,
too, half of the Experimental children were tested in French first, and
the other half in English first. The same procedures for 'counts' and
'ratings' as used in (8) above were applied here.

(12) Listening Comprehension in French. A French version of test
(6) described above.

(13) Picture Vocabulary Test in French. This is a translated version
of test (5) described above. Since there are two forms of the original
English test, the Experimental classes had an original English version
and the alternate form translated into French.

(19) Lorge-Thorndike Intelligence Scale. This intelligence test uses
pictorial materials and oral instructions. Level 1 was administered to

Grade 1, consisting of 3 subtests. The first, containing 25 items, tests vocabulary. The child must circle one out of the five possible pictures which represents the word which is read aloud to him. The second sub-test (25 items) consists of circling the one picture (out of five) which does not belong (e. g. basketball, football, cat, baseball, tennisball). The third subtest (25 items) consists of drawing circles around the two pictures (out of five) which go together. The children were allowed to rest between tests. Scores for the number of correct responses on each section are presented along with the total correct score, which had a maximum value of 75.

Results: Follow-up classes at Grade I

Our major interest in replicating was to examine the reliability of the results obtained with the pilot groups of first graders by comparing their performance with a second group of first graders following the same types of curricula. Important differences do exist, however; there are different teachers, school buildings, and principals involved with the Follow-up Experimental class. Furthermore, the team of university students conducting the testing, the interviewing and analysis of test data are all different, as are many of the testing procedures. Nevertheless, the majority of achievement tests are essentially the same as in the first year, although they have been modified or simpli-fied wherever possible, as is apparent in the description of procedures for last year's and this year's study. Thus, if the same pattern of re-sults as last year is found again, with all these variations, we will be assured that the conclusions drawn are reliable and of general value to others contemplating similar language training programs. Also, if the results for the first year are reliable in this sense, one can then have more confidence in the Grade II results, to be presented later.

   1. Reading ability and word knowledge in English. On tests 1, 2, and 3, all requiring ability to read and make judgments about English words, the Experimental children are significantly poorer than those in the two English Control classes; (see the first three entries in Table 3). This outcome is not unexpected since the Experimental children had no academic training in English at all. In fact, the interesting result is that, when compared with the North American norms for large groups of first grade children of normal intelligence, the Experimental class falls between the 20th and 40th percentiles. These results, essentially the same as those found with the Pilot classes, add strong support to the hypothesis that children trained to read in a nonnative language are very efficient at transferring these skills to the native language.

   2. Vocabulary and listening comprehension in English. When mea-sured for passive command of English by means of the Picture Vocabu-lary and the Listening Comprehension tests (tests 5 and 6), the Experi-

mental class demonstrates a capacity in English as advanced as that of both English Control groups, even for concepts that they would likely only have encountered through their French training. In this respect, too, the results square nicely with those of the Pilot classes.

3. Speaking skills in English. With regard to speaking skills in English (measures 8 and 9), the Experimental children were rated as competent in overall expression, grammar, enunciation, rhythm and intonation as the English Controls, both when retelling a story (No. 8) and when creating a story with the aid of comic strip pictures (No. 9). In fact their grammar was rated significantly more favorably on test No. 8. When their oral productions were analyzed statistically, it was found that they had fuller descriptions than either control (i.e. most number of words, significant at the .05 level), including most adjectives, nouns, and verbs (each statistically significant), and a more diversified repertoire of adjectives than at least one of the control classes. They made no more grammatical errors in retelling the story than did the controls, and their story comprehension was judged reliably better than that of either control class. When asked to create a story without the aid of a verbal model, they were still indistinguishable from the controls except that they used fewer adjectives and had a less diversified range of nouns than one control class. Still, their story comprehension was significantly better than either control class. Thus, there is no reflection of trouble with English grammar, as was noted with the Pilot classes; in fact, the Follow-up Experimental group had better comprehension and a richer descriptive repertoire in English than did the controls, at least when retelling a story.

4. English word associations. The children's word associations in English are used as an index of both linguistic and cognitive development. The results are essentially the same as those of the Pilot classes, even with major changes made in methods of analysis. They are as rapid at associating in English as the controls, and they produce no more idiosyncratic responses. Although they do give reliably more syntagmatic responses in both English and French, their proportion of paradigmatic responses is equivalent to the controls in both languages. Thus, as with the Pilot classes, there is evidence for a greater reliance on common verbal sequences in both languages, but none for an underuse of paradigmatic responses, which means that there are no conclusive symptoms of cognitive or linguistic retardation. It is of special interest nonetheless that we have found this same pattern two years running. It may be the expression of a transition period in the development of bilingualism wherein the Experimental children concentrate and rely on the sequential properties of both the native and target languages, and on the semantic properties of the native language, as is suggested by their significantly greater use of semantic clusters. Since this emphasis on semantic clusters does not appear in their French associations (see measure 15), the Experi-

mental children may rely on the semantic structure of English, even when using French. Apparently, the attention focused on semantic clustering is compensated for by giving reliably fewer transformations than the control groups. A similar but less pronounced trend was noted with the 1969 classes. Thus, rather than producing transformational variants of the stimulus words to the same degree as the controls, the Experimental children give semantically related associations instead.

As with the Pilot class, the Follow-up Experimental class produces reliably fewer rhyming responses in English; this may be interpreted either as a lack of playfulness with their native language, or, following Ervin (1961), as a sign of maturity, since they are less tied to the sound properties of words. In any case, as we shall see in Table 4, the tendencies to overstress syntagmatic and understress rhyming responses are no longer apparent by Grade II, suggesting that the period of transition which affects associational structures is short-lived.

5. Reading, word knowledge, vocabulary and comprehension in French. When one considers the Experimental class's competence in French, one finds similar patterns of results for Pilot and Follow-up groups. In their reading and word discrimination skills (measures 10 and 11), the Experimental class scores as well as the French Control class, making them as competent, after one year of training, as native speakers in these two aspects of the passive control of French. However, they are reliably poorer in French listening comprehension (test 12), a measure requiring competence in attending to, storing, and answering questions about details of a story related to them in French. They also fall short of nativelike command of French vocabulary, judging from their scores on the French Picture Vocabulary Test (test 13). However, there is actually not a great difference between the groups: there are only ten concepts which the control class knew that the Experimental class did not, and these may not yet have been encountered in their schooling. For example, they missed the following concepts: acrobatie 'stunt', communication 'communication', délice 'delight', entonnoir 'funnel', diriger 'to direct', comptoir 'counter', tache de rousseur 'freckle', insigne 'badge', and cueillette 'pinking'. Thus, the Experimental class' mean score on test 13 indicates that they have developed a substantial vocabulary in French.

6. Speaking skills in French. With regard to their skill in producing French sounds, the Experimental class' score of 38.35 out of a possible 57.00 on the test of French phoneme production is also below that expected of native children (for example, the Pilot first grade French Control class scored 56.08). Still, in terms of the linguistic judges, their mean score reduces to a judgmental rating of 2.01, or a score of moyen, with French native speakers as the point of reference, essentially the same figure as found with the Pilot class. The sounds that give the class as a whole particular difficulty are those listed first

in the following series: pn, pt, â, in, eille, ô, i, cl, eur, é, un, u, an, alle, ot, è, on, r, eu. The ratings range progressively from poor to good, with a sharp break between the first two (pn and pt) rated significantly lower (poorest average ratings) than all others, with the last three (eu, r, on) clearly the best under control.

The relative ability of the Experimental class to retell or create stories in French is presented in rows 16 and 17 of Table 3. Considering first the statistical counts of the children's spoken French, the Experimental class has reliably more grammatical errors, especially errors of gender and agreement, and a more stereotyped stock of verbs than the French Control class, both in retelling and in creating stories in French. At the same time, they have as large an active vocabulary as the controls and as varied a range of nouns and adjectives in French. Although they reliably less able than the controls to comprehend a story told to them, they nevertheless score as well as the controls on story comprehension when creating a story themselves. In general, then, their verbal production in French is extremely good when compared with that of the control class.

Two teams of judges were used to evaluate the tape-recorded productions of each child as he retold or created stories in French. One team comprised two perfectly bilingual French-Canadian university students who rated the English and French productions of children in all groups, thus assuring between-language comparability of ratings. In the practice period when they discussed how they would rate the French productions, they decided to be severe in the sense that they would use perfect bilinguals, such as themselves, as examples of how bilingual children can control their two languages. On the five-point rating scale, they reserved position 5 for 'superb' productions, 4 for those 'very good or worthy of note', 3 for 'passable or good', 2 for 'below average, more mistakes than should be, but not poor', and 1 for 'poor in construction, redundant, and needing prompting, etc.'. Incidentally, it was their opinion that the average French Canadian, adult or child, would likely fall between positions 2 and 3, whereas the continental French speakers would typically fall between positions 3 and 4.

The second team consisted of two very experienced French-Canadian teachers who specialize in teaching French at the elementary school level. Their frame of reference was the typical French child whom they had taught for 15 years in one case and 25 years in the other. Their scale also ranged from poor (1) to excellent (5), but as can be seen in rows 16 and 17 of Table 3, their ratings differed substantially from those of the bilingual judges. The bilingual judges rated the Experimental children, in general, between positions 1.3 and 2.2, and the French controls between 2.1 and 3.3. The French teacher judges rated the Experimental children, on the average, between the 2.0 to 2.7 positions, and the French controls between 2.9 and 3.5. Both teams found the most consistent between-group differences for rhythm and intonation and the smallest differences for enunciation and liaison. Thus, the children's command of French is rated about one position lower on a 5-point scale than that of the controls, that is, somewhere between the subjective positions of poor and average, with native speakers as the point of reference. They are relatively good in their enunciation and liaison and relatively poor in their rhythm and intonation and, when creating stories without a model, in grammar as well. All four judges summarized their general opinions by stating that the Experimental children would likely be indistinguishable from natives after a month or two if placed in a completely French environment, and they had rarely encountered English high school students with as good a command of French language sounds after seven years study as most of those in the Experimental group.

7. Word associations in French. The associations in French of the Experimental class are reliably slower than those of the natives (with the Pilot classes there was no significant difference in latencies), and as was found with the Pilot class, they emphasize syntagmatic responses significantly more than the control children do while giving significantly fewer transformation responses. It is of interest that the Experimental class' tendency to favor common sequential runs appears in both languages and was noted with two different samples of children. This reliable, but transient, characteristic deserves more careful study.

8. Skill in arithmetic. When tested for arithmetic ability to compute or solve problems presented orally in English (test 4), the Experimental class is as competent as the controls, all groups falling between the 75th and 80th percentile on national norms, with the Experimental class the highest. This result is impressive since all arithmetic concepts were taught through French, and here they are being tested through English. Apparently the concepts were well assimilated; in fact, they may have been assimilated 'through' French and given substance 'in' English.

9. Measures of intelligence. The end-of-year reassessments of intelligence are presented in rows 18 and 19 of Table 3. Contrary to the 1969 findings, the Experimental children show no intellectual retardation at all when compared with the two English Control groups on the Raven's Matrices Test. On the other hand, they show no intellectual advantage, but again Kittell's results (1959, 1963) would suggest that one should not expect an advantage to show itself so early in the development of bilingual skill. On the Lorge-Thorndike measure, the Experimental class scores the same as the controls on the picture vocabulary subtest, is significantly poorer than one control but equivalent to the other on the subtest measuring the comprehension of items and events that do not belong together, and is at the same level on the subtest dealing with the comprehension of items and events that go to-

gether. On the total test, there is no difference among groups in intelligence as measured in June.

10. Sensitivity to foreign language sounds. Finally, when tested in June for their sensitivity for the sounds of a totally foreign language, Russian, the Experimental class is somewhat better at discriminating Russian phonemes but the difference is not significant, nor was it for the Pilot class. Thus, one cannot argue, even though the results are in the expected direction, that children have developed, after one year's academic experience with a second language, a sensitivity for foreign languages in general.

Summary of findings and conclusions. In view of the substantial degree of similarity of results from two different classes of first year students, for whom the methods of instruction, the teachers, the forms of tests and the analysis of test results differed from one year to the next, one can make a very similar but more forceful set of conclusions than was the case in the Lambert and Macnamara report, with one experimental class only.

1. If one asks whether a first year of schooling conducted entirely in a foreign language retards children's development in their native language, it seems that, for children with the intelligence and home backgrounds of those studied here, the answer is a qualified No. In the first place, the Experimental class' breadth of vocabulary and listening comprehension in English were at the same level as those of the control classes. When reconstructing a story related to them, their expression, enunciation, rhythm and intonation were also as good as that of the controls and their grammar was better (a finding that contrasts with the Pilot class whose grammar was poorer). Their stories were fuller, more descriptive and diversified, and they showed more comprehension of the story than was the case for the controls. When creating a story on their own, their overall comprehension is still better, although in this instance they show less descriptive diversity than one of the control classes. Thus, with regard to oral productions and passive command of English they are generally as competent or more so than the controls.

Secondly, their thinking processes when associating in either English or French indicate, as was the case in the Pilot study, that they rely relatively heavily on common sequential patterns in English (syntagmatic responses), a tendency noted also in French. However, there is, for the second year running, no evidence of linguistic or cognitive retardation, since the Experimental children are not different from the controls in the number of paradigmatic responses given. They also distinguish themselves from the controls by over-emphasizing semantic relationships in their associations and underemphasizing transformation and rhyming responses (a possible symptom of rigidity or lack of 'play' with English). These differences form the basis of the qualifications attached to the No given above. As we shall see, after two years' experience in French, this qualification is lifted completely, but it is nevertheless of great interest to have a very reliable index of the type of cognitive effect brought on by this mode of developing bilingual skill, ephemeral as it now appears to be.

In the third place, it is apparent again this year that the reading skills, word knowledge, and word discrimination of the Experimental children is statistically poorer than that of the controls, as would be expected since they have had no training at all in reading English and have been discouraged from reading English on their own. Since they nevertheless fall at between the 20th and 40th percentiles on North American norms for these three skills, we interpret this amazing skill with the written forms of English as a fascinating instance of transfer from French to English, and offer the hypothesis (which merits special study) that the learning of French may take place 'through' English for these students. We assume that the children start the program with a good deal of translating from French to English and that they become very efficient at both translating and comparing the two languages. Furthermore, we interpret this transfer and the remarkable ability displayed at the end of the second year as a unique example of getting to know as well as know about one's 'own' language through the study of a second language. This claim, often made by teachers of classical languages, takes on great significance in this situation.

2. How well do children progress linguistically in a foreign language when it is used as the medium of instruction for the first year of schooling? The answer is, <u>Remarkably well</u>. Drawing on the results from both years of testing, their reading and word discrimination skills in French are at the same level as those of the French control group. At the same time, they are significantly poorer than the controls in listening comprehension and in passive control of vocabulary, although the same test of vocabulary showed that they have nevertheless attained a substantial depth of understanding of complicated concepts in French. Similarly, their mastery of French phonemes was clearly not as good as native-speaking children, and yet their average rating for phoneme production was considered average when judges used native speakers as a reference point. When retelling or creating stories in French, they compare surprisingly well with the controls on overall comprehension and on vocabulary depth and diversity. When their taped productions in French are analyzed, they are definitely not mistaken for native speakers of French, and yet they do surprisingly well, relatively, on enunciation and liaison, although relatively poorly on rhythm and intonation.

3. How do children trained in this fashion compare on tests of a subject matter such as mathematics, taught only in French? The fact that they scored as well as the two English control groups, falling at the 80th percentile on national norms, with the testing conducted in

English, strengthens the notion that the information they receive in French transfers extremely well into English, suggesting that the information may be thought through in English, via French, or processed simultaneously in the two languages.

4. Does the bilingual experience encountered by the Experimental children affect their sensitivity to the sounds of a completely novel third language? Although the results on the measure of sensitivity for Russian phonemes favor the discrimination ability of the Experimental class, the difference is not a statistically significant one. Thus, there is no reliable evidence, at the end of Grade I, for a generalized language aptitude derivable from bilingual training.

5. Finally, does the bilingual experience affect the measured intelligence of the Experimental children? In the Pilot study the Experimental class was significantly lower on their June retest of intelligence than one control group, but not different from the second control class. This year there was no difference among groups on the retest nor on the overall scores of a second comprehensive measure of intelligence. Thus, there is no evidence of intellectual confusion or retardation attributable to the training received. On the other hand, there is no evidence either for an intellectual advantage after Grade I.

Part II. The Pilot classes at Grade II

General procedure. The purpose and experimental plan as presented in Part I and in last year's report (see Lambert and Macnamara 1969) apply as well to the second year classes. In fact, in this section we follow the Pilot class, who were first graders last year, into their second year of schooling. The children were all in the same schools as last year, and these schools were the same as those described in Part I. In their second grade work, the English and French control classes continued their schooling in their respective native languages, while the Experimental Pilot class followed a normal French second grade curriculum except for two 25-minute periods of English language arts taught by a regular teacher of English. Her purpose was to cover the essentials of the standard second-year program in English in as concise and summary a fashion as possible. That is, the Experimental class was taught English, not as students of a second language, but as regular second-grade English-speaking students. Otherwise, they followed an all-French academic program, the content of which was appropriate for their grade level according to the standards set by the school board. All textbooks and readers were in French (except those used for English) and were published in Canada. The weekly courses in physical education, music, and plastic arts were, however, conducted in English.

The school setting of the Experimental Grade II class was the same as it had been for them in Grade I, that is, their class was situated in a typical English-Canadian elementary school where English was the only language of interaction at recess and in walking to and from school. Still, the principal and other teachers were sympathetic to the experiment, making the atmosphere for the Experimental children a friendly and considerate one.[4] Judging from discussions with teachers, visits to the classes, and measures of the amount of absences, there are no signs that the Experimental program was oppressive or unpleasant. For example, the mean numbers of days missed in the year, corrected for total number of school days, are: Experimental class, 4.38; English Control I, 5.78; English Control II, 6.14; and French Control, 2.17; ($F = 4.03$, df 3,56, p<.02). Thus, the Experimental class falls between the French Control class which has reliably fewest days absent and the two English Control classes.

All classes involved in the study had moved up to new, second-grade teachers and all of these, with one exception, met all required professional standards and were experienced elementary school teachers. The one exception was the teacher of the Experimental class who, apparently because of some administrative oversight, was engaged even though she had not completed her own secondary schooling and had no previous teaching experience. This is not to say that the teacher in question was not effective or appreciated by the students, but merely to indicate that there was certainly no bias in the study favoring the Experimental class with regard to teacher qualifications and experience. That teacher, incidentally, was French-Canadian, meaning that the Grade II Experimental Pilot class had had French-Canadian teachers for Grades I and II except for a replacement teacher from France who took over the last two months of the first year.

The covariance procedure, described earlier, was applied to the children's scores on various measures of English, French, and arithmetic competence collected at the end of Grade II; it adjusted these scores for initial differences amont students in measured intelligence and socioeconomic background as of the beginning of Grade I. With these adjustments, we can be confident that the comparisons to be made below are not attributable to differences in measured intelligence or social-class background which are known to influence school achievement and language development.

The interviewing, testing, and analyses of results were conducted by small groups comprising graduate and undergraduate students at McGill and L'Université de Montréal, and teachers from the English and French school systems. Disrupting as testing is, we were nevertheless given permission to keep the testing in the various schools approximately in lock-step, and to properly administer the tests, e.g. giving as many rest periods as called for, etc. In order not to abuse the cooperation extended by the various school authorities, we did not make all possible group comparisons. For example, we did not take the time of the French Control class for collecting new data on French phoneme production, because we knew from last year's study that Grade I French children in the control class had nearly perfect scores, as would be expected. Similarly, it would have taken too much time to ask for the word associations and the speech productions of all children in the French Control class; thus, only some students were given these tests.

Measures used with the Grade II Pilot classes

In general the tests and measures used with the Grade II children were standard extensions or simple up-aging of those used with the first graders. This is clearly so for the standardized tests such as the Metropolitan Achievement (Primary II Battery), or the Peabody Picture Vocabulary. Others, such as the Word Association and Speaking Skills measures, were identical in format for both grade levels, but with scoring provisions that accommodate age differences in expressive capacity. Others, such as the Lorge-Thorndike Intelligence Test and subtests of the Metropolitan series, however, are changed in format to be appropriate for the Grade II level, e.g. the ability to solve arithmetic problems required the older children to read problems themselves rather than listen to an adult present the problems and the questions to be solved. Certain tests that are substantially different in structure from those described earlier are referred to below, with numbering corresponding to the entries in Table 4.

1. English Word Knowledge. Similar to item 1 for Grade I (see corresponding section in Part I), but standardized for second graders. For the last 20 items, written descriptions rather than pictures were used as stimuli to be matched with printed words. Standard scores are used for Tests 1-6 in Table 4.

4. English Spelling Skills. Consists of 30 dictated words, each presented in a context to make its meaning unmistakable. 5. Arithmetic Concepts (English). Consists of 42 items that provide a comprehensive measure of ability to use basic numerical and quantitative concepts. 6. Arithmetic Computation (English format). Consists of 30 exercises in addition and subtraction. 7. Peabody Picture Vocabulary Test, English and French. One hundred items were presented in both English and French. Total score possible was 100. Same crossover procedure used for Experimental class (half starting with English version, half with French) as with first graders. 12. French Reading Skills. A relatively difficult test, even for the French Control children. In the first section, measuring word recognition and spelling ability, children read in unison a story with certain words deleted,

and are asked to fill in the missing words which they hear the teacher read aloud one time only. Spelling must be perfect; there are 18 items. In the second section, testing sentence comprehension, they read a story, silently, twice and are asked 12 rather difficult questions, requiring an understanding of the meanings of words. Children give spontaneous one-word answers. Section three is similar to the Grade I test of word order but with longer sentences and higher level vocabulary. Total score possible is 40. 19. June retest of Intelligence; Raven's. Note that for all classes involved, this was the third time they had taken the Progressive Matrices Test (i.e., September, 1966; June, 1967; and June, 1968). The maximum total score is 36.

Results: Pilot classes at end of Grade II

The results to be reviewed are all presented in Table 4 where the average performance scores of various classes are compared and tested for statistical significance. The following results were obtained with the Pilot second grade classes.

English language competence

Reading Skills, Spelling, and Vocabulary in English. There is an extremely impressive array of evidence showing that the Experimental children at the end of Grade II, with a very minimum of training in English, are at least equivalent and in no way inferior to the English Control classes in the development of native language skills. In fact, there are certain instances where the Experimental class shows relative superiority in English. Taken together, these results, as we shall see, throw an entirely new light on the whole experiment.

With regard to the tests of word knowledge and word discrimination (items 1 and 2 in Table 4), requiring a facility in matching printed words with either their meanings or their sounds, the Experimental class scores as well as either English Control group, all three groups falling between the 85th and 90th percentiles on nationwide norms. In reading skills (item 3), measured by tests of comprehension of English sentences and paragraphs, the Experimental class score is equivalent to Control II but reliably lower than that of Control I. In this instance, then, their relative standing is intermdiate, but the class as a whole nevertheless falls above the 80th percentile. Even on the Metropolitan Spelling Test (item 4), an ability one might not expect the Experimental children to have developed to an equivalent degree because of lack of experience with English sounds or because of so-called 'interference' of languages, the Experimentals are equivalent to both Control groups, scoring at the 87th percentile. Their performance on the Peabody Picture Vocabulary Test (item 7), which demands a knowledge of complex concepts in English, is also equivalent to that of either Control, as is their facility at storing and recalling the details of a story read to them, as measured by the English Listening Comprehension Test (item 8).

If we keep in mind that all of these skills are the ones normally taught and drilled in school, the performance of the Experimental class becomes especially enlightening. The results may mean that the normal pace of elementary education in North America is so slow, even in the best of schools, that children who have had a year or more 'vacation' of one sort or another can catch up rather easily. This may or may not be true, but in either case it is not clear how this group of students could catch up with such apparent ease. One might also argue that maturation may be playing a large role here, that is, simply delaying the formal teaching of native language reading skills and conceptual development for a year provides a shortcut in the time needed for learning. We cannot, within the limits of this study, argue strongly against these possibilities, except to emphasize that we noted a similar catching up process in operation even at the first grade level. The hypothesis that we favor in trying to understand the results is that the Experimental children may never have been on vacation in English at all, but rather have transferred basic skills of reading, concept development, word manipulation, and verbal creativity through French to English. The interesting speculation that derives from these results, and one that may give orientation to further experimentation, is that children of normal intelligence, trained as these children were in French, process new information encountered in class both in French (thereby developing great skill with that language) as well as in English, by drawing on and relating to their reservoir of English conceptual knowledge, built up through infancy and childhood, to help themselves comprehend and understand both the content of the new material and the nature of the new code through which that content is presented. In other words, it is our hunch that these children become aware of the new language as a code and, through contrasts made with their native language, become skilled at relating and translating academic content between French and English, and at relating and contrasting linguistic codes. It has often been argued, more or less convincingly, by specialists of the classical languages that training in Latin or Greek develops a deeper awareness of and understanding of one's native language (at least for speakers of those languages which are linguistically related to Latin or Greek). A similar argument is being proposed here, that learning through a second, linguistically related language appears to have affected favorably children's performance in their native language. The possibility will also be discussed that this contrastive language experience may have affected favorably the mastery of academic content as well.

An example of this favorable effect can be drawn from the Peabody test. Consider some French concepts that the third and fourth grade child is expected to understand, according to the age norms of the Peabody test: meringue, excaver, arctique, cérémonie, assaillir, chimiste, escarpement, lamentation, sentinelle, submerger, canine, évaluation, confiné, précipitation, and amphibie. As the child develops the meanings of these new words in French, he will certainly draw on past experiences and basic notions already symbolized and given substance with English names. For example, the context in which the concept canine is introduced and the amplifications provided by the French teacher will prompt the Experimental children to draw on their past experiences with dogs and dog-related events. Then as the notion is developed in French and the use of this new word is stabilized in a child's memory, he will incidentally have developed an equivalent concept in English, i.e. canine. Note the English possibilities in this list of concepts taken directly from the Peabody test: canine, excavate, arctic, ceremony, assail, chemist, escarpment, lament, etc. Thus, when given the English version of the Peabody test, with similar conceptual demands made on him, the child is able to score as well as the English Control classes. In addition to concepts that are cognates in English and French, the third grade children also must come to understand such concepts as pignon 'gable', sondage 'probing', hisser 'hoist', déchirement 'bereavement', planer 'hover'. As the meanings of these words are developed, a sharp contrast between languages is incidentally offered, and the child may be prompted to seek out on his own the English translation-equivalents of such new notions given substance with French symbols.

Speaking Skills in English. Further supportive evidence for this general view is found when the classes are compared in their capacities to retell or create stories in English (items 10 and 11 in Table 4). When retelling a story, the Experimental class is rated equivalent to both Controls on overall expression and grammar, and as equivalent to one Control and better than the other on enunciation, rhythm, and intonation in English. When creating stories in English, they are rated as equivalent to one Control and better than the other on both expression and grammar, the same as both English Controls on enunciation, but poorer than one Control and better than the other on rhythm and intonation. Except for this instance (rhythm and intonation) where they are judged poorer than one Control class, they are, in general, either as efficient as, or better than, one Control class or the other at retelling and in spontaneously creating stories in English.

When their individual stories are transcribed and analyzed in detail, we find that the Experimental class has a vocabulary in English as rich and varied or more so than that of the Controls. In retelling stories, they generally show a richer and more varied vocabulary than English

Control I, and they are similar to English Control II in depth and range of vocabulary except that they have a reliably more varied stock of adjectives than either Control class. Furthermore, they have as good a command of English grammar and are as able to comprehend the material presented them as is either Control. The same general picture emerges when the story inventions of each group are compared: the Experimental children use as many and as many different words as those of one of the Control groups, and are statistically better in this regard than the other Control class. However, the Experimental subjects comprehend the stories they invent significantly better than either of the Control groups do. Thus, the Experimental children's capacity to use English spontaneously is definitely developed as well as or better than one Control class or the other.

Encoding and Decoding Skills in English. There is one other indication of how well the Experimental children handle English. A separate experiment was conducted with the Grade II Experimental and English Control I children (see Samuels, Reynolds and Lambert 1969) on the relative ability of these children to communicate spontaneously and creatively in English. In that study, attention was directed to both their decoding and encoding abilities, that is, their skill in understanding descriptive messages relayed to them by children their own age and in communicating messages to others. In the decoding task, a child hears a taped version of another child describing which block out of six should be put next in order on a peg. For example, the one that looks like a girl with hair and hands and no feet and no tummy would describe the next block to place. The encoding task would have the same child describe in his own words which blocks he is putting on the peg in any order he chooses. This task calls for knowledge of children's everyday language, and the finding of special interest is that the Experimental class was as efficient as the English Controls in both decoding and encoding in English.

Word Association in English. As one examines the children's English word associations (item 9), the same pattern of comparability between classes becomes evident, and the relative overuse of syntagmatic responses that characterized two first-year Experimental classes is no longer in evidence. The Experimental class is as rapid in giving their associations as the Control class is, and they give proportionally no more paradigmatic, syntagmatic, semantic clusters or rhyming responses than do the Controls. However, the Experimental children do give reliably more idiosyncratic and reliably fewer transformation responses than do the Controls. It is difficult to interpret the meaning of this overuse of idiosyncratic responses; it could signify a relative lack of inhibition or a carelessness when thinking in English, especially when set to respond quickly, or it could mean that, as their facility with French progresses, there are more between-language routes along which associations can pass. Since there was no such tendency at the end of Grade I, it will be of interest to see if it occurs again when new classes of Grade II children are compared. The major outcome, though, is the similarity between the classes in the process of associating in English. The tendency for Grade I Experimental classes to give disproportionately more syntagmatic responses than the English Controls is not apparent at the Grade II level. If this outcome is replicated, we will be able to argue with greater assurance that the peculiar associational pattern noted after one year's academic experience with a foreign language passes away in a relatively short time. Of course, other peculiarities could show up at other points in time as one develops deeper degrees of bilingual skill, and it will be necessary to be on guard for such eventualities as the program is extended beyond Grade II.

Arithmetic competence

A third line of evidence suggesting beneficial transfer from French to English is to be noted in the Experimental class' performance on tests of arithmetic skill (items 5 and 6 in Table 4). Keep in mind that mathematics, a nonlinguistic academic subject, is taught to the Experimental children exclusively in French. The results of their comparative knowledge of mathematical concepts, when tested in English, are especially enlightening: on test 5 (arithmetic concepts and problem solving ability), the Experimental children score as well as either Control class and rank, as a class, above the 90th percentile on national norms. On test 6 (measuring speed and efficiency in mathematical computation), they are significantly better than either Control class. These results suggest very strongly that their French training in math had 'got through' to them, so that they are either amazingly clever in transferring the fruits of this training and/or are stimulated by their foreign-language experience to relate new notions and concepts to their English reserve of basic meanings while in the process of developing more complex, new ideas. The fact that they are even more skilled than the Controls in the application of these ideas suggests that such a tendency to transfer and relate may make the new concepts encountered more vivid and meaningful, thereby speeding up the learning process itself. Although the results obtained support such an hypothesis, much more research of a detailed, experimental nature is called for to verify it.

French competence

Reading Skills and Listening Comprehension in French. The results to be discussed next describe the progress of the Experimental class in

French, relative to the French Controls.[5] On the very demanding test of French Reading Skills (item 12), the Experimental class scores as well as the Controls and on one subtest, that concerned with word order, the Experimental class is significantly better ($F = 6.63$, df 1, 24, p<.02). Likewise on the French Listening Comprehension Test (item 13) there is no difference between the two groups. Thus, in terms of these two passive aspects of French, the Experimental class is as good as native-speaker Controls.

Vocabulary in French. On the French version of the Picture Vocabulary Test (item 14) the Experimental children are significantly behind the Controls, but it should be noted that the two group means differ only by 5 units (71.66 and 76.13) meaning that the Experimental class on the average did not know 5 or so concepts which the control group knew. These concepts are: attirail 'junk', 'superfluous baggage', or 'funny attire', cérémonie 'ceremony', entonnoir 'funnel', assaillir 'to assault', hisser 'to hoist'. It is very likely that these concepts have not yet been encountered in their reading or schoolwork. Incidentally, the Experimental children knew certain concepts which the French Controls missed, e.g. non dressé 'bronco', meringue (as on a lemon pie), and excaver 'excavate', and both classes had equal difficulty with the final 25 items given them (i.e. numbers 75 to 100). Thus, the Experimental children have actually developed an extensive vocabulary of complex concepts in French, even when compared with native-speaker Controls.

French Phoneme Production. Their control of the essential sounds of French is reflected in their score on the French Phoneme Production measure (item 15). There is evidence here for progress over the first graders (42.23 for Grade II versus 38.00 for Grade I), when rated by the same judges on the same scales. Their average score works out to a mean rating of 2.22 (42.33/19) on a 3-point scale, signifying a judgment between moyen and bon, with native speakers of French as a point of reference. Impressive as this outcome is, it may have a quite different significance for the experiment as a whole. Perhaps we have here an indication that the Experimental children, by the end of Grade II, have leveled off in their progress with French sounds and with each year will have progressively fewer chances of reaching perfect, native-like control. This possibility should be considered seriously because it may reveal that starting French at kindergarten age and sustaining it in a classroom environment only is both too late and not enough, from one point of view. The four linguistic judges spontaneously commented on this feature of the children's pronunciation by saying that they felt the children would be indistinguishable from native speakers if placed in an all-French environment for a 'month or so'. At the same time, the judges felt that the children's command of the sounds was extremely good and that, as a group, they certainly did not have the 'typical' English accent in their French. For many parents and educators, perfect control of French sounds may not be a high-priority goal compared to the other real advantages already emerging from the program as it is now designed.

The phonemes that presented the greatest difficulty to the Experimental children are listed at the start of the following list: p̲t̲, i̲n̲, p̲n̲, a̲, a̲l̲l̲e̲, e̲u̲r̲, é̲, ô̲, e̲i̲l̲l̲e̲, i̲, o̲n̲, a̲n̲, u̲n̲, c̲l̲, u̲, r̲, o̲t̲, è̲, e̲u̲. The order progresses from poorest performance to best, but there is a distinct break after p̲t̲, the sound that is significantly least well controlled, and another break before è̲ and e̲u̲, the two sounds best under control.[6]

Speaking Skills in French. The analyses of the children's oral productions when retelling or creating stories in French (items 17 and 18, Table 4) also reveal an extremely high level of skill on the part of the Experimental class. The statistical counts of the story retelling indicate that they have as good comprehension of the stories as the controls do, and they have as rich and varied a vocabulary in French. Still they make significantly more grammatical errors than the controls. The same two sets of judges, as discussed in Part I, rated the tape recordings of each story and, as with the first graders, the same types of discrepancies between the bilingual and the French-teacher judges are apparent. The bilingual judges find the Experimental children reliably poorer on overal expression, grammar, and enunciation and liaison, but no different from the Controls in their rhythm and intonation in French. The French-teacher judges, in contrast, have a different mode of perceiving and rating since they find the Experimental class comparable to the Controls on all aspects except rhythm and intonation where they are rated reliably poorer than the Controls. The mean ratings assigned by the bilingual judges range between 1.61 and 2.28 for the Experimental class, and between 2.70 and 2.89 for the French Control class. This constitutes less than a scale point of difference, i.e. an overall 'low average' for the Experimentals compared to a 'passable' for the Controls on a 5-point scale ranging from 'poor' to 'excellent'. The ratings of the relatively more lenient French teachers ranged from 2.59 to 3.13 for the Experimental class and from 3.09 to 3.46 for the French Control class, a remarkably close comparison.

The picture is only slightly different when the judgments deal with the children's spontaneous creations (item 18). Here the statistical counts show that the Experimental children make relatively more grammatical errors than they do when simply retelling a story. In both instances, they make significantly more errors of grammar than do the Controls. They also have a less diversified stock of adjectives than do the Controls, which was not the case for story retelling. Otherwise, the overall size of their vocabulary, the diversity of nouns and verbs used, and the degree of comprehension of the stories told is the same as that of the Controls. The ratings of the bilingual judges in this case show a larger difference between classes and in no aspect is the Experimental class rated as high as the Controls. The French-teacher judges also make a greater differentiation of the two classes in this case, especially with regard to grammatical correctness: the Experimental class is significantly poorer than the Controls in their command of grammar and in their rhythm and intonation. In terms of expressivity, and enunciation and liaison, however, the French teachers find no difference between the classes when story creation is involved. In summary, then, the Experimental class, when evaluated by two teams of judges, each with its own criteria, are surprisingly well rated in comparison with native speakers of French. As a group, they are placed about one step lower on a 5-point scale than the control class, somewhere between positions 2 and 3 on the scale. They are particularly poor in their knowledge of French grammar, especially when creating stories on their own, but are relatively good in terms of enunciation and liaison, and overall expression.

Decoding and Encoding Skills in French. The same measures of decoding and encoding skills as described above were used to assess the Experimental children's ability to communicate in French with children their own age. Note that their normal experience in French is restricted to the classroom and to interaction with an adult, the teacher. They have very few opportunities for informal interaction in French with children their own age, except for their contacts with one another in the classroom, mostly school related ones. Consequently, we anticipated that they might well be less efficient than native-speaker Controls at decoding and encoding. The procedure was the same as described for the assessment of English; they had to follow descriptive instructions given to them by children who were native speakers of French, for example, ça ressemble à deux 3 colés ensemble (the decoding task), and to give their own descriptive directions so that French children could understand (the encoding task). Because the French Control class was not available for retesting, we selected a new Control class of French children, equated for intelligence and social class background. It was rather amazing to find that the Experimental class performed as efficiently as the native-speaker Control class on both the decoding and encoding tasks (Samuels et al. 1969). Thus, with this nonacademic measure of communicational skill, the Experimental class is equivalent to the Control class.

Word Associations in French. With regard to the children's thinking processes in French, as reflected in their word associations (item 16), the Experimental class does not differ in any respect from the French Control class. This means that their associations in French come as rapidly as those of the controls, [7] they have no more idiosyncratic responses and, perhaps most important of all, they do not give proportionally more or less syntagmatic responses or semantic clusters than the Controls. Thus, by the end of Grade II the Experimental children have become indistinguishable from the native-speaker Control class in the structure of their French associations and in their speed of associating. This is an important trend that should be checked on for its reliability with another set of Grade II classes.

Intelligence measures

Two different measures were taken of the children's intelligence at the end of their second year in the experiment; one was a retest using the Progressive Matrices Test (item 19), the other, the Lorge-Thorndike battery (item 20). On the Matrices test, there is no difference among group means, indicating that the slight depression in IQ noted with the Experimental class at the end of Grade I is no longer apparent. On the Lorge-Thorndike scales, the Experimental class is equivalent to English Control I on the vocabulary subtest, but both are significantly poorer than the English Control II class. On the other two subtests and on the total scale, the Experimental class scores as well as either Control. Thus, we have no symptoms at the end of Grade II for any intellectual deficit associated with the experimental program of instruction. It should be noted again, however, that we also have no evidence at this stage for any intellectual advantage that can be ascribed to the experimental program. Whether such an advantage will appear in the next year or so, as Kittell's work (1963) would have us expect, will only be known in time.

Foreign language sensitivity

The same Russian phoneme discrimination test as used at the end of Grade I was administered again at the end of Grade II. The comparison is made between the sensitivity of the Experimental class and a Control group comprising children taken from the English and French Control classes who had no second language experience in their homes. The results indicate that the Experimental class, as predicted, makes fewer errors in discrimination than does the Control group, but the difference is not a statistically significant one. The same pattern was found with the Follow-up Grade I classes, also with no statistically reliable difference. Thus, we do not have strong evidence here for a generalized sensitivity to foreign language sounds as of the end of Grade II, even though there is a consistently small trend favoring the Experimental classes. It could be that in Montreal most children have some contact with two languages and thus our Control children are not fully monolingual; for example, the English Control children have French as a subject matter from Grade I on. Nonetheless, we would expect, in light of the study of Parver and Rabinovitch (1966), that at some point the Experimental classes would show a marked superiority over the more monolingual Control classes. Accordingly, we plan to continue testing Pilot and Follow-up classes on a yearly basis.

Summary of findings and conclusions

We shall summarize and integrate the various findings and interpretations made throughout the paper around the basic questions that oriented the original design of the study, giving attention to both the Grade I and the Grade II results. Our answers to these questions, of course, should only be generalized to English-speaking children of the same intelligence range and socioeconomic background as those studied here, and with a French program of training similar to that used here, including the very important kindergarten preparation. Also, more weight should be given to answers about first graders because these results have been tested with two different sets of classes.

Do children taught through a foreign language for the first two years of school suffer in the linguistic development of their native language?

After the Grade I experience, the children following the French program of study were found to be as competent as native English-speaking Controls in their passive command of English and in their speaking ability. In certain aspects they were more competent. Their reading skills and word knowledge in English were poorer than those of the Controls, but, nonetheless, they were surprisingly good when compared with national norms for English-speaking first graders. This replicated finding suggests that a good deal of favorable transfer of skills takes place across languages, presumably from French to English as well as from English to French. Their modes of expressing thoughts through the English language, as reflected in their English word associations, reveal that they overemphasize (relative to the Controls) the more common sequential patterns in the language and the semantic relationships among concepts in English, while underemphasizing, relatively, verbal transformations and rhymes.

After a second year of experience in the French program, with only a minimum of training in English, there is an impressive amount of evidence that the Experimental class is at least as efficient in English, and in certain instances more so, than English Control classes. They are equivalent in word knowledge and discrimination, reading skills, spelling, vocabulary development, and listening comprehension, and on all of these tests for which national norms are available, they rank between the 86th and 90th percentiles. This remarkable performance adds strong support to the notion that very beneficial transfer takes place through French to English, affecting favorably the development of skills in both languages and in academic content as well. The second graders are also either as efficient as, or better than, the Control classes in retelling or spontaneously creating stories in English, with vocabularies as broad and varied as the controls, or more so, and with as good or better comprehension of the story content. When tested for their capacity to understand other children's everyday language and to communicate efficiently with other children, they are as able as the Control classes. In their English word associations, they are as swift in associating ideas as the Controls, and the structure of their associations shows no deficiencies (relative to the Controls) as was the case at the Grade I level. This contrast between Grade I and II performance in English raises the possibility that the difficult transition period for this method of developing bilingualism is passed by the end of the second year.

How well do children progress in the development of foreign language skills when that language is used as the sole medium of instruction for the first year of schooling and as the major medium for a second year?

At the end of Grade I, the Experimental class was at the same level in French reading and word discrimination ability as the French Controls, and although they were significantly below the level attained by the Controls in listening comprehension and vocabulary depth, the mean differences were actually small, indicating that they had really attained a substantial degree of conceptual knowledge in French. On the production side, the class as a whole was judged to be average in their control of French phonemes. In story retelling and story invention, they compare very well with the controls in their comprehension of the material and the depth and diversity of their vocabulary in French. The evaluations of their taped productions in French, made by trained judges, indicate that they have not attained a native-like style apparently because their rhythm and intonation are relatively poor. However, their enunciation and liaison in French compare favorably with the Controls. The pattern of their associations in French is essentially the same as it was in English: they overstress, relative to the Controls, commonly occurring verbal sequences in French, and they underuse transformation-type responses. Thus in both languages at the end of Grade I, they are distinguished from the Control classes by this reliance on common verbal and ideational patterns.

After two years in the program, their French competence is substantially improved in most characteristics. For example, they are at the same level as the second-year Controls in French reading skills and listening comprehension. Their vocabulary knowledge is statistically poorer than that of the Controls, but the groups actually differ by only 5 or 6 concepts out of 100, and the concepts missed were likely not yet encountered in their schoolwork. Thus they have developed an extensive vocabulary of complex concepts in French by the end of Grade II. Their control of French phonemes shows improvement over the Grade I level, moving to an average rating between moyen and bon. However, the actual improvement over the first year results is small, raising a question as to their chances of ever attaining perfect, native-like command of French pronunciation, starting the language at the age they did and under the special circumstances that characterize this experiment. Those phonemes that give them particular difficulty are pt (as in petit), in, pn, â, alle; those best under control are eu, è, ot, r, u. Their spontaneous speech shows an extremely high level of attainment. They have as good comprehension as the Controls of the content of the stories they retold or invented, and their active French vocabulary is as rich and varied as that of the Controls, although they do make reliably more grammatical errors, especially errors of gender and agreement. Their spontaneous French productions were rated extremely high when compared with native-speaker Controls. As a group, they are placed about one step lower than the Controls on the 5-point scale, that is, between positions 2 and 3, with the Controls between 3 and 4. They are rated relatively low on grammar, especially when inventing stories without a model, but they are especially good in enunciation, liaison, and overall expression. Their efficiency at understanding the everyday descriptive language of French children their own age, and at communicating to them in French, is at the same general level as that of native-speaker Controls. Their flow of ideas in French, as measured by their word associations, does not differ in any respect from that of the controls; their associations are as swift, and they have the same proportions or paradigmatic, syntagmatic and idiosyncratic responses as the controls. The peculiarities noted after Grade I, in other words, are no longer in evidence after the second year of the program.

How well do children achieve in a nonlanguage subject matter such as mathematics, when it has been taught through a foreign language for a two-year period?

At the end of Grade I, they attained the same level as the Controls in standard tests of mathematical achievement, falling at the 80th percentile on national norms for both problem and computational arithmetic, with the testing conducted in English. This is a noteworthy outcome, suggesting that the information received through instruction and reading in French had got through to the child sufficiently to permit him to apply it effectively, even in an English context.

At the end of Grade II, they were somewhat ahead of the Control classes in mathematical achievement. On tests of arithmetic concepts and problem solving, also in an English format, they are at the same level as the controls, falling at the 90th percentile on national norms, and on tests of speed and skill in computation, they are significantly better than the Controls. These findings lend strong support to the hypothesis that the children transfer information through French to English, thereby improving their memory and understanding of the content.

Does bilingual experience of the sort described here affect children's intelligence?

After Grade I, there is some ambiguity about the relative standing of the Experimental classes on measured intelligence. With the Pilot first grade classes, the Experimental class was significantly below one Control and equivalent to another on June retests of the Raven's Progressive Matrices measure. With the Follow-up first grade classes, however, the Experimental children scored as well as both Controls. Thus, at the end of Grade I it seems safe to conclude that there is no evidence of intellectual retardation attributable to the experimental program.

At the end of Grade II there was again no difference among classes on June retests of the Progressive Matrices test, nor on the Lorge-Thorndike battery, administered to all second-year classes for the first time this year. Thus, there are no indications of cognitive retardation at either grade level that can be attributed to the experimental program. Nor is there any sign of intellectual advantage at either grade level, although certain researchers suggest we should expect such an advantage to show itself in time.

Does bilingual experience of the sort described here develop a generalized sensitivity for linguistic sounds, even those of a linguistically unrelated language?

The measure of sensitivity for novel linguistic sounds was a test of ability to discriminate Russian phonemes, administered to both Grades I and II Experimental classes, comparing their performance with that of those children from English and French Control classes who had no experience with foreign languages at home. At both grade levels, the Experimental classes had better scores than the monolingual Controls, but neither comparison was statistically significant. However, there was no increase from Grades I to II in sensitivity for Russian phonemes. Thus there is no strong indication of a generalized sensitivity to linguistic sounds of another foreign language, at least at the Grade II level, although earlier research would lead us to expect such a development as the children increase in bilinguality.

In conclusion, the results of this experiment to date indicate that the type of bilingual training offered these children is extremely effective, even more so than was originally expected. The similarity of the findings for two different sets of first grade classes, involving changes in teachers, methods of instruction, and modes of testing and analysis, speaks well for the stability and generality of the effects produced by the experimental program. These effects demonstrate a very high level of skill in both the receptive and productive aspects of French, the language of instruction; a generally excellent command of all aspects of English, the home language of the children; and a high level of skill in a nonlanguage subject matter, mathematics, taught through the foreign language only. The results for the second year of the French program, during which a minimum of training was given in English, show a general improvement in French and English language achievement and in mathematics so that the second-year Experimental class performs as well as, and in some respects better than, either English or French Control classes in most abilities examined. Impressive as the Grade II results are, however, they should be considered as tentative until they are replicated with the Follow-up classes. Their significance will become clearer, too, as the scope of the research is broadened to include an examination of the impact of the experimental program on the ethnic attitudes of the children and their parents, relative to the Control children and their parents. It would be surprising if a program of the sort offered these children did not affect their self-conceptions, since they have become progressively more bicultural, perhaps much more so than their parents. These topics are dealt with in the report now in preparation (Lambert, Tucker, d'Anglejan and Segalowitz 1970).

Finally, it is felt that plans should be made to study the effects of the same type of experimental program on English-speaking children in Montreal from somewhat lower social class backgrounds and on children with an even broader range of intelligence scores. To be of general value to a region or nation that is serious about developing a bilingual and bicultural citizenry, children from working-class backgrounds and those of limited intellectual endowment should be given every opportunity to capitalize on a program as promising as this one now appears to be. In other words, it should not become a program for children from privileged backgrounds exclusively. Similarly, it is hoped that French Canadian educators will see the possible advantages of such a program for their children. There is, of course, nothing peculiarly Canadian about the program described here, and other bilingual communities may see some value in adopting it, at least on an experimental basis. Similarly, the program might be seen as a possible alternative to standard methods of teaching second languages at the elementary and secondary levels.

NOTES

[1]This research was supported in part by grants to McGill's Language Research Group from The Canada Council, The Canadian Defense Research Board (Grant Number 9401-10), and from the Department of Education of the Government of Quebec. We are indebted and grateful to many institutions and people for making this study possible: (1) the authorities of the South Shore Protestant Regional School Board, the Municipalité Scolaire Catholique de St. Lambert, and The Protestant School Board of Greater Montreal who strongly endorsed the experiment and permitted us to contact school principals; (2) the four school principals who assisted us in conducting the testing and evaluations (Mrs. Grace Walker, Margaret Pendlebury Elementary School; Mrs. Barbara Murdock, Victoria Park Elementary School; Mlle Estelle Landry, Ecole Rabeau; and Mr. S. Kneeland, Roslyn School; (3) Alison d'Anglejan and Miriam Klein who organized the testing, and Andrée Esterez, Renée Stevens, Danielle Groven, Sylvie Lambert, Georgette Lapointe, Marie-France Esterez, Steven Rosenberg, Sharon Kelly, Robert Frender and Marilyn Samuels who conducted the interviews and helped with the testing and analyses; (4) Mr. Sidney Segalowitz who assisted with the statistical analyses, and (5) Dr. Richard Tucker and Allan Reynolds who helped in the planning of the study and in the final interpretation of results. We are especially indebted to The St. Lambert Bilingual School Study Group, especially Mmes Murielle Parkes and Olga Melikoff who assisted us on many occasions throughout the year.
[2]Now at Stanford University.
[3]Now at Oxford University.
[4]We have not yet examined the attitudes of other children in the school toward those who are following the Experimental program. These other children may create a quite different climate of feeling toward the Experimental children.
[5]Certain of these comparisons involve only part of the French Control class. For example, item 12 on Table 4 has only 24 degrees of freedom; this means that there are 33 children in the comparison, since 9 degrees of freedom are lost because of the statistical covariance adjustments made, 1 df lost for each variable adjusted and for each group compared. What happened is that the French control children have been placed in various second grade classes in their school and we were able to take the time of only a part of the total for certain

tests. In these cases, there was no selection of the better or poorer children, so that the smaller numbers are likely representative of the total. Because small samples are involved, the need to replicate this study with another set of second grade classes is obvious.

[6]A detailed statistical breakdown of the whole range of ratings can be obtained from the first author at McGill. It would be of interest and value to study why certain phonemes show improvement from year to year, while others apparently don't, e. g. why is it that certain sounds such as alle and eille, and an and on shift in relative positions from one year to another?

[7]Note, however, that the Experimental class is much slower in associating in French (5. 85 secs.) than they are in English (2. 81 secs.). If this difference at the Grade II level proves reliable after next year's replication, it would be of interest to look into the reasons why associating in French takes more time than in English for both the French Control and the Experimental classes. Similarly, it would be of value to examine the year-by-year changes in associations of all groups, especially those of the Experimental children.

REFERENCES

Bloom, B. S. 1964. Stability and change in human characteristics. New York, Wiley.

Dave, R. H. 1963. The identification and measurement of environmental process variables that are related to educational achievement. Unpublished Ph. D. thesis. University of Chicago.

Dunn, L. M. 1959. Peabody Picture Vocabulary Test. Tennessee, American Guidance Service.

Entwistle, Doris R. 1966. Word associations of young children. Baltimore, The Johns Hopkins Press.

Ervin, Susan M. 1961. Changes with age in the verbal determinants of word association. American journal of psychology, 74, 361-372.

Kittell, J. E. 1959. Bilingualism and language. Journal of educational research, 52, 263-268.

_____. 1963. IQ performance of children from bilingual environments. Elementary school journal, 64, 76-83.

Lambert, W. E. , and John Macnamara. 1969. Some cognitive consequences of following a first-grade curriculum in a second language. Journal of educational psychology 60, 86-96.

_____, G. R. Tucker, A. d'Anglejan, and S. Segalowitz. 1970. Cognitive and attitudinal consequences of following the curricula of the first three grades in a foreign language. McGill University Mimeo.

Lorge-Thorndike Intelligence Tests, primary battery, level 2. 1959. Boston, Houghton Mifflin Co.

Metropolitan Achievement Tests, primary I and primary II batteries. 1959. New York, Harcourt, Brace and World, Inc.

Peal, Elizabeth, and W. E. Lambert. 1962. The relation of bilingualism to intelligence. Psychological monographs 76, 1-23.

Rabinovitch, M. S., and L. M. Parver. 1966. Auditory discrimination in monolinguals and polyglots. Unpublished undergraduate honors thesis, McGill University.

Raven, J. C. 1956. Coloured progressive matrices: sets A, Ab, B. London, Lewis.

Samuels, Marilyn, A. G. Reynolds, and W. E. Lambert. 1969. The communicational efficiency of children schooled in a foreign language. Journal of educational psychology 60, 389-393.

Snedecor, J. W. 1956. Statistical methods. Ames, Iowa, Iowa State College Press.

Winer, B. J. 1962. Statistical principles in experimental design. New York, McGraw-Hill.

Wolf, R. M. 1963. The identification and measurement of environmental process variables related to intelligence. Ph. D. dissertation, University of Chicago.

Yeni-Komshian, Grace. 1965. Some training procedures applicable to teaching the sound systems and vocabularies of foreign languages. Unpublished Ph. D. dissertation, McGill University.

TABLE 3: Means and Adjusted Means for Grade I Follow-up Experimental and Control Classes

| Test Name | Experimental Class | | English Control I | | English Control II | | French Control | | Grand | F | |
English Competence	Mean	Adjusted	Mean	Adjusted	Mean	Adjusted	Mean	Adjusted	Mean	Ratio	df
1. Word knowledge[b] (S.S.)	42.44	42.87	59.00	58.67	56.88	56.59			51.37	29.40**	2, 72
2. Word discrimination (S.S.)	45.94	46.59	58.90	58.35	58.00	57.58			53.09	20.20**	2, 73
3. Reading skills (S.S.)	39.17	39.89	58.48	57.50	56.78	56.57			49.65	40.48**	2, 75
4. Arithmetic concepts (S.S.)	55.86	55.88	54.05	53.65	54.96	55.25			55.12	0.91	2, 75
5. Picture vocabulary	64.00	64.26	62.85	62.37	65.11	65.13			64.09	0.92	2, 73
6. Listening comprehension	22.17	22.34	22.37	21.93	22.15	22.23			22.21	0.19	2, 72
7. Word association analysis: associational latency (secs.)	4.06	4.15	3.86	3.69					3.98	0.96	1, 48
paradigmatic (%)	60.94	60.80	62.93	63.18					61.67	0.15	1, 49
syntagmatic (%)	19.50	20.14	13.89	12.79					17.43	4.15*	1, 49
semantic clusters (%)	7.35	8.07	4.96	3.73					6.47	7.79**	1, 49
idiosyncratic (%)	9.49	9.64	9.03	8.77					9.32	0.05	1, 49
rhymings (%)	0.35	0.16	2.48	3.35					1.13	5.61*	1, 49
transformations (%)	1.27	1.18	4.07	4.22					2.30	10.29**	1, 49
8. Speaking skills; story retelling ratings: overall expressive ability	2.36	2.42	2.03	1.95	2.15	2.13			2.21	1.48	2, 69

TABLE 3 (Cont.):

Test Name	Experimental Class		English Control I		English Control II		French Control		Grand F		
	Mean	Adjusted	Mean	Adjusted	Mean	Adjusted	Mean	Adjusted	Mean	Ratio	df
grammar	3.00	3.04	2.74	2.68	2.80	2.79			2.81	3.29*	2, 69
enunciation	2.80	2.86	3.00	2.88	2.87	2.87			2.87	0.00	2, 69
rhythm and intonation	2.39	2.35	2.13	2.11	2.46	2.52			2.35	1.73	2, 69
Counts											
number of words	63.47	63.36	49.80	50.19	48.27	48.12			55.11	3.85*	2, 71
number of adjectives	4.59	4.58	4.10	3.93	2.46	2.61			3.77	4.37*	2, 71
number different adjectives	3.26	3.27	3.40	3.33	1.92	1.97			2.86	4.47*	2, 71
number of nouns	14.00	14.01	10.45	10.40	10.77	10.79			12.06	3.90*	2, 71
number of different nouns	9.44	9.49	8.05	8.14	8.12	7.97			8.66	2.24	2, 71
number of verbs	11.21	11.10	8.20	8.23	8.58	8.70			9.60	3.58*	2, 71
number different verbs	8.32	8.23	7.30	7.40	7.00	7.04			7.64	0.92	2, 71
number of grammatical errors	0.12	0.05	0.05	0.10	0.31	0.36			0.16	2.46	2, 71
story comprehension	2.18	2.23	1.45	1.36	2.19	2.19			2.00	11.24**	2, 71
9. Speaking skills; story creation ratings:											
overall expressive ability	2.56	2.65			2.89	2.78			2.71	0.41	1, 52
grammar	2.64	2.62			2.93	2.94			2.77	3.96	1, 52
enunciation	2.56	2.55			2.61	2.62			2.58	0.13	1, 52
rhythm and intonation	2.55	2.63			2.94	2.85			2.72	1.37	1, 52

Counts											
number of words	44.29	46.48	49.45	49.94	54.85	51.64			49.02	0.43	2,73
number of adjectives	1.14	1.23	0.75	0.71	2.41	2.32			1.46	4.68*	2,73
number different											
adjectives	0.89	1.03	0.75	0.73	1.33	1.17			1.00	0.63	2,73
number of nouns	6.97	7.43	8.95	8.99	10.52	9.89			8.62	2.29	2,73
number different nouns	4.54	4.77	5.60	5.65	7.59	7.26			5.80	6.94**	2,73
number of verbs	8.94	9.27	9.15	9.08	8.74	8.37			8.93	0.34	2,73
number different verbs	6.97	7.34	7.10	6.99	6.74	6.34			6.93	0.84	2,73
number of grammat-											
ical errors	0.46	0.44	0.05	0.10	0.11	0.10			0.24	1.13	2,73
story comprehension	2.89	2.88	2.60	2.60	1.93	1.93			2.50	21.34**	2,73
French Competence											
10. Reading skills	15.29	15.36					17.11	16.98	15.93	2.05	1,46
11. Word discrimination	25.28	25.35					25.60	25.47	25.39	0.01	1,48
12. Listening compre-											
hension	15.15	15.15					19.45	19.45	16.74	19.79**	1,46
13. Picture vocabulary	53.85	53.81					63.48	63.54	57.53	27.45**	1,47
14. Phoneme production	38.35	38.35			1967 –		56.14	56.08	–	–	–
15. Word association											
analysis:											
associational latency											
(secs.)	5.78	5.76					3.76	3.79	4.90	12.58**	1,52
paradigmatic (%)	42.55	42.50					49.43	49.49	45.39	2.36	1,55
syntagmatic (%)	16.71	16.73					11.60	11.58	14.60	4.52*	1,55
semantic clusters (%)	10.67	10.60					6.86	6.95	9.09	2.72	1,55
idiosyncratic (%)	12.11	12.17					10.54	10.45	11.46	0.36	1,55
rhymings (%)	2.87	2.88					4.90	4.89	3.71	1.86	1,55

TABLE 3 (Cont.):

Test Name	Experimental Class		English Control I		English Control II		French Control		Grand F		
	Mean	Adjusted	Mean	Adjusted	Mean	Adjusted	Mean	Adjusted	Mean	Ratio	df
transformations (%)	3.81	3.91					13.47	13.32	7.81	8.36**	1, 55
16. Speaking skills; story retelling counts:											
number of words	57.91	57.13					57.27	59.54	57.74	0.07	1, 35
number of adjectives	2.78	2.68					2.18	2.49	2.63	0.05	1, 35
number different adjectives	0.94	0.93					0.73	0.75	0.88	0.18	1, 35
number of nouns	11.69	11.55					9.82	10.21	11.21	0.62	1, 35
number different nouns	5.62	5.54					5.55	5.79	5.60	0.10	1, 35
number of verbs	10.00	9.86					10.82	11.23	10.21	0.57	1, 35
number different verbs	6.31	6.18					7.82	8.19	6.70	4.94*	1, 35
number grammatical errors	3.78	3.76					1.00	1.06	3.07	13.76**	1, 35
story comprehension	1.69	1.63					2.27	2.45	1.84	5.47*	1, 35
Ratings: bilingual judges:											
overall expressive ability	1.48	1.44					2.00	2.13	1.62	10.85**	1, 33
grammar	1.53	1.49					2.18	2.29	1.71	26.48**	1, 33
enunciation and liaison	1.97	1.94					2.45	2.54	2.10	5.42*	1, 33
rhythm and intonation	1.65	1.58					2.27	2.45	1.82	10.83*	1, 33
Ratings: French teacher judges:											

					F	df
overall expressive ability	2.10	2.05	2.73	2.86	2.26	7.23*	1, 34
grammar	2.39	2.36	2.82	2.90	2.50	5.62*	1, 34
enunciation and liaison	2.58	2.54	3.05	3.17	2.70	4.16*	1, 34
rhythm and intonation	2.06	2.00	3.00	3.18	2.31	18.93**	1, 34
17. Speaking skills: story creation counts:							
number of words	56.18	56.00	64.18	64.72	58.18	1.35	1, 36
number of adjectives	2.00	1.88	2.55	2.89	2.14	1.33	1, 36
number different adjectives	0.55	0.52	0.73	0.81	0.59	0.70	1, 36
number of nouns	12.42	12.36	12.18	12.36	12.36	0.00	1, 36
number different nouns	6.61	6.56	7.36	7.45	6.80	0.65	1, 36
number of verbs	9.03	8.96	11.00	11.21	9.52	3.46	1, 36
number different verbs	6.39	6.39	8.82	8.84	7.00	12.38**	1, 36
number grammatical errors	6.82	6.78	1.09	1.20	5.39	24.68**	1, 36
story comprehension	2.45	2.49	3.00	2.88	2.59	2.14	1, 36
Ratings: bilingual judges:							
overall expression	1.71	1.70	3.14	3.16	2.08	39.87**	1, 34
grammar	1.34	1.33	3.00	3.02	1.77	83.19**	1, 34
enunciation and liaison	2.21	2.24	3.00	2.92	2.42	9.35**	1, 34
rhythm and intonation	1.98	1.98	3.32	3.32	2.33	28.39**	1, 34
Ratings: French teacher judges:							
overall expression	2.66	2.65	3.41	3.43	2.85	7.28*	1, 36
grammar	2.26	2.27	3.02	2.98	2.45	28.42**	1, 36

TABLE 3 (Cont.):

Test Name	Experimental Class		English Control I		English Control II		French Control		Grand F		
	Mean	Adjusted	Mean	Adjusted	Mean	Adjusted	Mean	Adjusted	Mean	Ratio	df
enunciation and liaison	2.67	2.70					3.05	2.97	2.77	0.90	1, 36
rhythm and intonation	2.42	2.40					3.48	3.54	2.69	12.96**	1, 36
Intelligence Measures											
18. June retest, Raven's	24.00	24.61	24.05	23.48	25.11	24.74			24.38	0.82	2, 73
19. Lorge–Thorndike											
a. vocabulary	17.86	17.99	17.89	17.96	18.12	17.89			17.95	0.01	2, 72
b. not-belonging	17.03	16.98	18.00	17.86	18.08	18.24			17.59	3.67*	2, 72
c. go-together	14.58	14.81	14.84	14.63	14.65	14.49			14.67	0.10	2, 72
Totals	49.19	50.07	48.26	47.42	50.85	50.26			49.51	1.55	2, 72
Foreign Language Sensitivity											
20. Russian phoneme discrimination (errors)	14.03	14.21	17.22[c]	16.98[c]					15.42	2.19	1, 54

(a) This table is comparable to that describing the Pilot Classes which can be found in Lambert and Mac-namara 1969: 92.

(b) Entries for the first four tests are mean Standard scores. They are based on different norms and are not comparable to the corresponding entries for the Pilot Classes.

(c) Control students who had no second language experience were selected from the English Control Group I and from the French Control. Their scores are combined to form these means.

TABLE 4: Means and Adjusted Means for Grade II Pilot Experimental and Control Classes

	Experimental Class		English Control I		English Control II		French Control		Grand Mean	F Ratio	df
	Mean	Adjusted	Mean	Adjusted	Mean	Adjusted	Mean	Adjusted			
English Competence											
1. Word knowledge[a] (S.S.)	56.33	56.40	55.35	57.69	57.48	55.69			56.49	0.20	2,51
2. Word discrimination (S.S.)	55.00	55.06	55.35	56.54	55.39	54.46			55.25	0.24	2,51
3. Reading ability (S.S.)	53.59	54.52	55.71	59.63	55.61	51.82			54.92	3.58**	2,52
4. Spelling (S.S.)	57.41	57.65	58.18	61.75	58.22	55.35			57.92	2.48	2,52
5. Arithmetic concepts (S.S.)	54.60	55.54	51.06	52.73	57.48	55.42			54.70	0.47	2,50
6. Arithmetic computation (S.S.)	62.30	63.27	48.71	49.36	57.30	55.98			56.53	9.05**	2,50
7. English picture vocabulary	75.24	74.69	75.00	76.41	75.21	74.87			75.17	0.39	2,49
8. English listening comprehension	22.68	22.66	22.81	22.53	23.09	23.32			22.87	0.65	2,50
9. Word association analysis, English: associational latency (secs.)	2.70	2.81	3.54	3.46					3.19	1.00	1,20
paradigmatic (%)	61.41	59.73	70.10	72.18					65.30	3.70	1,29
syntagmatic (%)	16.17	16.28	11.76	11.63					14.20	1.33	1,29
semantic clusters (%)	6.94	6.94	5.51	5.52					6.30	0.73	1,29
idiosyncratic (%)	12.99	14.90	4.06	1.70					9.00	8.98**	1,29
rhymings (%)	0.30	0.33	1.22	1.19					0.71	1.06	1,29

TABLE 4 (Cont.)

	Experimental Class		English Control I		English Control II		French Control		Grand F		
	Mean	Adjusted	Mean	Adjusted	Mean	Adjusted	Mean	Adjusted	Mean	Ratio	df
transformations (%)	1.88	1.90	4.41	4.39					3.02	7.66**	1, 29
10. Speaking skills: story retelling, English:											
Ratings											
overall expression	2.98	3.05	2.32	2.50	3.07	2.91			2.88	0.96	2, 45
grammar	2.84	2.85	2.64	2.68	3.00	2.97			2.86	0.56	2, 45
enunciation	3.20	3.17	2.73	2.75	3.55	3.57			3.25	3.42*	2, 45
rhythm and intonation	3.11	3.11	2.09	1.94	3.09	3.17			2.90	7.88**	2, 45
Counts											
number of words	80.27	78.27	51.73	50.93	69.14	70.69			66.25	5.19*	2, 38
number of adjectives	6.09	6.01	3.00	2.91	4.27	4.37			4.29	6.21**	2, 38
number different adjectives	4.91	4.90	2.07	2.09	3.36	3.35			3.31	8.41**	2, 38
number of nouns	17.18	16.87	11.53	11.12	14.68	15.12			14.27	4.89*	2, 38
number different nouns	11.73	11.48	7.87	7.79	10.68	10.86			10.04	4.71*	2, 38
number of verbs	14.36	14.03	8.00	8.28	11.82	11.79			11.21	6.31**	2, 38
number different verbs	10.73	10.51	6.53	6.61	9.32	9.37			8.77	5.00*	2, 38
number grammatical errors	0.18	0.19	0.13	0.10	0.14	0.16			0.15	0.18	2, 38
story comprehension	2.27	2.18	2.00	2.01	2.45	2.50			2.27	1.51	2, 38
11. Speaking skills: story creation, English:											
Ratings											

overall expression	3.35	3.26	2.70	2.68	3.47	3.58			3.22	3.85*	2,45
grammar	3.05	2.99	2.60	2.59	3.22	3.29			2.99	5.75**	2,45
enunciation	2.97	2.91	2.60	2.63	3.20	3.24			2.95	3.33*	2,45
rhythm and intonation	3.30	3.17	2.63	2.56	3.57	3.76			3.22	6.96**	2,45
Counts											
number of words	67.67	68.55	42.06	38.59	66.23	67.91			60.19	6.74**	2,49
number of adjectives	1.52	1.48	0.56	0.37	1.77	1.95			1.36	2.98	2,49
number different adjectives	1.52	1.50	0.56	0.49	1.36	1.43			1.20	1.83	2,49
number of nouns	12.86	13.07	6.12	5.33	11.55	11.92			10.54	13.77**	2,49
number different nouns	7.10	7.20	4.37	3.86	7.36	7.64			6.46	10.79**	2,49
number of verbs	12.90	13.28	6.56	6.64	11.59	11.18			10.69	7.20**	2,49
number different verbs	9.00	9.09	5.62	5.56	9.55	9.51			8.29	5.12*	2,49
number grammatical errors	0.33	0.32	0.06	0.12	0.18	0.15			0.20	0.90	2,49
story comprehension	3.00	2.99	2.25	2.21	2.23	2.26			2.51	12.70**	2,49
French Competence											
12. French reading skills	17.86	18.73					18.33	16.80	18.03	0.64	1,24
13. French listening comprehension	18.95	19.15					21.38	21.09	19.94	2.33	1,23
14. French picture vocabulary	71.23	71.66					76.92	76.13	73.24	6.08**	1,25
15. French phoneme production	42.23	42.23					—	—	—	—	—
16. Word association analysis, French: associational latency (secs.)	4.97	5.85					7.34	6.37	6.10	0.05	1,31

TABLE 4 (Cont.)

	Experimental Class		English Control I		English Control II		French Control		Grand F		
	Mean	Adjusted	Mean	Adjusted	Mean	Adjusted	Mean	Adjusted	Mean	Ratio	df
paradigmatic (%)	54.06	55.64					58.92	57.33	56.49	0.09	1, 33
syntagmatic (%)	19.89	17.79					13.91	16.01	16.90	0.20	1, 33
semantic clusters (%)	7.09	6.40					8.87	9.57	7.98	3.78	1, 33
idiosyncratic (%)	12.79	14.34					9.90	8.35	11.34	1.45	1, 33
rhymings (%)	1.21	0.76					1.96	2.41	1.59	2.70	1, 33
transformations (%)	3.36	3.64					5.13	4.85	4.25	0.30	1, 33
17. Speaking skills: story retelling, French: Counts											
number of words	75.50	74.58					72.09	72.65	73.38	0.02	1, 28
number of adjectives	2.14	2.21					2.04	2.00	2.08	0.05	1, 28
number different adjectives	1.14	1.32					0.96	0.85	1.03	0.77	1, 28
number of nouns	16.36	15.50					12.39	12.92	13.89	1.62	1, 28
number different nouns	7.14	6.73					7.22	7.47	7.19	0.75	1, 28
number of verbs	13.36	13.10					12.22	12.38	12.65	0.12	1, 28
number different verbs	9.07	8.39					9.13	9.55	9.11	0.66	1, 28
number grammatical errors	4.86	4.91					0.83	0.79	2.35	46.57**	1, 28
story comprehension	2.79	2.71					2.96	3.00	2.89	0.43	1, 28
Ratings: bilingual judges											
overall expression	1.93	1.94					2.73	2.72	2.42	7.82**	1, 27

					Mean	F	df
grammar	1.61	1.61	2.70	2.70	2.28	20.22**	1, 27
enunciation and liaison	2.21	2.28	2.93	2.89	2.65	5.39*	1, 27
rhythm and intonation	2.21	2.19	2.80	2.81	2.57	3.53	1, 27
Ratings: French teacher judges							
overall expression	2.86	2.91	3.45	3.42	3.22	3.41	1, 27
grammar	2.82	2.93	3.16	3.09	3.03	0.44	1, 27
enunciation and liaison	3.04	3.13	3.18	3.12	3.12	0.00	1, 27
rhythm and intonation	2.68	2.59	3.41	3.46	3.12	9.76**	1, 27
18. Speaking skills: story creation, French: Counts							
number of words	76.05	76.91	68.44	67.43	72.54	0.61	1, 30
number of adjectives	1.24	1.25	3.33	3.32	2.21	10.67**	1, 30
number different adjectives	0.57	0.49	1.28	1.37	0.90	2.66	1, 30
number of nouns	16.00	16.25	12.33	12.04	14.31	2.69	1, 30
number different nouns	8.24	8.48	7.61	7.33	7.95	1.15	1, 30
number of verbs	13.00	12.89	11.33	11.46	12.23	0.59	1, 30
number different verbs	9.33	9.27	7.67	7.74	8.56	1.78	1, 30
number grammatical errors	7.57	7.76	1.06	0.84	4.56	45.12**	1, 30
story comprehension	3.52	3.49	3.33	3.37	3.44	0.15	1, 30
Ratings: bilingual judges							
overall expression	2.00	2.04	3.03	2.98	2.46	19.80**	1, 29
grammar	1.40	1.40	2.85	2.86	2.05	62.62**	1, 29
enunciation and liaison	2.29	2.30	3.18	3.16	2.68	16.57**	1, 29

TABLE 4 (Cont.)

	Experimental Class		English Control I		English Control II		French Control		Grand F		
	Mean	Adjusted	Mean	Adjusted	Mean	Adjusted	Mean	Adjusted	Mean	Ratio	df
rhythm and intonation	2.24	2.26					3.26	3.24	2.70	29.75**	1, 29
Ratings: French teacher judges											
overall expression	3.24	3.31					3.79	3.70	3.49	2.58	1, 30
grammar	2.57	2.57					3.28	3.28	2.90	12.97**	1, 30
enunciation and liaison	3.02	3.06					3.32	3.28	3.16	2.20	1, 30
rhythm and intonation	3.14	3.16					3.71	3.69	3.40	4.20*	1, 30
Intelligence Measures											
19. June retest, Raven's	28.27	28.27	28.94	30.23	27.65	26.76			28.21	2.03	2, 51
20. Lorge-Thorndike:											
a. vocabulary	15.68	15.52	14.59	14.71	17.09	17.15			15.90	4.35*	2, 52
b. not-belonging	17.23	17.44	18.65	18.85	17.22	16.86			17.61	2.42	2, 52
c. go-together	17.41	17.58	17.06	16.98	17.35	17.24			17.29	0.58	2, 52
Totals	49.86	50.14	50.29	50.73	49.83	49.24			49.97	0.20	2, 52
Foreign Language Sensitivity											
21. Russian phoneme discrimination (errors)	13.27	13.01	15.21[b]	15.63[b]					14.03	1.08	1, 27

(a) Entries for tests 1-6 are mean Standard scores.

(b) Control subjects who had no second language experience were selected from both English and French Control classes. Their scores are combined to form these means.

DISCUSSION

Virginia Hodge, Catholic University: I'm extremely fascinated by Dr. Lambert's talk on two scores: first, as a student of psychology, and secondly, because I have spent the last 18 years with my husband abroad in the Foreign Service. We have four children who have had various combinations of attempts at getting them to be bilingual. One of them now is bilingual, the other three are not. In the course of watching these children in their attempts to become bilingual (I might add that my husband is multilingual), I have been amazed and astonished at the fact of what a difference personalities make on the language-learning ability and, more important, on the motivation of these children. I came back to school to look into this matter, and find that there is an extraordinary lack of information in this field of personality variables correlated with language learning. Dr. Lambert's is the first that has gotten close to my interest in this field. I was wondering if in your study you have come up with any information on ego development in these bilingual children and what are the effects of various personal variables, personal style, etc., on the language learning of these children.

Lambert: Yes, and this is discussed in a report just completed, especially a section on attitude development, etc. The overall openness and lack of prejudice of these children who have followed the experimental program is impressive, even though their parents generally have less open and charitable views.

There is one other matter your question brings to mind. I think a program like this one has to be evaluated carefully. It also has to be designed so that, in a sense, it is teacher 'proof' and student 'proof'. Certainly there are individual variations in speed of acquisition (there was no screening done to keep below average children out of the program). Some children have perceptual motor problems, and yet we urged psychiatrists to leave them in the program. Now, at Grade 4, you would have a hard time finding them in the group, possibly because they were late starters. In fact, we now feel that the perceptually and motorically retarded child may have a second chance, almost, in a program like this. That is, his peers who have been showing greater skill than he are in this program set back to zero with him at the start. Thus, we tried to design a program that would permit us to talk about the consequences for all who might be included. So far we have studied only middle class children, but current studies are introducing the program in a lower class area. But we would like to have it student proof and also teacher proof, so that one could put any other teacher or student in the program. In this way, one can get a better, harder test of the program because one has controlled out any special features of the teacher or the student. We are happy to be able to state, for example, that one of the teachers at Grade 2 was a French Canadian lady who had never taught before and had never finished high school herself. Her only special skill was the ability to speak French. Her pupils nevertheless did a fabulous job at the end of Grade 2, and I don't think we can attribute this to that particular teacher. Thus, if there is anything special about a teacher, even if she is especially good, try to get her out of the program because she spoils the test of the program itself. If she is especially bad and you think you can afford it, leave her in.

Xavier Albó, Cornell University: I wonder whether you would like to make any comparison between your study and those studies, or even the UNESCO recommendations which deal with teaching literacy to people who speak a vernacular different from the official language—the first question.
And the second question is related to that one: As I understand it, these English-speaking children going to French schools were a minority within the school where the experiment was done. In other words, there was a majority of French-speaking children—

Lambert: of English-speaking children, rather. It was an English school that introduced these experimental classes.

Albo: Ah, so, all of them were English-speaking. Good. So this is similar to the situation in these vernacular areas. So the final question: What was the place of English as a second language in these schools, if any?

Lambert: To start with the last point: English was not taught as a second language, rather English was taught as a native language with an English language arts program starting with Grade 2, but no introduction of English at all at kindergarten or Grade 1.
The major question you bring up is an important one, Fergy and I talked about this last summer. The contrast, let's say, between Spanish American children who are coming into a school system in the United States and learning through English is not a valid parallel. For the minority group in the United States, giving up the home language and entering an American school is like kissing his home language goodby. In the case we are dealing with, however, English is clearly the most powerful language, so much so that these parents can be sure to have English skilled children who can afford to learn some French. The contrast is a strong one.

Albo: I had in mind another group, a group of Quechua monolinguals in Andean areas where this native language is much more commonly spoken than Spanish. Yet the school system is intended to teach them Spanish, the official language. So it happens that everybody in the classroom is a monolingual Quechua speaker. But, when the teacher is there, everything is supposed to be taught in Spanish, the official language, and not in vernacular Quechua.

Lambert: Yes, that is interesting. I think each of your examples has to be considered separately because the richness of the sociolinguistic and sociocultural settings involved. Drawing from our study, the parent can persuade the child not to worry at all about language development. Go and do as well as you can; the more you can get of that other language the safer you will be as a teenager in this community, the way things are now going. So it's that particular sociolinguistic or psycholinguistic climate that is the driving motivation, if you like. You would have to study each community in a similar manner, but that is the fun of it all, trying to figure each one out and directing research that evaluates or attempts to modify the problems uncovered.

Gillian Sankoff, Université de Montreal: I'd like to know, given the fact that Canadian French presents some significant differences from standard French, and also the fact that in the Montreal situation the social implications of speaking one or the other are quite important, I would like to know what your position was on this issue and why, in fact, you didn't have only Canadian French teachers.

Lambert: Good question. And it is not really a local, Canadian question. It sounds as though these are two Montrealists talking to one another, but there is a general problem touched on here. First of all, the Pilot group I talked about has, by chance, had, except for kindergarten, only French Canadian teachers all the way through. But the Follow-up group has, by chance, had only European French teachers all the way through. If it were local French only, parents might well feel it doesn't have the social value an international French might have. The proper solution is to use both versions and make sure that the children get both type teachers. But the parents, too, want a bit of assurance that the French they get is not provincial or parochial in any sense. At the same time, to limit the program to Canadian French instructors would limit the cultural factor as well. Mind you, DeGaulle tried to construct a big bridge across that ocean, but there is still a tremendous cultural variance between what French Canada represents and what France represents.

A second point to keep in mind is that a tremendous majority of French Canadians, as they go up the socioeconomic scale, move toward French French in their language style. Thus, why shouldn't we help these kids, coming from the English Canadian community, master the

higher status version of French? I think it would be shortsighted to
teach them only a local language, even though one must develop a command and facility in the local language.

Dorothy Goodman, Washington International School: My question
is about syllabuses and textbooks. I am Director of the Washington
International School, which is only a few hundred yards from here and
which is, as far as we know, the only genuinely bilingual school in the
metropolitan area, and one of the few on the North American continent.
We have 180 children of more than 40 nationalities. They range between the ages of three and eleven, and everyone, from the age of five,
studies half the day in English and half the day in French or Spanish.
What do you do about texts and syllabuses in Montreal? And what
about teaching methods? You have mentioned that you have French
Canadian, Swiss, Belgian, and French French teachers. In our experience these pedagogical traditions may vary considerably among
themselves and usually contrast markedly with the Anglo-American,
except at the nursery-kindergarten level. (We find that a French
French jardinière fits in well with the North American idea of the
'free' nursery-kindergarten. But a French French or a Belgian
French primary teacher usually does not. Of course in many cultures
there is a big break between the kindergarten and primary levels.) In
our school with its half-day pattern, all children from five up have both
methods—'formality' and 'freedom'—in the course of the day, which
works quite well with most children. But what do you do in Montreal
where the English Canadians work in French all day? Do you ask
French Canadian teachers to use AAAS science materials? French
Belgian teachers to use Zacharias or Nuffield? Or do you ask teachers simply to do leçons de choses as does the San Francisco French
American School during the first three grades? I understand San Francisco finds leçons de choses very effective for the development of
French vocabulary.

Lambert: I see. This is a good set of questions. Briefly, what we
have been trying to teach the teachers is to look at the children as
crazy little North American kids and to try and introduce a different
kind of craziness. You can't slap them or, if you do, you've got to be
very fast at it. You can teach them your type of respect; these kids
should stand up when an adult comes into class if that's what you want.
With regard to the text materials, we have found that the Pre-Saklier
method is an interesting one. It's a very important kindergarten program that works through physical education in order to develop perceptual motor skills that lead to the first starts of reading and writing.
The Saklier method is the reading method used in France and in middle-class French Canadian schools, and we have been using it to ad-

vantage. All our texts are collaborative works by French and Canadian authors. The ones we've found valuable for the early years are Je veux lire and Je sais lire.

There are no systematic controls placed on vocabulary level; we stress a phonemic-type reading approach rather than a global method and we don't let them print. Instead they learn from the start to write. The critical point, though, is that none of this material is second-language in format—it is all designed for native speakers of the language.

June Hutchinson, Georgetown University: Sir, have you done any attitudinal studies on the parents of your controlled groups? Do you know what the parents' attitudes toward the children are?

Lambert: Yes. We have checked out the attitude of parents and children each year. There are quite interesting differences between the attitude profiles of parents and children. It is clear that the children will question any prejudiced statements they hear around them, even from parents. The fascinating thing is that the European teachers get a satisfaction from proselytizing, no question about it. They love to talk about France, just as the French Canadian teacher loves to have them read French Canadian stories about the earth and about the Canadians' attachment to the earth and to the family. These are some of the shapers of attitudes that clearly influence the children in the program.

AN ALTERNATE DAYS APPROACH TO BILINGUAL EDUCATION

G. R. TUCKER, FE T. OTANES[1] AND B. P. SIBAYAN[1]

McGill University

The paper was presented by the first author at the Twenty-first Annual Round Table Meeting on Linguistics and Language Studies, Georgetown University, 1970.

Abstract. Educators in diverse countries, including the United States, are often faced with the problem of teaching their pupils via a weaker language. This situation may arise, for example, in a multilingual country when some foreign language or an indigenous national language is adopted as the medium of instruction, when immigrant children enter a monolingual school system, or perhaps even when speakers of nonstandard dialects attend schools where teachers use only a more prestigious standard form. In these situations it would seem appropriate to consider the adoption of some form of bilingual instruction.

The effectiveness and practicality of an alternate days bilingual approach to education is now being evaluated in the Philippines. The language proficiency and content mastery of students in classes instructed bilingually has been carefully compared with those instructed monolingually using either English or Tagalog. The results of the first year analyses were positive and exciting; and the classes are now being followed during the second year. This approach could maximize advantages inherent in native language instruction and provide solid grounding in the language of wider communication. The relevance of these results for North American educators and social scientists will be discussed.

The Language Study Center at the Philippine Normal College in Manila is now collaborating with the Laboratory School of the College in an experiment to assess the effectiveness and practicality of a particular type of bilingual education. In this paper, we would like to briefly describe the factors which prompted the research, the design and results of the first year's evaluation, and the current state of the project during its second year.

The Republic of the Philippines comprises a chain of approximately 7, 000 islands stretching from close to Taiwan in the north to Borneo in the south. The 'official' languages are Pilipino, popularly called Tagalog, English, and Spanish. There are, however, at least 75, and perhaps as many as 150, mutually unintelligible languages used in the country although many of them are spoken by relatively few people. In fact, one or more of the eight major languages are spoken by approximately 90% of the population of 36, 000, 000 (see Pascasio 1967).

The Philippine language policy for education is neither coherent nor successful. For many years, English was the sole medium of instruction in schools although Pilipino has been studied as a subject since 1940. Prator (1950) has provided a comprehensive report of language teaching in the country through 1950. In 1957, a decision was made to use the prevailing local vernacular as the medium of instruction in Grades 1 and 2, with the result that primary classes are now taught using many of the major and minor languages. English is introduced as the principal medium of instruction in Grade 3.

The Curriculum Committee of the Board of National Education is now considering a proposal to adopt Pilipino as the medium of instruction in Grades 1 through 4 throughout the country. Much of the current discussion of Philippine language policy proceeds on guesswork. There now exists no base line from which to evaluate the success or failures of policy decisions. With an aim to presenting the Board of National Education and other interested groups with a core of facts and documented opinions, the staff of the Language Study Center has recently conducted a national Language Policy Survey.[2] The results of this survey will provide a relatively complete picture of various aspects of language usage and preference in the Philippines.

When the Board adopts its new language policy, regardless of the specific details, it seems clear that either a local vernacular or Pilipino will be used at the primary level with a switch to English as the main medium of instruction occurring by the secondary level.

A number of language teaching experiments, conducted in the Philippines (e. g. Davis 1967, Ramos, Aguillar, and Sibayan 1967) support the observation made by most Filipino educators and visiting specialists that the exclusive use of one language, either a local vernacular or Pilipino, as the chief medium of instruction in the first two grades results in transition difficulties for pupils when an abrupt change is made to English as the medium of instruction in Grade 3.

In the early Iloilo and Rizal experiments (Davis 1967), the language of instruction in the primary grades was systematically varied, and the effects of these variations were evaluated. A bilingual alternate days approach such as that used in South Africa (Malherbe 1946) was, however, never tried. This untried approach which would appear to maximize the advantages inherent in native language instruction coupled with solid grounding in English, the language of wider communication, may prove to offer a very attractive alternative to Filipino educational planners. Such an approach has also been used, with apparent success, in other settings (e.g. Montreal); but most of these other programs have not been critically evaluated. By training Filipino pupils via both Pilipino and English, we hope to reduce—perhaps eliminate—the transition difficulties mentioned earlier; but retain the advantage of introducing them to content material in their own vernacular. That is, we want to capitalize on the early enthusiasm of children for their school activities and the educational process and complement their Tagalog experiences with similar English language experiences.

Our primary concern was to critically assess, over a period of several years, the success of the program by comparing the language skills and content mastery of bilingually instructed pupils with those of monolingually instructed controls. The periodic sharing of our experiences via reports such as this will perhaps interest educators from diverse countries who are considering changes in their own language policies.

The design of the research program

The program began in July, 1968 with the opening of the Philippine academic year. Since the composition of the four participating Grade 1 classes had been set during the summer before the plans for the experiment had been finalized, a meeting was held with the children's parents in late June to explain the purpose and details of the investigation and to solicit their cooperation.

Students. Four classes of Grade 1 students participated in the pilot program. Class 1 (N = 32) followed a standard Pilipino curriculum. Class 2 (N = 35) followed a standard English curriculum. Class 3 (N = 33) followed an alternate days bilingual approach. The majority of the children in these three classes had attended kindergarten. The children in Class 4 (N = 29) had not attended kindergarten. They also followed the alternate days bilingual approach, although their test results were not included in the analysis of the second semester testing. Boys and girls attend class together in the Philippines. Most were from middle-class families.

Curriculum. All possible steps were taken to insure that the curricula for the classes would be similar, with language of instruction as the main independent variable (see Table 1). All classes began each day with opening exercises and a short period devoted to good manners and right conduct. Each class had a daily period for social studies, science, and mathematics, and a daily period devoted to either music, art, or physical education. These subjects were taught via Pilipino, English, or bilingually. In addition, all classes regardless of their method of instruction had one period each day devoted to Pilipino Language Arts, one to English Language Arts, and one for English as a second language. In summary, all pupils received formal language training in both Pilipino and English; but studied their content subjects in Pilipino, English, or bilingually.

Materials. All classes were taught using the materials developed at the Science Education Center (SEC), University of the Philippines, for mathematics and for science and health. These materials had been developed in English, and a Language Study Center specialist supervised their adaptation to Pilipino as well as the integration and transition required for bilingual materials. The prescribed Grade 1 materials were used for other subject areas. The potential problem of book choice or format for written presentation was not relevant at this level.

Method of instruction. In the bilingually instructed classes, an 'alternate days approach' was followed. For example, all subjects except Language Arts were taught on Day 1 using Pilipino as the medium of instruction; on Day 2 using English; Day 3, Pilipino; Day 4, English; etc. The material covered on Day 2 was not simply a repetition of that covered on Day 1; but was instead a continuation of the previous day's lesson. Apparently, this switching caused no appreciable or continuing difficulty to students or teachers. A sign posted on the door of the classroom indicated English Today, or Pilipino Ngayon.

Teachers. Each class had a home room teacher who taught most subjects. Specialists taught ESL, social studies, music, art, and physical education. Unlike many of the North American Bilingual Education programs where separate teachers are typically used for each language (e. g. one teacher for Spanish, another for English), in the present program the same teachers taught alternately using English or Pilipino as required. The teachers were not specifically prepared for bilingual teaching, although code-shifting occurs very frequently in the Philippines. They all, of course, spoke Pilipino and English fluently.

All teachers at the Laboratory School have been selected after rigorous screening from among experienced candidates in the field; thus, although the four home room teachers were not specifically equated on particular variables, it is probably safe to assume that they were equally competent.

TABLE 1: Philippine Normal College Laboratory School, Manila
Experimental Classes, School Year 1968-69, Grade 1

Time	Min.	1 Pilipino with kindergarten	2 English with kindergarten	3 Bilingual with kindergarten	4 Bilingual w/o kindergarten
A.M.					
8:00- 8:15	15	GMRC	GMRC	GMRC	GMRC
8:15- 8:55	40	Pilipino	Pilipino	Pilipino	Pilipino
8:55- 9:35	40	English	English	English	English
9:35- 9:55	20	Recess	Recess	Recess	Recess
9:55-10:35	40	(9:55-10:25) Soc. Studies	Math	Math	Science
10:35-11:15	40	(10:25-11:05) Music, Arts, P.E.	ESL	(10:35-11:05) Soc. Studies	Math
P.M.					
1:00- 1:40	40	ESL	Music, Arts P.E.	Science	(1:10-1:40) Soc. Studies
1:40- 2:20	40	Math	Science	Music, Arts P.E.	ESL
2:20- 3:00	40	Science	(2:20-2:50) Soc. Studies	ESL	Music, Arts P.E.

Note: In this revised program, the changes are: (1) Social Studies, originally for 40 minutes, is now taught for 30 minutes; (2) Social Studies, originally taught by the respective home room instructors, is now taught by Mrs. N. Baira; and (3) Work Education has been removed.

In addition, the four teachers were sent to the University of the Philippines as faculty development scholars during the summer preceding the program to be trained to use the science teaching materials.

Background Information. Because the experimental plans were finalized after the class groupings had been completed, it was not possible to match pupils from the various sections before instruction began. During the first two weeks of school, all students were given the Raven Progressive Matrices (Raven 1956), English and Pilipino Science Readiness Tests developed by the SEC, and Tagalog Picture Vocabulary, English Picture Vocabulary, and Language Aptitude Tests selected from the Rizal test battery (Davis 1967). During the course of the year all parents were interviewed, following a schedule adapted from Bloom (1964), to determine their socioeconomic status and their educational aspirations for their children.

Research Council. After classes began, meetings were held approximately every two weeks to discuss the experimental program and problems that had arisen. The meetings were attended by the Language Study Center staff, the teachers and school administrators involved in the program, and various college staff from related departments (e. g. Pilipino, English, and Child Study). This group prepared a series of working papers which they distributed to all interested educators during the year.

The topic which recurred most frequently at our meetings concerned the translation of scientific terminology from English to Pilipino. Some specialists favored borrowing already existing terms; others, the derivation of 'pure' Pilipino terms (e. g. the English word set may be translated as set or tangkas; magnet as magneto or balani). Consultants from the Institute of National Language served as arbiters.

Since this type of program had never before been tried in the Philippines, we proposed to assess the pupils' progress before the end of the academic year. We decided to conduct a preliminary evaluation at the end of the first semester. If things had been going badly for the bilingually instructed pupils, we would have made immediate alterations in their program.

The first semester evaluation

First Semester Tests. Since all of the tests had to be specially developed for this experiment, a brief description of each and of the testing procedure may be appropriate. The instruments were pretested before use.

Oral English Test. This 30-item test developed by the ESL specialist sampled such skills as listening comprehension, picture vocabulary, production of plurals and pronoun usage. The test required approximately four minutes per pupil to complete. The children were tested individually in alphabetical order in a quiet room.

English Reading Readiness. A 30-item test composed of two parts was developed by members of the staff. In Part I (15 items) the pupil selected for each item the one picture out of four that matched a sentence read aloud by the teacher. Each sentence was read two times. In Part II (15 items) the pupil selected for each item the one word out of four that was different (e. g. dig, big, dig, dig). These items were not read aloud by the teacher. However, the teacher paced the pupils' progress by saying, Number 1 ... (15-20 second pause) Number 2, etc.

For testing purposes, the pupils in each of the four classes were randomly divided into three groups. All Group 1 pupils were tested by one teacher. Therefore, she tested pupils from the other three classes in addition to a portion of her own pupils. Likewise, all Group 2 and all Group 3 pupils were tested together by one of the teachers.

Pilipino Reading Readiness. A 30-item test composed of four parts was developed by staff members. In Part I (eight items) the pupil selected for each item the one word out of four that began with a different letter (e. g. upo, opo, oho, oto). In Part II (eight items) the pupil selected the one item out of four that was the same as a given stimulus item (e. g. Aba — Ada, Apa, Aha, Aba). Part III (eight items) was a three-choice picture vocabulary test. Part IV (eight items) complemented Part III. In Part IV, the pupil selected the one picture of three which matched the stimulus sentence.

The students were again tested in their respective groups with a rotation of teachers.

Mathematics Test. A 30-item test was developed by staff members, which consisted of five parts. Part I (five items) was essentially a picture vocabulary test; Part II (five items) required the child to select which of two sets contained more (three items) or less (two items) than the other. Part III (ten items) directed the child to circle a numeral to indicate the number of objects in each set. Part IV (five items) required the child to complete numerical sequences. In Part V (five items), the child was asked to group a number of objects by tens and then to give the total.

Three separate, but equivalent, forms of this test were prepared— a monolingual English form, a monolingual Pilipino form, and a bilingual form in which questions were asked both in Pilipino and in English. All oral directions were presented twice. With the bilingual format, the directions were given once in English and once in Pilipino. On this form, the language order was systematically varied.

The students were tested in their respective groups with another rotation of the teachers.

Nonverbal Social Studies Test (SSN). A 15-item nonverbal social studies test was developed by the staff. A series of questions were asked (e. g. Which is used by mother for cooking?) and the pupil selected the one picture out of four that best answered the question. Three forms of the test, bilingual, Pilipino and English, were prepared. All questions were asked twice. Pupils from Group 1 were tested bilingually, those from Group 2 in Pilipino, and those from Group 3 in English.

Verbal Social Studies Test (SSV). A 'verbal' social studies test consisting of 30 items (two parts) was prepared. Part I (26 items) consisted of four alternative multiple choice items such as Who connects the water tubes in the house?, engineer, plumber, electrician, carpenter. Part II (four items) consisted of more complex word problems to be answered by selecting the best of four given alternatives.

Again, three forms of the test were prepared. All questions were asked twice orally. The testing arrangements for this test were the same as those for the nonverbal form of the social studies test.

Science Test. In addition, a Science Achievement Test developed by the SEC was administered. All children received both an English and a Pilipino version of the test with a week's interval between administration. One half of the children from each class received the English version first, the other half the Pilipino.

The results of the first semester testing

Language Tests. The responses to the three language tests and the two science tests were analyzed using five separate one-way analyses of variance (Winer 1962). The data are summarized in Table 2. Significant differences occurred on all three language tests. On each test, however, it was clearly the class without prior kindergarten experience that performed most poorly. This fact was confirmed by a posteriori tests which revealed that on all three measures Class 4 pupils were significantly poorer than the others which did not differ. Kindergarten preparation clearly affects the performance of the pupils, at least during their first semester of formal schooling.

TABLE 2: Mean Number of Errors on Midyear Achievement Tests

Test	Class				
	1	2	3	4	F (3/120 df)
Oral English	3.06	2.51	2.90	5.61	5.74**
English Reading	2.07	2.00	1.88	4.87	8.72**
Pilipino Reading	4.88	3.85	3.97	9.97	10.57**
English Science	4.48	2.36	5.42	4.59	7.33**
Pilipino Science	2.80	2.09	4.06	5.26	12.55**

Note: 1 = Pilipino, 2 = English, 3 = Bilingual with kindergarten, 4 = Bilingual without kindergarten. ** indicates p<.01.

Science Tests. Significant differences also occurred on both forms of the science test. The English monolingually instructed class did better than either bilingual class or the Pilipino class. The Pilipino form of the test was not significantly easier than the English form.

Nonverbal Social Studies Test. The data for the two social studies tests and the mathematics test were analyzed using three separate 3 x 4 analyses of variance (Winer 1962). Three forms of each test were given—English, Pilipino, and bilingual—to subgroups from each of the four classes. The data for the nonverbal social studies test are summarized in Table 3. Both method of instruction (F = 3.60, 3/96 df, p<.05) and language of testing (F = 21.36, 2/96 df, p<.01), were

TABLE 3: Mean Number of Errors on Midyear SSN Test

Form	Class				
	1	2	3	4	Total
Bilingual	3.22	2.11	2.22	5.11	3.16
English	1.33	1.33	1.56	2.00	1.55
Pilipino	0.22	1.33	1.11	1.00	0.91
Total	1.59	1.59	1.63	2.70	

TABLE 4: Mean Number of Errors on Midyear SSV Test

Form	Class				
	1	2	3	4	Total
Bilingual	10.56	4.67	4.44	12.44	8.02
English	5.89	2.44	5.56	10.44	6.08
Pilipino	4.78	5.78	7.56	10.33	7.11
Total	7.08	4.30	5.85	11.07	

TABLE 5: Mean Number of Errors on Midyear Mathematics Test

Form	Class				
	1	2	3	4	Total
Bilingual	2.78	0.56	2.22	3.44	2.25
English	4.33	0.44	1.67	6.44	3.21
Pilipino	2.11	0.22	0.89	5.67	2.21
Total	3.07	0.40	1.59	5.18	

significant sources of variation, as was the interaction between the two (F = 2.69, 6/96 df, p<.05). In general, the pupils performed best on the Pilipino version of the test, and poorest on the bilingual version. Contrary to expectation, the Pilipino class performed as well as the English class on the English form of the test. Again, the pupils without kindergarten preparation clearly performed more poorly than the others.

Verbal Social Studies Test. The method of instruction was a significant source of variation on this test (F = 11.12, 3/96 df, p<.01). Again, the class without kindergarten training performed significantly more poorly than the others. The language of testing was not a significant source of variation, nor was the interaction significant. The results are summarized in Table 4.

Mathematics Test. Once again, the children instructed bilingually who had not attended kindergarten seem to be responsible for the significant difference among the four classes (F = 9.42, 3/96 df, p<.01) on the Mathematics test. This was the only significant effect. These results are summarized in Table 5.

Summary of Results. The test results at the end of the first semester indicated that the class with kindergarten training instructed using an alternate days bilingual approach performed similarly to the monolingual control classes on language and content tests. These findings, together with the favorable impressions of the participating teachers and many observers, encouraged us to continue the experimental program into the second semester.

The second semester evaluation

Second Semester Tests. Toward the end of the school year, three language tests and four content tests were administered to all pupils. The language tests, specially designed by staff members and graduate students for use in the experiment, were an English Oral Production Test, an English Reading Test, and a Pilipino Reading Test. A science test was developed by members of the SEC and both English and Pilipino versions were administered. Likewise, English, Pilipino and bilingual versions of Social Studies Verbal, Social Studies Nonverbal, and Mathematics Tests were developed and pretested. The tests were similar to those described previously with appropriate content modifications. Again, the classes were randomly divided into three groups for testing with teachers being rotated through the groups. Because of the fact that the class without kindergarten training had consistently lagged behind the other three classes, their results were excluded from the analyses of the second semester data.

The results of the second semester testing

Language Tests. The average scores on the language and science tests for the pupils from the three classes included in the second semester analyses are presented in Table 6. The data were analyzed using five separate one-way analyses of variance. There were no significant differences among the groups for English Oral Production or

TABLE 6: Average Number Correct of Final Achievement Tests

Test	Class			
	Pilipino	English	Bilingual	F(2/100 df)
Oral English	14.81	15.77	14.38	2.97
English Reading	40.69	40.91	40.41	16.70**
Pilipino Reading	39.31	44.85	37.82	0.30
English Science	12.63	13.53	11.50	6.08**
Pilipino Science	13.66	13.44	13.16	0.27

Note: The bilingual class without kindergarten training has been excluded from the final analyses.

for Pilipino Reading. There was a significant difference, however, for English Reading (F = 16.70, 2/100 df, p<.01) with pupils in the English class performing better than those in the Pilipino or bilingual classes. This result was not surprising, since the English class spends the majority of every day working via English whereas the bilingual class spends only about one half their time in English.

Science Tests. As the data in Table 6 indicate, there were no significant differences among the groups on the Pilipino version of the science test. On the English version, however, there was a significant difference among groups (F = 6.08, 2/100 df, p<.01). A multiple comparison test showed that the English class performed significantly better than the bilingual. The Pilipino class, however, did not differ significantly from the bilingual class.

Social Studies Nonverbal Test. The results for the SSN test are presented in Table 7. There were no significant main effects for either method of instruction or language of testing; but a significant interaction did occur (F = 5.74, 4/60 df, p<.01). A strange pattern of results emerged with the bilingual class performing best on the bilingual test, but the English class doing best on the Pilipino version, and the Pilipino class doing best on the English version. The overall effect for method of instruction was not, however, significant.

TABLE 7: Average Number Correct on the Final SSN Test

Test	Class			
	Pilipino	English	Bilingual	Total
Bilingual	22.50	25.00	25.75	24.42
English	25.25	24.25	22.38	23.96
Pilipino	23.12	24.87	22.87	23.62
Total	23.62	24.70	23.67	

TABLE 8: Average Number Correct on the Final SSV Test

Test	Class			
	Pilipino	English	Bilingual	Total
Bilingual	23.15	27.00	26.25	25.50
English	28.00	27.37	25.38	26.92
Pilipino	21.75	27.00	23.00	23.92
Total	24.33	27.12	24.87	

Social Studies Verbal Test. The results for the SSV test are summarized in Table 8. There were significant main effects for method of instruction (F = 6.34, 2/60 df, p<.01), and language of testing (F = 6.52, 2/60 df, p<.01), as well as a significant interaction between the two factors (F = 3.26, 4/60 df, p<.05). In general, the English class performed somewhat better than either the bilingual or the Pilipino class. Again, the pattern of results followed that for the SSN test with the bilingual class scoring best on the bilingual test, but the English class doing best on the Pilipino version and the Pilipino class doing best on the English version.

Mathematics Test. The results for the mathematics test are presented in Table 9. Method of instruction was a significant source of variation (F = 8.53, 2/60 df, p<.01) with the English class performing best. There was no significant difference between the Pilipino and the bilingual classes. Furthermore, language of testing was not a significant source of variation nor was there a significant interaction.

TABLE 9: Average Number Correct on the Final Math Test

Test	Class			
	Pilipino	English	Bilingual	Total
Bilingual	42.12	43.25	38.50	41.29
English	42.50	42.13	38.13	42.25
Pilipino	37.88	43.00	37.88	39.58
Total	40.53	43.12	38.17	

Summary of Results. Three language and five content tests were administered to the pupils to assess their performance at the end of the school year. After one year of instruction, there were no significant differences in performance on tests of Oral English, Pilipino Reading, Pilipino Science, and Nonverbal Social Studies among classes of children instructed via Pilipino, English, or bilingually using an alternate days approach. Significant effects due to method of instruction were found on tests of English Reading, English Science, Verbal Social Studies, and Mathematics. Although the English class demonstrated consistently superior performance relative to the others, there is reason to believe that their slightly better performance may have been due to the influence of certain uncontrolled variables. The tests administered during the first two weeks of school which were intended to be used for equating purposes revealed that, in fact, the English class performed better than the other two on English Picture Vocabulary and English Science Readiness. These equating measures were not used as the basis for an analysis of covariance since several basic statistical assumptions underlying this type of adjustment were not satisfied.

The results of the second semester testing together with the observations by teachers and visitors indicate that the alternate days bilingual approach to education does not result in confusion or retardation. Rather, the bilingually instructed pupils at the end of one year appear to be developing language and content skills comparable to their control counterparts.

Implications of these Results. The implications of these results, after one year of instruction, are positive and exciting. Two factors must be considered when interpreting the data. The Board of National Education probably will never seriously consider returning to predominantly English instruction at all primary grade levels. However, a solid grasp of English will continue to be a prerequisite to social and economic mobility in the country. Second, there now appears to be a nonproductive transitional period during Grade 3 when the rather abrupt shift is made from the vernacular to English as the medium of instruction. With these facts in mind, it should be understood that the main reason for including an English control group in the experimental program was for comparative purposes. The main question for the program during the first two years is whether the bilingually instructed children can compete with those taught in the vernacular. A more crucial test will come, under present policy at Grade 3, when the bilingual and Pilipino classes both switch to English. We predict that the bilingually instructed class will not suffer from the same transitional problems as the Pilipino class. The bilingual class would not really change their medium of instruction since they will have built up habits and expectations in both Pilipino and English.

At the end of the first year, then, we were sufficiently satisfied with the progress of the bilingually instructed pupils to recommend the continuation and expansion of the project. This recommendation was adopted by the college trustees.

New Directions for the Program in its Second Year. The Pilot Classes entered Grade 2 in July, 1969. They are now following a program of instruction similar to that described earlier with modifications, of course, to include appropriate second grade material.

In addition, six new Grade 1 classes started the program. Three classes (one Pilipino, one English, one bilingual) included children who had attended kindergarten, and three classes (Pilipino, English, and bilingual) were made up of children who had not. This year they were equated in terms of nonverbal IQ before class lists were finalized. We plan to continue to follow the Pilot Class this year, and then at least through next year's transition. In addition, we will pay particular attention to the results with the Follow-up Classes over the next several years for two reasons. First, since a bilingual alternate days approach had never before been tried in the Philippines, special attention was naturally being focused on the pupils and teachers. This extra attention could, of course, have affected their performance. Some of this novelty will have worn off by the second and subsequent years and we will be able to assess the pupils' performance under more natural conditions (see Lambert and Macnamara 1969; Lambert, Just, and Segalowitz 1970). Secondly, since most pupils outside the Manila area do not have the opportunity to attend kindergarten, the second year's design will provide a more general test of the effectiveness of such a scheme of education.

At the end of the academic year, April 1970, we will again evaluate the English and Pilipino language skills and content mastery of the pupils. In addition, the attitudes held by the pupils, parents, and teachers will be systematically evaluated.

In this report we have tried to describe a research program currently under way in the Philippines. Because we have really only just begun, our description and conclusions can only be tentative; but we feel that this program is an exciting one that will interest educators from diverse settings who are contemplating changes in language policy.

NOTES

[1] This research was supported by a grant from the Ford Foundation to the Language Study Center of the Philippine Normal College, Manila. The project was begun while Tucker was a Foundation Project Consultant at the Center. It continues under the direction of Otanes and Sibayan of the Philippine Normal College. We would especially like to thank R. Cena, R. C. Gardner, and D. M. Taylor for their assistance in every phase of this study.

[2] A summary of the methodology and results of the Philippine Language Policy Survey may be obtained by writing to B. P. Sibayan, Philippine Normal College, Manila.

REFERENCES

Bloom, B. S. 1964. Stability and change in human characteristics. New York, Wiley.

Davis, F. B. 1967. Philippine language-teaching experiments. Quezon City, Philippines, Phoenix Press.

Lambert, W. E., and J. Macnamara. 1969. Some cognitive consequences of following a first grade curriculum in a second language. Journal of educational psychology 60: 86-96.

Lambert, W. E., M. Just, and N. Segalowitz. 1970. Some cognitive consequences of following the curricula of the early school grades in a foreign language. Georgetown University MSLL No. 23: 229-274.

Malherbe, E. G. 1946. The bilingual school. London, Longmans.

Pascasio, Emy M. 1967. The language situation in the Philippines from the Spanish era to the present. In A. G. Manuud, ed., Brown heritage: essays on Philippine cultural tradition and literature. Quezon City, Ateneo de Manila University Press, 225-252.

Prator, C. H. 1950. Language teaching in the Philippines. Manila, U. S. Educational Foundation in the Philippines.

Ramos, M., J. V. Aguillar, and B. P. Sibayan. 1967. The determination and implementation of language policy. Quezon City Philippines, Phoenix Press.
Raven, J. C. 1956. Coloured progressive matrices: Sets A, Ab, B. London, Lewis.
Winer, B. J. 1962. Statistical principles in experimental design. New York, McGraw-Hill.

DISCUSSION

Madeline Ehrman, Foreign Service Institute: This paper was very interesting. I have a few practical questions only. First of all, in what language was the kindergarten training conducted? Was this in Tagalog?

Tucker: The kindergarten training was in Tagalog, that's right, with English introduced approximately ten minutes a day by a Peace Corps Volunteer.

Ehrman: There are some very special things about classes in the Manila area. First of all, it is an area where English is frequently spoken. The kids are going to hear it a lot just in their daily lives. The other thing is, of course, that Tagalog is the vernacular language of the children, and when you get out to the provinces this is not the case. Have you any plans for how you would change this program to account for the difference between the provinces and Manila?

Tucker: Essentially, for reasons such as this, because the Manila situation may be atypical, because of the fact that their kindergarten training may be atypical, we have extended the program this year to study systematically children who have not had kindergarten training. We would also envision carrying on this type of program in other language areas together with English. It depends, of course, on Philippine national language policy. When they make a change and say this is what the language situation will be, we'll have to go with that. But, essentially, based on results from the Iloilo experiment and other experiments, the suggestion is that schooling by the vernacular at the early years, if nothing else, gets the children enthused about the process of going to school. But yet at some stage—Professor Campbell will talk about these results—you are faced with the inescapable fact that your success in English, at least in the Philippines, appears to be directly related to the number of years' exposure you have had to the language. If you were introduced to English at an early age, you will do better at a later stage. So we see no reason why a bilingual scheme of education like this could not be combined with instruction via Tagalog in the Philippines or Spanish in the Southwest United States or whatever, depending upon the local situation.

Ehrman: No, probably not. But there would have to be changes, wouldn't there?

Tucker: There would have to be some changes. We do not think, however, that a situation such as you found, for example, should be continued. Miss Ehrman was working in a very isolated area of the Philippines, and there was a local language which was perhaps spoken by 15,000 people. This language, Bolinao, was used as a basis of instruction in Grades 1 and 2. This, I think, may be an unworkable situation because of control features, preparation of materials, training of teachers, etc.

Ehrman: Well, what they used were materials translated from Pangasinan, a language used by a far greater number of speakers.

Tucker: Right. We do not see that as a workable type of solution.

Vera John, Yeshiva University: I am concerned and confused about the purpose of the experiment, about the commitment that you express again and again towards a particular kind of outcome. Some of the reports I have received from the Philippines have been that students who do better on testing in a second language like English, still, even at college level, do very poorly when they are asked to compose or do some kind of freer, original task. They do better in their native language on that. I am wondering whether educational policies should be based upon an interlocking system of testing and instruction that is limited, very often, to certain kinds of tasks that require relatively little structured thinking from the child. The system uses basically multiple choice or completion kinds of examples. In other words, the utilization of a native language as a fundamental source for the development of cognitive activity does not really get explored in this kind of an examination procedure.

The second question is: How do you explain the lack of superiority of the Filipino-educated child in Filipino reading and so on? Could that not be also an artifact of relying upon English as the basis for instruction? To what extent are these really two equal languages, or again, what are the artifacts of the experiment?

Tucker: Let me first answer your second question, looking at artifacts, etc. There are several possible explanations for the lack of superiority of the Pilipino-instructed group. One factor, for example, might be associated with the translation or change of the materials from their original English preparation into Pilipino; another might be the fact that these particular elementary school teachers had received all of their own training via English; that is, they received their orientation to materials via English so that they were in the process of making the transfer at that time. During the course of teaching the material, we tried to help them over the transition difficulties; but factors such as these may have affected the outcome. From our point of view, this situation didn't bother us because that was, in fact, the situation they are faced with in the country, but from a generalizability point of view, you would worry about that.

With regard to your other question. This, of course, is a crucial question which is involved in the evaluation and assessment of the effectiveness of any type of program or any type of change in policy. We want, of course, to take advantage of getting children into the school system, enthused about the education process, and to capitalize on any advantages that might come from native language instruction. We try in assessing their performance to include real life communication type situations, communication with peers and this type of thing. As you know, there are variations of the Glucksberg procedure that we can use to test their English oral production skills.

The question that Dr. John raised is certainly a valid question with regard to any of these programs. The fact, nevertheless, remains that in the Philippine setting where planners and educators demand, and job opportunities require, that a switch be made to English at some point with those who are proficient in English being the ones who will be hired, the goal which you set for yourself is to teach English as effectively as possible. Dr. John's point is certainly well taken that this, perhaps, should not be the guiding criteria in formulating policy or in making decisions of this type, but that was what we were faced with. I know this is really not a sufficient answer to you, but your question really cannot be answered at this time.

Dorothy Goodman, Washington International School: You mentioned you were encouraged by the fact that the children instructed in English had done better than the other two groups, and I see that this would be a cheerful finding for Montreal. But from our point of view here in Washington it is depressing, because the bilingually-instructed children ought to do better! Otherwise I ought to abandon my school, send the French section to the Ecole française (the French French school here in Washington) and set up a Spanish Spanish school for the children who want Spanish and English.

My question is whether the teaching of the bilingual teachers in the bilingual section is perhaps less effective than that of the English teachers teaching only in English, with Tagalog as simply a subject. Is it perhaps, as we have found in the Washington International School, that the monolingual teacher is a better teacher in that language than the person who is fully bilingual and able to work to a very high standard in two? We find, for instance, that some of our most sophisticated French teachers who are bilingual with English often do not know which language they are talking and are less forceful in communicating with the children than teachers who are decidedly dominant in one or the other.

Tucker: This is an important question. Let me highlight three areas in response. First, all the teachers would be characterized as dominantly Tagalog or dominantly Pilipino. They would also speak English very well, and be able to use it in the classroom. Second, we have started and have in progress an interesting video-tape survey. We move into a classroom and spend approximately one week there recording everything that goes on (e. g. in social studies every day for a week between 10 and 11 o'clock; or mathematics, etc.). Then we plan to do a content analysis of the video-tape to find out whether there is, in fact, a progression of material; that is, does the English teacher move along at the same pace that the Pilipino teacher moves along, that the bilingual teacher moves along? Our first impression is that the bilingual teacher does in fact move along continuously, rather than spending a lot of time going back and working on the transition, but we will be able to document that, I think, in a little while for you.

You probably should not be discouraged in terms of the Bilingual Education program you have going on. We would like to get to the point of the development of balanced bilinguality. Although Professor Lambert didn't get a chance to go into this, we see other advantages inherent in or associated with bilinguality; in terms, perhaps, of certain cognitive advantages or more open or broader perspectives toward both cultural groups, rather than the anomie or culturelessness.

Charles E. Terry, Yeshiva University: I just wanted to add a comment about the extension of this discussion to other areas of the Philippines. I know that in the village I was in, you would have to consider the fact that there were really no functional usage settings for children in English, or for teachers for that matter; and a great number of children at that point were becoming either fishermen or rice farmers, and they didn't have the need for English. Not that I would want to rule out the possibility of their choosing to learn English since this introduces choices of mobility and different work, but there would have to be some consideration of this, that's all.

Tucker: This is one reason, in fact, why the Board of Education is now considering a change to the use of a vernacular or Pilipino as the primary medium of instruction at the Grades 1, 2, 3, and 4 levels, with a switch to English a little later on. Many children do not now continue in school past Grade 4. The Board feels that they can provide them with a better education in those first four years, better training for citizenship in a limited period of time, via the vernacular, which I'm sure ties in with your experience in a rural community.

Robert Lado, Georgetown University: I would like to make two comments. One concerns whether or not the experiment has anything to say to the situation where you have only 15,000 speakers of the home language. I don't think the experiment has anything negative to say about that situation. Whether or not you use a bilingual approach when there are only 15,000 speakers apparently will be a logistic and economic decision. If the government wants to spend the money in developing the materials, then you would do it. I don't think the experiment has anything to say about that.

The other is that I don't think we can conclude—I know you don't want to conclude—that monolingual teaching is better. Your results seem to be showing that monolingual teaching in English is better; that bilingual or monolingual in the home language is a little bit less, only you are willing to discount the differences. I think that this can be interpreted differently: either we have to think that there is some magic about English that makes monolingually-taught students superior, or perhaps the evaluation instruments gave some bias in favor of English.

Tucker: Professor Lado's comments are, of course, right on target. The first, with regard to the size of the language community, is not a matter of the experiment, but is an economic question, a matter of feasibility or practicality tied up with the investment that the government is willing to make.

With regard to the second, I think that it would probably not be bias on the part of the testing instruments, because we were careful to pull out random selections of the children for testing, some via Pilipino, some via English, some bilingually, and we looked carefully at the interaction between language of testers and medium of instruction. I think, though, that the results may be an artifact or bias associated with the tendency in the school system for so many years to teach via English, to prepare materials mainly via English, to train these teachers mainly via English, etc. I would say that in the next couple of years as these experiments are repeated, as there is more development of materials in the local vernacular, as teachers in the normal schools are better trained to teach via the local vernacular, that we would see a similarity in the results of children taught with English or a vernacular.

ENGLISH CURRICULA FOR NON-ENGLISH SPEAKERS

RUSSELL N. CAMPBELL

University of California, Los Angeles

Abstract. Recent research by Lambert et al (Some Cognitive Consequences of Following the Curricula of Grades One to Four in a Foreign Language) has revealed the possibility of successful scholastic
achievement for students studying in a foreign language as well as the
successful acquisition of the foreign language. In this paper it will be
argued that emphasis on the development of partial or parallel curricula
in the students' native language, say for Navajo or Mexican-American
children, is not a necessary prerequisite for successful academic
achievement or acquisition of English. It will further be argued that
success or failure can be accounted for in terms of the expectations
held by the human participants in the educational process and other
non-linguistic factors including the socioeconomic status of the community represented by the students.

A review of the hearings before the House Committee on the Bilingual Education Act will show that a large number of educators and
school administrators consider the teaching of English as a Second
Language (ESL) to be one of the components of a bilingual education
program. As a member of, but not necessarily speaking for, a professional group of several thousand American ESL teachers, I would
like to use this opportunity to define as clearly as possible the actual
as well as the potential role of ESL in the education of nonnative speakers of English in the United States.
My remarks will center around four categories of students who
might be thought to profit from ESL instruction, namely (1) university,

(2) secondary, (3) nonuniversity adults, and (4) children entering our elementary schools.

The needs of these diverse groups vary considerably. Foreign university students generally have already completed 12 to 16 years of formal education and usually have had a number of years of experience with English before coming to this country and they are assumed to have previously reached a high degree of English-language proficiency. That this is not always the case is reflected in the large number of elementary ESL courses that have been established in nearly every large university from New York to Hawaii. This group of nonnative speakers of English in our educational institutions has received more attention from ESL experts than any of the other groups mentioned above. That so many of them failed to learn sufficient English in their home countries to succeed in American universities has been a blessing in disguise. For the major contributor to the development of a set of assumptions about the optimal conditions for second-language acquisition has been our collective experience with this particular group.

This experience, coupled with the acceptance of the concepts held by descriptive linguists as to the nature of language and language acquisition can be said to account for the ESL profession's support and propagation of what has come to be known as the audio-lingual or aural-oral approach to second-language teaching. We will want to keep this orientation in mind as we discuss the role of ESL in the education of the other groups.

Nonnative speakers of English who enter our secondary schools are similar in some ways to the foreign students who enter our universities. Like university students, secondary students are probably recent arrivals in this country who have had considerable previous academic experience and they are probably literate in at least one language. However, the high school student may still be in the process of gaining certain fundamental skills and knowledge prerequisite to either obtaining a job or entering college. They differ also in that we cannot assume that they have substantial previous experience with the English language. That is, we cannot assume that they have a basic knowledge of English upon which we can build as we do for university students. Furthermore, whereas we have over a quarter of a century of experience behind us in dealing with foreign university students, we have all but ignored the special problems of the secondary school student. In those instances when high school personnel have sought the guidance of university ESL experts, we frequently see the imposition of essentially the same methods and techniques that have been found suitable in the university programs. Quite frequently this results in the establishment of special ESL classes for these high school students some time during the school day while the remainder of their program is identical to that of their native English-speaking peers.

Bringing to bear both our experience with university students and a common sense comparison, we can see that the wholesale adoption of university tactics for the solution of English-language deficiencies of high school students has little to recommend itself. We have found that university students who come to us with minimal knowledge of English, even though they receive our most sophisticated ESL instruction, are quite likely to perform badly in their academic pursuits during the first two or three terms at the university. Given that high schools are even less prepared to teach ESL and that the foreign student is less likely to have as much previous experience with English, then we cannot be very optimistic that such a program will greatly facilitate the students' academic careers in our high schools.

It also helps me to appreciate the plight of foreign teenagers in our secondary schools if I try to imagine what would have happened to me academically if I had been abruptly enrolled in a secondary school in Tokyo or Mexico City when I was, say, 15 years old. Even if I were given special instruction in Japanese or Spanish for a period every day—I cannot imagine that I would have been able to continue my studies in math, history, biology, etc., without serious difficulty. I certainly would not have had any hope of competing with my Japanese or Mexican classmates.

It seems perfectly clear to me that we have two alternatives if we are truly going to assist foreign secondary school students. One, we must develop full-time English-language programs for them and delay the continuation of their normal educational program until such time as they demonstrate an ability to pursue academic studies without major hindrance from English-language deficiencies. Or, two, we must develop for these students parallel academic courses in the student's native language which he would pursue along with special ESL courses. This second alternative seems perfectly feasible to me for this age group, at least for students who are members of large non-English-speaking groups in this country, e.g. Spanish or Chinese. To find teachers and teaching materials for these students in most urban areas would not appear to be an insurmountable task. Such instruction would permit the student to rather comfortably and securely enter our educational system without the massive opportunity for frustration and failure that he would face otherwise. Although an ESL course would be of some benefit to a foreign high school student who was forced to study in the normal English curriculum, it clearly cannot prepare the student to compete immediately with his English-speaking peers in academic coursework.

It is very difficult to describe the adult foreigners who flock to evening ESL courses. For those who have read Leonard Ross' Hyman Kaplan, not much more need be said. They range from highly educated professionals to illiterate manual laborers. Their most common need is a rapid acquisition of enough English to permit them to be mobile in the community and to establish themselves in an appropriate job. Once again, ESL professionals have been slow to attend to the needs of those attempting to teach students in this situation, and when they have, they again (usually) bring their university-oriented solutions to bear.

Adult education presents so many problems that it is difficult to generalize. An article by Sue Ervin-Tripp may provide some guidance. She describes the possible linguistic needs of a newcomer to San Francisco's Chinatown as follows:

> Virtually all of his roles in adult life can be conducted in Chinese, and it is common to find long-term residents of the United States knowing virtually no English. Let us suppose a man conducts a business with some non-Chinese customers. In that case he may learn some English words, but the necessary interchanges can be extremely limited in vocabulary and syntax. He may have to make some purchases outside the Chinese community. But on the whole his situation is very much like that of a tourist. It may be a general fact that the first and most rudimentary forms of speech demanded of an adult in an intercultural situation are usually request forms with a vocabulary specific to goods or services exchanged. The reason is that the roles involved are typically economic—customer, employer, and so on. If we know what the functions of such speech are, we can find how much of the language need be learned, or will be learned first. It is clear, for example, that even phonemic distinctions are not needed for communicating request forms in a highly redundant context.

A more precise understanding of these limited needs would suggest priorities to be considered by the ESL teacher or textbook writer.

In those instances where the adult student is needful of instruction that would lead to the mastery of some skill or trade, then it would again seem most appropriate that such instruction be given in his native language. The alternative would be to postpone such instruction until the student had acquired a high degree of proficiency in English. For most adults such a postponement would be to his great economic disadvantage. We, again, must recognize that current ESL methods cannot simultaneously teach the adult student English and give him technical or complex instruction in that language.

Now to turn to the group of students who have been uppermost in the minds of those who are concerned with bilingual education; namely, the young five or six-year-old speaker of some language other than English who enters our elementary schools. In the following remarks

I shall have in mind particularly the Mexican-American children of
Southern California and the Navajo children on the Navajo reservation.
Traditionally, these children have been expected to enter our schools
and perform as if they were native speakers of English. That is, their
teachers taught in English, the teaching materials used were written
for English speakers, and the children were tested in English. The
results of such instruction and testing are well known. By the end of
the six years of elementary school, a great number of these students
were tragically behind their English-speaking counterparts in their
academic achievement and were prime candidates to drop out of school
within an additional few years. To explain these results, the most
common assumption has been that it is unreasonable to expect a child
to acquire the fundamentals of education in a language he does not understand. Educators, with this assumption in mind, turned to the
ESL profession for help and found a sympathetic ear. Over a 10 or
15-year period a substantial number of ingenious courses and teaching devices have been developed to teach English to these children.
Underlying nearly all of these efforts we again find the same limited
assumptions that were found acceptable in the preparation of materials
for university students. Although one can hardly doubt that such programs have to some degree alleviated the problem, there is very little
concrete evidence that they have made it possible for the student to
perform any better scholastically than did his older brothers and sisters who received no such instruction.

While this plan continues to be employed in a number of school systems, an alternate solution has emerged, essentially, the same solution that we came to earlier for high school and adult students. Why
not initiate the student's education in his native language, say, Navajo
or Spanish, and teach him English at the same time? Then, at some
point, after two or three years, after he has fully learned English, we
can switch the child to an all-English curriculum. This solution is
intuitively extremely attractive and, indeed, were it implemented,
might well result in a number of favorable benefits for the child. But
there are several aspects of such a program that should be considered
carefully before accepting it as a solution to the problems of scholastic achievement and the acquisition of English as a second language.
First, as suggested earlier, there is little evidence that our current
ESL methods can adequately prepare students of this age to assume
their studies in English after two or three or even four years of ESL.
There is no doubt that we can teach him a great deal of English, but
whether it will be enough to permit him to compete with his English-
speaking peers in their third and fourth grade studies is at least in
doubt.

Another important concern is the availability of sufficient materials
and teachers to teach children of this age in their first language, es-

pecially if we have in mind the Navajo child. I am not sure whether this concern is as serious for Mexican-American children in California. I suspect, however, that we assume a uniformity of proficiency in Spanish on the part of these children that may be illusory. There is some evidence that their competence in Spanish ranges over a broad continuum from complete competence to only passive knowledge of a small amount of Spanish. If this be the case, then we at least must take it into consideration before accepting this plan as if they were all equally prepared to receive this education in Spanish.

We have, so far, recognized that our success at teaching the Mexican-American and Navajo child as if he were a speaker of English has not been maximally beneficial to the child. We have also considered briefly two alternative plans and seen that neither is without inherent problems. However, it seems apparent that our major efforts will continue along variations of these two solutions unless we reexamine our first assumption, i.e. that it is unreasonable to expect a child to gain the fundamentals of education in a foreign language.

In an earlier paper at this conference (Lambert 1970) we heard the results of an extensive experimental program in St. Lambert, Canada. We heard that a number of Anglo children were taught as if they were French-Canadian children, and we further learned that, contrary to our intuitive expectations, they not only acquired near-native-speaker competence in French, but they have performed in all but one scholastic area (verbal expression) as well as both Anglo and French-Canadian control groups in both languages. Without further repetition of the remarkable results reported by Lambert, one can at least suspect that the previous accounting for our failure with Navajo and Mexican-American students may have been extremely narrow. It apparently is not the fact that it is unreasonable to expect children to acquire the fundamentals of education in a foreign language. Once one accepts this as a possibility, additional evidence in its favor can be brought into focus.

From 1960 to 1966 extensive research was carried out in the Philippines 'to determine the effect on language and subject matter achievement at the end of grade four and of grade six of beginning English as the language of instruction in grade one, in grade three, or in grade five'. Among other conclusions, as reported by Frederick B. Davis, the following were reached:

(a) Proficiency in English is directly related to the number of years in which it is used as the medium of instruction.
(b) The effect of increasing the amount of time devoted to teaching English in classes where it is not used as the language of instruction is likely to accomplish relatively little.

(c) At the end of Grade 6, the group that used English as the medium of instruction in Grades 1-6 (as compared to those in which English became the medium of instruction in the third or fifth grades) displayed, on the whole, the highest level of achievement on subject matter tests whether the tests were given in Tagalog, English, or bilingually. (These texts were on social studies, science-health, arithmetic computation, and arithmetic problems.)

In this Philippine study, the concern was with Tagalog-speaking children who would later have to carry out their secondary school studies in English, i.e. a situation in some ways similar to that of our Navajo and Mexican-American children. I again quote from Davis:

It is clear that any change in the number of years in which English is used as the medium of instruction will effect the facility and effectiveness with which the pupils can profit from instruction in English in secondary schools and colleges.... It is likely that if the Philippine Public Schools made a drastic change and used, say, vernacular languages in different areas as media of classroom instruction in Grades 1-6, most public school pupils who entered secondary schools would be so handicapped, if the language of instruction in the classroom, texts, and references continued to be in English, that the schools would have to lower their academic standards and increase the time devoted to teaching English.

A second bit of evidence, admittedly of indeterminate importance, that we tend to ignore when thinking about the child's capacity to assimilate to a new linguistic environment, is the massive anecdotal evidence we have that children of this age who are set in a foreign language environment, almost without exception, perform in that language on the same level as do their native-speaker peers within a matter of weeks.

Finally, the success reported by those bilingual education projects which have initiated a scholastic program with more-or-less fifty percent of the curriculum in English and fifty percent in the foreign student's native language are to a large extent dependent upon the assumption that English is most efficiently acquired when used as the language of instruction.

The nagging question that now must be surfaced is the following: If children can succeed academically in a foreign language, then how do we account for our rather miserable performance in educating Mexican-American and Navajo children in an English curriculum? That is, what are the factors that differentiate the scholastic and language-learning success of those Anglo students in Lambert's study and the success attained by minority students in our schools? At this point one can only speculate, but at least a number of hypotheses suggest themselves:

(1) Teachers hold low academic expectations for these children and the children respond accordingly.
(2) The students' (and their parents') attitude toward the culture represented by the English language are such that they are detrimental to the acquisition of English.
(3) Because of socioeconomic conditions, the preschool opportunities for concept-development on the part of these children is in some significant way different from those of the students in Lambert's studies.
(4) Rather than given the feeling that their adjustment to foreign language instruction is proceeding in a normal fashion, these children are subjected to unwarranted feelings of failure, fear, and frustration during the earliest days of their schooling.

One or another of these or related hypotheses may account for our relative lack of success in educating nonnative speakers of English in our elementary schools. What appears to be nearly certain is that for whatever reason we reject an English curriculum for non-English speakers, it should not be on the basis that children are not innately capable of succeeding in such a program.

We began by asking what the actual and potential role of ESL is in bilingual programs. It is apparent that with our current knowledge we cannot compete with the language acquisition results gained by the children in Lambert's study or in the Philippine experiment. It may be that our accumulated knowledge would suggest solutions to some of the persistent structural problems that these students had, but by and large, it appears that their overall gains in competence in the foreign language exceed those we would hope for in an ESL program.

With our current knowledge of ESL, we can, under certain conditions, continue to make important contributions to students in the other three categories discussed above. However, our potential contributions to second-language learning are, in fact, much more interesting.

Not too long ago, the typical kind of research carried out by members of our profession was the addition of yet another contrastive analysis of English and Spanish phonemes. Our questions, almost without exception, were asked within the confines of something called applied linguistics. As suggested by the hypotheses listed above, we are now seeking to broaden our basis for research both by developing an awareness of the accumulated findings of psychology, sociology, and education and by stimulating members of these fields to direct their atten-

tion, along with ours, to specific questions that we have identified on
second-language acquisition.

REFERENCES

Davis, Frederick B. 1967. Philippine language-teaching experiments,
    Philippine Center for Language Study Monograph Series No. 5.
    Alemar-Phoenix Publishing House.
Ervin-Tripp, Susan. The study of language learning in social contexts.
Lambert, Wallace. 1970. Some intellectual consequences of following
    an elementary school curriculum in a foreign language. Paper given
    at the Twenty-first Annual Round Table Meeting on Linguistics and
    Language Studies, March 12-14.

DISCUSSION

Shaligram Shukla, Georgetown University: Perhaps you are aware
of the findings of Eric Lenneberg. He has tried to prove—and he sounds
very convincing—that in children between the ages of 18 months and 36
months, language capacities of speech production and related aspect of
acquisition develop. Parents, although they try very hard, can't teach
them because they don't know how to. Till they are 12 years or thereabouts the capacity to acquire language in children is still turned on,
after that it is turned off. Now if you are teaching a second language
to children who are under 12 years of age, why don't you provide a
conducive social atmosphere in which they pick up the language? Why
do you have to have teachers to tell them, when we know that in children language develops according to built-in biological schedules?

Campbell: There are about four people here on the stage who could
answer that question better than I. It seems to me that one of the points
of my paper was, precisely, that we should reconsider the question of
whether or not special instruction in ESL was necessary for very young
children. It has appeared, in the evidence cited from the research done
in Canada and the Philippines, that early education in the target language
resulted in the most substantial gains in the acquisition of the target language. It appears that, given the exposure, the communicational experience, children apply their own language acquisition device and learn the
new language.

Einar Haugen, Harvard University: I was very happy that Mr.
Campbell brought out certain points that are often confused in discussions of bilingualism. We tend to see bilingualism in an educational environment, as the teaching of a second language to someone

who has a first language. But obviously that is an oversimplification of the problem, because there is another dimension which rarely gets mentioned but was implied in some of what Mr. Campbell said. He was faced with a situation in which the second language was the dominant language. This was brought out in the kind of charts which Mackey has made and which were used on the board yesterday by Father Ó Huallacháin. These charts show the home language surrounded by a totally different language, with the school being the intermediary between these two parts of the environment. We need to think in terms of dominant and nondominant, but these are terms we don't like to talk about because they are ultimately political. They are matters of power, which teachers don't enjoy discussing. In the United States I think everyone would agree that English is the dominant language. In Canada there are differences within the country, but overall English is dominant there also. It makes a great deal of difference whether the schools are teaching the children a language that is nondominant or one that is dominant, because children are sensitive to the pressure of society through their parents and their peers. I think the opposition of dominant and nondominant is so important that I wonder if Lambert's good results may not be accounted for by the fact that he is teaching the members of a dominant group a nondominant language which has potentialities of dominance, while in Texas or New Mexico we are teaching the dominant language to a nondominant group. This alters the educational picture totally.

Campbell: I appreciate the suggestions very much.

Question: Don't we have to take the environment into consideration?

Campbell: Certainly it would have to be; you couldn't ignore it, I would think. I think the experiment in Canada is all the more remarkable in that the children speak English when they go out for recess, when they go home they speak English, and yet just with the exposure in the classroom five or six hours a day, they acquire such proficiency in French. This fact should be in our favor in teaching the Chicano kids in Los Angeles. They turn on television and they (probably) listen to English programs; there is English all around them, so this should make our task easier. Yes, obviously you do have to take into consideration the environment outside of the classroom.

Robert Lado, Georgetown University: I just want to clarify the term 'teaching', because otherwise we may fall into a cliche here and burn all the teachers at the stake, and that would be a terrible thing.

I think we also have another clarification. There is the old saying that one swallow does not make a summer, and nothing could be truer in research. We know that one experiment is very seldom definitive; we should have more. We mustn't jump too quickly to conclusions here. I am entirely in sympathy with and support of Professor Campbell that we should broaden the basis of our question concerning the problem of English and bilingualism. I myself am carrying on research with a broader base.

On the matter of teaching. We are faced with this situation: either we don't teach, in which case we leave them in their natural surroundings (and that hasn't worked), or we teach in certain ways. I think it is in the meaning of the word 'teach'. One way is to provide certain tokens that will result in learning. That is teaching.

Campbell: I appreciate those remarks very much. My objective in this paper was to suggest that we should in fact consider additional ways of 'teaching' that go beyond what we as ESL professionals have adhered to in recent times. We have, I believe, interpreted second language teaching and learning rather narrowly. I am simply pleading for research that will explain our successes and failures in ESL that cannot be explained by the theoretical assumptions currently held by most ESL experts.

Vera John, Yeshiva University: It is a sad fate to be an advocate. But it is back in fashion to be a scientist as well as a person who is a thinking, active member of this society. As you knew I would and I hoped I wouldn't, I would like to remind you of a few considerations that we have to think of when advising others about their educational policy. You and I can no longer decide on educational policy for Navajos and Chicanos. They are going to make their own educational policy, and they are going to consider research as part of that decision. Part of their decision is based on the thought: How shall we give the best possible education to our children to compete, if they wish, in a society toward which we have ambivalent feelings? Regardless of their decision they no longer feel that they will be the victims of that society. Mr. Nakai was elected because he spoke in Navajo on the radio. He was heard by every member of that tribe who has a radio. His election as Chairman of the tribe was very deeply related to his proficiency in Navajo, not to his income, which may have been related to his proficiency in English. These are important factors to consider in a sociolinguistic, sociological, political, psychological and educational context. I think we have to, when we are educational advisors to minority groups, rethink our role. Our role should be to try to present as objectively as we can—and none of us are objective—the outcomes of various research findings. At the same time we should seriously consider the national and social aspirations of the groups with which we work. Language is a small part of success. We are speaking this morning as if language is the determining aspect of how and why a human being is successful in this society. I don't think that that is a realistic assumption. It may be indeed an assumption that we should also reconsider as we relate ourselves to research in this area.

Frank Ponce, Jr., District of Columbia Teachers College: I must say that I had not expected to disagree with the young lady who just spoke. I think that although some very, very good points have been made, there is a certain amount of naivete involved. Having been an examiner for ETS Princeton, I can say that no matter what you bring to a system, the system dictates its terms. I do believe, however, not along with the young lady from Yeshiva, that it is the community which must first speak out its own issues and then be heard. I think one of the things that perhaps has not been emphasized here is the fact of cross purposes. The bilingual child wants to learn the language of his father and mother, but his father and mother are in another direction, becoming new Americans, and therefore may not want to encourage the child in speaking the language.

And now I think I would like to project Dr. Haugen's idea a little bit. If we do have to consider the dominant, what about the subdominant languages, such as Spanish in New York? It's unofficial but it's still the second strongest language in New York, English being the first. If we take Spanish being taught in the Midwest, we have Spanish in 'isolation' (relative isolation), let's say; or we can take Montreal where the French that's being spoken is not the same French as in middle Canada. The people who have come over have come over with an educated French. The others, perhaps, are white collar workers or farmers or blue collar workers. Therefore these are some of the aspects that I think have to be taken into consideration.

Now, if I may bore you with just one more comment. At ETS when I arrived I found that the three people in charge of college board exams were three ladies, all bilinguals and all specialists. They were in charge of Spanish exams, and they were specialists in French and German—two from Germany, one from Belgium. Needless to say, the animosity which was felt was great when a person arrived who was not only bilingual but tricultural. Then we had to meet with committees on which sat foreign bilingual professors along with American professors. Now the professor who comes from Spain or Latin America or elsewhere may feel that in order to succeed he must fit the mold prescribed by a certain system. In other words, you 'play by the rules', or pressures are brought to bear for not concurring with established practices and policies. I would be interested in hearing the comments of Dr. Campbell or any other member, perhaps Dr. Lambert.

(Dr. Campbell expressed his wish to comment to Mr. Ponce individually after the meeting was adjourned, because of the lack of time.)

STRUCTURE AND PROCESS IN LANGUAGE ACQUISITION[1]

SUSAN ERVIN-TRIPP

University of California, Berkeley

Abstract. Our knowledge of the effects of exposure to second languages in natural situations is limited in many ways. a) We have very little information about the specific kinds of competence children have for the varieties of language in the repertoire of their community. b) We have defined language far too narrowly, omitting just those skills in the social use of language which may have more to do with social acceptability and communicative success than knowledge of school vocabulary. c) We lack well-developed theories of the processing of linguistic information which can account for changes in children's ability to understand, imitate, or produce appropriate speech as they learn. The applied orientation of most work on second language learning has resulted in the lack of a strong theoretical framework for designing empirical studies. On the other hand, many of the theoretical issues and concepts in psycholinguistic work on grammatical processing, and in child language research are relevant to studies of bilingualism.

Wallace Lambert's recent experimental program in which Canadian Anglophones learn French presents a dilemma to American advocates of bilingual education. Lambert took a group of English-speaking children and put them into kindergartens in which for two years French was the sole medium of instruction. The pupils were all monolingual. In an astonishingly short time, their achievements in language and in other subjects were equal to those of French and English monolinguals.

If this could happen, why do Chicanos have problems in our California schools? Since the overt linguistic circumstances seem entirely parallel, it seems to me the differences are social. In the Montreal environment, English-speaking children have no sense of inferiority or disadvantage in the school. Their teachers do not have low expectations for their achievements. Their social group has power in the community; their language is respected, is learned by Francophones, and becomes a medium of instruction later in the school. In the classrooms, the children are not expected to compete with native speakers of French in a milieu which both expects and blames them for their failures, and never provides an opportunity for them to excel in their own language.

If the root problems of Chicano children in our schools are social, rather than linguistic, we can expect that the comparable structure here would provide a fully bilingual program, as in Miami. Thus the Chicano children could see their own language respected as a medium of instruction, and see Anglophones struggling to learn it as they learn English. It would not be surprising if in such fully bilingual programs they eventually learn school English better than children in schools where English is the sole medium of instruction—even though they hear and speak less English in the course of the school day.

I think two major changes have taken place in our views of language acquisition in recent years. One is that we now are beginning to see the functions of language in the life of the speaker as of far more importance in its acquisition than we had realized, and the other is that the mechanical view that practice makes perfect has given way under the impact of the evidence that speechless children can have well developed language. Studies of first language acquisition have grown rapidly and undergone some major theoretical changes. It is my purpose in this paper to bring the current views of child language acquisition and of language processing strategies to bear on some issues of second language learning.

If one is to study how people change, how they learn to understand, imitate, or emit sentences, then one must at least start with some notions of how they handle such linguistic material at a given point in development. The study of change then is a study of change either in their processing procedures or in the stored structures—for example their vocabulary—as it is employed in that processing.

Recent work on children's language acquisition has brought out strongly that the child is not just a passive vessel of sense impressions. He actively strains, filters, reorganizes what he is exposed to. His imitations are not exact duplications or even random reductions of input, but reflect knowledge similar to that revealed in his other uses of language. In this respect, first and second language learning must be quite alike; the learner actively reorganizes, makes generalizations, simplifies. Any learning model which predicts language learning on the basis of input without regard to the selective processing by the learner will not work, except for trivial problems. [2] And yet most of our rationales for procedures in second language instruction have been based on assumptions that organization of input, plus practice, will have predictable results.

The processing or strategy analyses currently discussed differ from linguistic descriptions in that they are concerned with actual behavior occurring in time, so that questions of how long a process takes, and what processes are simultaneous make sense. In testing hypotheses about processing we are concerned to use a maximum range of criteria. Linguists rely on native speakers' judgments of grammaticality, paraphrase equivalence, and structural parallelism. In addition we would use other criteria, such as effects of memory, time to process, mistakes in repetition, and differences between types of performance.

There are at present no processing models in existence except as general schemata. You can imagine that filling in the details will take many years, since the program is so ambitious. I plan to illustrate the relation of such approaches to second language learning in a few instances.

If we begin by looking at processing of the auditory surface, it is important to think about some of the interactions involved. For example, speakers of English interpret pitch and intensity cues to differentiate meanings. But when judges are asked to draw or identify the details of the contours, they often reconstruct on the basis of the full, completed sentence interpretation (Lieberman 1965). It is this reconstruction of which Chomsky and Halle (1968) speak in describing the cyclic rules of stress and the impact of grammar on prosodic judgments. They are not talking about the initial perception and utilization of pitch and intensity. Otherwise it would be totally baffling how infants under one year discriminate these properties and imitate them long before they interpret grammatical features.

It is perfectly clear that lexical, grammatical, and pragmatic contexts can influence the interpretation of phonological features. These interpretations are a final outcome. Any model must account for the fact that a preparatory set or some input information may effect an interpretation powerfully relative to other information. Yet it is the case that people can analyze and remember isolated syllables independent of lexical and grammatical information—how else could we repeat nonsense or expect students to write down new technical vocabulary? Or, for that matter, learn a new language.

The implications of these effects are merely that the overall model will not take the form of a series of equally important, irrevocable decisions ordered from phonology to syntax, but will be far more complex and may include short-term surface structure memory and provisional analyses.

One way of looking at second-language learning is to assume that the first encounters with a second language will be handled by the apparatus of structure and process already available. But there is an additional factor to consider. An adult who has changed his linguistic system only in minor ways—by adding new vocabulary, for example— for many years may not have available ready strategies for change. An adult who has already learned other languages, or a child who is constantly in the process of reorganizing his processing system and adding to his storage at all levels will have quite different approaches to new input. 'Learning to learn' is an established notion in psychology. The most adaptable, sensitive language learner we can find is a young child. Surely we can expect that his second language learning will reflect many of the same processes of development as he used to discover his first language. On the other hand, in the case of inexperienced adults we can expect the system to be most adaptable just at the point where it changes most readily in adult life—the lexicon. But we can expect the typical adult to be ready to process both the sounds and syntax of what he hears as if his usual processing devices were appropriate.[3]

Three different kinds of performance have been the bases for making inferences about mental processes. For example, we often use imitation to assess knowledge of language. At a minimum, it can be shown that imitation requires perception, storage, organization of output, and motor output. In addition, before the storage phase there will be interpretation if the material is interpretable.

It is a common practice in reporting imitations to say that speakers 'perceive' in a certain way. But I think it is clear that even someone who clearly could hear a difference between two input items might not differentiate them in his own pronunciation.

When a person listens to an utterance, and then answers it, acts on it, paraphrases it, or just stores up its message, we say he has interpreted its meaning. The components of interpreting and imitation are in part the same. In interpreting, components may be perception, short term storage while various kinds of processing occur, and an outcome which may result in immediate action of some kind, in long-term storage of the message, or both. If the outcome options are limited, the surface structure in short-term memory is erased very rapidly, and even linguistic processing may be minimal. There are several kinds of good evidence that when the task is to understand, surface structure features like exact words, passive vs. active, are rapidly forgotten though they must have been utilized for the interpretive task.

In the task of production the processing is far more difficult to analyze because the input is not known. It must overlap with interpretation in including lexical and syntactic processing, but the nature of the input is quite different so it remains to be seen how the processing can be similar. In terms of organization and motor output the processes are like imitation.

It is often pointed out (e. g. Fraser, Bellugi, and Brown 1963) that during language acquisition interpretation appears to be more advanced than production. For example, a child who frequently gives in production nouns unmarked for number may consistently correctly interpret plurality. In the case of phonology, the difference may merely lie in the articulatory demands absent in interpretation. In syntax, there are other reasons. One may be that in organizing the production of a sentence, the speaker must make many explicit choices. He cannot rely on redundancy. He cannot hope mumbling will be correctly interpreted —unless, as we all know, he is in his family or close peer group and can rely on their assumptions regarding his meanings. But the listener frequently expects such a narrow range of alternatives—or in picture tests he may be given such a narrow range—that he need process very little input to know what is going on—he can listen with half an ear. Further, as McNeill has suggested, the time available to the listener is longer since normally nobody paces his decisions, but sentence production forces linear output and the unskilled orator has no preprogrammed material to plug in while he prepares. We have evidence that listeners may still be processing an earlier sentence when exposed to later material.

The comparison of interpreting skill and production skills can of course only be made when topic and structure are carefully controlled; we can find the opposite result if they are not. For example, foreign students with control of topic can produce pre-organized sentences like skilled producers of English. But if you make rapid topical and structural switches you may find their comprehension is poor. At an extreme, some linguists learn questions and greetings in a new language so well they are taken for native speakers—but then nobody shows them the way when they can't understand directions.

These three processes, imitation, interpretation or comprehension, and sentence production are obviously intercalated in various ways. We have reason to believe, for example, that interpretation may routinely accompany imitation since it can often occur very rapidly and does not interfere. We find that children given a series of sentences of various types to imitate will often answer the questions or act out the imperatives if they can easily. If the sentence to be imitated surpasses the memory span for the period of delay before the imitation is to be produced, it is likely to be interpreted first. Then the sentence is put out through the normal sentence production device and looks very similar in many respects to spontaneous utterances. We see in two-year olds that imitations are grammatically like free speech. The Harlem teenagers who worked with Labov, for certain forms like imbedded questions, translated standard English into their normal equivalent when asked to imitate (Labov et al. 1968).

I am sure that the appropriate sentence processing models will not show one route, but many, available to account both for the speed and power of human sentence processing. It is clear that we have heuristic devices which allow us to listen with minimal attention, to process with great rapidity and minimal analysis. But at the opposite extreme we can discover the multiple ambiguities in context-free sentences thrown at us by linguists. If linguists tend to be most impressed with the power of our occasional performance (from which they want to infer competence), psychologists are more likely to want to account for the speed of our usual interaction. But we can't ignore either. The decoding of triply-imbedded sentences can be viewed as a special instance of a logical puzzle, since such sentences even when they are decoded cannot be apprehended like ordinary sentences. But within the range we can call normal sentence processing, there seem to be a family of strategies available to us as a result of task definition, set, or as alternatives when the quickest route fails. One intuitive clue is the experience of telling a speaker we didn't understand what he said; we may find we have done so by the time he opens his mouth to repeat. In this case it appears that a quick route has failed but an alternative succeeds.

Sound system processing

Children discriminate different terminal contours by the middle of the first year (Kaplan 1970) and can imitate a few months later. The first differentiations that identify speakers from different language milieux seem to be these tonal features and other global qualities of timing and stress (Nakazima 1962). This is the time, near the end of the first year, when parents report that their children seem to converse, read the paper, to talk to to their dolls. Bever (in press) has identified meaning in one of these recurrent long sequences, which may indeed be first words, but represent a level of unit analysis different from the conventional word level.

An example from a three-year old Chicano child learning English in nursery school is this (from Hernandez' material).[3]

What's his name?   [hətltæ]

What's his name?   [həsinéi]

The stress-pitch qualities of the contour are retained in both imitations. The first imitation correctly retains basic vowel qualities and locates consonants, the second adds information on sibilant and nasal, differentiating the internal consonants. The simplest structure, CVCVCV, is used. In this case the repetition gives information on the level of difficulty of the features for storage of a relatively complicated sequence, where some selection was required.

In Malmberg's report (1945, 1964)[4] of a 4-1/2 year old Finnish girl moved into a Swedish environment we find that the child produced Swedish words like 'marmalad' with the stress on the first syllable as in the Finnish cognate. In this case, since the word is stored as a Finnish cognate, we can suppose that the stored lexicon lacks stress marking since it is predictable, and that in spontaneous production she generates the stress as a feature of her organizational processing in producing sentences. We can expect that any conditions which distract, which make more difficult the task of imitation, might foster reliance on already available organizational strategies and reduce the accuracy of production of timing and prosody.

Children treat prosodic contours as additional material to be stored for imitation. If they are asked to imitate grammatically difficult utterances, some do better if they are produced in a singsong. One reason may be that easy-to-remember prosodic input may release processing capacities for other tasks. Another reason may be that the additional stress provided by such patterns supplies more stressed vowels as cues for the child.

In a detailed study of the imitations of a well-trained 2-1/2 year old girl, Slobin and Welsh (1968) report the following:

Chómsky and véritâs are crýing — Cýnthia and Tásha crý.
(1)   s í n   tâs a   krái
(2) č ms i an   tâs a   krái

In the second case, we account for the consonants in Cynthia by metathesis. The recency effect is clearly illustrated, the retention of the main stress, the conversion of nasality and the features composing the sibilants and fricatives into components allowing recombination—e.g. [m] becomes [n], [s] becomes [š]. The pressures for change relate to stored lexical material, so that this example illustrates another stage of imitation, not merely processing of the surface structure.

Bruce (1956) has presented words at very low intensities to listeners. He found that the guesses were primarily influenced by the stressed vowel. However, if the words presented were drawn from a category, the guessers soon used this additional clue. They guessed words at far below their thresholds in random sequences. But if they chose a wrong guess, they perseverated beyond the contextless threshold, so that a pre-established hypothesis could make one less attentive to sensory cues. Thus in redundancy conditions the influence of phonetic input may be reduced.

In imitations, vocalic similarity tends to be retained. In addition, nasals tend to be preserved, even if they are displaced, and voiceless friction as well. Miller and Nicely (1955) also found these were acoustically easily identified.

Some of this selectivity is vividly illustrated in a recurrent sequence of my 35-month old son, which was clearly nonsense to him:

[ˈjao ffyə ˈjáyns wǽs]   or: [wǽyɬθ]

After he had produced it on command with some minor variations, I finally recognized it as a line he had heard a few times from a story in which Milly Whipple outwits a giant, who says to her:

If once more thou cross my path
Thou shalt feel the giant's wrath!

He normally of course by this age used definite articles in standard fashion, so the loss reflects the lack of syntactic processing of the sentence. The stressed material only was retained.

In sum, it seems possible to predict that certain features are more salient in unanalyzed input, and hence are preserved in imitation and recall. They may also be better candidates for perceptual cues for interpretation:

(1) In English, peak pitch, what is stressed or not stressed, and terminal fall or non-fall; Lieberman (1965) has shown that the physical signal presents this information.
(2) Timing and length in terms of stressed syllables, for short utterances within memory span.
(3) Approximate quality of stressed vowels, especially unrounded vowels.
(4) Approximate location of marked features such as friction and nasal consonants.

As the input becomes longer and more complicated relative to the hearer's capacities, we can expect that these factors of saliency, along with locational markedness such as first word, and recency, will most often show up in imitations (Blasdell and Jensen, in press).

It is common to make a distinction between ability to perceive contrasts or recognize features, and ability to articulate that sound with the appropriate constellation of features. But we do not ordinarily take into account that in almost all the discrimination tasks there may be various amounts of storage required and that the storage may affect the retention of phonological information.

A standard way to test perception of contrasts is to use either a same-different judgment between pairs, or to present a third and ask which it matches. In such tasks, short-term storage is required to permit the comparison through time, since dichotic comparison is normally not employed. The amount of information that can be retained in these testing conditions can be very high.

In the Haskins laboratory procedures the subjects are well-trained and sophisticated. They know how to sit still, to ignore internal and external distractions, to orient to the acoustic input only. The input is very brief so the memory load is minimal, and even the location of attention within the syllables presented is likely to be highly focussed through long experience with similar stimuli. Even under these optimal conditions, judgments of stimuli which are near on acoustic continua but reflect articulatory discontinuities—e.g. ba vs. ga vs. da are no better than the categorial assignments. That is, the judgments appear to reflect coding into categories, as defined by the phonemic system of English. On the other hand, for vocalic ranges, discrimination is relatively fine, and much information on vowel quality is available in storage for comparisons (Lisker, Cooper, and Liberman 1962).

Why, then, do Spanish speakers often have trouble with classroom or examination aural discrimination of bit vs. beet? Obviously the testing conditions are quite different, and it may be that the additional distractions and anxiety may lead to more reliance on categorial storage than in the Haskins testing conditions.

In this explanation, we raise the question of the difference between what is heard and what is stored. Lengthened delays and more complicated input may demand different types of storage than brief, simple discriminations. More categorial storage reflecting experience with the most useful coding dimensions will occur the longer the delay or the more complex the material. Another distinction in process occurs when storage may be influenced by lexical recognition, in which case comparisons or reproduction may be affected by the analytic dimensions employed in lexical storage. Foreign or nonsense input is less subject to such effects, though the Slobin and Welsh example of 'Chomsky and veritas are crying' shows that in complex cases even nonsense can be assimilated to available lexicon.

It is reasonable to assume that some kind of analytic process is necessary to permit matching a relatively fully specified string in immediate memory with the features of lexical items as they are stored. It has been argued by linguists in terms of efficiency that lexical storage contains only the minimal features required to differentiate lexical items, and nothing more. The features specifiable by general phonological rules, including redundancies within segments (e.g. that nasality implies voicing) or phonotactic obligations, need not be stored in the lexicon.

The ready availability of an analytic category set must speed up learning of new lexicon. Paul Menyuk (1968) showed that with age, children were increasingly efficient in recognizing and recalling the semantic association to a referent if the name they were taught to recognize conformed to English rules for monosyllabic words. Messer (1967) showed that by 3-1/2 children say these are more like words than, e.g. [dlek].

The features employed in storage may, of course, be neutralized in production. Roger Brown has used the example of a child who says fis for fish but is indignant when an adult says fis. The child's irritation shows that he has an internal model of the word fish which allows him to recognize it when produced by others and to recognize incorrect production by others.

Edward Hernandez has recently analyzed in detail the phonological development of a bilingual Chicano of three. The child produced a great variety of substitutions for adult /r/s. On internal grounds, such as distributional differences between word-final and intervocalic location, he was able to identify three underlying forms. In certain positions, such as word-finally, the contrasts were neutralized in production. The three underlying forms turned out to correspond to English /r/ and Spanish /r/ and /rr/. For example, in intervocalic position flaps might appear for señores, but never for here is, (even though the latter is based on Spanish syntax).

In picture-naming by Japanese who learned English as adults, the second naming was usually better in the cases of the most able speakers, suggesting that they compared their own output to a stored criterion.

When information is coded for purposes of matching to lexical storage, in the case where interpretation occurs, what happens to phonetic information superfluous to interpretation? In some cases it probably is lost, but it clearly is often retained. We employ cues of social class, ethnicity and so on to classify speakers, but generally in a categorical fashion, as Labov has shown (1966). Listeners to lower class speakers from New York assume they always say da for the and fa for far, and lose probabilistic information which is in fact the basis for correct class assignment. As Geohegan has shown (1969) various prosodic and phonological features may be employed in marking rules to indicate deference, affection, distance, and anger. We assume that the decoding of this information, too, may be stereotyped. In 'imitation', it is possible that accent, dialect, and mood imitations are in fact reconstructions accomplished via these stereotypes rather than accurate reflections of input features.

If information in lexical storage has been reduced to an efficient minimum, then considerable reorganization arises not only in the process of producing lexical items in isolation, but of course out of the combination which occurs in normal continuous speech. This reorganizing we assume to be a level of processing which occurs prior to the sending of motor commands which are realized as actual motor output.

It is a puzzling fact about the acquisition of English as a second language that the same 'input'—e.g. the interdental consonants—may be quite differently realized by speakers with varying first languages. If we take only languages containing both apical stops and sibilants, we find a preference for one or the other to the point that it can be a reliable means of identifying 'accent'. A possibility proposed by Carter (n. d.) and cited in a stimulating discussion by Kathleen Connors (1968), is that there is a feature hierarchy that differs even though the same features may be present.

Many speakers can hear a difference, and when monitoring their speech carefully are able to articulate the interdental. For these reasons, we assume that it is identified distinctively in lexical storage. Therefore we assume the selectivity occurs whenever in naming, spontaneous speech, or reconstruction during imitation, material in lexical storage is turned into strings of fully specified motor commands. Presumably also included at this level are some of the alternation patterns which regulate contrasts between formal and allegro speech, including which features dominate in assimilations and simplified output. If this is the case, it should be possible to find instances of language-internal style alternations which will reveal the greater importance, for example, of continuant properties to a French speaker relative to a Russian or French-Canadian and thus account for $\theta \rightarrow s$ and $\theta \rightarrow t$. This kind of evidence may provide some insight into language processing, if such adaptations can be isolated procedurally.

If experience in a variety of phonological rule systems aids learning of new rules, then bilinguals should in general have more ability to imitate sequences which violate the phonological rules of the languages they already know. Cohen, Tucker, and Lambert (1967) tested adult bilinguals in this respect by developing monosyllabic test words which began with consonant clusters not acceptable in either French or English. The most common error in all groups was simplification by loss of the first consonant. The bilinguals made fewer errors in imitation than the monolinguals.

Brière was the first to provide systematic experimentation on the issue of the relative difficulty of different types of new phonological learning in adults. Learning a contrast between cat and cot requires learning a set of acoustic ranges to be identified as one or the other class, in a given consonantal context—i.e. learning, not a discrimination, but the limits for categorial identification, for absolute judgment. As Harlan Lane has pointed out (1966) the task is similar to learning semantic ranges. I have examined the progress of learning narrower and narrower semantic overlap, so that categories have a relatively steep slope to the 50% overlap point. Of course, even if one performs this task well, mistakes can be made in recognizing natural speech. Native speakers may deviate quite far in natural conditions, but are intelligible because of lexical and syntactic information which a new learner may lack.

Kathleen Connors, giving English-speaking children Hindi words for imitation, found that they recognized the inadequacies of their imitations. She found that the Hindi /o/ in a CVC context, which is phonetically close, was imitated on first hearing most often as English /u/, next as /o/, and least often as /U/. It seems clear that some of the time the listeners were storing the information in English categorial ranges.

When a new discrimination is developed, and the coding categories to go with it, the lexicon must be reorganized. In such instances there may be hypercorrections, or there may be layered lexicon in which recently acquired items represent a distinction reliably but older items do not. The latter must be relearned and appropriately tagged.

Is it always the case that perceptual discrimination and categorial absolute judgments precede productive accuracy? This must be the case if the only available route for monitoring the produced form is auditory. Brière has commented (1968) that by articulatory instructions he was able to teach experimental subjects to produce pharyngeal fricatives and initial, heavily aspirated, lenis unvoiced stops before they could be reliably distinguished from laryngeals and other unvoiced stops, respectively. But one would guess that unless kinesthetic feedback is very reliable, the production would not be trustworthy for these consonants. We do know, from vocal training of the deaf, that it is possible to maintain intelligible speech with only kinesthetic feedback. In addition, new lexicon could be added which was learned from reading and produced through motor commands without auditory monitoring.

Brière's data provide information on both discrimination and imitative output, comparing segmental material related in systematic ways to the English mother-tongue. He found shifting of vowel ranges for categories to be the easiest to make in imitative output. New sounds were most difficult, but even they varied. The pharyngeal fricative from Arabic was extremely difficult, as was a back unrounded vowel. On phonemic grounds it is puzzling that back unrounded vowels should be much more difficult than front rounded vowels, even once discrimination has been learned. The typical error was to round the back vowel, rather than produce a front unrounded vowel, as though producing a back vowel was most controllable, but the acoustic impression of lack of rounding was less so. In terms of the unity of a motor set, rounding is much more definable than not rounding, and perhaps more easily under voluntary control.

Brière found also that unvoiced velar fricatives were learned more rapidly than their voiced counterpart. One reason was that apparently the Arabic-speaking judges tolerated a far greater range of variability in [x] as long as the friction was sufficient. Another factor may be the additional complexity in production in adding the voicing command, since voicing is a marked feature in fricatives. Substitutions for voiced fricatives included even the English /r/, which suggests that they are interpreted or decoded as French or German /r/ and translated.

Brière's most interesting finding is that redistribution of existent allophones is of only moderate difficulty. Placing [ŋ] in initial position, employing nasalized [ɛ] before stops, using voiced [h] initially, and fortis unaspirated [t] initially, proved of about the same level of difficulty, given the task of imitating isolated words. In contrast, heavily aspirated, lenis initial [tš] was relatively difficult to learn.

Mrs. Roengpitiya, a Berkeley student (1969), found that English of a Thai student showed no new sounds at all yet in spontaneous speech, but redistributions on the model of English. In both the Brière study and Mrs. Roengpitiya's analysis, phonological rule changes are acquired more readily than sounds employing new feature combinations.

In the following cases, the English form is represented by the Thai phone, not only in syllable initial position, but occasionally in syllable-final position, where it does not occur in Thai:

English	Thai	Examples
voiced affricate [ǰ]	unvoiced [ts]	judge [tsəts]
	[s]	because [bikhɔɔt]˜
		[bikhɔɔs]
		rose [root]˜
		[roos]
[š], [ž]	aspirated affricate [tsh]	garage [garaat]˜
		[garaatsh]

The speaker appears to have discovered that there are equivalences between English and Thai initial consonants, and in English contexts he replaces the Thai initial consonants with the Thai consonants which are closest to English! These might be said to be lexical redistributions. They seem to reflect realization of lexicon through the new organizational process, and new phonological rules, with no changes yet in the resulting feature combinations available to him as segmental output. For example, the place names pronounced in Thai [paaklat] and [tsanburii] when mentioned in an English context receive initial aspiration, [phaaklat] and [tshanburii].

In sum, it appears that the most permeable processes are the learning of new discriminations, and the development in imitated articulation at least of new phonetic locations. Second in difficulty is the development of new phonological rules. The hardest aspect of acquisition of a new sound system is the articulation of new feature combinations, with considerable over-generalization occurring in the process.

It has commonly been noted that children are more adept than adults in learning new sound systems. They do not lack problems, of course —witness, for example, the difficulties of the 4-1/2 year old child studied by Bertil Malmberg in acquiring voiced stops. And there are children with articulatory difficulties in their native language at that age.

On the theory that the attentional focus and learning strategy applied to a second language is a function of the most recent learning problems in a prior language, one would expect that most adults attend primarily to learning a new lexicon. One of the children studied by Hernandez rejected parallel lexicon in English and Spanish, and insisted one word could do for both, in the case of new words at least, such as animal names. Adults, unlike children, have a large investment in lexical alternations as a means of conveying information. For children, a great deal of interaction remains affective, and therefore is carried by articulatory and prosodic variations.

Children often hear adult speech which is unintelligible by virtue of lexicon or grammar. The fact that a foreign language is lexically or grammatically unintelligible is not distinctive. What is distinctive is the sound surface. Hernandez noted that some Spanish-speaking children first 'speak English' by using English phonological features with Spanish lexicon and grammar. Similar instances have been observed in English-speaking children.

For a variety of reasons which are not well understood, children show more interest in sounds than do most adults. They play with sounds, make up nonsense games, generalize between words that sound alike more than words alike in meaning.

It was a vivid feature of the difference in Hernandez' corpus between the Chicano child's responses in speaking English and in speaking Spanish, his first language, that he imitated English far more often. In Spanish, he usually replies rather than imitates. The difference, of course, is that he understands English less well. Shipley, Smith, and Gleitman (1969) found that children around two to three exposed to short utterances with nonsense in various locations often spontaneously imitated the nonsense word. In our work on language development in monolinguals, we found imitating was very frequent around two, but diminished later.

One way to describe the function of spontaneous imitation for the learner is that it enables him to hold the strange object a moment longer before him, to look at it from all angles, before it fades from view. Whether from curiosity or delight, children in such cases seem to treat words as they do objects. It is not clear what the effects of this spontaneous behavior may be on learning. Perhaps the new distributional patterns become better recognized in this way. Perhaps the meaning of new lexicon may be learned, for imitation enables the child to tie the arbitrary new sound sequence to a discerned meaning for a moment longer, much as repetition of a new name helps us store it while we stare at its owner.

Experienced language teachers report that in large groups in organized language programs discrimination generally proves not to be a problem, but rather output is the issue, and in output large individual differences persist. The difference between adults and children, and between different adults, might lie in part in the skill in utilizing kinesthetic feedback, and relating it to what is heard, or recalled.

Here is a Chicano child, practicing alone:

hayuse. ʔayo. xáy xáy xáyú xáyǿ háwaryÛ
əháwaryú xay xou
háwryú
xawyu . . .
Another child hears him and says:
hàwiryú
hâwyú hâwəyú
And so on.

Lexical processing

Information about vocabulary has to be approachable either from phonological input or semantic input, to allow for both interpretation and sentence production. An example of how word-searches in production may work is given in Brown and McNeill's ingenious experiment with the 'tip of the tongue' phenomenon (1966). When you try to remember someone's name, you may have the following experience: You may, in the United States, recognize the national origin of the name. Such general categorial groups are efficient for American names; Orientals otherwise fluent in English sometimes have trouble remembering American names because they lack a full array of European name-sorting clues. In addition to such semantic groupings, you may remember how many syllables the name had, the location of stress, and the first sound or letter. Brown and McNeill, giving meanings of rare words, evoked partial recall. These same features appeared during recall stages, and in addition final letters; a serial position effect was revealed as is common in arbitrary sequences, and in addition 'chunking' of units like suffixes.

In accounting for their results, the authors propose (1966: 355) an analogy to a card storage device. 'Suppose that there are entries for sextant on several different cards. They might all be incomplete, but at different points, or some might be incomplete and one or more of them complete. The several cards would be punched for different semantic markers and perhaps for different associations so that the entry recovered would vary with the rule of retrieval.... The more accessible features are entered on more cards or else the cards on which they appear are punched for more markers; in effect, they are wired into a more extended associative net.'

The problem, of course, is that if we assume that at one computer 'address' there is a matrix of phonological features, enough to separate one lexical item from others, a set of syntactic markers, and semantic features, we have no way of accounting for partial recall. It is clear that on the separate, rare occasions of exposure to low frequency words only a partial array of semantic features and of phonological features may be stored, and there is, of course, no reason to assume that they will be identical on all occasions. The features selected by the device include some we have reason to believe, from imitative behavior, are most salient to perception. One major difference is that Bruce's recognition data make vowel quality dominant; Brown and McNeill speak of 'first letters'. The difference implies that for perception, vowels may be clearer, but that once identification and interpretation has occurred, long-term lexical storage may employ more consonantal information. From the standpoint of informational efficiency, consonants would be better. If words are rare, and stored primarily via consonants, they should not be accessible to Bruce's subjects until a signal level is reached that makes consonantal information audible.

During sentence production anticipations can indicate lexical selection ahead of time, whereas hesitations occur not only at points of syntactic encoding but at points of maximum lexical uncertainty. In Goldman-Eisler's clever experiment (1964) it was found that when words were clipped from an otherwise intact tape (as they might be on a bad phone connection) the least predictable items elicited the longest hesitation pauses both for the original speakers and those who correctly guessed them.

Interestingly, those morphemes which were most predictable were also least audible, which of course proves English is the most efficient of all languages since its stress and timing rules permit producer economy just when there would be least loss!

In addition to phonological and semantic features of variable detail, lexical storage must contain information regarding selectional restrictions. The storage of he contains a restriction to subject position in the surface structure. One might simply assume that the selection of pronouns for gender and number occurs directly from semantic information. But what happens when someone speaks of washing the spinach and uses a pronoun? In French, one would say lavez-les, in English, Be sure to wash it well. But we would not say wash them, like a Frenchman. This difference suggests that even exophoric pronouns, those referring to external referents not previously specified in discourse, may yet require passage through the noun-storage device. Is it possible to use the the correct pronoun gender, say in German, but forget the noun? Brown and McNeill's experiment implies that it might be.

In addition to single lexical items there must be similar devices for higher order units of many kinds, like United States of America, how are you, and idiosyncratically frequent sequences.

Processing theories vary in whether they locate lexical processing before or after grammatical analysis in interpretation. Thorne et al (n. d.) describing a device for interpretation of the phrase markers of input sentences, utilize no dictionary at all except a list of finite items like function words and affixes. It is clear that syntactic information could make far more efficient the recognition device for lexicon by narrowing the search. But the process is not assumed by anyone to involve one stage for a whole utterance (except very short ones), and then another stage, but rather it is ordinarily assumed that processing of earlier material cooccurs with input later, and may in fact influence the thresholds for features of that input.

Evidence from child language favors the priority of lexical processing, since children for some years make little use of cues other than order and syntactic features of lexicon in grammatical processing. In handling jabberwocky, for example, they are more influenced by order than by affixes and grammatical morphemes (Porter 1955).

Some years ago, Einar Haugen (1955: 7) developed the very fruitful concept of the diamorph. 'If two morphemes have phonemic shape or semantic function in common, they will often be identified by bilingual speakers.' The identification is manifested in semantic and syntactic shifting, in which the two items are treated as equivalent in meaning, syntactic features, selectional restrictions, and so on. For example, in Je cherche pour le livre the French child carries over the distribution of the English look into French, and in il est un garçon the syntactic features of he and il, which largely overlap, are assumed to be equivalent.

We would in fact assume that a plausible first step in second language learning is to map matched synonyms onto the elaborate structure of semantic and syntactic features already available. This is the classic case of compound bilingualism, with common semantic features and categories employed in both languages. Differentiation of features occurs as the items are experienced in different verbal and nonverbal contexts, just as differentiation within the lexicon of a single language occurs, though some items in early vocabulary, like big and strong, are treated as synonyms by young children. Indeed, such differentiation may be so fine that in bilingual communities supposed translation equivalents may coexist in both codes because the nuances of connotation have added dimensions of discrimination not available to monolinguals. Japanese women in the United States often use the word husband among themselves since it lacks the 'lord and master' feature of the Japanese translation.

Some diamorphs reveal features of the syntactic development of second language learners. For example, when a Frenchman says, That's a book who is on the table, we wonder if generally who = qui. A similar case is He held his hat in her hand, in which (if we ignore the anomaly of her for inalienable possession), we find son = his, and sa = her, although of course the basis for gender of possessives is entirely different in the two languages, concerning the possessor in English, the possessed in French.

A 6-year old French child in an English milieu, described by Paul Kinzel (1964) and grammatically analyzed by Kathleen Connors, gives excellent evidence of diamorphs for pronouns, in sentences like these:

'She is all mixed up.' (pendule)
'I got her.' (serviette)
'I'm going to jump her.' (crepe)
'Who likes them?' (épinards)

Here again we see that pronoun selection requires processing via a gender- and number-marked unit of some sort rather than directly from semantic information.

What is the relation between the stored French lexicon and stored English lexicon for such a child? If the storage of phonological features and of lexicon involves merely an additional tag designating language, register, or affective connotations, then one would assume that the tagging process goes to the morphophonemic matrix only for the lexicon at first, and leaves semantic and many syntactic features unmarked, undifferentiated, appropriate to both codes of a bilingual. Through additional learning, perhaps dependent on differentiated contexts, whether verbal or nonverbal, these semantic feature constellations also could acquire such code and register tags. I would not want to assume that entirely separate environments, e.g. Montreal vs. France, are necessarily required for such differentiation. It is well known that even within the life of linguistic enclaves in the United States there may be quite distinctive usage complexes for items if they have a 'home and kitchen' implication in one language, and a 'work' implication in the other. Indeed, my work with Japanese bilinguals on this issue suggests that the differentiation of meaning constellations is extremely complex and may not work the same way for different domains of lexicon (Ervin-Tripp 1967).

There has, however, been some confirmation of the effect of acquisition milieu in developing more differentiated semantic systems and associative networks (Lambert, Havelka, and Crosby 1958; Gekoski 1968).

One of the advantages of using feature marking rather than separate locations in the brain as a way of handling code differentiation is that in bilingual communities shifting between languages is frequently a reflection of nuances of social meaning (Gumperz and Hernandez 1969). For this reason, one would not want to make the apparatus for shifting more elaborate than that required for style shifting of monolinguals.

The structure of meaning and hence of lexical mapping appears from the little evidence we have to change a good deal with age. The earliest lexical items at the beginning of language development are global semantically, and change significance with context. For example, the word coat may mean coat, hat, dress, going for a walk, baby carriage, let's go! Gradually both semantic and syntactic specificity increase, the latter depending on the differentiation of syntax and the elaboration of selectional rules. The similarity in these features in the early lexicon of both languages of bilingual children is evident in their ability to switch in midsentence, as in esta Chicqui coming? ves este in here? and Un de tes blooms sont dead.

The semantic complexity of adult lexicon is far greater in terms of elaboration of features, knowledge of distributional probabilities, and analytic abstractness of features, as in the development of taxonomic hierarchies. All of this development takes place within a context of enriched conceptual discrimination, which may affect far more than direct verbal functioning. For these reasons, we can assume that acquisition of new lexicon by adults could occur extremely rapidly. It does not have to wait upon conceptual maturation. To the extent that semantic universals exist, a large part of the work in the acquisition of structure has already occurred. In addition, as we have suggested earlier, adults continue throughout life to add lexical items both in terms of entirely new semantic features and constellations of features, and in terms of stylistic and affective nuances of selection. As Geohegan found in his extraordinary study of address rules in Samal, changes continued to enrich the address alternatives and complexity of rules of selection throughout adult life. This is one domain of language in which children appear to have no particular advantage in acquisition. To the extent that languages acquired in childhood appear to have some semantic differences (e.g. one can be angrier or sadder in

one's mother tongue), they may simply reflect the fact that the affective life of the child is different; lexicon acquired in childhood may retain connotations from that time. My work with adult bilinguals has
revealed that adults can acquire emotional connotations in the adult
language depending on their 'resocialization'. Child rearing in a second language can have a profound impact, for example, on semantic
differentiation and connotative elaboration in that language.

Syntactic processing

The order of relationship in ability between comprehension, imitation, and production of syntax is not the same at all ages. Normally,
it is true, comprehension is superior to production for features under-
going change. The reasons have been discussed earlier. However,
the relative ease of imitation depends on age, memory span, and the
features to be imitated. For example, children below two have very
brief productive capacities. The mean utterance length of their free
speech shows surprising reliability over samples and grows at a constant rate. After the beginnings of ellipsis, of course, this measure
becomes an increasingly poor index of both complexity and level of development because deletions and compressions requiring sophistication
may result in a shorter sentence. At the age when produced sentences
are short, so are imitations. In other respects as well, such as the
number of basic sentence elements present, imitations are like spontaneous speech. Presumably at this stage the immediate rote memory
span is quite short, and the processing abilities of the child are so
small as not to allow him to generate an imitated sentence longer than
his immediate rote span when he imitates.

On the other hand, research on comprehension at this stage suggests
that children may attend to connective items they do not produce, such
as articles, since their absence or replacement with nonsense disrupts
comprehension (Shipley, Smith, Gleitman 1969).

At a certain point, abilities become sufficiently advanced to permit
interpretation, storage, and reproduction to allow imitations to well
exceed rote memory span. For example, Labov noted that teenage boys
who could not imitate I asked him whether he could play baseball, were
able to interpret and translate I asked him if he could play baseball into
I axed him could he play baseball. They clearly interpreted the sentence
as containing an imbedded question and produced their version of such a
structure, but believed they had imitated verbatim.

As coding ability for storage increases, learners at first reproduce
deviant material according to their own grammar; later, they may be
able to store the information about deviance as well, and reproduce it,
as though they coded the basic syntax plus footnotes. Some building up
of the level of syntactic difficulty in imitated material can be obtained

by repeating, or gradually enlarging the complexity of a given utterance (by expansions). As an instructional device for altering grammatical skill this method (which is rather like many drill methods) is no more effective than giving replies, and thus increasing the learner's exposure to relevant heard sentences (Cazden 1965).

Models for syntactic processing have been forced to differentiate 'surface structure' processing from deeper levels. It has been repeatedly found that such surface features as subject vs. predicate location of information (e. g. passive vs. active), and prenominal vs. postnominal location of adjectives can make a difference in processing speed, latency in comprehension, and so forth. On the other hand information that requires more complex processing, like agent vs. direct object of action in passive vs. active sentences, or main vs. subordinate clause will alter the same processing measures. Smith has pointed out that the 'compression' of information into constituents, which sometimes arises, according to linguists, from reordering and deletion transformation, and sometimes does not, as in complex auxiliaries, can alter ease of imitation. It is obvious that the first level that the listener encounters is surface order and cues as to underlying structure, such as connectives. Sentences can sometimes be interpreted from this information alone with only lexical processing. For instance, truncated passives require minimal analysis because there is only one semantic relation possible.

There is some evidence of the existence of simple order processing heuristics in both children and adults. Troike (1969) has cited the following:

Coleman had matched groups of speakers
read, once, passages containing many passives...

The sentence would not mislead a reader were it not for the possibility of interpreting read as +past, but the initial readiness to fall into this trap arises from the structural preference for an agent-transitive verb-object sequence.

In center-imbedded sentences this strategy may also impede solutions.

The chef cooks oil signed the list.

Compare this sentence to the following:

The cat the dog chased ate the meat.

Welsh has suggested that following a lexical processing that yields syntactic and semantic features, a kind of storage loop keeps recycling the syntactic markers to subject them to 'templates' of 'encounter-operate rules'. For example, if a noun is encountered, look for a verb. If the verb is transitive, look for a noun. Interpret as agent-verb-object. His data from imitations of a 2-1/2 year old to some extent support this hypothesis.

In answering questions, children seem to employ the NVN and related strategies. For example, if they hear a question word followed by N+TV, they normally reply with a direct object of the verb, if the question word is not in their lexical repertoire, for instance <u>how</u> or <u>when</u>. If they hear a question word followed by an inanimate noun and an intransitive verb, they are more likely to give a missing locative phrase. That is, the children act as though they are completing a standard sentence frame (Ervin-Tripp 1970).

Young children often misinterpret passives which contain the agent. They will understand <u>The cat is chased by the moth</u> to refer to a picture in which a cat chases a moth. Since passives nearly always have the agent truncated, this unusual sentence sequence elicits the usual interpretation that the NVN sequence must mean standard transitive order.

In adult comprehension, Sachs (1967) has found that the formal contrast passive vs. active is forgotten almost as fast as the particular lexical item of paired synonyms chosen. Lorraine Novinski (1968) noted that children recognized passives, even in comprehension instructions, when they otherwise forgot surface details in immediate recognition tests. In this case it may be that the striking contrast of surface order was very vivid; it may be even more important to children than to adults, by whom meaning is rapidly interpreted.

The presence of clues to guide the conversion of surface structure into deep structure may alter the ease of processing. For example, Shipley and Catlin (1967) compared processing time for children imitating sentences with relative clauses. They tested processing time by adding a short list of arbitrary items to be remembered after the sentence. Reduction in recall of the first item on this list suggested sentence analysis still was going on when this word was heard. Such reductions happened more often when a relative pronoun was deleted (e.g. <u>I saw the cat the mouse liked</u>). One child who supplied the pronoun in his imitations did not have the reduction in list recall either.

The learning of syntax in children clearly begins with their development of analysis strategies in listening, when they are expected to make appropriate reactions to heard material. The evidence we have about their early syntax in a variety of languages suggests that it begins with a set of primitive and universal basic semantic relations: negation, conjunction, agent-action, action-object, attribution, location, identification, possession. Normally, these basic relations are represented by order relations in speech, but of course in inflecting languages children may develop morphological realizations of these relations much earlier than in languages like English, where affixes represent less basic features. Order relations seem to be very apparent to children. Where they are very consistent in adult speech—e.g. location of question words in English—they are the same in child speech. Numerous children have used consistent order in output, when input was less orderly. In the grammars of children I have worked with, it is more likely that action-object order can be permuted than that agent-verb order is changed. Order is almost always accurately reproduced in imitations.

The point in the development of English where semantic relations are no longer represented by simple orders in the surface structure is most strikingly the time, around 2-3, when the auxiliary and do system develops. This is also a system of great interest in second language learning since it is peculiar to English.

Klima and Bellugi (1966) have described the development of the negative and interrogative, and their results correspond closely to what we have found in Berkeley in these structures and in ellipsis. The negative goes through three stages: a negator external to the sentence nucleus, an internal negator placed before the predicate, and differentiated into no or not before nouns and adjectives, and these plus some monomorphemic negative verbs like don't or won't before main verbs—finally, the adult pattern. In the interrogative two stages are essentially characterized by use of intonation, and the prefixing of question words to otherwise complete sentences. In the third stage, do is differentiated and inflected for tense. It alternates with modals before main verbs in negatives, and the auxiliary is permuted with the subject in yes-no questions and occasionally in wh-questions. It appears alone with pronouns in ellipsis.

Children who speak other languages seem to have difficulty differentiating the English system from their own, but in some respects they follow the same order of development. Hernandez noted that one of the Chicano children produced no can and no could on the model of Spanish. This order would only occur in English monolinguals at the very early stage when subjects ordinarily are not present.

An excellent analysis by Ravem (1968) of the auxiliary system of his 6-year old Norwegian-speaking son, who acquired English in Scotland, points to compromises between Norwegian and English. In Norwegian and English interrogative and negative sentences, modals are alike. For this reason, an underlying structure might be available to the child for developing the English rule easily, simply generalizing modals to all auxiliaries. But in the early stages, do was omitted, perhaps because it is meaningless.

In English-speaking children before do or copulas are systematically present, negatives are marked by a variety of negators between subject and main verb or predicate. Ravem's son often produced similar sentences: I not looking for edge, I not like that, I not sitting on my chair. In acquiring negatives, the boy followed a developmental sequence similar to English-speaking children, with the negator before the main verb regularly, as in the Norwegian sentence with a modal.

However, in the case of interrogatives, before do appeared, inversion of the main verb and subject occurred as in Norwegian: Drive you car to-yesterday? Like you ice-cream? Like you me not, Reidun? These inversions are not usually found in American children. But like American children, he inverts less often in wh-questions: What you reading to-yesterday? What you did in Rothbury? When the do-form appeared, Say it you not to Daddy? was replaced by Did you not say it to Daddy? The formality of this version probably represents the parental English the child heard.

Thus when do appeared, the child acquired normal English, but prior to that time he employed a negative pattern unlike Norwegian (except for modal sentences) and like younger English-speaking monolinguals. In the case of the interrogative, on the other hand, the Norwegian inversion pattern dominated, whereas at the comparable stage American children rely solely on intonation without inversion. A good account of the reason for this difference would rest on developmental studies of Norwegian negation and questions. One might guess that in the case of interrogation an inversion locating subject second is a very reliable question cue in listening, particularly important in yes-no questions to indicate meaning from the start of the utterance whether a modal is present or not. Thus the inversion may be a strong and stable pattern by six. In the case of the negative, location is not important to meaning, and a separate rule is used for modals and nonmodalized verbs—one could see English as simpler in this sense. For this reason the child may move more readily to the English order. In other respects we see the same features that we find developmentally in monolinguals.

A rich source of information on the contrast between child bilingualism in a truly bilingual context, and adult second-language learning, appears in the research reported by Lance and his colleagues in Texas (1969). In their studies, the adults showed the usual array of problems arising from processing of English through existent Spanish syntactic rules. However, the authors make the important observation that from one-third to two-thirds of the deviant features of the foreign students' speech could not be traced to identifiable features of Spanish. I found also in doing detailed statistical counts of errors coded according to their relation to French in adult bilinguals that a large percentage had no clear basis of this sort. What are these errors, then? Some are of course production slips of one sort or another. Monolinguals make mistakes, too. These are nonrandom and revealing of production processes. Others are what I would call learner's simplifications. They are developmental features which often are shared with other learners—for instance, lack of tense inflection. Uninverted wh-questions in the Ravem study seem to represent this kind of developmental pattern.

Lance points out that amost all of the highly frequent deviations from standard English in the migrant bilingual children in their study were not based on Spanish. Many reflected the local English of their peers. Others seem to be developmentally based since they are common in English monolinguals, possibly at an earlier age. In Hernandez' data, too, Spanish-based structures were rare: <u>no can,</u> <u>here is</u>. The high incidence of switching in the everyday discourse of the bilinguals in the Lance study corresponds to observations elsewhere (see Gumperz' paper in this volume). Even where the social inhibitions about switching are low, language alternations are never random. We have very little evidence on how they are learned as sociolinguistic regularities.

Socially, there appear to be bases in the structure of discourse— switches to the language of quotations, boundary markers for greetings, and for arrivals and departures of participants. Referential content may generate switching; some lexical realizations may be common to both codes. Social allusions may generate switching. Where the latter is a conscious rhetorical device its linguistic location may be different, being at points where hesitation pauses for lexical input are most frequent—e.g. before nouns rather than noun phrases.

Where social constraints are few, switching may occur at major constituent boundaries in the case of social allusion and lexicon may shift with syntax with some vertical cooccurrence of codes. In some texts, the switches appear largely at underlying sentence boundaries; in others, smaller units may be switched.

In experimental situations where language is controlled by instruction, on the other hand, we often find that the conscious control exerted affects the output language, the morphophonemic realizations of lexicon, and 'switching' when it occurs is at the level of semantic categories, syntax, or surface order, with a resulting inconsistency in vertical code features. This has been the case in my research with Japanese and French-English bilinguals.

In communities with a long history of bilingualism, it sometimes happens that for social reasons the output language is constrained by situation. In these cases, the codes tend to merge except at the level of the phonemic entries in the 'dictionary'. Gumperz found such surface-only switching by situation in Marathi-Kannada bilingualism in India (1967) and Brugner in Slovenian-German bilingualism in Austria.

These seem to be historically different phases of the same psychological process of merger as my experimental studies showed.

The linguistic units shifted under both constrained and free conditions constitute excellent evidence of the units in language processing.
For example, in an unconstrained situation, we find nearby in the
same narrative in Yiddish and English: un er zol buy-n di haus ...
zogt er, 'vos darf ix keifn' ... so di shul bought di haus ... (text
collected and transcribed by David Argoff). Note that the quotations
are more consistently Yiddish, but when the borrowed lexical item
buy appears in a Yiddish context it is syntactically integrated with the
suffix.

The stages of development in such a systematic separation of affixes has been described by Malmberg for a child learning Swedish
after Finnish. At Stage 1, Finnish postpositions were attached to
Swedish nouns to designate location. Next, the Swedish case suffix
was used, followed by the postposition in Finnish. Next, the postposition was replaced by the Swedish preposition but followed the noun
as before. Thus the general syntactic frame remained the same until
the fourth stage, but Swedish 'diamorphs' gradually replaced their Finnish counterparts until a syntactic restructuring occurred. We do not
know what if any switching continued to occur.

Stage 0. $N_F + Gen_F + Po_F$

Stage 1. $N_S + Gen_F + Po_F$

Stage 2. $N_S + Suf_S + Po_F$

Stage 3. $N_S + Suf_S + Pr_S$

Stage 4. $Pr_S + N_S + Suf_S$

The child who lives in a bilingual environment hears a good deal
of switching. Then we may need to find out how he comes to tag the
features of his two codes and separate them in formal style. We
clearly need more process descriptions to see how these changes come
about. Malmberg's has the advantage of showing stages, but we know
very little about the conditions under which the utterances are produced,
and whether the patterns vary so that children develop situationally-
controlled switching rules.

Finally, I would like to return to the issue of how the learning takes
place. In the case of concurrent learning, as may happen with bilingual
children, there is evidence that code separation of lexical material can,
in experimental conditions, be better than in successive learning (Lambert and Witelson 1961). In the case of concurrent learning of two lan-

guages by children, we simply can assume we are dealing with primary language acquisition. In the case of successive or overlapping learning, we assume that some prior processes and structures will be employed during learning. There are dramatic differences in the learning conditions of natural second language learning and classroom second language learning that must have consequences for the kinds of changes that take place during learning. The evidence from natural learning suggests that manifest speech is largely secondary. That is, as long as the learner orients to speech, interprets it, and learns the form or arrangement that represents the meaning, he learns language as fast as someone speaking. Children have normal language development who cannot or do not speak. The only case where motor practice might have any merits is in articulation of new sounds or in writing letters in a new alphabet.

Secondly, it would appear to be impossible to learn to recognize what contrasts of sound or structure are important, or to learn to interpret either lexicon or structure, unless one knows what is meant. Children do not learn languages spoken as secret languages between adults. They do not learn languages from television, if their parents are deaf and use signs. They normally learn language if they hear simple, repetitive speech, which is what characterizes 'baby talk' style or speech to infants, and after the first few months this speech normally refers to meanings that are obvious from context. The first syntactic structures children interpret and produce are thos focused on basic semantic relations. There are picked out very early from the complex input.

Is the same true of language-learning adults in natural situations? I have observed that Japanese speakers, who have immense syntactic problems in learning English, for which almost every conceivable order is different from Japanese, do successfully signal basic semantic relations. There are cases when they will slip, and put the verb last.

Everybody together and 'omochi' and 'otoso' and other many
—big dinners, have, enjoy.
Every day I think come—all over the street and some funny
comics make—I don't know.

But these order problems are surprisingly few. Far more persistent are subject, preposition, and object deletions which do not disrupt intelligibility because the contexts make them clear. The assumption is that in learning to interpret English sentences the basic processing heuristics which permit identification of subject, verb, and object, and modifier—head units must be developed very early to permit even primitive communication to take place. In these respects the adult seems like the child learning his first language.

But we know that in formal instruction there is frequently emphasis on structure devoid of semantic context, practiced in instances where meaning is either unclear or trivial—e. g. in transformation drills. So it cannot surprise us when after an hour of practicing turning statements into questions a student intent on getting a question answered, after class, produces a question that is a word-for-word translation of his mother tongue and shows no impact whatever of the drill. <u>What means this word, Mrs. Tripp?</u>

Valerian Postovsky, of the Russian department at the Defense Language Institute at Monterey, recently compared two instructional methods which differed in the point at which speaking was introduced. In both, highly discriminative listening was required. For a month the experimental subjects performed various written drills from spoken input, but they did not speak except in the first few days when they were taught the Cyrillic alphabet. They heard speech only from native speakers. The audio-lingual group had oral drills along with their usual memorizing of dialogue and written work. They heard their own speech, and that of fellow-students. Both groups had six hours a day of class and laboratory drills in addition to homework. After a month, the experimental group was very superior in morphology, and somewhat superior in vocabulary even when tested by story telling aloud. Most surprising of all to the believers in oral drill is the finding that the experimental group had better Russian pronunciation. Most of the items were redistribution of sounds in their repertoire like dark and light [l], [l^y] and so on. This experiment suggests that a thoughtful incorporation of features we have found in natural language-learning may improve our pedagogical success. But to do this adaptation rationally, we need a much more analytic approach to the stages of development in language processing during learning. We need to be able to sort out for the adult learner the entirely different kind of processing skills he may need, and not blindly assume that there is one method for all ends, or even that the superficial features of skill practiced will inevitably match the knowledge acquired.

NOTES

[1] I am grateful for discussions on the materials in this paper to John Gumperz, Edward Hernandez, John Macnamara, and Martin Braine. Braine's superb paper (in press) on language acquisition aided me in seeing the relation between first and second language learning and how we might connect processing models with learning.

[2] An example of the devastating effects of an automatic operant view of language acquisition is provided in a Russian teaching program supervised by Morton, described by Valerian Postovsky (1970). The taped self-instructional material consisted of writing discriminatory

responses to phonemes, words, sentences, and then imitating them, then imitating sentences. Hints of meaning were finally given in the latter stage of the third of four stages in the materials. Students worked six hours a day for seventeen weeks. At the end of the period their Army Language Proficiency Test score in Russian was below the score achievable by random marking. They were subsequently enrolled in the regular Russian program at Monterey, but never caught up with the beginners in that course! Whether because Russian became hateful and meaningless to them, or because they created idiosyncratic meanings for the sounds they heard, this program actually interfered with their acquisition of a meaningful language. The idle brain does the devil's work.

[3]The distinction adult-child may be too sharp here. We have some evidence, mentioned later, that children as young as 4-1/2 may show transfer of earlier grammatical patterns into new languages, and in turn over-generalization back to the first language. We have too few close analyses of changing grammatical systems of children as they learn second languages to speak confidently of age changes.

[4]I am grateful to Loni Takeuchi for translating and summarizing.

REFERENCES

Bever, Thomas. 1970. The cognitive basis for linguistic structure. In R. Hays, ed., Cognition and language learning. New York, Wiley.

Blasdell, Richard, and Paul Jensen. n. d. Stress and word-position as determinants of imitation in first-language learners. Manuscript of the Communication Sciences Laboratory. Gainesville, Florida.

Braine, M. D. S. In press. On two types of models for the internalization of grammars. In D. Slobin, ed., The ontogenesis of grammar: facts and theories. New York, Academic Press.

Brière, Eugene. A psycholinguistic study of phonological interference. The Hague, Mouton.

Brown, Roger, and David McNeill. 1966. The 'tip of the tongue' phenomenon. Journal of verbal learning and verbal behavior. Vol. 5: 325-337.

Bruce, D. J. 1956. Effects of context upon the intelligibility of heard speech. In C. Cherry, ed., Information theory: third London symposium. London, Butterworth.

Cazden, Courtney. 1965. Environmental assistance to the child's acquisition of grammar. Unpublished doctoral dissertation. Harvard University.

Chomsky, Noam, and Morris Halle. 1968. The sound pattern of English. New York, Harper and Row.

Cohen, Stephen P., G. Richard Tucker, and Wallace E. Lambert. 1967. The comparative skills of monolinguals and bilinguals in perceiving phoneme sequences. Language and speech. Vol. 10: 159–168.

Connors, Kathleen. Phonological studies of borrowing. I. Aspects of a study of sound changes in borrowed words. II. Spontaneous 'borrowing' of Hindi words into English. III. Problems with feature substitution and minor strategies. Unpublished ms. University of California Phonology Laboratory. Berkeley, California.

Ervin-Tripp, Susan. 1967. An Issei learns English. Journal of social issues. Vol. 23, No. 2: 78–90.

_____. 1970. Discourse agreement: how children answer questions. In R. Hays, ed., Cognition and language learning. New York, Wiley.

Fraser, Colin, Ursula Bellugi, and Roger Brown. 1963. Control of grammar in imitation, comprehension and production. Journal of verbal learning and verbal behavior. Vol. 2: 121–135.

Gekoski, William Lee. 1968. Associative and translation habits of bilinguals as a function of language acquisition contexts. Report 54. Center for Human Growth and Development. Ann Arbor, Michigan, University of Michigan.

Geohegan, William. 1969. The use of marking rules in semantic systems. Working paper no. 26. Language-Behavior Research Laboratory. Berkeley, California, University of California. Mimeo.

Goldman-Eislar, Frieda. 1964. Hesitation, information, and levels of speech production. In A. V. S. de Reuck and M. O'Connor, eds., Ciba Foundation symposium: Disorders of language. Boston, Little Brown: 96–111.

Gumperz, John. 1967. On the linguistic markers of bilingual communication. Journal of social issues. Vol. 23, No. 2: 48–57.

_____ and Edward Hernandez. 1969. Cognitive aspects of bilingual communication. Language-Behavior Research Laboratory. Working paper no. 28. Berkeley, California, University of California. Mimeo.

Haugen, Einar. 1955. Problems of bilingual description. General linguistics. Vol. 1, No. 1: 1–9.

Kaplan, Eleanor, and George Kaplan. 1970. Is there any such thing as a prelinguistic child? In John Eliot, ed., Human development and cognitive processes. New York, Holt, Rinehart.

Klima, E. S., and Ursula Bellugi. 1966. Syntactic regularities in the speech of children. In J. Lyons and R. J. Wales, eds., Psycholinguistics papers. Edinburgh, Edinburgh University Press: 183–208.

Labov, William. 1967. The social stratification of English in New York City. Washington, D. C., Center for Applied Linguistics.

_____, Paul Cohen, Clarence Robins, and John Lewis. 1968. A study of the nonstandard English of Negro and Puerto Rican speakers in New York City. Final report. Cooperative Research Project No. 3288. Office of Education, Washington, D. C.

Lambert, Wallace E., J. Havelka, and C. Crosby. 1958. The influence of language acquisition contexts on bilingualism. Journal of abnormal and social psychology. Vol. 56: 239-244.

Lambert, Wallace E., and Sandra Witelson. 1961. Concurrent and consecutive orders of learning two 'languages'. Montreal, McGill University. Mimeo.

Lance, Donald. 1969. A brief study of Spanish-English bilingualism. Final report. Research Project Orr-Liberal Arts-15504. College Station, Texas, Texas A and M.

Lane, Harlan. 1966. Identification, discrimination, translation. The effects of mapping ranges of physical continua onto phoneme and sememe categories. IRAL, Vol. 4: 216-226.

Lieberman, Philip. 1965. On the acoustic basis of the perception of intonation by linguists. Word. Vol. 21: 40-53.

Liberman, Alvin M., Katherine S. Harris, Jo Ann Kinney, and Harlan Lane. 1961. The discrimination of relative onset-time of the components of certain speech and nonspeech patterns. Journal of experimental psychology. Vol. 61: 379-388.

Malmberg, Bertil. 1945. Et barn bytar sprak. Nordisk Tidsskrift. Vol. 21.

_____. 1964. Spra ket och människan. Lund, Aldus. 98-112.

Miller, George, and Patricia Nicely. 1955. An analysis of perceptual confusions among some English consonants. Journal of the acoustical society of America. Vol. 27: 338-352.

Menyuk, Paula. 1968. Children's learning and reproduction of grammatical and nongrammatical phonological sequences. Child Development. Vol. 38: 849-859.

Messer, Stanley. 1967. Implicit phonology in children. Journal of verbal learning and verbal behavior. Vol. 6: 609-613.

Nakazima, Sei. 1962. A comparative study of the speech developments of Japanese and American English in childhood. Studia phonologica. Vol. 2, 27-46.

Novinski, Lorraine. 1968. Recognition memory in children for semantic versus syntactic information. Dissertation. University of California, Berkeley.

Porter, Douglas. 1955. Preliminary analysis of the grammatical concept 'verb'. Cambridge, Harvard School of Education. Unpublished.

Postovsky, Valerian. 1970. Effects of delay in oral practice at the beginning of second language learning. Dissertation, University of California, Berkeley.

Ravem, Roar. 1968. Language acquisition in a second language environment. IRAL, Vol. 6: 175–185.

Roengpitiya, Karita. 1969. A contrastive analysis of Thai students' difficulties with English. Unpublished. Berkeley, University of California seminar paper (Rhetoric 155).

Sachs, Jacqueline Struck. 1967. Recognition memory for syntactic and semantic aspects of connected discourse. Perception and psychophysics. Vol. 2: 437–442.

Shipley, Elizabeth, Carlota Smith, and Lila Gleitman. 1969. A study in the acquisition of language: free responses to commands. Language. Vol. 45: 322–342.

Shipley, Elizabeth, and Jane Carol Catlin. 1967. Short-term memory for sentences in children: an exploratory study of temporal aspects of imposing structure. Technical report V, Grant No. MH 07990. Philadelphia, Eastern Psychiatric Institute.

Smith, Carlota. 1969. Children's control of some complex noun phrases: a repetition study. L. S. A. meeting, San Francisco, California.

Slobin, Dan, and Charles Welsh. 1969. Elicited imitation as a research tool in developmental psycholinguistics. Language Behavior Research Laboratory. Working paper no. 10. University of California, Berkeley.

Thorne, James Peter, Hamish Dewar, Harry Whitfield, and Paul Bratley. n. d. A model for the perception of syntactic structure. Edinburgh, English Language Research Unit. Mimeo.

Troike, Rudolph C. 1969. Receptive competence, productive competence, and performance. Round Table Monograph No. 20. Washington, D. C., Georgetown University Press.

Walker, Edward. 1969. Grammatical relations and sentence memory. L. S. A. meeting, San Francisco, California.

DISCUSSION

William A. Stewart, Education Study Center: Just a brief comment on the last experiment you mentioned. The way you put it makes it sound very dramatic. However, it seems obvious to me that delaying production in the foreign language should produce the kind of results you mentioned. Or, to put it the other way around, requiring the language learner to produce utterances in the language before he has come to perceive all the important contrasts, etc., is to encourage him to produce grossly nonnative utterances, and to reinforce these through practice. Anyone who has taught a foreign language, or observed one being learned, certainly knows that students often carry cases of early interference clear through their learning process, and retain these even after the mechanisms to avoid them have been learned.

For example, a foreigner just starting to learn English might learn why as /vay/, while later learning to produce English /w/, so that subsequently acquired words like weapon would have /w/ and not /v/. Yet he may well continue to pronounce the word why with a /v/. It is often the case that language teaching—even linguistically-sophisticated language teaching—does not follow through on such problems, since it is expected that learning the appropriate contrasts will have a retroactive effect on mislearned pronunciations. Maybe having the students avoid producing utterances in the new language until they show that they have learned to discriminate adequately is a better way to teach a foreign language. Maybe, therefore, the experiment you mention had hit on a good language-teaching device. But I don't think that it has the deep theoretical implications that you seem to imply.

Theodore Walters, S. J., University of Detroit: I would like to ask Dr. Tripp or Dr. Lambert or anyone else at the conference whether there is any general feeling now with regard to the proper age at which a young child should be introduced to a second language spoken in the home. Should it be from the very beginning, or should you wait until one language is fairly stable, say at 3 or 3-1/2 years of age?

Ervin-Tripp: I don't know any strong empirical grounds for answering that. The theoretical reasoning I have been talking about suggests—and certainly the evidence we see from the Chicano children is —that at a very young age, let's say at 2 or 3, you have considerable ease in learning a second language and no serious hazards to the first. John Carroll has summarized the effects of FLES programs. The evidence seems to point to the possibility that the phonological acquisition may be very easy early. From the standpoint of efficiency, there is another kind of consideration, which is that an older child has a very highly developed semantic system. To the extent that most of this system consists of semantic universals, he has an apparatus available for very rapidly learning a tremendously complex semantic system in the second language which he does not have as a young child. So, if you consider that accent in the second language isn't all that important in the practical sense, there may be efficiencies in later learning from the standpoint that a lot of the basic devices involving both syntactic and semantic processes are common to many languages, particularly if they are closely related languages in area or in history, so that one can be transferred to the other. There may be real advantages in waiting to the point with schooling where there is already a lot there, if it's a practical issue of the amount of time it takes to learn, so that you don't have to be learning the basics in second language learning. If you start from the beginning, as Lambert's program did, and don't settle for an hour a week, the system will be both very efficient from the time standpoint and very effective. For less committed systems, the evidence is not so persuasive.

Robert J. Di Pietro, Georgetown University: I have a few questions for Dr. Ervin-Tripp. First of all, are you always certain that you can distinguish between meaningless and meaningful material? You were very careful to say that you make this distinction. I was wondering how you go about determining if the material is meaningless or meaningful all the time.

Secondly, how can you state categorically that certain vowel consonant sequences are simplest to articulate? How do you account for language learning in a language that has an extremely reduced number of vowels? Hockett describes American Indian languages that have very few vowels, making it possible to utter sentences consisting entirely of voiceless sounds.

Thirdly, I don't know if you can say—unless you can prove it—that adults don't change their phonological patterns. I am sure that we are all constantly changing our phonological patterns. In total deafness, for example, one of the problems is that the afflicted person doesn't hear himself, can't monitor what he is saying, and is likely to become mute, depending on how early this happens. As an illustration of how phonological patterns can change, my original idiolect had the vowel [a] in fog and hog, and now that I've moved away from upstate New York, I find myself saying [fɔg] and [hɔg]. I reshaped this particular part of my phonology quite late.

You also mentioned Lenneberg. How does your model accommodate the distinction between that part of language which is innately endowed and therefore acquired by all children whether they are bilingual or monolingual, and that part which is acquired through multilanguage contact? I would assume that bilingual children have the same anatomical parameters and the same mental abilities as monolingual children. I would also make the claim that bilingual children might not even know at some stage of their development that they're really speaking two languages. I would suspect that the bilingual part is due to what Lenneberg and others would call learning by experience. Lenneberg seems to be saying that children are going to learn to speak, whatever you do to them, if they're normal children.

About your final reference to testing: I have been involved with foreign language work for a long time, and I'm always suspicious of the kinds of tests that language teachers give because I've given some suspicious ones myself. Are we really proving what we claim to be proving? From some of the reports that I've read, all I can deduce is that students tend to learn what you teach them.

Ervin-Tripp: On the last one, your comment bears, perhaps, on your suspicion about the difference between the speaking abilities of the two, and it seems to me the evidence is very nicely the reverse of what you say, because the fact that the nonspeaking group learned the better pronunciation is puzzling if you assume they learn what you teach them. They both heard a lot of input. Now if you are being asked to produce under pressure a lot of oral output, you may not, in fact, be attending quite the same way as if you are not under that particular kind of pressure. So you could argue that the difference is really in the kind of attention, that you are able to perceive more in this situation. I don't know what the differences are due to, but the study certainly doesn't reflect the traditional view that practice makes perfect and we are developing habits that very closely correspond to the kind of practice we have given people. I could talk more about what the specific tests involve, but let me turn to some of your other comments.

I'm glad to hear your comment about the change in your vocalic range, because it fits very nicely with Brière's finding that this is the easiest thing to learn. I didn't say that you don't change your phonology in adult life; I said probably the major changes in adult language, relatively speaking, are in lexicon. I can't imagine anyone disagreeing with the point that there are more changes in phonology and syntax in childhood than in adult life. It is a matter of relative change. It is very puzzling to account for the differences between individuals in their phonological adaptability. Postovsky commented that as far as the sound system went, discrimination was very easy for all of his students. They learned that very early in both groups. There were tremendous differences between individuals in their acquisition of pronunciation, and I think we've all had this experience who have been language teachers. We all know that even in their native language, people's ability to play with imitations, to joke with accents, varies a great deal. I am sure that is somehow related to their adaptability in second language learning.

The CVCV matter, going backward through your list, in part reflects some evidence we are getting about first language learning from Arlene Moskowitz. She suggests that before there is segmenting of phonemes there may be segmenting of syllables, so that development of a syllabary comes first, and that CV units are primary. So it is not surprising in a young child that in imitating he may simplify to very simple CVCV sequences. I've simply used that as an example, relating to the 'what's his name?' illustration of the Chicano child. I think it is probably based on things that are language universals.

As to what is meaningful and what is meaningless, obviously the Chomsky and veritas are crying example shows that the child converted something that could not be interpreted, through her own lexicon. She gave it a meaning, and that is what we often do. People who deal with nonsense materials find that that happens. If you know the verbal learning literature, you know that you can in fact devise measures for finding out how meaningless things are. You can give people input that they have great difficulty in imitating or learning, partly because it is totally senseless and hard to give meaning to. As a matter of fact, I might mention a good example of meaninglessness and how people give meaning to it. There was an operant conditioning program developed here in Russian. The gist of it was that for over a month or so (this is a self-instructional program) there was meaningless teaching. People learned to write Russian, they learned to judge whether their accent was good, they imitated words and sentences, but they never learned the meaning. After many weeks they were given some glosses on some of the input. Then, after they finished the self-instructional program of 17 weeks they were taken to Monterey and put into the regular Defense Language Program. They were tested as to their language knowledge at that point, and they scored lower than chance on the test. They then went through the entire Russian language program at Monterey, and after 30 weeks, I guess, they never caught up to the people who started from scratch. I think this program ought to be labelled 'Dangerous to Health'. There are several possible explanations. It may have taught people that this language is meaningless. Another interpretation is that the students generated meanings. The idle mind does the devil's work. They created meanings for these syllables, and as you say, we may think it is meaningless, but people will find meanings and, of course, those meanings were not the conventional ones.

John Macnamara, McGill University: I do want to support Dr. Ervin-Tripp on two very important points which, perhaps, need little support at this meeting. One is that comprehension precedes production, something which should be obvious but which hasn't always been attended to in the study of language learning. The second is that language is a system of communicating. If I may just give you a hunch, the reason that new methods of teaching languages are not really much improvement on the methods they replace is that language is not being used to communicate. Nobody in a language class wants to say anything to the teacher, and the teacher has nothing to say to the children that they want to hear. I think linguists and psychologists too have neglected this point. I suspect that progress will be made when the classroom is so organized that the teachers will have something to say to the children and the children will have something to say to the teacher. Only then will the Faculté de Langage be engaged; at the present time it seems hardly to be engaged at all. Such was my own experience as a language teacher; the sort of mistakes the students made were incredible. They seemed not to come from the Faculté de Langage.

Just one final word. Communication is not conducted only by means of language. I think we must remember what Susan Philips said in her splendid paper, what John Gumperz has been saying, and other people have been saying here: that it is the entire communication system which must be mobilized, of which formal language is but a part.

Shaligram Shukla, Georgetown University: I have this funny feeling that in your paper you have equated human sentence-processing, adult sentence-processing, and child sentence-processing. If you did, I think you were wrong; and if you didn't would you please comment on that?

Ervin-Tripp: What I'm suggesting is that probably the components may be similar in gross outline, but of course the whole point is to study what those components consist of. For instance, the heuristics in syntactic analysis are very different for adults. Obviously I was talking in a very gross schematic outline. You have quite a different linguistic system depending on the stage of first language acquisition, at the point at which you come into second language acquisition, and a different knowledge of how to adapt that linguistic system. I don't equate them at all except in this very, very gross sense.

Shukla: I think that even in that sense they should not be equated.

Esperanza Medina-Spyropoulos, Georgetown University: I would like to ask Dr. Ervin-Tripp three questions and offer brief remarks on the first two. First of all, it seems to me that the term 'imitation' has been used loosely in your presentation. The notion of imitation has a twofold difficulty as far as defining the term, since it involves, on the one hand, rather complex cognitive processes, and on the other it also represents a miscellany of behavior, i.e. response, repetition, echoic behavior, mimicry, mockery, impersonation, etc. Will you elaborate on your use of the term 'imitation'?
Secondly, please make the distinction, if applicable to your investigation, between phonetic and phonological imitation. For it is often the case in experiments on phonetic imitation that the imitative response given by the subjects resembles the realization of some item in their native language more than the vocal-verbal stimulus given. I am thinking in particular of the lexical item [losperos] given to a group of six-year-olds to imitate this item was invariably imitated as [lɔ+spæroʷs], thus resembling the realization of the English word <u>sparrows</u> much more than the stimulus, that is the subjects responded with the particular corresponding variants which they habitually pronounce in their native language; the features of sound that the S̲s heard as stimulus were indubitably perceived as variants of their own language as well as members of correspondence sets. Do we speak in cases like this of phonetic, or phonemic, imitation?

And lastly, what is the size of the population as well as age and socioeconomic status?

Ervin-Tripp: Some of our conclusions are highly speculative and are based on an N of zero, or on home observations. Some are based on studies and so on, with a paper where I put together every bit and shred of ideas that I could find.

On the mimicry and imitation, of course one finds in any spontaneous test that young children spontaneously repeat what other people say. Some people say this is just a triggering device and it is different from telling somebody to repeat what somebody else says. The latter is, of course, what we do in the classroom, and one can make distinctions along that line. In both cases we find that certain features are salient. They are more salient the more distracting things you have in the situation. Of course the quality and accuracy of the repetition is much greater if you have a very, very constrained situation with very few distractions on the channel. It would take very long to answer all of those questions.

Dorothy Goodman, Washington International School: My question has to do with the relation, if any, between the learning of mathematics and the learning of languages. Is any research going on anywhere in the world having to do with the relation between language-learning and mathematics-learning? I understand that the Ecole active bilingue in Paris believe they have proved that any bilingual child, any child with a real competence in a second working language, has an advantage in mathematics over the monolingual child, even though the bilingual child has been taught by a very dull old-fashioned method and the monolingual child has had the benefit of all methods, old and new. The bilingual child, according to these findings, still has an advantage. Does this have something to do with bilingualism or multilingualism as a factor contributing to abstract thinking? For instance, here is a chair, it is also a chaise, and thence to an abstract idea in the child's mind. Has any serious work been done on this?

Another point. Is there any research on the effect of studying in a particular language upon the learning of mathematics? I have heard from Singapore—and I have no idea whether there is any significant collation of data here—that in the Chinese language schools where Malay and English are taught as subjects of instruction but are not vehicles of instruction, children do better in mathematics than in Malayan or English schools where Chinese is merely a subject of instruction. Has superior mathematical achievement something to do, perhaps, with the learning of Chinese characters? I asked the Singapore teacher (a Chinese, but teaching in an English language school) who told me of this what she thought might be the explanation. They thought in Singapore, she replied, that it was a question of training the memory, of the children having to memorize the Chinese characters. This is quite contrary, I remarked, to all the evidence about mathematical learning of the last half century: it is supposed to come about through logic and reasoning, not memory. Yes, they knew this. Of course Chinese ideographs are like complicated puzzles and do involve logic, although there are many irregularities. Is there any research? Perhaps Chinese success is due to the sequence of the syllabus, not ideographs at all.

Wallace Lambert, McGill University: You made a reference to this Ecole active bilingue in Paris. The study is out now as a Ph. D. thesis by Rachael Cohen, and the facts aren't exactly as you presented them. One thing is that she had an incomplete design, although overall it is a very interesting study. Basically she studied several classes of kindergarten and Grade 1 children, picked at random and equated as to intellectual capacity at the prekindergarten level. It would have been nice if she had completed the design so that she could have controlled each of three factors. One was the method active, a second was a bilingual introduction to English taught as a second language, and the third was modern mathematics. The flaw is that she did not have all combinations where you could observe the influence of bilingualism all by itself. Bilingualism always came up in a combination with mathematics. Now it is true that the results are very interesting in that there were marked jumps in IQ, measured in various ways, but one cannot attribute these changes to the mathematics or to the bilingualism because they were always confounded in her design. Thus, one can't conclude that learning the second language early does have an effect. It would be nice now to untangle those two factors.

While I have the microphone, I would like to add one comment to an earlier question as to the best age to introduce the second language. Although it is a complicated problem, I think the question was asked in the sense of understanding what happens if two languages are available at home. When the question was asked: Wouldn't it be better to wait until one language was stable before introducing the second? I feel it would really be a crime not to capitalize on the possibility that both languages can be stabilized early if very simple things are done in the home. For example, one parent uses one language and the other presents the other, and does so consistently and for understandable reasons. If there is a naturalness and appropriateness of usage as when the mother expresses a need to keep the Italian background that she brings with her alive, or the Ukrainian mother who wants to make sure that the child becomes Ukrainian even though her English Canadian or French Canadian husband is equally anxious to make the child Canadian. Thus, to the extent that both parents make attempts to communicate both ways among themselves so that the child learns that she can turn to one in one language and one in the other, there is nothing in the literature to suggest any harm will be done. That is, if there is a predictability created so that the child can count on appropriate use of both languages, I see nothing to worry about with this scheme. In fact, if parents wait too long for one language to stabilize, they run into the age when negative attitudes towards the foreign language show themselves. The child can comfortably learn both languages in early childhood with no difficulty at all.

Ervin-Tripp: I think on that point that I was thinking more in a second-language class context, and I completely agree with Dr. Lambert about a bilingual home context. I think part of the age issue in the school is how much societal maintenance there will be. If you decide to go in for very early instruction and there is no maintenance of it, it seems to me that there could be some arguments against it both from the standpoint of efficiency and the fact that it will get lost later. Children do not maintain languages well without societal support. On the other hand, there are probably significant savings in later second-language learning arising from the earlier exposure which could make it worthwhile. Personally, I wish my own children could attend a bilingual school early.

Wilga Rivers, Teachers College, Columbia: I would like to ask Professor Ervin-Tripp whether she feels that listening comprehension and production can be separated in any absolute way. It seems to me that the listening and the production are interrelated processes, and that there is some experimental evidence that listening does involve some form of matching for identification; in view of this fact, unless we take production in a very crude way as being production which is loud enough for other people to hear, maybe in the Monterey situation there was a considerable amount of production going on, at least at subvocal level. This would perhaps explain why, when it came to pronunciation, the pronunciation didn't just suddenly appear out of the blue, but was related to the prolonged practice in listening with some form of personal participation.

Ervin-Tripp: Two things on that. One is that one gross social difference is that there is no pressure to produce, there is no reward or punishment for it, there is no sense that this is a production. Production is a more strenuous thing than listening; it taxes your organizing capacities much more, so that it is a socially very different situation if the demands made are not for production. Postovsky's argument is that you don't hear nonnative pronunciation in this situation. I quite agree with you about subvocal practice being present; speechless children or people who have articulatory defects have an ability to do phonological processing from the input side which is perfectly normal. That is against the motor theory of how this develops.

Lorand Szalay, American Institutes for Research: I have a question which relates to numerous presentations. The question is based on my experiences derived from research on cultural differences in meanings. The presentations and discussions have generally focused on bilingualism, but I think that some of the apparently conflicting findings could be explained by considering the circumstance that occasionally not merely two languages interfere, but also two cultures. For example, in instances where children come from different cultural milieu (e. g. Indian reservations) and learn English in a U. S. cultural milieu with meanings which are partially also 'white American', we may face a problem which is both bilingual and bicultural. I have no easy solution for this situation; I don't raise this as a question to be answered, but merely as a matter for future consideration.

Ervin-Tripp: May we discuss that with you later, since we are under such time pressure right now.

THE ROLE OF ARABIC IN ETHIOPIA:
A SOCIOLINGUISTIC PERSPECTIVE

CHARLES A. FERGUSON

Stanford University

Abstract. First, the language situation in Ethiopia is summarized in a national sociolinguistic profile formula with commentary. Second, the major kinds of variation in Arabic as used throughout the world are characterized briefly. Then the main section of the paper examines the use of Arabic in Ethiopia as mother tongue, lingua franca, religious language, and trade jargon. Finally, a report is given on attitudes toward Arabic on the part of users of the language in Ethiopia, based on impressionistic observations and the replies to about 100 questionnaires.

As I understand the purpose of my paper in this discussion of second language learning in formal education contexts, it is to call attention to the wide variety of multilingual situations in which bilingual education may take place.[1] It seems clear that hypotheses or conclusions about second language acquisition will be affected by such factors as the nature of the linguistic environment, the relative dominance of the relevant languages in the society, their degree of standardization—indeed by the whole range of issues involving the respective roles of the languages and their means of acquisition outside the educational system. Some of the other speakers at this Round Table have already emphasized the variety of multilingual situations, but the presentation of one particular setting—Arabic in Ethiopia—may still be of value, since the kinds of decisions needed for the teaching of Arabic in the schools of Ethiopia are different in many respects from those needed in more familiar situations.

1. National sociolinguistic profile formulas. One method of presenting the sociolinguistic setting of a language is to include it in a formula representing the sociolinguistic profile of a nation or other political entity (Ferguson 1966, Uribe Villegas 1968). This method differs from others in that it selects a political entity rather than any other demographic, societal, cultural, or psychological framework, and in that it uses a particular taxonomy of language types and functions (Stewart 1968). This method makes no strong claims for predictive value and omits important sociolinguistic data relevant for assessment of the 'roles' of languages in a nation; it does, however, offer a convenient way of making gross sociolinguistic comparisons among nations and it seems to have considerable heuristic value in suggesting lines of investigation and data collection often overlooked in the establishment of national language policies.

Briefly summarized, the method consists of (1) identifying the number of major and minor languages and languages of special status in the nation and (2) representing them in an additive formula using capital and lower case letters standing for language types and functions respectively. A third, more informative, expansion of the formula specifies the languages by name, so that a separate key can provide information on degree of linguistic distance among them and dialect diversity within them; if necessary, information can be added on the diversity of writing systems used. A sample national profile formula in alternative expansions might read:

(1) 2Lmaj + 6Lmin + 1Lspec
(2) (Sow + Sei) + (5Vg + Sge) + Crl

Formula (1) states that in the nation in question there are two major languages, six minor languages, and one language of special status. Expanded formula (2) specifies the major languages as two Standard languages (S) one of which is official (o) and also serves as an important lingua franca within the country (w) and the other is used extensively in education (e) and serves as the nation's means of communication with other countries (i). It further specifies the minor languages as five vernaculars (V) which primarily serve to identify their speakers as members of particular ethnic or other sociocultural groups (g) and one standard language which not only serves this function but is also used in education. Finally, it specifies the language of special status as a Classical (or dead Standard) language used chiefly for certain religious (r) and literary (l) purposes. Further details of the method, with more precise defining criteria for the various categories, can be found in the articles cited.

2. Language situation in Ethiopia. Like many other nations of Africa, Ethiopia is a highly multilingual country, although it differs

from most other African nations in having an indigenous language constitutionally recognized as its official language. The currently available body of data is not adequate for definite identification of the major and minor languages of the country, but an approximation can be made on the basis of the present estimates of the Language Survey of Ethiopia, subject to correction as more extensive and accurate information becomes available.

The Ethiopian profile formula reads:

(1) $5\,Lmaj + 13\,Lmin + 3\,Lspec$
(2) $(3S + 2V) + (13V) + (1C + 1S + Arabic)$
(2a) $(Sowe + Sie + Sgw + Vgw + Vg) + (13Vg) + (1Cr + 1Sw + Arabic)$

L maj: (in approximate order of sociopolitical importance)

Sowe	Amharic	(Ethio-)Semitic
Sie	English	Indo-European (Germanic)
Sgw	Tigrinya	(Ethio-)Semitic
Vgw	Galla	E. Cushitic
Vg	Somali	E. Cushitic

L min: (in alphabetical order)

V_1g	Afar	E. Cushitic
V_2g	Anyuak	Nilo-Saharan
V_3g	Beja	N. Cushitic
V_4g	Chaha Gurage	(Ethio-)Semitic
V_5g	Derasa	E. Cushitic
V_6g	Gumuz	Nilo-Saharan
V_7g	Hadiyya	E. Cushitic
V_8g	Janjero	Omotic
V_9g	Kefa	Omotic
$V_{10}g$	Kembata	E. Cushitic
$V_{11}g$	Sidamo	E. Cushitic
$V_{12}g$	Tigré	(Ethio-)Semitic
$V_{13}g$	Wellamo	Omotic

L spec:

Crl	Geez	(Ethio-)Semitic
Sw	Italian	Indo-European (Romance)
Arabic	Arabic	Semitic

Amharic is a standard language, with a writing system of its own (the Geez syllabary with a few additions) and literature going back to the 14th century; it serves as the medium of instruction in all government primary schools, the primary language of oral and written communication in the government and the armed forces and the only Ethiopian language whose function as a lingua franca is national in scope; it is declared in the Constitution of 1965 as the official language of the Empire.

English is the medium of instruction in all government secondary schools and higher education; it is an important spoken and written medium in government communication; it is the language of upward socioeconomic mobility. It has been publicly recognized by the government as the nation's second language, and serves as its chief medium of communication with other countries.

Tigrinya is a standard language, using essentially the same writing system as Amharic; it has a small literature, and the publication of newspapers in Tigrinya antedates that of Amharic. Formerly the medium of instruction in primary schools in the Eritrea region, in which role it is being replaced by Amharic, it still serves as a lingua franca in many parts of that area.

Galla is a vernacular with considerable dialect diversity which does not seem to be moving toward standardization; it is not normally written, but is spoken as a mother tongue by more people than any other language in Ethiopia. In certain parts of the country it serves as a lingua franca.

Somali is a vernacular spoken over a large but sparsely settled area. It has considerable dialect diversity, but mutual intelligibility is high among them and there is some trend towards standardization. It has a large oral literature but is rarely written; in neighboring Somalia where it is the mother tongue of 90% of the country, Arabic or European languages are used for writing (Andrzejewski 1962).

The minor languages are all vernaculars used by ethno-linguistic communities of at least 100, 000 members. Most are clearcut languages, but several, e.g. Wellamo (-Gofa-Gemu-Kullo- ...) and Gumuz (-Sese-Disoha-Dakunza-Sai- ...) might be regarded as dialect clusters. Afar is often considered together with the closely related language Saho. Chaha Gurage may not be spoken by 100, 000, but it is included as probably the most important representative of the cluster of languages called Gurage which taken together may have nearly a million speakers.

Geez is a classical language known from inscriptions as far back as the 4th century B. C. ; its periods of literary flowering were between the 7th and 13th centuries, long after it had ceased to be a spoken language. Today it serves as the liturgical language of the Ethiopian Orthodox Church; it is the vehicle of traditional Ethiopian ecclesiastical and historical literature and is still used for the composition of poetry. Geez uses a syllabary of some 250 characters derived from the writing system of South Arabic inscription.

Italian has no official or publicly recognized status in the nation, but there are several thousand for whom it is their mother tongue and there is a fairly active Italian press. In its standard form (with some dialect differences brought from Italy) it serves as a lingua franca among some sections of society, particularly in the Eritrea area. In a pidginized form it serves as a lingua franca at a different level in scattered areas of Ethiopia. The use of Italian seems to be declining in favor of English and Amharic.

3. Varieties of Arabic. Arabic, as a great world language spoken by some hundred millions of people over the enormous area from Morocco to the Persian Gulf and attested in literature for nearly a millennium and a half, offers a bewildering range of variation. First there is the Classical written language extending from pre-Islamic poetry to modern technical journals: this variety shows essentially the same sound system and morphology but with considerable variation in vocabulary, syntax, and forms of discourse. Next there is Colloquial Arabic, the chain of regional dialects which constitute the Arabs' mother tongue today. The extent of variation among these dialects is greater than that between what are recognized in other circumstances as separate languages (e.g. Norwegian and Swedish), but the speakers of these dialects have a strong sense of linguistic unity, and a speaker of Arabic recognizes that speakers of other dialects are also speaking Arabic. These two varieties, Classical and Colloquial, exist side by side in the Arabic speech community in a diglossia relationship (Ferguson 1959a, Gumperz 1962, Fishman 1968).

Among the regional dialects some may be regarded as 'prestige dialects' (cf. Johnstone 1967: xxix-xxx), notably those of important urban centers such as Cairo, Beirut-Damascus-Jerusalem, Baghdad (Muslim variety), northern Moroccan cities. Arabic speakers within the areas of influence of these prestige dialects may in the course of their lives adjust their own dialect in the direction of the prestige dialect or even be bidialectal (e.g. Blanc 1964).

Intermediate between the two varieties or sets of varieties, relatively 'pure' Classical and Colloquial, there are many shadings of 'middle language'. These intermediate forms, some highly fluctuating and transitional, others more stable, represent two tendencies: classicization, in which a dialect is modified in the direction of classical, and koineization, in which dialects are homogenized by the modification or elimination of features which are felt to be especially distinctive of a particular regional dialect (Blanc 1959).

Some of these intermediate varieties may be viewed collectively as a 'pan-Arab koine' (cf. Johnstone 1967, xxv-xxx), and indeed the Arab world seems to be developing such a koine for at least the third time in its known history (pre-Islamic poetic koine, koine of early centuries of the Muslim era, modern koine; cf. Ferguson 1959b).

Finally, in certain areas and under certain social conditions where Arabic has been used for limited purposes by people of other mother tongues, it has developed pidginized forms in which the lexicon and overt grammatical categories of the language have been drastically reduced. The best known examples are the Turku of the Lake Chad area and Central Africa and the 'Bimbashi' Arabic which spread southward from the Sudan (Heine 1968 and references). [2]

4.0 Arabic in Ethiopia. Having reviewed the method of sociolinguistic profile formulas, the general language situation in Ethiopia, and the nature of sociolinguistic variation within Arabic, our task is now to identify the kinds of Arabic and their respective functions in Ethiopia in such a way that this information can be represented in the total profile formula for the nation.

Since at least as far back as the fourth millennium B. C. there has been traffic and communication across the Red Sea, between southern Arabia and the coast of eastern Africa including the Ethiopian area. And since at least the seventh century of the Christian era, this has involved the appearance of speakers of Arabic (as opposed to South Arabian languages) on African soil. This process of temporary and permanent immigration of Arabic speakers from Yemen and the southern coast of Arabia has continued into the 19th and 20th centuries. The immigrants have brought both language and religion, and Arabic and Islam have spread to African populations, partly separately and partly in close connection.

Also, peoples further south along the East African coast and inland who have become Muslim, as a result of influence from Yemen and southern Arabia, have moved northward, bringing with them the use of Arabic for various purposes within their basically non-Arabic-speaking-society. The best example may be the constantly expanding population of Somali tribes all of whom have been Muslim since the beginning of the 16th century.

Since at least as far back as the second millennium B. C., there has been traffic and communication between Egypt and the Ethiopian area. With the coming of Christianity into Ethiopia in the fourth century, religious ties with the church in Egypt formed a special line of communication and in medieval times a large part of the literary production in Geez consisted of translations from Arabic works used by the Coptic Christians of Egypt. In the 19th century, Egyptian political influence extended down the Red Sea onto the Eritrean lowlands and the city-state of Harar, and this also directly affected the spread of Arabic and Islam, separately and together.

Finally, since at least the 19th century there has been movement of Arabic-speaking Muslims from the Sudan into Ethiopia. In addition to groups of Arabic mother tongue, many have been speakers of other languages who used Arabic as a lingua franca.

This rapid and drastically oversimplified historical account of the spread of Arabic into Ethiopia cannot do justice to the complex story,

which deserves research and study in itself, but it can give some indication of the varied strands of influence involved in the present-day use
of Arabic in the nation. One aspect of Arabic influence on Ethiopian
language—the presence of Arabic loanwords—has received treatment
in a number of studies by Leslau (e. g. Leslau 1957).

4.1 Arabic as mother tongue. It is not possible to estimate with
any high degree of accuracy the number of native speakers of Arabic
resident in Ethiopia, although it must run in the tens of thousands.
The total number is, however, relatively small, and by this criterion
Arabic cannot be included in the L min of the formula.

The varieties of Arabic in use by the mother tongue speakers are
roughly comparable to those in use in other parts of the Arabic-speaking
world, i. e. there is a diglossia situation in which the speakers acquire
the Colloquial in childhood and then superpose some amount of Classical
Arabic for written and formal oral use. The kinds of Colloquial in use
in Ethiopia seem to cluster around two norms, one of which may be labeled 'Yemeni', the other 'Sudanese'. Neither of these two varieties is
homogeneous in Ethiopia and there is fluctuation and use of intermediate
varieties, but Arabic speakers generally recognize the existence of the
two major types, which differ in pronunciation, certain details of morphology, and in a considerable number of lexical items, including some
items of basic vocabulary. The two varieties in any case are to a high
degree mutually intelligible.

As an illustration of the nature of the difference, we may cite material elicited from two Ethiopian speakers of Arabic. Both had essentially the same sound system but differed, for example, in their re-
flexes of Classical /qð θ/:

Classical	'Yemeni'	'Sudanese'
/q/	/q/	/g/
/ð/	/ð, d/	/d/
/θ/	/θ, t/	/t/

In matters of morphology, for example, the 'Sudanese' had the
ending -ta for the first and second person singular of the past tense
while the 'Yemeni' had -t for both, but in some styles of speech used
-tu for the first person and -ta for the second. Or, the equivalent of
this was da after the noun for the 'Sudanese' and haða before the noun
for the 'Yemeni'. On the standard 100-word list of basic vocabulary
used in the Survey, the two informants had different words on about
30 items, although this may be misleading, since for a number of
these the other word would also have been familiar either as a
synonym or from Classical use. Examples of the differences:

	Yemeni	Sudanese	Classical
'foot'	xuff	riǰil	riǰl
'man'	raǰul	zōl	raǰul
'sit'	ǰalas	ga^{c}ad	ǰalisa, qa^{c}ada
'water'	mōya (masc.)	mōya (fem.)	mā'
'what'	'ēš	šunu	mā

4.2 Arabic as a religious language. Every Muslim in the world, regardless of mother tongue, learns at least a few expressions in Arabic, such as greetings (e.g. some version of As-salāmu 'alaykum 'Peace be on you'), invocations (e.g. Bismillāh 'in the name of God'), a statement of faith ('There is no god but God, and Muhammad is God's messenger.'), and prayers, including the Fātiḥa, the opening surah of the Qur'an. Additional study of Islamic precepts requires memorization of further Arabic material, especially the Qur'an, and ideally the mastery of Arabic to read the traditional works of theology, jurisprudence, ethics, traditions of the Prophet, and so on.

In Ethiopia there are great differences from one region to another, one ethnic background to another, and one individual to another, in the amount of Arabic a Muslim acquires for primarily religious reasons. The mastery of a few greetings and so on is relatively insignificant in the total language economy of Ethiopia, but certain aspects of the religious use of the language deserve special attention. In the first place, many thousands of Muslims every year become literate in Arabic by studying with a traditional teacher (mu^{c}allim) or attending some kind of traditional school (madrasa);[3] typically this is their initial (or, in some cases, only) acquisition of literacy since it normally takes place before entry into a 'modern' government or private school. Secondly, there may be more than a hundred thousand Muslims in Ethiopia who do not speak Arabic well, but who make use of Arabic to the extent of reciting long passages from Arabic works, carrying on stereotyped conversational exchanges in a religious context, or following to some extent a sermon or exhortation in Arabic.

4.3 Arabic as lingua franca. More important than the preceding two points, in terms of extent of active use of Arabic in Ethiopia, is the widespread use of Arabic as a means of oral communication between speakers of different languages. There is no doubt that Amharic is the most important lingua franca in Ethiopia as a whole, but a number of other languages serve as lingua francas in limited areas, not only major languages like Tigrinya and Galla as mentioned in No. 2 above, but even quite minor languages such as Wetawit (Berta) in the Beni Shengul region of western Ethiopia. The use of Arabic as a lingua franca only partially follows regional lines; it tends to coincide more with religious boundaries. Arabic is used as a lingua franca mostly among Muslims of various mother tongues. Some indication of the range of use of Arabic as a lingua franca is given by the questionnaire replies of twenty freshmen at Haile Selassie I University who claimed knowledge of Arabic (October 1969). These twenty students, of about 21 years of age, came from six different provinces, and represented ten different tongues. Twelve of the students claimed to speak Arabic 'fluently', six 'with difficulty', and two 'only a little'. While we cannot assume that these findings are representative of the users of Arabic throughout the country, they clearly show that Arabic can function widely as a lingua franca.

There are of course many Muslims in Ethiopia who are unable to converse in Arabic, so that the latter cannot be regarded as a normal secondary language for Muslims, but it is probably true that hundreds of thousands (as high as a million?) Muslims in the country are able to use some kind of spoken Arabic as a means of oral communication, whereas the number of non-Muslims able to do so is very small. The kind of Arabic spoken in this way tends to cluster around 'Yemeni' and 'Sudanese' norms, but it often fluctuates more than mother tongue Arabic, mixes regional dialects, and incorporates features of Classical Arabic. Finally, we must take note of the fact that an indeterminate (although fairly small) number of Muslims who cannot use Colloquial Arabic as a means of conversation have learned enough Classical Arabic in madrasa, mosque, radio, and reading to be able to use it to a limited extent as a lingua franca, and with some hesitation we may add 'w' also to the 'C' part of Arabic in the formula: Crlw:Vgw.

4.4 Arabic as trade jargon. Many of the Arabic-speaking immigrants to the Ethiopian areas through the centuries have been merchants, and Arab traders, shopkeepers, and small merchants can be found in many parts of Ethiopia. In communication between Arab merchant and customer, often a rudimentary, pidginized form of Arabic is used, and this use of Arabic is not so strongly limited to Muslims as the more general lingua franca use just described. Although there has been as yet no systematic study of this kind of Arabic, impressionistic observation notes some of the usual features of pidginized Arabic, such as the m. sg. for all persons of the verb, and so on. Some indication of the use of Arabic in trade transactions is given in the freshman student responses. Of the twenty students, eighteen checked 'usually use Arabic' or 'may use Arabic' in the market, in shops, or both (one student did not answer the question). Next to religious use (prayers, preaching), the trade use (market, shops) was most often checked in the 'usually use Arabic' column (religious use: 12 checks; trade use: 9).

4.5 Arabic in the Ethiopian formula. The material presented above on the types and functions of Arabic in Ethiopia may be summarized by an entry for Arabic in the national profile formula as

Crlw:Vgw(:Pt)

This formula is to be interpreted as follows: there is a Classical form
of the language which serves religious and literary purposes and is in
a diglossia relationship with vernacular varieties of the language, the
use of which serves as a mark of social group identity (i. e. Islam);
both forms of the language, as well as the intermediate varieties characteristic of diglossic languages, serve as a lingua franca in the country. Less certain is the existence of a pidginized form of the language
used primarily as a trade jargon.

   5. Attitudes toward Arabic. We may assume that every community
has some shared beliefs about language and attitudes toward language.
In multilingual countries we can assume that some of these beliefs and
attitudes will be about the appropriateness of the use of particular languages for different purposes as well as about esthetic and moral values inherent in one language and its uses in comparison with another.
In order to understand fully the role of Arabic in Ethiopia, it would be
desirable to have information on the attitudes of Ethiopians toward Arabic and its use in comparison with their attitudes toward other languages.

   Previous studies of attitudes toward Arabic (Ferguson 1959, Nader
1962) have been based on participant observation in communities of
Arabic mother tongue, and studies of the role of Arabic in a multilingual society have been concerned with Arabic as a national language in
relation to a European former colonial language (e. g. Gallagher 1968)
or to a local minority language (e. g. Jernudd 1968). Accordingly,
there is little precedent for a study of attitudes toward Arabic in a
nation where it serves as a secondary lingua franca and religious language. A few predictions might be hazarded on the basis of the description in No. 4 above, but field investigation is required for any
dependable conclusions.

   Some meagre indications of the attitudes toward Arabic held by
users of the language in Ethiopia can be found in the results of the
questionnaire. To the question 'What languages would you like your
children to know?' the twenty university freshmen and the seventy
Dire Dawa respondents gave overwhelming preference to English, Arabic, Amharic, and French (82, 81, 61, 57 votes respectively), the
other languages named being mostly mother tongues. This at least
testifies to the importance they attach to knowledge of Arabic. The
responses to the questions about which languages seemed most pleasant and most unpleasant gave preference to Arabic and English as the
most pleasant, and apart from 17 votes for Gurage gave no clear pattern of languages regarded as unpleasant (scattered votes or no language named). Again, this gives some indication of a favorable attitude toward Arabic.

   The answers to a complex question on language preferences for different uses give some slight additional information. Arabic was not

consistently preferred to English, mother tongue, or Amharic for any use, although the largest number of top preference votes for use of Arabic was for talking about religion. This suggests that the use of Arabic as a lingua franca is not out of some kind of preference for that language, but because it is favored by the existing language competences of the people communicating. [4]

Finally, the answers to the questions about the use of Arabic in government schools and on the radio are of interest. The votes were overwhelmingly in favor of the teaching of Arabic as a subject in government schools, the use of Arabic in broadcasting to Ethiopians, and the recitation of the Qur'an over the Ethiopian radio. The vote was indecisive on the question of teaching the Qur'an in the schools (8 yes, 9 no, 3 no vote). Whatever else may be their attitudes about Arabic, the students seemed to want more use of Arabic under government auspices.

This very little bit of information about language attitudes is tantalizing, and points to the need for a broader investigation with other techniques. Even with fuller information on the attitudes of Ethiopians who use Arabic as a secondary language, any attempt at characterizing the position of Arabic in the nation or predicting future trends would fail without investigation of the attitudes of those in the country who have Arabic as their mother tongue as well as the attitudes of the vast majority of Ethiopians who have little or no knowledge of Arabic at all.

NOTES

[1] This paper is in the nature of an interim report on one subproject of the Language Survey of Ethiopia. The Survey is part of the five-nation Survey of Language Use and Language Teaching in Eastern Africa supported by the Ford Foundation. This paper was presented in preliminary form at the Conference on Ethiopian Languages held in Addis Ababa, October 1969. Even in its present form it provides very little information not already well-known to many Arabists and specialists in Ethiopian affairs. What merit it may have probably lies in the attempt to communicate this information in such a way that it can be readily assimilated by social scientists, linguists, or interested laymen and can thereby serve as the basis for more extended research or policy making.

[2] The entire range of linguistic variation in Arabic has been studied chiefly by descriptions of 'pure' varieties and studies of local variation in a given dialect area. (For a summary of the research see Abboud, in press.) Studies of variation in some kind of social context have been extremely rare (e.g. Blanc 1960 and 1964, Mitchell 1957. We are certainly far from having sociolinguistically sophisticated studies of verbal interaction of small groups, studies of the sociolinguistic patterns of

whole communities such as villages or social institutions, or large-scale studies of whole nations or the whole Arab world. It may be hoped that the new generation of Arab linguists will undertake studies which will utilize such fruitful sociolinguistic constructs as domain, network, social situation, role relationship, and interaction type (Fishman 1968).

[3]Of twenty university freshmen who claimed knowledge of Arabic (Addis Ababa, October 1969), all but three claimed some reading knowledge. Fourteen reported having learned to read in a <u>madrasa</u>, which they reported having attended for periods ranging from two to eight years (mean five).

[4]The preferences for other languages are of some interest: English was the most strongly preferred for the largest number of uses: 15 out of the 20 gave it top preference for seeing movies and reading books for fun, and 11 and 13 respectively for reading newspapers and listening to news broadcasts. Amharic was not consistently given preference above mother tongue or English for any use, but was preferred by five respondents for talking during sports or for writing letters. As might be expected, the mother tongue was strongly preferred for listening to songs; more surprising was the vote on talking about religion, in which mother tongue preferences exceeded Arabic.

REFERENCES

Abboud, Peter F. 1969. Arabic dialects. In Thomas A. Sebeok et al, eds., Current trends in linguistics V: Southern Asia and North Africa. The Hague, Mouton.

Andrzejewski, B. W. 1962. Speech and writing dichotomy as the pattern of multilingualism in the Somali Republic. In Colloque sur le multilinguisme. Brazzaville.

Bender, Marvin L., and Robert L. Cooper. 1969. The prediction of between-language intelligibility. Mimeo. Addis Ababa.

Blanc, Haim. 1960. Stylistic variations in Spoken-Arabic: a sample of interdialectal educated conversation. In C. A. Ferguson, ed., Contributions to Arabic linguistics. Harvard University Press. 79-161.

_____. 1964. Communal dialects in Baghdad. Harvard University Press.

Ferguson, Charles A. 1959a. Diglossia. Word 15: 325-40. Repr. in D. Hymes, ed., Language in culture and society. New York, 1964.

_____. 1959b. The Arabic Koiné. Language 35: 616-30.

_____. 1969. Myths about Arabic. Languages and linguistics monograph series 12: 75-82. Georgetown University. Repr. in J. A. Fishman, ed., Readings in the sociology of language. 1968. The Hague, Mouton: 375-81.

_____. 1966. National sociolinguistic profile formulas. In W. Bright, ed., Sociolinguistics. The Hague, Mouton.

Fishman, Joshua A. 1968a. Societal bilingualism: stable and traditional. In Bilingualism in the barrio. Washington, D. C., U. S. Office of Education. Rev. version of Bilingualism with and without diglossia; diglossia with and without bilingualism. Journal of social issues. 23. 2: 29-38, 1967.

_____. 1968b. Sociolinguistic perspective on the study of bilingualism. In Bilingualism in the barrio. Washington, D. C., U. S. Office of Education.

_____. 1968c. The relationship between micro- and macro- sociolinguistics in the study of who speaks what language to whom and when? In D. Hymes and J. J. Gumperz, eds., Directions in sociolinguistics. New York City.

Gallagher, Charles F. 1968. North African problems or prospects: language and identity. In J. A. Fishman et al, eds., Language problems of developing nations. New York, Wiley.

Gumperz, John J. 1962. Types of linguistic communities. Anthropological linguistics, 4. 1: 28-40. Repr. in J. A. Fishman, ed., Readings in the sociology of language. The Hague, Mouton, 1968.

Heine, Berndt. 1968. Afrikanische Verkehrssprachen. Infratest Schriftenreihen zur empirischen Sozialforschung Bd. 4. Köln.

Jernudd, Björn. 1968. Linguistic integration and national development. In J. A. Fishman et al, eds., Language problems of developing nations. New York, Wiley.

Johnstone, T. M. 1967. Eastern Arabian dialect studies. London, Oxford University Press.

Leslau, Wolf. 1957. The phonetic treatment of the Arabic loanwords in Ethiopia. Word 13: 100-23. Arabic loanwords in Amharic BSOAS 19: 221-44, Arabic loanwords in Argobba JAOS 77: 36-39.

Lukas, J. 1936. The linguistic situation in the Lake Chad area in Central Africa. Africa 9: 332-49.

Mitchell, T. F. 1957. The language of buying and selling in Cyrenaica; a situational statement. Hesperius 44: 31-71.

Nader, Laura. 1962. A note on attitudes and the use of language. Anthropological linguistics 4. 6: 25-29. Repr. in J. A. Fishman, ed., Readings in the sociology of language. The Hague, Mouton, 1968.

Stewart, William A. 1968. A sociolinguistic typology for describing national multilingualism. In Joshua A. Fishman, ed., Readings in the sociology of language, 531-45. The Hague, Mouton. Rev. version of an outline of linguistic typology for describing multilingualism in F. A. Rice, ed., Study of the role of second languages. Washington, D. C., Center for Applied Linguistics, 1962.

Trimingham, J. Spencer. 1952. Islam in Ethiopia. London, Cass.

Uribe Villegas, Oscar. 1968. Instrumentos para la presentación de las situaciones sociolingüísticas. Revista Mexicana de sociología. 30: 863-84.

DISCUSSION

William L. Higgins, U.S. Office of Education: As I understand it, Dr. Lambert is teaching the nondominant language to pupils of the dominant group without having any French Canadian pupils present in the class as representatives of the less prestigious culture. There is thus a minimum of intercultural conflict; there is only language conflict or interference. This circumstance may be of particular significance in accounting for the high acceptance of the learning situation by parents and pupils which he reports. Rarely will this be the case in the bilingual areas of the United States.

The crux of the problem, as I see it, is that although the dominant Anglos and the nondominant minority recognize that the bilingual minority must be brought into the mainstream of American society, an English-speaking society, both groups believe that it is the minority who must solve the problem as a unilateral learning task, chiefly English language learning. Very little more than lip-service, if that, is given to our professional contention that to be successful this must be a reciprocal bilingual and bicultural learning effort, for the Anglo as well. Unfortunately the nondominant group almost always concurs in the dominant group's deprecating attitude towards the ethnic language and the culture it represents, including the inferiority of that language as a vehicle of instruction. Granted the ideal—public recognition of the desirability of bicultural and bilingual goals for both groups, these mutual goals for disparate groups increase the problems and their complexity. The problems are different for each group, and the approaches must be different, even in the same classroom.

In my mind motivation is the key. All of these attitudes and circumstances affect the level of student motivation and thus the chances of ultimate success. How can motivation be effectively nurtured? Dr. Lambert is consultant for a project directed by Sister Ruth Adelaide Jonas at the College of Mt. St. Joseph on the Ohio which is supported by the U.S. Office of Education. In this experiment involving the preparation of unique teaching materials for African studies in French for the elementary grades, the principal investigator has explicitly attempted to increase and maintain pupil motivation by bringing in the parents one evening a month for a cultural but nonlanguage program, with the children acting as instructors. Even in the control group, this and other measures have successfully maintained high motivational levels after four years. (This will be a six-year program, to be articulated into the existing local junior and senior high school French curriculum.)

Can this example of the involvement of parents, and by extension the Parent Teachers Association and other organized and unorganized elements of the community, perhaps be emulated in bilingual situations?

As an aside, please allow me a comment, or even a warning, concerning this morning's papers and discussion. Full focus seems to be falling on the micro-details of language and language-learning, with very little attention being given to the communicative and cultural goals of bilingual and bicultural education, for which ends language is only a tool—however important. Our professional association with linguistics must not blind us to the broader and more important nonlinguistic perspective. The low aptitude pupil, especially the Anglo, who fails to meet our stringent language requirements must not thereby be allowed to fail in appreciating and communicating with the opposite group and its culture. In such an event it will be we, his teachers, who fail and not the student. The loss will be great for both.

Shaligram Shukla, Georgetown University: I would like to know if this Arabic situation in Ethiopia is something like Hindi in India, where in Calcutta, Bombay, or in South India people have their own languages, still sometimes they speak Hindi. They do have different varieties of Hindi, perhaps like different varieties of Arabic. Is it something like that?

Ferguson: I'm sure there are some similarities, but the more fundamental differences are what strike you first. Hindi at least has the support of the national government and recognition in the constitution and a whole set of people who are trying to further its use, etc. Whereas Arabic is not only not recognized in the constitution, but its use in public education would be strongly opposed by the government. Where it serves as a signal for membership in the Muslim community, it has a very different function from Hindi even in South India.

Pierre Calve, Georgetown University: Dr. Ferguson, could you say a few words about the pattern of influence among all these languages in Ethiopia, especially from English into Arabic? Do you see a trend of unification, or are all these languages well established?

Ferguson: There are two important considerations, I think. First is that the languages now used in Ethiopia have for the most part been used side by side or in various forms of multilingualism for a number of centuries. Also, most of them are ultimately genetically related, although sometimes very distantly, so that in the first place because of genetic relation, and in the second place because of the contact over a number of centuries, there has emerged what we might call an Ethiopian language type. That is, there are certain fundamental

similarities in syntax and pronunciation, etc., which characterize
Ethiopian languages. This may not be very helpful when you compare
two languages which are mutually unintelligible and at first sight seem
to be very different, but it is a factor.

The other consideration is that since about the turn of the century
there has been a gradual penetration through French, Italian, and English of a great deal of technical vocabulary and Western European
ways of looking at things, and this is happening to a number of languages in the country.

But as to the other influences back and forth among Ethiopian languages, that is a very complex question. There is to some extent
Amharization of many of the minority languages, since Amharic is so
widely used, widely learned by all educated people, etc. In the past,
there have been borrowings from Arabic by local languages, including
Amharic, but there is relatively little influence nowadays from Arabic to the other languages.

BILINGUALISM AND THE
NATIONAL INTEREST

ROBERT F. ROEMING

University of Wisconsin, Milwaukee
Editor, Modern Language Journal

Abstract. Bilingualism in the United States has historically had
two orientations, one cultural and economically beneficent, one acul-
tural and detrimental. The former in two major manifestations, the
German in the North and the French in the South, supported non-English
languages as common speech because they represented dominant cultures, participation in which became the aspiration of all individuals
and exclusion from which was economically disadvantageous to only
English-speaking individuals.

Such bilingualism was all pervasive, non-English speech expressed
all aspects of life, religious and humanistic as well, while the economic
power was in the hands of those of non-English heritage. Strong and
vibrant bilingualism accompanied entrepreneurial success and mer-
cantile progress. Spanish in the Southwest failed to assert this ascendancy because it was fundamentally rooted in feudal concepts.

The second orientation is that of the economically depressed, in
which culture, in an anthropological sense and its accompanying linguistic expression, marks individuals or ethnic groups as either restricted or marginal economically. In this group two large sub-groups
can be identified. One is at the upper level, the Italian and the Polish,
which maintains a wavering bilingualism as a means of internal cohesion, but gains economic ascendancy only when it is abandoned. The
second sub-group includes those of Latin American Spanish and Portuguese background marked by native Indian mixture. This group shares
the economic disadvantages of the Negro and the American Indian be-

cause they fail to acquire a functional economic use either of their own
language or dialect or of standard English.

In this historical and economic context this paper analyzes the Bilingual Education Program, Title VII, Elementary and Secondary Education Act of 1965 and subsequent amendments of 1967, to identify what
is valuable to the individual beneficiary of this act and what can be detrimental to his economic welfare. This analysis underscores the thesis
that bilingualism, associated as it is in this Act of the Congress with
economic depression, cannot be construed nor dealt with in the cultural
contexts of the past manifestations of bilingualism.

I am taking advantage of my position as last speaker to act as 'anchor man'.

As usual at meetings such as this, we have made assumptions, argued and come to no conclusions. We have also avoided problems which
are more than academic differences of opinion. We have viewed the
problem of bilingualism emotionally but carefully avoided irrationality.
There were moments when we came perilously close.

We have considered bilingualism without agreeing on a definition.
If bilingualism is total behavioral functioning in society through the medium of two or more languages, then we have some means of judging
whether that behavior affects the national interest. The national interest again is a total concept in which bilingualism may or may not be a
contributing factor. In these discussions we have never considered the
totality of national interest. At this time my reading assures me that
consideration of the national interest must involve population growth,
environmental pollution, recognition of violence as a weapon of social
change and like any weapon potentially uncontrollably destructive, bur-
dening taxation, and innumerable other problems. In a world that offers
us a possibility of contemplating total disaster, we have heard no mention of it.

It has also been assumed that an act of Congress establishes an interest in bilingualism. The most innocent in our society know that
every act of Congress is designed to keep a Senator or Congressman
in his post and that the sponsors of the Bilingual Education Act found
it a good means for nailing down votes. It represents no commitment
at all to bilingualism any more than the National Defense Education Act
of recent memory was a national commitment to support the study of
foreign languages.

The Bilingual Education Act is an anti-poverty measure. It is specifically concerned with families which do not speak English as their
first language and have an income of $3,000 or less. This is repeatedly
stated in the Act. It is Title VII of an act which amended the Elementary
and Secondary Education Act of 1965. I wonder how many of us have

read the Act or have read the 584 pages of the report on the House of Representatives hearings of June 28 and 29, 1967. The latter is a compendium of information relating to the economic desperation of ethnic groups, who are failing to acquire salable labor potential because of major deficiencies in acquiring proficiency in English.

As an anti-poverty measure the Bilingual Education Act has as its basic purpose the upgrading of the economic status of those who are beneficiaries of this Act. To assume that the bill supports bilingualism as this Round Table discussed it is an illusion. It is directed really towards functional non-English speaking monolinguals.

These people need bilingual education because this is the only way they can be reached. If any system of communication doesn't work, we do not certainly rely upon it. For this reason, we throw away television and radio receiving sets. But if we cannot communicate with others in English, we have placed the blame and responsibility on the noncommunicator. It is impossible to educate—by that I mean literally lead out—those with whom we cannot communicate.

Bilingual education has the virtue of establishing viable means for making contact so that language can convey love, compassion and understanding to those in want of it. Back in 1919 approximately, Pastor Franz Uplegger, a German Lutheran pastor from Leipzig, friend of the Stockbridge Indians of Wisconsin, left his post in Milwaukee as Director of the Lutheran High School to establish himself among the Apache Indians of Arizona near Rice on the San Carlos Reservation. In his time he did more fieldwork as an anthropologist, linguist, and missionary than most Ph. D. 's have done as research specialists in a lifetime. He died not too long ago at 96; he still rode his horse at 93. This story has significance, I believe, because it epitomizes what can be accomplished by love and interest in others. The failure of most education, the current failure on our own campuses and in our high schools, the moral decay even in our grade schools, is attributed to a lack of communication, but it is really a lack of demonstrable interest on the part of teachers in their students.

Unfortunately, in this area of controlled research, we do not speak of the spirit of man, of the qualities of fantasy and festivity which Harvey Cox describes as an increasing loss in the current pollution of men's minds. The quality that bilingualism in the final analysis affords man is an expansive spiritual communication with others of his own kind which cannot be measured—in fact, I believe it cannot even be consciously determined by an individual himself. But some of us have the experience of spiritual renewal in communication with others and often find it intensified when we can surmount the barriers of language, or of spiritual frustration when we find ourselves totally alienated in a foreign environment.

But bilingual education will defeat itself if it attempts to focus upon a language or a heritage which is not worth preserving and from which the child or youth yearns to escape. Each non-English language enclave has its own causes for existence; very often these are rooted in religion which has found linguistic isolation a practical ally. The longer paper which I originally prepared for this Round Table details such an experience of my own in which I was isolated in a German Lutheran enclave. To be sure, I possess today a rich background in German language and culture. But I am certain that I would have had quite a different career and a far more agreeable and benign personality had I been trained in public school as an English-speaking monolingual. If you can in wildest fantasy picture me as a completely isolated introvert at a critical stage in my life, you will not even approach the image of what I was. I have been very fortunate in that I was able to convert all my disadvantages to good purposes, but many others coming from the same environment were not equally successful in doing so.

It is, therefore, of utmost importance that we constantly consider that we are dealing with human beings, that as educators we have no way of remaining to see what good or harm we do to individuals as we affect their lives.

Let us also remember that bilingualism perpetuates itself only because social groups can isolate themselves into enclaves for political, economic, or social reasons. On the other hand, it normally tends to disappear into monolingualism under the impact of the same forces. The reasons why this country is English-speaking are obvious to any student of history, and no attempt by us to make it anything else will succeed unless we can change all the economic, social, and political forces. I pointed out in my original paper how these forces perpetuated and then obliterated the German language in Milwaukee. The oversimplification of 'war hysteria' had only little to do with it. In an era when separatism is gaining strength, multilingualism in this country will solidify special-interest and ethnic groups. When the revolution or chaos arrives, order will have to be restored as a natural progression, and those most easily identified because of group cohesion will be the victims—since someone has to be guilty.

As a nation, we are so ignorant of history that we cannot see the reflection of 20th century Russian history, Italian history, German history, Czech history, Chinese history and so on, in the events of violence at our own doors. In those countries also, without exception, tyranny and persecution followed in the wake of violence; and very commonly linguistic separation focused attention on the victim. The lesson of the Sicilian Vespers should be a signal for us to think out carefully the problem of the degree to which bilingualism can serve the national interest or detract from it. At that time in the 13th century, men died because they mispronounced <u>ceci</u>.